Techniques of
PROLOG PROGRAMMING

Techniques of

PROLOG PROGRAMMING

with implementation of logical negation and quantified goals

T. Van Le, Ph.D.
University of Canberra

JOHN WILEY & SONS, INC.
New York * Chichester * Brisbane * Toronto * Singapore

Acquisitions Editor	Steven Elliot
Marketing Manager	Debra Riegert
Production Supervisor	Charlotte Hyland
Manufacturing Manager	Andrea Price
Copy Editing Supervisor	Richard Blander
Illustration	T. Van Le
Cover Art	Marjory Dressler

This book was set in Times Roman by the author and printed and bound by Malloy Lithographing. The cover was printed by Phoenix.

Library of Congress Cataloging in Publication Data:

Le, Tu Van
   Techniques of Prolog programming with implementation of logical negation and quantified goals / Tu Van Le
      p. cm.
   Includes bibliographical references and index.
   ISBN 0-471-57175-X (paper)
   1. Prolog (Computer program language) 2. Negation (Logic)
I. Title.
QA76.73.P76V36 1993   92-90399
005.13'3--dc20   CIP

Printed in the United States of America

10 9 8 7 6 5 4 3 2

To
Phuong-Mai, Joelle and Vivienne

Preface

Prolog: power and weakness

The rapid increase in both the number and power of Prolog-based systems developed in the past ten years (since the adoption of Prolog as the base language for the Japanese Fifth-Generation Computer Project in 1981) is a strong indication that Prolog has been recognised as an effective programming language for software engineering and artificial intelligence.

The power of Prolog lies mainly in its combination of the declarative style of predicate calculus and a simple but powerful inference mechanism based on resolution. The declarative nature of Prolog allows knowledge to be expressed explicitly, whereas program control is left implicit. Thus, some Prolog programs are precisely executable problem specifications, which is what software engineers have always longed for. Other strengths of Prolog include its flexibility in accepting data (as variables in Prolog are untyped), its built-in mechanisms for pattern matching and backtracking, and its powerful means for meta-programming.

Prolog is weak, however, in its handling of negation. In fact, the technique of negation-as-failure used in standard Prolog requires negated goals to be ground (that is, having no uninstantiated variables) at the time of evaluation; otherwise, the answers may be incorrect. This requirement disallows negative finding queries and makes it very difficult to represent universally quantified goals. So, a stronger form of logical negation is needed and is provided in this book.

The book: purpose and organisation

The purpose of this book is twofold. First, it aims to provide a comprehensive exhibition of the techniques of Prolog programming in four stages: declarative, procedural, advanced, and meta-programming. Unlike many current books on Prolog that describe the Prolog constructs and mechanisms before discussing their use in programming, we adopt the approach normally used in successful (natural) language courses. Namely, we guide the students to express their knowledge in the language of Prolog by writing simple but typical programs; then we base on these programs to discuss the language's features and programming techniques. These techniques are reinforced by fully solved exercises, which are followed by similar problems for practice.

The second aim of the book is to present a simple and efficient implementation of logical negation and quantified goals, which are needed in expert systems and which, so far, are not available in any existing books on Prolog. The powers of these new features are demonstrated in the construction of a multilingual expert system shell that supports negative and quantified queries, and subtypes.

The book is organised as follows.

The first five chapters contain the basics of Prolog programming.

Chapter 1 gives a brief introduction to Prolog and Prolog programs. A sample program is given to show what a typical Prolog program looks like and what it means.

Chapter 2 presents the techniques of declarative Prolog programming, that is, how to write a Prolog program to solve a problem without having to know *how* to solve it. Prolog is presented as a descriptive language for problem defining. The topics of recursive programming, list processing, data structures, and databases are discussed, and practical and interesting problems are used to demonstrate the techniques.

Chapter 3 presents the techniques of procedural Prolog programming, that is, how to translate algorithms into Prolog programs. This chapter focuses on the operational aspects of Prolog, including program execution, unification and resolution, parameter passing and backtracking. These topics are studied from a practical point of view and for the purpose of achieving program efficiency. The theory of unification and resolution, which is more useful to researchers than to programmers, is covered with details in Appendix A; also a Pure-Prolog interpreter is given in Appendix B.

Chapter 4 discusses the explicit forms of control and the side-effect features of Prolog and their use in the development of correct and efficient programs. The themes include prevention of backtracking, forcing of backtracking, control of repetition, negation-as-failure, input-output, and other environment manipulating facilities.

Chapter 5 gives a summary of the fundamentals of program development in Prolog, including the combination of declarative and procedural approaches for large and complex applications. The three main issues, namely program style, programming techniques, and program validation, are discussed in detail and practical guides are given.

The remaining six chapters contain advanced programming techniques and applications.

Chapter 6 presents the techniques of nondeterministic programming and second-order programming. Also discussed in this chapter are the representation and manipulation of many useful data structures, including queues, frames, AVL-trees, and B-trees, and the aspects of user interface.

Chapter 7 is devoted to search techniques that have wide application in artificial intelligence. This chapter provides a complete set of search procedures, including nonguided searches such as depth-first, breadth-first, wave and inter-wave search, and guided searches such as hill-climbing, best-first, best-cost (branch-and-bound), best-path (A*), minimax, and alpha-beta search. For each search procedure, we explain when and how it is applied. Also, an analysis of the performance of search procedures is given.

Chapter 8 describes many powerful techniques of developing meta-programs (that is, programs that manipulate other programs). These include the methods of inspecting formulas, modifying formulas, generating new formulas, and executing goals in some specific way other than the normal process of standard Prolog. In particular, we present a collection of Prolog meta-programming tools that are useful in developing large meta-systems. But most significantly, we point out the serious problem of the meta-predicate *not* (or \+) of standard Prolog, and we present the implementation of a simple but powerful form of logical negation represented by a new predicate *non*. We then combine the two predicates *not* and *non* to represent various forms of quantified goals. The power of the given techniques and tools is demonstrated in the construction of three complete systems: a full Prolog meta-interpreter, a complete Prolog debugger that can detect the erroneous clause in a program that gives incorrect (positive or negative) answers, and LnProlog, a Prolog system with logical negation.

Chapter 9 is devoted to application of meta-programming to expert systems. The logical negating predicate *non* developed in Chapter 8 proves to be particularly powerful when it is used in the environment of an expert system where every object has a *type*. This chapter presents two full meta-interpreters for expert systems: one contains no certainty assessment and the other does. The construction of ESSLN, a multilingual expert system shell that supports negative and quantified queries and subtypes, is described in detail. This system serves as a demonstration of the techniques and tools presented in the preceding chapters.

Chapter 10 studies natural language processing. Here, the forms of quantified goals described in Chapters 8 and 9 also prove to be very useful in the representation and interpretation of natural languages, particularly in database query languages.

Chapter 11 presents a special technique of programming which is a combination of nondeterministic programming in Prolog and the object-oriented system modelling approach. The result is a powerful technique of system simulation. We also show in this chapter the main features of POSS, a Prolog-based object-oriented simulation system. It turns out that several typical simulation problems, which normally result in very complex programs in the traditional simulation languages, such as GPSS, SIMULA, and SIMSCRIPT, can be programmed quite straightforwardly in POSS.

All programs given in this book are written in standard Prolog and were tested with Arity-Prolog and LPA-Prolog. (These systems provide different programming environments, but they use the same Prolog syntax as in DEC-10 Prolog.) A few minor points that need to be pointed out are the following. We use the predicate symbol *not* instead of the symbol \+ of DEC-10 merely for its nice appearance. Also LnProlog and ESSLN (described in Chapters 8 and 9) employ some special predicates of Arity-Prolog designed for environment and string handling (such as *create_world, code_world, read_string, concat, string_length* and *string_term*); these predicates can be replaced by their counterparts in other Prolog systems, or can be avoided altogether (with the price of efficiency) as explained in the text and in Appendix G.

Accompanying this book are two diskettes containing the programs presented in the book. (For common use, the diskettes are supplied in the form of 3.5 inch low-density disks, but the publisher also provides 5.25 inch floppy disks on request.) For easy search, the programs are stored on the diskettes in files named after the chapters and figures (or problems) in which they are given. For example, the file `\chap4\figure9.pro` contains the program given in Figure 4.9 of Chapter 4, and the file `\chap6\problm5.pro` has the program presented in Problem 6.5 of Chapter 6. For programs that spread over several figures, we store the whole program in the file named after the first figure in which the program occurs. Each file on the diskettes also contains the instructions on how to run the program in the file and how to perform experiments with the program. Thus, the diskettes are ready for use in the practical sessions.

The audience

This book is intended to serve as a textbook on Prolog programming for second and third-year students of Computer Science courses. The book can also be used by postgraduate students and researchers in artificial intelligence.

For students of a first course on Prolog, the first five chapters establish a firm background for Prolog programming and provide the fundamental techniques of problem-solving using Prolog. The book's tutorial style makes it easy to follow, and the large number of fully solved exercises provide gainful practices. Students should attempt these exercises before reading the solutions, and should try to relate the solutions to the techniques previously presented. By doing this, skill in Prolog programming develops smoothly and naturally.

For advanced courses in artificial intelligence and expert systems, Chapters 6 to 10 provide a comprehensive collection of techniques and tools for the development of large and complex applications. Many techniques presented here are new and powerful. In particular, the implementation of logical negation and quantified goals is very useful in expert systems and natural language processing. The systems LnProlog and ESSLN presented in Chapters 8 and 9, and the database query-answering system given in Chapter 10 demonstrate the power of the techniques given. Many tasks of these systems are common to a large class of applications, and the developed procedures can be used to build similar systems.

For system simulation courses, Chapter 11 provides a favourable alternative to conventional simulation programming. The simulation system presented in this chapter, namely POSS, is easy to use. In fact, simulation programming in POSS is almost reduced to system modelling. In spite of its small size, POSS attains many powerful features of the traditional simulation systems such as GPSS and SIMULA.

Reading sequence

The first five chapters that contain the basics of Prolog should be read in the given order. The remaining chapters can be read in the sequences indicated by the following diagram in which the initial numbers refer to chapter numbers, and the extensions are section and subsection numbers.

$$
1 \to 2 \to 3 \to 4 \to 5 \to 6
\begin{cases}
6.2.(1,2) & \& & 6.3.(1,3) & \to & 7 \\
6.2.(1\text{-}4) & \& & 6.3.(1,2) & \to & 8 \to 9 \\
& & & & \to 10 \\
6.1.1 & \& & 6.2.5 & & \to 11
\end{cases}
$$

For those readers who are familiar with the materials in the first five chapters and who wish to read Chapters 9, 10 and 11 immediately, the following backward-chaining indications may be useful.

$$9 \quad \leftarrow \quad 8.(1\text{-}4)$$
$$10 \quad \leftarrow \quad 6.2.(1\text{-}2) \ \& \ 8.2.4 \ \& \ 8.(3\text{-}4) \ \& \ 9.8$$
$$11 \quad \leftarrow \quad 6.1 \ \& \ 6.2.(1,5) \ \& \ 8.2.4$$

Acknowledgements

The author is greatly indebted to many colleagues and reviewers whose constructive comments and suggestions have led the book to its present form. The list includes the following professors: David Clark (University of Canberra), Norman Foo (University of Sydney), Roy Freedman (Polytechnic University of Brooklyn, New York), Christopher Hogger (Imperial College, London), Jan Newmarch (University of Canberra), Kevin Reilly (University of Alabama at Birmingham), Neil Rowe (Naval Postgraduate School at Monterey, California), Geoffrey Roy (University of Western Australia), Claude Sammut (University of New South Wales), Clint Smallen (University of Tennessee), Quang Van Tran (Oklahoma State University), Zerksis Umrigar (State University of New York at Binghamton).

Special thanks to Professor Kevin Reilly of the University of Alabama at Birmingham for many helpful and highly inspiring suggestions and advice.

I am also grateful to Steven Elliot (Computer Science Editor), Katy Rubin (Production Manager), Laura Nicholls (Designer), Richard Blander (Senior Copy-editor), and Charlotte Hyland (Senior Production Supervisor) of John Wiley & Sons, who have given their utmost care to ensure that the book appears in its best form.

I also thank my wife, Phuong-Mai, and my daughters Joelle and Vivienne for their constant support and understanding during my busy time of preparing this book.

T. Van Le
University of Canberra, 1991

Contents

Chapter 4   Control and side-effect features of Prolog

Chapter 5   Development of Prolog programs

Chapter 6   Advanced programming techniques and data structures

Chapter 7   Search techniques

Chapter 8   Meta-programming in Prolog

Chapter 9   Building expert systems in Prolog

Chapter 10   Natural language processing in Prolog

Chapter 11   System simulation in Prolog

Appendices

Chapter 1

Introduction to Prolog

1.1 What is Prolog?

Prolog stands for

Programmation en Logique,

which is French for Programming in Logic. As its name indicates, Prolog is a programming system in which logic is used as a programming language as well as a framework for program interpretation.

Basically, the system works as follows. The user submits a description of her problem written in Prolog language. The Prolog interpreter then applies logical reasoning to find answers for the problem. Thus, Prolog can be used either as a software tool for development of intelligent systems (such as expert systems and robot control systems) or simply as a general-purpose programming language with a powerful mechanism for problem-solving.

The first Prolog system was introduced in 1973, by Alain Colmerauer and his Groupe d'Intelligence Artificielle de l'Université d'Aix-Marseille, with the

1

initial purpose of translating natural languages. This system brought great
excitement to European computer scientists, and in 1977 David Warren of
the University of Edinburgh successfully implemented a very efficient version of Prolog, called Prolog-10. Warren's various experiments on Prolog-10
demonstrated the power of Prolog in many applications, ranging from sophisticated artificial intelligence applications to productive software engineering.

In spite of all those impressive results, we had to wait until 1981, when
the Japanese National Conference announced its adoption of Prolog as the
base language for their Fifth-Generation Computer Project, to see the full
recognition of Prolog within both the academic and commercial computer
communities. There is now a wide range of available Prolog systems, designed to meet the needs of all kinds of users. These systems may differ
from each other in speed, price, or system environment, but most of them
are compatible with Prolog-10 (also known as Edinburgh Prolog), which has
been unofficially recognised as the standard Prolog.

So, Prolog is now a practical alternative to conventional programming.
The main advantages of Prolog are highlighted in the following comparison
of the two schools of programming.

1.2   Prolog versus conventional programming

John Backus, in his 1977 Turing lecture, made the following comment:

> "Conventional programming languages are fat and flabby."

In fact, during the past three decades we have witnessed the fast growth
of conventional programming languages. Each successive language contains
all the features of its predecessors plus a set of new constructs designed to
meet the ad hoc demands of new applications. This led to an enormous
increase in size with little gain in power. Indeed, conventional programming
languages are particularly weak in the fields of natural language processing,
vision and speech recognition, and automatic program construction and verification. The weakness of conventional programming, in general, is due to
its concentration on instructing the machine how to solve a problem, instead
of dealing directly with the problem.

To overcome the above-mentioned weakness, logic appears to be an excellent candidate, for logic is a formalisation of natural languages, and logic
has been used for many centuries in Mathematics and Philosophy to describe
problems and to reason about problems. Prolog is then a first successful

attempt in this new direction. Thus, the fundamental difference between programming in Prolog and conventional programming is as follows.

In conventional programming:

- The programmer instructs the machine *how* to solve a problem by performing a given sequence of actions;
- The machine carries out the instructions in a specified order.

In logic programming:

- The programmer defines *what* the problem is, using the language of logic;
- The system applies logical deduction to find answers for the problem.

So a Prolog program is basically a problem specification, which is also executable. For this reason, Prolog is regarded as a very-high-level programming language. Therefore, Prolog programs are usually much shorter than programs written in other languages for the same purpose. Let us now see what a Prolog program looks like, and how it is activated.

1.3   Prolog programs

Generally, a Prolog program is a description of a world (that is, a collection of objects that are related to each other in some way), written in the language of Prolog. The purpose of the program is to provide information on the world it describes. In particular, the information required could be an answer to a given problem.

EXAMPLE 1.1   The world of Ann and Sue is described below.

Ann likes every toy she plays with.
Doll is a toy.
Snoopy is a toy.
Ann plays with Snoopy.
Sue likes everything Ann likes.

The above description is translated into a Prolog program, which is shown in Figure 1.1.

```
likes(ann,X) :- toy(X),plays(ann,X).
toy(doll).
toy(snoopy).
plays(ann,snoopy).
likes(sue,Y) :- likes(ann,Y).
```

FIGURE 1.1 A Prolog program.

Each line of the above program is called a (*definite*) *clause*. The first and the last clauses are called *rules*, and the remaining ones are called *facts*. Thus,

> In a Prolog program:
> ⬦ A *fact* represents a unit of information that is assumed to be true;
> ⬦ A *rule* represents a conditional assertion.

The symbols appearing in the above program are classified into five different classes:

X and *Y* are called variables;
ann, doll, snoopy, and *sue* are constants;
likes, toy, and *plays* are called predicates;
":-" and "," are logical symbols, which are read "if" and "and" respectively;
and finally, "(", ")" and "." are delimiters.

From this classification we note that

> In a Prolog program:
> ⬦ A *variable* represents an unspecified element of a world;
> ⬦ A *constant* represents a specific element of that world;
> ⬦ A *predicate* represents a relationship between elements or a property of a class of elements.

Observe also that the variables X, Y are written in capital letters, and all other symbols begin with lowercase letters. In general, we have the following syntax rule (for most Prolog versions):

- User-defined symbols begin with a letter, which may be followed by zero or more (lower- or uppercase) letters, digits, or underscores.

- Variables, and only variables, begin with a capital letter or an underscore. Anonymous variables are allowed and are represented by single underscores; each sole occurrence of the underscore symbol represents a different variable (even in the same clause).

In logic, clauses are special forms of formulas. A clause is composed of a number of elementary formulas that are called *atomic formulas*. For example, the program of Figure 1.1 contains eight atomic formulas, namely,

```
likes(ann,X)       toy(X)        plays(ann,X)
likes(sue,Y)       toy(doll)     plays(ann,snoopy)
likes(ann,Y)       toy(snoopy)
```

In general, an atomic formula may contain symbols other than variables and constants. For example, consider the formula

```
likes(sue,husband(ann)),
```

which is read "Sue likes Ann's husband". Here, *husband* is not a constant or a variable, it is a *function symbol*. Function symbols are used to represent a *way of referring* to an element indirectly, via other elements. In the above formula, *husband(ann)* refers to an element, not by its name, but by its relation to (another element represented by) *ann*.

In appearance, *husband(ann)* and *toy(doll)* have the same form. But the former represents an element (a man, in this case), whereas the latter represents a property, which may be "true" or "false". Hence *husband(ann)* is called a *term*, to be distinguished from an atomic formula.

Syntactically: *a term never stands alone, but always appears within some atomic formula.*

In summary, we have the following formal definitions.

⋄ A *term* is either a variable or a constant or an expression of
the form $f(T_1, \ldots, T_n)$ where f is a function symbol and
$T_1, \ldots, T_n$ $(n > 0)$ are terms. The symbol f is called the
functor, n the *arity*, and $T_1, \ldots, T_n$ are arguments of the term.

⋄ An *atomic formula* is an expression of the form $p(T_1, \ldots, T_n)$,
where p is a predicate symbol and $T_1, \ldots, T_n$ are terms. If $n = 0$,
that is, no arguments exist, then the parentheses are omitted.

Thus, the distinction between symbols of different kinds in an atomic formula
is quite clear. In fact, the predicate is always the outermost (nondelimiter)
symbol. Inside the formula are variables, constants, and functors: the variables are distinguished by their initial capital letters or underscore; constants
have no arguments, while functors do.

There is a minor point that should be mentioned here. In logic, predicate
symbols (as well as function symbols) used in a language are assumed to be
all different (e.g., see Enderton, 1973). Many Prolog systems allow the use
of the same symbol to name predicates of different arities. This practice
should be avoided, however, so as not to obscure programs' readability.

Let us now summarise the syntax of a Prolog program.

⋄ A *Prolog program* is a finite set of clauses of the form

$$A \ :- \ B_1, \ldots, B_m.$$

where $m \geq 0$ and A and the B_i's are atomic formulas. The
above clause is read "A if B_1 and ... and B_m". The atomic
formula A is called the *head* of the clause and $(B_1, \ldots, B_m)$
is called the *body* of the clause. If $m = 0$, then the clause,
with the symbol "$:-$" omitted, is called a *unit clause*.

Note that the above definition makes no mention of the order of clauses in a
Prolog program. That is, in general, the order of clauses in a Prolog program
is unimportant. It is a good practice, however, to group together the clauses
having the same head predicate; such a group is called a *procedure*. Thus,

the program of Figure 1.1 has three procedures: *likes, toy,* and *plays.* So,

---

In a Prolog program:

⋄ A *procedure* is a group of clauses having the same head predicate. This common predicate is referred to as the procedure's name.

1.4 Queries

Given the program of Figure 1.1, which describes the world of Ann and Sue, one may seek information by asking questions such as

"What does Sue like?"

In Prolog language, the above query is written as follows:

```
?- likes(sue,X).
```

Invoked by such a query, the Prolog system is put into action, applying logical deduction to find an answer for the query. For the above query, Prolog's answer will be:

```
X = snoopy
```

which means "Sue likes Snoopy".

We shall examine in detail how Prolog answers a query in Chapter 3 (Section 3.3). At this stage we can give an outline of Prolog's reasoning process, for the above given query, as follows:

1. Sue likes X if Ann likes X.
2. Ann likes X if X is a toy and Ann plays with X.
3. Snoopy is a toy and Ann plays with Snoopy.

Therefore Sue likes Snoopy.

Observe that the above given query is composed of a single atomic formula. In general, a query may contain several atomic formulas. For example, the query

```
?- toy(X),likes(sue,X).
```

means "What toy does Sue like ?". As you may expect, Prolog's answer to this query is again "X = snoopy". So, in general,

> ⋄ A *query* has the form ?- $A_1, \ldots, A_n$, where each A_i is an atomic formula. In this query, $(A_1, \ldots, A_n)$ is called a *goal*, and each A_i is a *subgoal*. If $n = 1$, then the goal is called a *simple goal*. If $n = 0$, we have an empty goal, which is denoted by □.

For clarification of terminology, let us summarise some definitions. An *atomic formula* is a unit clause, which represents a unit of information. If this information is given and is stored in a program, then it is called a *fact*. If the information is to be sought, then it is called a *simple goal*. A *goal* is a finite list of simple goals, and a *query* is a goal preceded by a question mark.

1.5   Working with Prolog

When a Prolog system is invoked, a prompt symbol appears on the screen. For most Prolog systems the prompt is

```
?-
```

This prompt indicates that the system is ready to receive instructions from the user for execution.

Normally, the first thing the user must do is to provide Prolog with a program. This can be done in two ways: if the program already exists and is stored in some file, then it can be loaded into memory; otherwise, the program can be entered directly from the keyboard.

> ▷ To load a program from a file named *c:filename*, say, we use the following query:

```
?- consult('c:filename').
yes
```

Prolog's response "yes" indicates that the program has been successfully loaded. Otherwise, a message would be displayed to the screen advising the user of an error.

▷ To enter a program directly from the keyboard, we must *consult* a file representing the keyboard, which is named "*user*" or "*con*" (for console) in most systems, before typing in the program.

Figure 1.2 shows an example of entering a program from the keyboard.

```
?- consult(con).
likes(ann,X) :- toy(X),plays(ann,X).
toy(doll).
toy(snoopy).
plays(ann,doll).
plays(ann,snoopy).
likes(sue,X) :- likes(ann,X).
<Ctrl-Z><Enter>
yes
```

FIGURE 1.2 A program entered from the keyboard.

Again, the system's response "yes" indicates that the program is syntactically correct. Otherwise, an error message will be displayed.

Having provided the system with a program, the user can now ask questions by entering goals. For example, consider the following query to the program of Figure 1.2 and Prolog's answer:

```
?- likes(sue,X).
X = doll ->
```

The symbol -> (or some symbol in this place) is a prompt for request of alternative answers. If the user wants alternative answers, he should type ";", otherwise, simply press the return key. For example,

```
?- likes(sue,X).
X = doll ->;
X = snoopy ->;
no
```

Here, the answer "no" means that there are no more answers to the given query.

Queries can be classified into three categories:

- A *finding query* asks for values of some variables such that the entered goal is true in the context of the program currently in memory. For example, the query ?- *likes(sue,X)* is a finding query, which can be read as "Find values of X such that *likes(sue,X)* is true".

- A *confirming query* seeks confirmation of a ground goal (i.e., a goal having no variables). For example,

```
?- likes(sue,doll).
yes

?- likes(sue,ann).
no
```

- An *action query* requests the system to perform some action. Thus, an action query causes some side effect such as changing the environment or performing input-output. For example, the first query we use in this section, *consult('c:filename')*, is an action query that requests the file *c:filename* to be read into memory.

Below is another example of an action query that allows the user to leave the Prolog system:

```
?- halt.
```

At this stage, the user should use the first method of creating a program, that is, use an editor to create the program as a text file, then load the file into memory by means of the *consult* predicate. If the program needs to be changed, then the user should leave Prolog and use the editor to make changes. (Many Prolog systems are supplied together with an editor, and the user is allowed to switch between the editor and the Prolog environment.) By using this method, the user can minimise the use of Prolog's action queries in file editing and concentrate on the task of defining the problem, which is the main stream of Prolog programming, namely *declarative programming*.

More details on Prolog's file editing facilities, such as consulting several files, checking and changing clauses in a program, and saving programs in files, are presented in Section 4.7 of Chapter 4.

1.6   Predefined functions and predicates

In Prolog programming, the programmer is entrusted with full authority in defining the symbols used in his program. There are, however, a number of standard symbols that most of us would define in the same way. Therefore, most Prolog systems provide these standard symbols as predefined functions and predicates. A full list of such symbols is given in Appendix C. In this section, we present some frequently used predefined functions and predicates in Prolog.

Most frequently used are the following arithmetic functions and predicates that Prolog recognises for arithmetic computation.

Arithmetic functions:	+	−	*	/	//	mod
Arithmetic predicates:	<	=<	>	>=	=:=	is

The reader is probably familiar with most of the above-listed symbols, with the possible exception of the functors "//" (for integer division) and *mod* (for remainder of integer division), and the predicates "*is*" (is the value of) and "=:=" (have the same value).

Like other programming languages, Prolog allows arithmetic terms and formulas to be written in infix order, instead of prefix order. So, $+(1, *(2, 3))$ is equivalent to $1 + 2 * 3$, and $is(X, +(Y, 1))$ is equivalent to X *is* $Y + 1$.

It is very important, however, to distinguish between a term such as $1 + 2$ and its value 3. In Prolog, these are two *different terms*, having the *same value*. In fact, the first term represents an indirect reference to the second one. To show this, consider the following Prolog queries and answers.

```
?- 3 = 1 + 2.
no
?- 3 is 1 + 2.
yes
```

The answer to the first query indicates that 3 is not the same term as $1 + 2$, whereas the second query's answer shows that 3 is the value of $1 + 2$. Here, the predicate symbol "=" does not represent the normal "equality", but it represents a special relation in Prolog called "*unifiability*", which is defined as follows.

> ⬦ Two terms T_1 and T_2 are *unifiable* (written $T_1 = T_2$) if they can be made identical by a substitution of their variables with appropriate terms.

For example:

```
?- X + 2 = 1 + Y.
X = 1
Y = 2
```

The above answer shows that the terms $X + 2$ and $1 + Y$ are unified by the substitution $X = 1$, $Y = 2$. Now, returning to the previous query, we note that "3 is not unifiable with $1 + 2$". In fact, there is no variable substitution that can make those two terms become identical. So, the difference between the predicates "=" and "*is*" is summarised as follows:

> ⬦ The predicate "=" unifies its two arguments with no arithmetic computation involved.
>
> ⬦ The predicate "`is`" unifies its first argument with the (computed) value of its second argument.

Unlike "=" and "`is`", the predicate "`=:=`" (which is read "has the same value as") and <, =<, >, >= compare the values of the two sides. For example, consider the following queries and answers.

```
?- 4 - 1 is 1 + 2.           ?- X + 2 = 1 + 2.
no                           X = 1
?- 4 - 1 =:= 1 + 2.          ?- X + 2 =:= 1 + 2.
yes                          no
```

Besides the above-mentioned comparing predicates, Prolog provides another predicate symbol "==" that represents *identity*. The following table provides a collating list of Prolog's comparative predicates, with indication whether variable substitution or arithmetic computation may take place. A number i following the "yes" indicator means the indicated operation is applied to the ith argument of the predicate.

Predicate	Relation	Variable substitution	Arithmetic computation
`==`	identical	no	no
`=`	unifiable	yes(1,2)	no
`=:=`	have the same value	no	yes(1,2)
`is`	is the value of	yes(1)	yes(2)

A final note on arithmetic function symbols: they can be used for non-arithmetic purposes. For example, a corner of two streets can be represented by a term such as `john_st + manuka_ave`. Of course, in this case the only relations that can be used are identity and unifiability.

1.7 Summary

In this chapter, we have given a brief introduction of Prolog and Prolog programs. We have presented a sample program to show what a typical Prolog program looks like and what it means. Let us now summarise the main features of these two aspects of Prolog programs.

- Syntactically, a *Prolog program* is a set of clauses. Each *clause* in the program is either a fact or a rule. A *fact* takes the form of an atomic formula $p(T_1, \ldots, T_n)$, where p is a predicate symbol and $T_1, \ldots, T_n$ are terms. A *rule* has the form A :- $B_1, \ldots, B_m$, where A and the B_i's are atomic formulas.

  A *term* is either a variable, a constant, or an expression of the form $f(T_1, \ldots, T_n)$, where f is a function symbol and $T_1, \ldots, T_n$ are terms.

- Semantically, each term represents an object: a variable represents an unspecified object; a constant represents some specific object; and a term of the form $f(T_1, \ldots, T_n)$ represents an indirect reference to an object, via the objects represented by $T_1, \ldots, T_n$.

  A fact, in a Prolog program, states that a certain relationship between some objects is true. A rule is a conditional assertion about objects.

  A Prolog program is regarded as the conjunction of its clauses, and its *logical semantics* consist of the truths of its clauses.

In the next chapter, we shall discuss the questions of how to write a Prolog program and how to check its logical semantics. Chapter 3 studies the operational semantics (i.e., the execution) of Prolog programs. The control and side-effect features of Prolog are presented in Chapter 4. The rest of the book contains advanced techniques of Prolog programming and their applications.

Solved problems

1.1 Translate the following sentences into a Prolog program:

> Everyone who teaches a computing unit is smart.
> John teaches the unit MA1.
> John's wife teaches the unit SA1.
> MA1 is a mathematics unit.
> SA1 is a computing unit.

(a) From the above Prolog program, identify the facts, rules, terms, and atomic formulas. Also list the variables, constants, functions, and predicates.

(b) Load the program to a Prolog system and enter a query to ask if anyone is smart. What is the logical meaning of the answer?

Solution:

The given sentences are translated into the following Prolog clauses:

```
smart(X) :- teaches(X,Y),computing(Y).
teaches(john,ma1).
teaches(wife(john),sa1).
mathematics(ma1).
computing(sa1).
```

(a) In the above program, only the first clause is a rule, all other clauses are facts. The first clause contains three atomic formulas: they are $smart(X)$, $teaches(X,Y)$, and $computing(Y)$. Each of the remaining clauses is an atomic formula. In general, each argument of any atomic formula is a term. Here, the terms include: variables X, Y; constants *john, ma1, sa1*; and the term *wife(john)*, which contains the function symbol *wife*. The predicates used in the program are *smart, teaches, mathematics,* and *computing*.

(b) To ask if there is anyone smart, we use the Prolog query:

```
?- smart(X).
X = wife(john) ->;
no
```

Prolog's response shows that there is only one answer to the given query. This answer means the formula *smart(wife(john))* is a logical consequence of the given program. That is, in common sense, according to the given information, John's wife is smart. In fact, Prolog's reasoning in finding the above answer is as follows:

> X is smart if X teaches some computing unit Y;
> John's wife teaches SA1, and SA1 is a computing unit.
> Therefore, John's wife is smart.

1.2 The use of functions in a Prolog program greatly increases the expressing power of the program. Consider the following English sentences:

> Every mother likes her child if her child is good.
> Every mother is a woman.
> Ann is a woman.
> Ann's husband is good.

Following are attempts to translate the above sentences into two different Prolog programs: one contains function symbols, the other does not.

Program 1:

```
likes(mother(X),X) :- good(X).
woman(mother(X)).
woman(ann).
good(husband(ann)).
```

Program 2:

```
likes(X,Y) :- mother(X,Y),good(Y).
woman(X) :- mother(X,Y).
woman(ann).
good(X) :- husband(X,ann).
```

(a) Give reasons why program 1 is more expressive than program 2. That is, program 1 can provide more information than program 2.

(b) Write a Prolog query to ask if there is any woman who likes some-one's husband. If that query is put against the above programs, what will be the output?

(c) Is there anything missing in program 2? If yes, suggest changes to fix the program.

Solution:

(a) Program 1 is more expressive, because its functions allow reference to a large number of entities such as Ann's husband, Ann's mother, and Ann's mother-in-law, whereas in program 2, the only entity that can be displayed is *ann*.

(b) For program 1, to ask if there is any woman who likes someone's husband, we enter the following query:

```
?- woman(X),likes(X,husband(Y)).
X = mother(husband(ann))
Y = ann
```

Prolog's answer shows that Ann's mother-in-law likes Ann's husband (not surprising!). For program 2, to ask the same question, we use the following query:

```
?- woman(X),husband(Y,Z),likes(X,Y).
no
```

Here, the answer is "no", because the system is unable to find anyone's *husband*.

(c) Program 2 does not indicate the existence of Ann's husband, Ann's mother-in-law, etc. To do this we must introduce new constants (called Skolem constants), say *anns_husband* and *anns_mother_inlaw* and add the following facts to the program:

```
husband(anns_husband,ann).
mother(anns_mother_inlaw,anns_husband).
```

Now, let us enter the above query again:

```
?- woman(X),husband(Y,Z),likes(X,Y).
X = anns_mother_inlaw
Y = anns_husband
Z = ann
```

This time we have the expected answer as in program 1. Note, however, that in order to make program 2 as expressive as program 1 we have to introduce an infinite set of constant symbols representing *mother(mother(ann))*, *husband(mother(ann))*, etc. On the other hand, if we do know the names of Ann's husband and his mother, then it is slightly easier to express this knowledge in the way of program 2 than as in program 1 (see Problem 1.7).

1.3 The unification process of Prolog assumes every function is one-to-one, that is, $f(x) = f(y)$ only if $x = y$. Consider the following pairs of expressions and determine if they are unifiable. If so, find the appropriate variable substitutions (also called *unifiers*).

(a) `loves(X,husband(Y));`   `loves(mother(Z),Z);`
(b) `loves(X,husband(X));`   `loves(mother(Z),Z);`
(c) `mother(john);`   `mother(sue);`
(d) `min(log(X),Y);`   `min(U,exp(V));`
(e) `X + 1;`   `Y + 2;`
(f) `2 + 1;`   `1 + 2.`

Solution:

(a) Yes. `X = mother(husband(Y))`, `Z = husband(Y)`.
(b) No, because `husband(mother(Z))` is not unifiable with `Z`. (In some Prolog systems, the process of unifying these two terms may be non-terminated.)
(c) No, because `john` is not unifiable with `sue`.
(d) Yes. `U = log(X)`, `Y = exp(V)`.
(e) No, because 1 is not unifiable with 2.
(f) No, for the same reason as in (e).

Supplementary problems

1.4 What is Prolog? In what way does Prolog programming differ from conventional programming such as programming in Pascal, COBOL?

1.5 Answer the following:

(a) What is a Prolog program? What is the purpose of a Prolog program?

(b) Convert the following information into a Prolog program:

Everyone born in Australia is an Australian citizen.

Children of Australian citizens are Australian citizens.

Peter is John's father and was born in New Zealand.

Mary is John's mother and was born in Australia.

(c) Write Prolog queries to ask the following questions: Is John an Australian citizen? Who are Australian citizens?

(d) Run the program to find answers for the above queries.

1.6   Translate the following sentences into Prolog:

John likes all kinds of food.

Apples are food. Oysters are food.

Anything anyone eats and still alive is food.

Tom eats snakes and still alive.

Sue eats everything Tom eats.

(a) Do you represent *apples* and *oysters* as constants or predicates? Give your reasons.

(b) Run the program with appropriate queries to find out if John likes snakes, and also what Sue eats.

1.7   Consider the following information:

John is Ann's husband.

Katy is John's mother.

Lucy is Katy's mother.

(a) Express the above information as Prolog facts in the following cases:

  (i)   Use the symbols *husband* and *mother* as predicate symbols.

  (ii)   Use the symbols *husband* and *mother* as function symbols and a predicate symbol *is_* to express the (nonnumeric) relation "*X is Y*".

(b) Write a query to ask "Who is the mother of Ann's mother-in-law?" (i.e., a grandmother-in-law) for each of the programs obtained in part (a). Run the query in each case and check the answers.

1.8 Examine whether the following pairs of expressions are unifiable. If they are, give the appropriate variable substitutions:

(a) `admires(X,father(X));`   `admires(father(U),V);`
(b) `corner(X+Y);`   `corner(wall_st+perth_ave);`
(c) `X+1-Y*2;`   `U-(1+2)*Z;`
(d) `1+0;`   `1.`

Check your answers using a Prolog system.

1.9 What will be Prolog's answers to the following queries:

(a) `?- X = 2, Y is X+1.`
(b) `?- X = 2, Y = X+1.`
(c) `?- X = 2, Y == X+1.`
(d) `?- X = 2, Y =:= X+1.`
(e) `?- X = 2, 3 =:= X+1.`

Check your answers using a Prolog system.

Chapter 2

Declarative
Prolog programming

2.1 Writing a declarative Prolog program

As defined in the preceding chapter, a Prolog program is a description of a world in the language of Prolog. The purpose of a Prolog program is to provide information on the world it describes. The world under study is possibly a problem and the information sought is a solution to that problem. Each clause of a Prolog program is either a *fact* or a *rule*. A fact expresses an affirmative knowledge, and a rule represents a conditional assertion. Thus,

▷ To write a declarative Prolog program is to write facts and rules to describe a world or a problem.

For example, let us consider how to describe the following problem in Prolog.

20

EXAMPLE 2.1   Three musicians of a multinational band take turns playing solo in a piece of music; each plays only once. The pianist plays first. John plays saxophone and plays before the Australian. Mark comes from the United States and plays before the violinist. One soloist comes from Japan and one is Sam. Find out who comes from which country, plays what instrument, and in what order.

To solve this puzzle, we first identify the relevant entities, namely, the soloists. Each soloist is represented by a term $soloist(N, C, I)$, where N stands for the soloist's name, C his country, and I his instrument. (The definition of *term* is on page 6 of Chapter 1.) Then a solution to the problem is represented by the term

$$band(soloist(N1, C1, I1),\ soloist(N2, C2, I2), soloist(N3, C3, I3))$$

where the position of each soloist in the band represents his turn to play.

The problem is now described in logic-style English as shown in the following Figure 2.1.

S is a solution to the musicians problem *if*
    S is a band of three soloists,
    in which the first member X of S plays piano, and
    there are two ordered members Y, Z of S such that
        Y's name is John, Y plays saxophone,
        and Z comes from Australia, and
    there are two ordered members Y1, Z1 of S such that
        Y1's name is Mark, Y1 comes from the US,
        and Z1 plays violin, and
    there is a member U of S who comes from Japan, and
    there is a member V of S whose name is Sam.

FIGURE 2.1 Description of the musicians problem.

The description of Figure 2.1 is then translated into a Prolog program, which is shown in Figure 2.2.

```
musician_solution(S) :-
    band_soloists(S),
    first(X,S),plays(X,piano),
    order_mbers(Y,Z,S),
        named(Y,john),plays(Y,sax),
        country(Z,australia),
    order_mbers(Y1,Z1,S),
        named(Y1,mark),country(Y1,us),
        plays(Z1,violin),
    member(U,S),country(U,japan),
    member(V,S),named(V,sam).
```

FIGURE 2.2 Prolog program for the musicians problem (top level).

The next step is to define the predicates used in the program of Figure 2.2. These definitions are straightforward and are presented in Figure 2.3 below. (Observe that each occurrence of the symbol % starts a line of comment.)

```
band_soloists(band(soloist(N1,C1,I1),
    soloist(N2,C2,I2),soloist(N3,C3,I3))).
named(soloist(N,_,_),N).          % Soloist's name is N
country(soloist(_,C,_),C).        % His country is C
plays(soloist(_,_,I),I).          % His instrument is I
first(X,band(X,_,_)).             % X is first member
order_mbers(X,Y,band(X,Y,Z)).     % X plays before Y
order_mbers(X,Z,band(X,Y,Z)).     % X plays before Z
order_mbers(Y,Z,band(X,Y,Z)).     % Y plays before Z
member(X,band(X,Y,Z)).            % X is a member
member(Y,band(X,Y,Z)).            % Y is a member
member(Z,band(X,Y,Z)).            % Z is a member
```

FIGURE 2.3 Prolog program for the musicians problem (lower level).

Now a query can be put to Prolog asking for a solution to the given puzzle:

```
?- musician_solution(X).
X = band(soloist(mark,us,piano),soloist(john,japan,sax),
soloist(sam,australia,violin)) ->;
no
```

The result shows that this puzzle has a unique answer. From Example 2.1, we have the following observations.

Notes

1. The program made up of Figures 2.2 and 2.3 does not indicate *how* to solve the problem, it merely defines *what* the problem is. The task of applying logical reasoning to solve the problem is left to the Prolog interpreter.

2. In defining an entity (or a group of entities), we use the following pattern:

   An entity is said to be of certain type *if*
       it is something in general
       that is characterised by some special properties.

3. Whenever we mention the *existence* of some unspecified entity (as shown in Figure 2.1), a new variable is introduced.

4. In Prolog, variables are untyped, that is, a variable can stand for anything. Therefore, the use of single-letter variable names is quite common. Sometimes, indicative variable names are desirable, especially in data structures and program schemes. In such a case, a variable name should be chosen to indicate its intended type. For example, it might be clearer to write *soloist(Name,Country,Instrument)*, but this would make the term representing the band too long.

2.2 Recursive programming

In a Prolog program, a rule is said to be *recursive* if the predicate symbol of its head reoccurs in its body as a predicate symbol. For example, the assertion "X is a citizen of Southland if X is a child of a Southland-citizen" is expressed by the following Prolog clause:

```
southlander(X) :- child(X,Y), southlander(Y).
```

Recursion is a powerful technique of programming in Prolog, which enables the programmer to do programming at a very high level. That is, for a given problem, the programmer need only define:

- the trivial case for which a solution exists;

- the reducibility of the general case toward the trivial case.

We present in this section a number of examples and three general schemes of recursive programming.

EXAMPLE 2.2   Consider the problem of travelling between cities, which is described as follows:

Travelling from A to B is possible *if*
    either   direct-travelling from A to B is possible
    or   direct-travelling from A to some place C is possible, and
               travelling from C to B is possible.

This description is translated into the following recursive Prolog program.

```
travel(A,B) :- direct_travel(A,B).
travel(A,B) :- direct_travel(A,C),travel(C,B).
```

The program is to be completed with a list of facts giving the cities between which direct travelling is possible. The second clause above is said to be *tail-recursive* since the head's predicate symbol reoccurs in the last subgoal of the body. (Tail recursion is most efficient in recursive programming, as most versions of Prolog apply *tail recursion optimization* to save stack space.)

EXAMPLE 2.3   The factorial of a nonnegative integer n is defined to be $n \times (n-1) \times \cdots \times 1$ if $n > 0$, and is 1 if $n = 0$. This definition is expressed as follows:

F is factorial of N *if*
    either $N = 0, F = 1$
    or $N > 0, F = N \times F1$, where
                  $F1$ is factorial of $(N - 1)$.

This definition is translated into the Prolog program of Figure 2.4, the simplified version of which is given in Figure 2.5.

```
factorial(N,F) :- N = 0, F = 1.
factorial(N,F) :- N > 0,
                  N1 is N-1,
                  factorial(N1,F1),
                  F is N*F1.
```

FIGURE 2.4 A program for the factorial function.

```
factorial(0,1).
factorial(N,F) :-
    N > 0, N1 is N-1,
    factorial(N1,F1),
    F is N*F1.
```

FIGURE 2.5 Final program for the factorial function.

There are a few things that should be noted from the development of the programs in Examples 2.2 and 2.3.

Notes

1. A recursive definition takes the following form:

   > An entity is said to be of certain type *if*
   > *either*   it is something trivial
   > *or*   it is something in general
   >   that is characterised by a recursive relation.

2. Since *A if (B or C)* is logically equivalent to *(A if B) and (A if C)*, a definition of the form *A if (either B or C)* is translated into two Prolog clauses *A :- B* and *A :- C*. Most Prolog systems also accept the clause *A :- B ; C*, where the symbol ";" is read "*or*", and treats the clause in the same manner as dealing with the above two clauses. (Recall that the clauses of a Prolog program are regarded as being *and*ed; see Chapter 1, Section 1.7.)

3. In English, a sentence of the form *(A,where B)* means *B* holds before *A* is considered. Hence, such a sentence is translated into Prolog as the goal *B,A*.

4. Prolog does not perform computation during unification (see the end of Section 1.6 of Chapter 1). That is, in general, arithmetic expressions appearing in the arguments of a goal are not evaluated. Therefore, in the program *factorial* of Figure 2.4, we must write `N1 is N-1,factorial(N1,F1)` instead of `factorial(N-1,F1)`.

5. The clause `factorial(N,F) :- N=0,F=1` is logically equivalent to `factorial(0,1)`. In general, when an equation $X = T$ appears in the body of a clause, all occurrences of X in the clause can be replaced with T. We shall see later (in Chapter 4, Section 4.2) that the practice of writing equalities in a clause's body before expressing them in the clause's head is particularly useful in ensuring the correctness of a program containing the *cut*. In this case, however, the aforementioned replacement is valid only under certain conditions.

The program *factorial* of Figure 2.5 has been developed using the mathematical recursive definition of the factorial function. The program computes the factorial value of a given nonnegative integer. We note, however, that the factorial relation is one-to-one (except the first two pairs). That is, we should be able to find a nonnegative integer whose factorial value is given. To achieve this, we reexpress the relation as follows:

> F is factorial of N *if*
> > *either* $N = 0$ and $F = 1$
> > *or* $N = N1 + 1$ and $F = N \times F1$, where
> > $F1$ is factorial of $N1$.

This definition is translated into the program of Figure 2.6, applying the rules set out in the above notes.

```
factorial(0,1).
factorial(N,F) :-
    factorial(N1,F1),
    N is N1+1,
    F is N*F1.
```

FIGURE 2.6 A program for the factorial relation.

Now we can enter queries to find the factorial value of a given number, or to find a number whose factorial value is given.

```
?- factorial(7,F).
F = 5040 ->

?- factorial(N,5040).
N = 7 ->
```

Here, we must press the return-key to terminate the evaluation process, because a semicolon would cause the Prolog interpreter to be stuck in an infinite loop (the reader is recommended to find out why). This nontermination can be prevented, however, by using the predicate *once* (which is defined in Chapter 4, Figure 4.6) to ensure that the goal *factorial(N,F)* will be executed only once.

The development of the programs of Figures 2.5 and 2.6 shows the advantage of representing a one-to-one relationship as a relation rather than a function. In the program of Figure 2.5, we consider N as an independent variable (N is not computed in the program), and F as a function of N, whereas, in the program of Figure 2.6, N and F are expressed as being interdependent. Thus, one can be computed from the other. From these programs, we have the following observations.

Notes

1. The program of Figure 2.5 performs *recursive reduction*. That is, it reduces the problem, one step at a time, until the problem becomes trivial.

2. The program of Figure 2.6 performs *recursive generalisation*. That is, it starts with the trivial case, and generalises the case, one step at a time, until the given specification is met.

3. Both programs of Figures 2.5 and 2.6 are not tail-recursive. A recursive-generalisation program cannot be tail-recursive anyway, because it must check whether the generalised case has met the given specification. But the program of Figure 2.5 can be made into a tail-recursive program. This is shown in Problem 2.4.

In summary, we give two schemes for recursive programming in Prolog that reflect the above-studied cases. The schemes are shown in Figures 2.7 and 2.8. The scheme of Figure 2.7 is extended into one for doubly-recursive programs, which is presented in Figure 2.9.

```
recursive_reduction(X0,Y0) :-
    trivial(X0,Y0).
recursive_reduction(X,Y) :-
    reduce(X,X1,C1),
    recursive_reduction(X1,Y1),
    combine(C1,Y1,Y).
```

FIGURE 2.7 A scheme for recursive-reduction programs.

```
recursive_generalisation(X0,Y0) :-
    trivial(X0,Y0).
recursive_generalisation(X,Y) :-
    recursive_generalisation(X1,Y1),
    generalise((X1,Y1),(X,Y)).
```

FIGURE 2.8 A scheme for recursive-generalisation programs.

```
doubly_recursive_sol(X0,Y0) :-
    trivial(X0,Y0).
doubly_recursive_sol(X,Y) :-
    reduce(X,X1,X2,C1),
    doubly_recursive_sol(X1,Y1),
    doubly_recursive_sol(X2,Y2),
    combine(C1,Y1,Y2,Y).
```

FIGURE 2.9 A scheme for doubly-recursive programs.

EXAMPLE 2.4   Suppose that the nodes of a binary tree contain integers. The summing of all nodes in the tree is described below.

> Sum of all nodes in tree T is S *if*
> > *either* T is empty and $S = 0$
> > *or* T has the form *tree(Left,Node,Right)*,
> > > sum of all nodes in tree *Left* is *S1*,
> > > sum of all nodes in tree *Right* is *S2*, and
> > > S is *S1+S2+Node*.

The corresponding Prolog program is shown in Figure 2.10 and its simplified form is presented in Figure 2.11.

```
sum_tree(T,S) :- T = nil, S = 0.
sum_tree(T,S) :-
    T = tree(Left,Node,Right),
    sum_tree(Left,S1),
    sum_tree(Right,S2),
    S is S1+S2+Node.
```

FIGURE 2.10 A doubly-recursive program for *sum_tree*.

```
sum_tree(nil,0).
sum_tree(tree(Left,Node,Right),S) :-
    sum_tree(Left,S1),
    sum_tree(Right,S2),
    S is S1+S2+Node.
```

FIGURE 2.11 Final program for *sum_tree*.

Two matters of concern involving a recursive program are its correctness and termination. Actually, the correctness of a program written in any language is always a concern of the programmer. But in Prolog, the correctness of a program is assured by the independent correctness of every procedure in the program, and the task of verifying the correctness of a nonrecursive procedure is quite straightforward.

In order to establish the correctness of a recursive procedure in Prolog, it suffices to make the following checks:

1. Check that the clause that describes the trivial case is true.
2. Assuming all subgoals containing the head's predicate symbol are true, show that the recursive clause is true.

In considering termination, the programmer must ensure that for recursive-reduction programs, the trivial case must be reached at some stage, and for recursive-generalisation programs, the specified target must be hit at some recurrence. For instance, in the procedure *travel* of Example 2.2, we must include an extra argument to save the visited cities so that a check can be made to ensure that no city is visited twice. This guarantees that in the end either the cities have been exhausted, or we will be at a place from which direct travelling to the destination is possible (see Problem 2.6). In procedure *factorial* of Figure 2.5, the argument N is decremented by 1 at each recurrence. Thus, it will eventually reach 0 (or fail to meet the condition $N > 0$). The disadvantage of the procedure *factorial* of Figure 2.6 is that it lacks a safeguard for termination. If we enter a query such as `?- factorial(N,5).`, the process will be stuck in an infinite loop, because after a number of generalising recurrences, the target is missed and the process continues forever (the reader is recommended to list the trials up to the point where the target is bypassed). Procedure *sum_tree* of Figure 2.11 has its first argument, which is expected to be a tree, reduced by one level at each recurrence, thus tending to *nil*.

To conclude this section, we note that while the recursive programs *travel* (in Example 2.2) and *sum_tree* (Figure 2.11) are elegant and easy to understand, the two programs for *factorial* (Figures 2.5 and 2.6) look clumsy and may be hard to comprehend. This is because in Prolog functions are used for building data structures rather than for arithmetic computation.

Thus, in Prolog recursive programming a structural reduction of the problem usually results in a neater program rather than a numerical reduction. In Prolog, the data structure that best suits recursion is *list*, which is studied in the next section.

2.3   List processing

List is the most frequently used data structure in Prolog. In general, the function *list* is defined as follows.

> ⋄ A list is either *empty-list* or a term of the form $list(X, Y)$, where Y is a list. The argument X can be any term and is called the *head* of the list; Y is called the *tail* of the list.

In most versions of Prolog, the function symbol for *list* is ".", and *empty-list* is represented by []. For simplicity, Prolog also allows the use of square brackets to represent lists. Thus, the following pairs of notation are equivalent:

Dot notation	List notation
·(X,Y)	[X|Y]
·(X,·(Y,Z))	[X,Y|Z]
·(X,·(Y,·(Z,[])))	[X,Y,Z]

Following are basic operations on lists. We begin with the membership relation between an element and a list. The program's development is presented in Figures 2.12 and 2.13.

> X is a member of *List*   *if*
>   *either* X is the head of *List*
>   *or* X is a member of the tail of *List*.

```
member(X,List) :- List = [H|T], X = H.
member(X,List) :- List = [H|T], member(X,T).
```

FIGURE 2.12 Development of program *member*.

```
member(X,[X|_]).
member(X,[_|T]) :- member(X,T).
```

FIGURE 2.13 Program *member*.

Queries can be put to the program *member* in three ways. A confirming query requests verification if a given element is a member of a given list.

```
?- member(b,[a,b,b]).
yes
```

We can use the program *member* to extract an element from a given list; for example,

```
?- member(X,[a,b,b]).
X = a ->;
X = b ->;
X = b ->;
no
```

or to save a given element in a list:

```
?- member(a,L).
L = [a|_00A5] ->;
L = [_0085,a|_00B5] ->;
  .
  .
  .
```

From the first answer, we see that the element *a* is stored as the head of a list *L* that has an unspecified tail (represented by a Prolog-generated variable). The second answer shows *a* stored as the second element of a list, and so on.

As seen above, the program *member* can be used to extract an element from a given list without paying attention to the remaining elements of the list. A similar program that describes the selection of an arbitrary element from a list, saving the remaining elements in another list, is developed as shown in Figures 2.14, 2.15 and 2.16.

Again, there are three ways of putting queries to the program *select*. A confirming query asks for a selection confirmation. For example:

```
?- select(b,[a,b,c],[a,c]).
yes
```

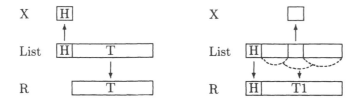

FIGURE 2.14 The process of selecting an element from a list.

X is a selected member of *List*, with R containing the rest *if*
   either   X is the head of *List* and R is the tail of *List*
   or   head of *List* is the same as head of R, and
            X is a selected member of the tail of *List*,
            with tail of R containing the rest.

```
select(X,List,R) :- List = [H|T], X = H, R = T.
select(X,List,R) :- List = [H|T], R = [H|T1],
                    select(X,T,T1).
```

FIGURE 2.15 Development of program *select*.

```
select(H,[H|T],T).
select(X,[H|T],[H|T1]) :- select(X,T,T1).
```

FIGURE 2.16 Program *select*.

A finding query asks for an element to be selected from a given list with the
remaining elements to be shown. For example:

```
?- select(X,[a,b,c],R).
X = a
R = [b,c] ->;
X = b
R = [a,c] ->;
X = c
R = [a,b] ->;
no
```

Lastly, a finding query can also be used to combine a given element and a list into another list. For example:

```
?- select(b,L,[a,c]).
L = [b,a,c] ->;
L = [a,b,c] ->;
L = [a,c,b] ->;
no
```

The next basic operation on lists is finding the length of a list. The program *length*, which has an interesting reverse effect to be described later, is developed as shown in Figures 2.17 and 2.18. (In some Prolog systems, the predicate *length* is predefined, but it is not as flexible as the one defined below. If the predicate symbol *length* already exists, then of course we must change the name of the procedure given below, before we can run it.)

Length of *List* is N *if*
    either   *List* is empty and $N = 0$
    or   *List* is not empty, and
               $N = 1+$ length of the tail of *List*.

```
length(List,N) :- List = [], N = 0.
length(List,N) :- List = [H|T],
                  length(T,M),
                  N is M+1.
```

FIGURE 2.17 Development of program *length*.

```
length([],0).
length([_|T],N) :- length(T,M),N is M+1.
```

FIGURE 2.18 Program *length*.

Obviously, a confirming query can be used to confirm the length of a given list. For example:

```
?- length([a,b,c],3).
yes
```

A typical query is to ask for the length of a given list. For example:

```
?- length([a,b,c],N).
N = 3 ->;
no
```

An interesting query, however, is a request for a list of variables of given length that can be used as a *frame* in expert systems. For example:

```
?- length(L,3).
L = [_0085,_0095,_00A5] -> <return>
yes
```

Here, we have to press the return-key to terminate the evaluation process, as a semicolon would cause the Prolog interpreter to be stuck in an infinite loop (the reason is the same as with program *factorial* of Figure 2.6).

A special list operation that has a wide range of application is appending two lists to create a third one. The development of program *append* is shown in Figures 2.19 and 2.20, and the simplified program is presented in Figure 2.21.

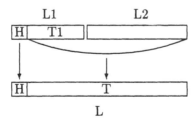

FIGURE 2.19 Appending two lists.

The program *append* can be used in many ways, either to join two lists into one, or to split a list into two parts, or to test if a given list is the prefix or suffix of another list. A confirming query can be used to confirm any of the above-mentioned operations. For example:

```
?- append([a],[b,c],[a,b,c]).
yes
```

L1 is appended to *L2* giving *L* *if*
 either *L1* is empty and *L2 = L*
 or *L1* is not empty,
    head of *L1* is head of *L*, and
    tail of *L1* is appended to *L2* giving tail of *L*.

```
append(L1,L2,L) :- L1 = [], L2 = L.
append(L1,L2,L) :- L1 = [H|T1], L = [H|T],
                   append(T1,L2,T).
```

FIGURE 2.20 Development of program *append*.

```
append([],L,L).
append([H|T1],L2,[H|T]) :- append(T1,L2,T).
```

FIGURE 2.21 Program *append*.

The following query asks for concatenation of two lists:

```
?- append([a],[b,c],L).
L = [a,b,c] ->;
no
```

An interesting query is to ask for all possible ways of splitting a given list into two parts. For example:

```
?- append(X,Y,[a,b,c]).
X = []
Y = [a,b,c] ->;
X = [a]
Y = [b,c] ->;
X = [a,b]
Y = [c] ->;
X = [a,b,c]
Y = [] ->;
no
```

The previous query is very useful in scanning a given list from left to right. Finally, *append* can be used to test if a given list is the prefix (or suffix) of another list. For example:

```
?- append([a,b],X,[a,b,c]).
X = [c] -> <return>
yes
```

An immediate application of the program *append* is the determination of sublists of a given list (Figure 2.22).

X is a sublist of L *if*
    there is a prefix $L1$ of L such that
    X is a suffix of $L1$.

```
sublist(X,L)  :- append(L1,L2,L),
                 append(A,X,L1).
```

FIGURE 2.22 Program *sublist*.

Like the preceding programs, *sublist* can be used either to test if a given list is a sublist of another list, or to extract an arbitrary sublist of a given list.

```
?- sublist([b,c],[a,b,c,d]).
yes

?- sublist(X,[a,b,c]).
X = [] ->;
X = [a] ->;
X = [] ->;
X = [a,b] ->;
.
.
.
```

By pressing the semicolon repeatedly, we will obtain all sublists of the list $[a, b, c]$ (some of them are duplicated). Note that $[a, c]$ is not a sublist of the list $[a, b, c]$. In fact, we may consider $[a, c]$ as a representation of a *subset* of $[a, b, c]$. Subsets represented in this form are defined by the program shown in Figure 2.23.

S is a subset of *L* *if*
    there is a subset *R* of the tail of *L* such that
    either *S* is *R*
    or   *S* is *R* together with the head of *L*.
The only subset of [ ] is [ ].

```
subset(S,[H|T]) :-
    subset(R,T),
    (S = R; S = [H|R]).
subset([],[]).
```

FIGURE 2.23 Program *subset*.

For example:

```
?- subset(S,[a,b,c]).
S = [] ->;
S = [a] ->;
S = [b] ->;
S = [a,b] ->;
S = [c] ->;
S = [a,c] ->;
S = [b,c] ->;
S = [a,b,c] ->;
no
```

The program *subset* of Figure 2.23 shows a case in which the use of the semicolon to express disjunction is quite appropriate. In fact, if the first clause of this program is split into two clauses, the program would be very inefficient, due to the repetition of the subgoal *subset(R, T)*.

As mentioned before, the list [*a, c*] is only one representation of the set {*a, c*}. Another representation of the same set is [*c, a*], which is a *permutation* of [*a, c*]. This establishes an equivalent relation between lists that is defined as follows, and is expressed in Prolog as shown in Figure 2.24.

Two lists *L* and *L1* represent the same set *if*
    L1 is a permutation of *L*.

L1 is a permutation of *L* *if*
    either both *L1* and *L* are empty
    or   head of *L1* is a selected member of *L*
              with *R* containing the rest, and
              tail of *L1* is a permutation of *R*.

```
setequal(L,L1) :- permutation(L,L1).

permutation([],[]).
permutation(L,[H|T]) :-
    select(H,L,R),permutation(R,T).

select :- % see Figure 2.16
```

FIGURE 2.24 Programs *setequal* and *permutation*.

For example, to test if $[c, a]$ is a subset of $[a, b, c]$ (i.e., $[c, a]$ represents a subset of the set represented by $[a, b, c]$), we use the following query:

```
?- subset(S,[a,b,c]),setequal(S,[c,a]).
yes
```

2.4   List sorting

List sorting is traditionally an algorithmic problem. This section presents some declarative sorting programs that are elegant but not very efficient. More efficient sorting programs are given in Chapter 3. For simplicity, we assume the lists contain only numbers, which are to be sorted into ascending order. The programs developed below can be easily extended to the general cases.

The most primitive sorting program is *permutation-sort*, which is purely declarative. The definition of permutation-sort is given below, and its expression in Prolog is shown in Figure 2.25.

L1 is the sorted list of *L* *if*
    L1 is a permutation of *L*, and
    L1 is ordered.

L is ordered *if*
> *either*   *L* has zero or one element
>
> *or*   *L* has at least two elements, and
> head of *L* is ≤ its second element, and
> tail of *L* is ordered.

```
permutation_sort(L,L1) :-
    permutation(L,L1), ordered(L1).

ordered([]).
ordered([X]).
ordered([X,Y|R]) :- X =< Y, ordered([Y|R]).

permutation :- % see Figure 2.24
```

FIGURE 2.25 Program *permutation_sort*.

The permutation-sort program is inefficient for long lists, since it blindly tests every permutation of the list until an ordered one is found. The following sorting program, called *selection-sort*, is far more efficient, as it considers only selected members of the list. The program is defined as follows:

L1 is the sorted list of *L* *if*
> *either*   both *L1* and *L* are empty
>
> *or*   head of *L1* is the least member of *L*, and
> tail of *L1* is the sorted list of the rest of *L*.

X is the least member of *L* *if*
> *X* is a selected member of *L*, with *R* containing the rest, and
> *X* is smaller than all members of *R*.

X is smaller than all members of *R* *if*
> *either*   *R* is empty
>
> *or*   *X* ≤ head of *R*, and
> *X* is smaller than all members of tail of *R*.

The definition of "selected member" has been given in Figure 2.15. The above definition of selection-sort is translated into the Prolog program of Figure 2.26.

```
selection_sort([],[]).
selection_sort(L,[H|T]) :-
    least(H,L,R), selection_sort(R,T).

least(X,L,R) :-
    select(X,L,R), smaller(X,R).

smaller(_,[]).
smaller(X,[H|T]) :-
    X =< H, smaller(X,T).

select :- % see Figure 2.16.
```

FIGURE 2.26 Program *selection_sort*.

We note that the procedure *least* of program *selection_sort* (Figure 2.26) can be made more efficient (for the price of elegance) by using a more specific definition: the least member of a list is the smaller member between its head and the least member of its tail. The formal definition is given below.

> X is the least member of L, with R containing the rest *if*
> *either* X is the only member of L and R is empty
> *or* Y is the least member of tail of L, and
> X is the smaller of Y and head of L, and
> R contains the rest.

So, we have a second version of the *selection_sort* as shown in Figure 2.27.

```
selection_sort([],[]).
selection_sort(L,[H|T]) :-
    least(H,L,R), selection_sort(R,T).

least(X,[X],[]).
least(X,[H|T],R) :-
    least(Y,T,S),
    (H =< Y,(X,R) = (H,T);
     H > Y, (X,R) = (Y,[H|S])).
```

FIGURE 2.27 Efficient *selection_sort*.

We conclude this section by noting that the list sorting programs shown in Figures 2.25, 2.26, and 2.27 are in decreasing order of generality and in increasing order of efficiency. This shows a very typical situation in computer programming: more effort from the programmer means less work for the system. The important point is to maintain a reasonable balance between these two trends. For this, Prolog appears to provide a higher potential than conventional programming languages.

2.5   Data structures

Conceptually, *term* is the only data structure used in Prolog. List is a special kind of term with a distinguished notation. For convenience, a term that is not a list or a constant (or a variable) is called a *compound term*. Thus, practically, data structures in Prolog can be classified into three categories: constants, compound terms, and lists.

As we have demonstrated in the preceding sections, in order to write a Prolog program to describe a world (or a problem), we first identify the relevant entities of the world and design data structures to represent them. Following are some guidelines on the choice of data structures.

1. If an entity can be uniquely identified by a single attribute, such as its name, position, or ownership, then it is represented by a *constant* symbol that expresses the identifying attribute. For example:

```
john, the_president, my_cat
```

are appropriate constants if there is only one John, only one president, and I have only one cat in the world of consideration. Besides user-defined constants, Prolog recognises three other kinds of constants, namely, integers (e.g., -2, 0, 39), floating-point numbers (e.g., 0.5, -12.5E4), and quoted strings of characters (e.g., 'Hello there!').

2. If an entity is identified by a fixed number of more than one attribute, then it is represented by a *compound term*. For example:

```
soloist(sam,australia,violin)
segment(point(1,2),point(3,4))
transaction(cust(bond,1024),order(p2,100),date(26,3,90))
travel(london,sea,travel(rome,air,newyork))
```

In case the functor of a compound term is unimportant, it can be omitted, and the term is treated by default as having the functor ",". For example, *pair*$(1, 2)$ can be simply represented as $(1, 2)$, which is the displayed form of ','$(1, 2)$. Likewise, *tuple*(a, b, c) is represented by (a, b, c), which is the contracted form of ','$(a,$ ','$(b, c))$.

3. If an entity is a sequence of arbitrary length of other entities, then it is represented by a *list*. For example, a sequence of moves in a chess game can be represented by a list

```
[Move|Next_moves]
```

where each move may have the form *move*(*Piece,Oldposition,Newposition*).

4. If an entity has hierarchical structure, then it can be represented by a tree. There are two cases. If each node of the tree can be represented by a single symbol, then the tree is represented by a compound term in which functors are node symbols. For example, consider the following simple grammar parse tree of the sentence "girls like music":

A *sentence* is composed of a *noun* followed by a *verb-phrase*;
A verb-phrase is composed of a *verb* followed by a *noun*;
Nouns are "girls" and "music";
Verb is "like".

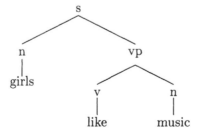

FIGURE 2.28 A simple grammar parse tree.

The parse tree of the sentence is shown in Figure 2.28, and is represented by the compound term

```
s(n(girls),vp(v(like),n(music)))
```

If some nodes cannot be represented by single symbols, then we have two subcases. A binary tree can be represented by a recursive structure

```
tree(Left,Node,Right)
```

where *Node* is a term of any type, and *Left, Right* have the same recursive structure. For example, the binary tree of Figure 2.29(I) is represented by the following term

```
tree(tree(nil,n(a,1),nil),n(b,2),tree(nil,n(c,3),nil))
```

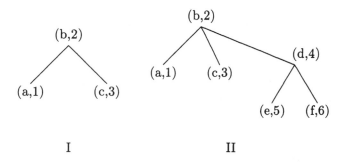

FIGURE 2.29 Tree structures.

A general tree is represented by a list in which the head represents the root of the tree and the tail is the list of its subtrees. For example, the tree of Figure 2.29(II) is represented by the following list

```
[n(b,2),[n(a,1)],[n(c,3)],[n(d,4),[n(e,5)],[n(f,6)]]]
```

5. If an entity is a network such as a bus-route map or an airline network, then it is represented by a *graph*. There are two ways (with numerous variations) to represent a graph in Prolog. If the graph is not frequently changed, then it can be represented as a set of facts to take advantage of Prolog's automatic searching. For example:

```
route(a,b,14).
route(a,d,10).
route(b,c,15).
route(c,a,20).
```

A major disadvantage of this representation is that the graph can only be changed by the use of the *assert* and *retract* predicates (to be studied in Chapter 4), which obscures the declarative reading of the program.

If the graph is frequently changed or is to be passed between programs, then it should be represented as a list of *arcs*. For example:

[route(a,b,14),route(a,d,10),route(b,c,15),route(c,a,20)]

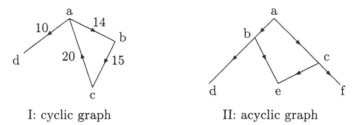

I: cyclic graph   II: acyclic graph

FIGURE 2.30 Graph structures.

Generally, a tree provides easier access to its nodes than a graph of the same complexity. Hence, acyclic graphs are sometimes represented as trees with duplicated nodes. For example, the graph of Figure 2.30(II) is represented by the compound term

a(b(d,e),c(e,f))

2.6   Databases

As mentioned before, a Prolog program is conceptually a description of a certain world. So, from this point of view, a Prolog program can be seen as a database. In practice, however, the word "database" is reserved for programs that have a large number of facts and only a few rules. The facts represent explicit data and the rules contain implicit information.

There are mainly four ways of organising a database in Prolog.

2.6.1   Database as a set of records

The simplest way to represent a database in Prolog is to use a set of facts, each of which represents a data record. For example, a supplier-part database can be represented as shown in Figure 2.31.

```
% SUPPLIER(SNUMBER,SNAME,CITY)
supplier(10,leman,newyork).
supplier(22,adams,london).
supplier(46,fuji,tokyo).
%
% PART(PNUMBER,PNAME,SIZE,PRICE)
part(k10,cam,6,20).
part(m15,shaft,14,50).
part(s21,wheel,25,132).
%
% SUPPLIER-PART(SNUMBER,PNUMBER,QUANTITY)
supplier_part(10,m15,300).
supplier_part(22,k10,200).
supplier_part(22,m15,100).
supplier_part(46,s21,500).
```

FIGURE 2.31 A database as a set of records.

Besides the basic relations that are explicitly expressed in the form of database records as shown in Figure 2.31, other relations between various attributes of the entities in the database can be established by combining these basic relations. For example, the relationship between parts and the cities where they are supplied can be defined as follows:

```
part_city(PName,City) :-
    part(PNumber,PName,_,_),
    supplier_part(SNumber,PNumber,_),
    supplier(SNumber,_,City).
```

Then, to find out "where a shaft can be ordered", the user can use the first query shown in Figure 2.32. It is interesting to note that the same procedure can be used to find out "what parts are available in London", for example. This is expressed in the second query of Figure 2.32.

```
?- part_city(shaft,City).
City = newyork ->;
City = london ->;
no

?- part_city(Part,london).
Part = cam ->;
Part = shaft ->;
no
```

FIGURE 2.32 Queries to the database using *part_city* relation.

Of course, we can ask a more general question such as "What parts are available and where are they supplied?", by leaving both *Part* and *City* to be variables in the above query. (The reader is recommended to try this query and to observe the answers.)

2.6.2   Database as a set of attributes

A disadvantage of representing a database as a set of records is that a large number of records may have to be changed if some entity is given additional attributes. A more flexible way is to represent a database as a set of key-attribute pairs. Figure 2.33 shows a representation of the supplier-part database in this way.

```
sname(10,leman).        scity(10,newyork).
sname(22,adams).        scity(22,london).
sname(46,fuji).         scity(46,tokyo).

pname(k10,cam).         supplier_part(10,m15,300).
pname(m15,shaft).       supplier_part(22,k10,200).
pname(s21,wheel).       supplier_part(22,m15,100).
                        supplier_part(46,s21,500).
```

FIGURE 2.33 Supplier-part database as a set of key-attributes.

Note that the facts that define the supplier-part relation are unchanged, since *Quantity* is an attribute of the pair (*Snumber, Pnumber*) and not of

Snumber or *Pnumber* alone. The relation *part_city* is now defined as follows:

```
part_city(PName,City) :-
    pname(PNumber,PName),
    supplier_part(SNumber,PNumber,_),
    scity(SNumber,City).
```

Then, the user can use the same queries as shown in Figure 2.32 to find out "where a shaft can be ordered" and "what parts are available in London".

For the database of Figure 2.33, when some entity is given an additional attribute, we simply add a new fact to the database. For example, suppose that supplier 46 is given a special status 1 representing its high reliability. Then the following fact is added to the database:

```
sstatus(46,1).
```

If there are several suppliers in Tokyo and all of them are given status 1, then instead of adding several separate facts to the database, we can use the following single rule:

```
sstatus(S,1) :- scity(S,tokyo).
```

2.6.3   Database as a collection of record lists

Representing a database as a set of records or attributes allows only access to individual records. To be able to pass a whole set of records between programs, we can organise the database into lists of records. For example, the above supplier-part database can be represented as shown in Figure 2.34. Here, the procedure *arecord* provides a means of retrieving a record from any specified *List*, which is identified by its *Type*.

The procedure *arecord* can be used to establish the relations between various attributes of the entities in the lists. For example, the *part_city* relation is defined as follows:

```
part_city(PName,City) :-
    arecord(part,p(PNumber,PName,_,_)),
    arecord(supplier_part,sp(SNumber,PNumber,_)),
    arecord(supplier,s(SNumber,_,City)).
```

Again, the queries about parts and the cities where they are supplied provide the same answers as shown in Figure 2.32.

```
datafile(supplier,
   [s(10,leman,newyork),
    s(22,adams,london),
    s(46,fuji,tokyo)]).

datafile(part,
   [p(k10,cam,6,20),
    p(m15,shaft,14,50),
    p(s21,wheel,25,132)]).

datafile(supplier_part,
   [sp(10,m15,300),
    sp(22,k10,200),
    sp(22,m15,100),
    sp(46,s21,500)]).

arecord(Type,Rec) :-
    datafile(Type,List),
    member(Rec,List).
member :- % see Figure 2.13
```

FIGURE 2.34 A database as a collection of record lists.

2.6.4 Database as a collection of sorted binary trees

All the above-described organisations of database allow only sequential search for individual records. This may be inefficient if the database is large. To allow fast searching, a database can be represented as a collection of binary trees each of which is sorted in infix-order of some specific key. That is, the value of the specified key in every node is greater than or equal to that in its left branch, and is less than that in its right branch. For example, consider again the supplier-part database. Suppose that supplier records are sorted according to supplier-number; part records: part-name; and supplier-part records: part-number. The database is shown in Figure 2.35. Here, the procedure *arecord* enables fast retrieval of a record from any specified *Tree*, which is identified by its *Type*. Note that X @=< Y is true if the term X is alphabetically before the term Y. As before, the relation *part_city* is defined by using the procedure *arecord* as shown in the program below Figure 2.35.

```
datatree(supplier,
    bt(bt(nil,n(10,s(leman,newyork))),nil),
        n(22,s(adams,london)),
        bt(nil,n(46,s(fuji,tokyo)),nil))).

datatree(part,
    bt(bt(nil,n(cam,p(k10,6,20))),nil),
        n(shaft,p(m15,14,50)),
        bt(nil,n(wheel,p(s21,25,132)),nil))).

datatree(supplier_part,
    bt(bt(nil,
          n(k10,sp(22,200)),
          bt(nil,n(m15,sp(22,100)),nil)),
        n(m15,sp(10,300)),
        bt(nil,n(s21,sp(46,500)),nil))).

arecord(Type,Rec) :-
    datatree(Type,Tree),tree_member(Rec,Tree).

tree_member(n(Key,X),bt(_,n(Key,X),_)).
tree_member(n(Key,X),bt(Left,n(Nkey,_),Right)) :-
    Key @=< Nkey,tree_member(n(Key,X),Left).
tree_member(n(Key,X),bt(Left,n(Nkey,_),Right)) :-
    Key @> Nkey,tree_member(n(Key,X),Right).
```

FIGURE 2.35 The supplier-part database as a collection of sorted binary trees.

```
part_city(PName,City) :-
    arecord(part,n(PName,p(PNumber,_,_))),
    arecord(supplier_part,n(PNumber,sp(SNumber,_))),
    arecord(supplier,n(SNumber,s(_,City))).
```

Again, the query *?- part_city(shaft, City)* draws the same answers as shown in Figure 2.32. Note, however, that the predicate *part_city* should not be used with its first argument uninstantiated, as the inequalities Key @=< NKey and Key @> NKey (in procedure *tree_member*) are meaningful only if both Key and Nkey have values. Of course, we can remove this restriction by deleting those inequalities. But this would annihilate the usefulness of the sorted binary trees and reduce the effect of the procedure *tree_member* to checking membership of an ordinary binary tree. (The reader is encouraged to try the query *?- part_city(Part, City)* after having removed the above-mentioned inequalities.)

In the foregoing, we have presented four different ways of organising a database in Prolog. Yet, for any of these databases, the same query can be used to obtain the required information. This effect is a result of *data abstraction*. More precisely, data abstraction is the process of organising information so that it can be accessed without having to know how it is stored. The purpose of a database system is to provide such an organisation and to present to the user only the conceptual representation of the database, together with the means of storing and retrieving information.

In this section, we have discussed the organisation of databases and the basic technique of arranging for information retrieval. The issue of information storing is deferred till Chapter 4, as the addition of new information to a database requires the use of side-effect predicates of Prolog.

2.7 Fundamental techniques of declarative Prolog programming

We conclude this chapter with a summary of the fundamental techniques used in the previous sections for declarative Prolog program development. Given a problem or a world to be described, the following steps of program development are to be followed.

1. Identify the relevant entities and design data structures to represent them. (For the choice of appropriate data structures, see Section 2.5.)

2. Describe the problem (or the world) by defining the entities and their relationships in the following pattern:

Entities are said to be of certain type *if*
        they are something in general
        that is characterised by some special properties.

The characterising part may contain joined properties and alternatives. That is, in general, a definition has the form:

$$A \quad if$$
$$either \quad B_1 \text{ and } \dots \text{ and } B_{n_1}$$
$$or \quad C_1 \text{ and } \dots \text{ and } C_{n_2}$$
$$\vdots \qquad \vdots$$
$$or \quad D_1 \text{ and } \dots \text{ and } D_{n_k}$$

where each of the A, B, C, D's expresses a relationship between the entities. The B, C, D's are called *conditions*, but if no conditions exist, then the definition is a factual assertion.

The problem description should be expressed in a top-down manner. That is, we begin by describing the problem as being made up of general relations between entities. We then describe these relations as combinations of more specific relations, and so on. This is to be continued until the relations used are trivial, such as "equal to", "less than", "is", etc., or are defined as facts (see Example 2.1 and Section 2.4).

3. Translate the description of step 2 into Prolog, employing the following rules:

- Each factual assertion is translated into a fact in Prolog;

- Each conditional assertion of the form given in step 2 is translated into k Prolog clauses

$$A \quad :- \quad B_1, \dots, B_{n_1}.$$
$$A \quad :- \quad C_1, \dots, C_{n_2}.$$
$$\vdots$$
$$A \quad :- \quad D_1, \dots, D_{n_k}.$$

Here, there are two important points to be noted:

- If a condition is expressed as $P, where\ Q$, then it is translated into Q, P (see Example 2.3).

- If a condition contains an arithmetic expression in the form $B(\text{expression})$, then it is translated into

$$X \text{ is (expression)}, B(X)$$

4. Simplify the Prolog program of step 3 by applying the following rule. If the body of a clause has a subgoal of the form $X = T$, where X is a variable and T is any term, then all occurrences of X in the clause can be replaced with T. This replacement should not be done, however, if the term T is too complex and X has many occurrences in the clause, as it may obscure the readability of the clause.

5. Finally, establish the correctness of the program by checking the correctness of each procedure. (For correctness of recursive procedures, see the end of Section 2.2.)

In conclusion, we highlight some important points on the approach of declarative Prolog programming.

A declarative Prolog program has the following advantages:

- It is elegant;

- It is easy to be checked for correctness;

- The input-output roles of variables may be reversible (e.g., *member, select, length, append*).

The usual drawback of a declarative program is its inefficiency due to the generality of the program. To write an efficient program, we must follow the trend of the program's execution, and that is the approach of procedural Prolog programming, which is studied in the next chapter.

Solved problems

2.1 A company is to settle in a new building having three floors. The first floor has 50 offices, the second floor has 40, and the third floor has 30 offices. The company has ten divisions for which the requirements are as follows. Division *dcr* needs 12 offices; *dhw*: 10; *dms*: 22; *dsw*: 8; *eme*: 14; *epr*: 11; *esn*: 9; *mem*:9; *mes*: 9; and *mex*: 16. All the offices for a given division must be on the same floor. Also, the following pairs of divisions that work closely together must be on the same floor: *dcr* and *dsw*; *dms* and *esn*; and *eme* and *mex*. Write a Prolog program to determine which divisions should move into which floors.

Solution:

In this problem, the relevant entities are the building's offices and the company's divisions. It is natural to represent the capacity of three floors by a list $[50, 40, 30]$. As for the company's divisions, each division is represented by a term (D, N, F), where D represents the division's name, N is the number of offices required, and F is the floor to be allocated. Thus, the solution to the problem has the form of a list

$$[(D1, N1, F1), \ldots, (D10, N10, F10)]$$

where the values of F1,...,F10 are to be found. Here, for any divisions that are required to be on the same floor, we use the same variable Fn. The problem is described below.

> S is a solution to the office-allocation problem *if*
>> S is the list of divisions,
>> A is the list of floor capacities, and
>> S is an allocation of A.

> S is an allocation of A *if*
>> the first division of S is assigned N offices on some floor F of A
>>> with the remaining offices in $A1$, and
>> the remaining divisions of S is an allocation of $A1$.

> A division is assigned N offices on floor F of A
>> with remaining offices in $A1$ *if*
>> *either* $F = 1$ and floor 1's capacity is reduced by N,
>>> other floors are unchanged
>> *or*   the division is assigned N offices on one of the
>>> next floors of A with remaining offices in $A1$.

The program:

```
office_allocation(S) :-
    divisions(S),
    capacities(A),
    allocate(S,A).

allocate([(D,N,F)|Rest],A) :-
    assign(N,F,A,A1),allocate(Rest,A1).
allocate([],_).

assign(N,1,[H|T],[H1|T]) :- N =< H, H1 is H-N.
assign(N,F,[H|T],[H|T1]) :- assign(N,F1,T,T1), F is F1+1.
```

```
divisions([(dcr,12,F1),(dhw,10,F2),(dms,22,F3),(dsw,8,F1),
          (eme,14,F5),(epr,11,F6),(esn,9,F3),(mem,9,F8),
          (mes,9,F9),(mex,16,F5)]).

capacities([50,40,30]).
```

The following query provides an answer to the problem:

```
?- office_allocation(S).
S = [(dcr,12,1),(dhw,10,1),(dms,22,2),(dsw,8,1),
     (eme,14,3),(epr,11,1),(esn,9,2),(mem,9,1),
     (mes,9,2),(mex,16,3)] ->
```

2.2 *Solving a murder case.* Someone was murdered last night, and you are sommoned to investigate the murder. The objects found on the spot that do not belong to the victim include: a pistol, an umbrella, a cigarette, a diary, and a threatening letter. There are also witnesses who testify that someone had argued with the victim, someone left the house, someone rang the victim, and someone walked past the house several times about the time the murder occurred. The suspects are: Miss Linda Ablaze, Mr. Tom Burner, Ms. Lana Curious, Mrs. Suzie Dulles, and Mr. Jack Evilson. Each suspect has a different motive for the murder, including: being harassed, abandoned, sacked, promotion and hate. Other clues are given below.

The *cigarette* belongs to Mr. Burner. Neither Ms. Curious nor the person who was *sacked* by the victim is the author of the *threatening letter*. Also, Ms. Curious does not own the *pistol* and she did not *hate* the victim. In fact, the person who *hated* the victim is the one who owns the *diary* that disclosed this information. The person who owns the *umbrella* is the one who *left the victim's house* without it. It is Mrs. Dulles who *walked past the house* several times. The person who *argued* with the victim is the *man* who stands a good chance of being *promoted* to the victim's position. As for Miss Ablaze, she had been often *harassed* by the victim, but she did not write the *threatening letter* and did not *commit the murder*. Finally, it is established that the people heard or seen by the witnesses are *different* people among the suspects and that they did not commit the murder; also each evidence-object belongs to a different suspect.

You are asked to find the motive, the evidence-object, and the activity associated with each suspect; in particular, the person who committed the murder.

Solution:

It is obvious that the relevant entities in this problem are the suspects. Each suspect is identified by a name and is associated with a motive for the murder, an object left behind, and an activity at the time the murder occurred. So, each suspect is represented by a term:

$$(\texttt{Name},\texttt{Motive},\texttt{Object},\texttt{Activity})$$

and the solution to the problem is a list of suspects in the form:

$$[(\texttt{ablaze},\texttt{MA},\texttt{OA},\texttt{AA}),\ldots,(\texttt{evilson},\texttt{ME},\texttt{OE},\texttt{AE})],$$

where the values of the variables *MA, OA, AA*, etc., are to be found. The problem is described as follows.

> *S* is a solution of the murder problem *if*
>> *S* is a list of suspects, in which
>> each suspect is associated with
>>> a motive for the murder,
>>> an object left behind, and
>>> an activity at the time of the murder,
>> such that:
>> suspect Burner owns the cigarette,
>> suspect Curious was not sacked,
>>> does not own the threatening letter,
>>> does not own the pistol, and
>>> does not hate the victim;
>> the suspect who was sacked by the victim
>>> does not own the threatening letter;
>> the suspect who hated the victim owns the diary;
>> the suspect who owns the umbrella left the house;
>> suspect Dulles walked past the house;
>> the suspect who argued with the victim is a man
>>> and has a good chance for promotion;
>> suspect Ablaze was harassed by the victim,
>>> does not own the threatening letter, and
>>> did not commit the murder.

The above description is translated into the following program, in which the goals representing positive information are listed first for reasons of efficiency. (Here, the symbol "\=" should be read "is not".)

```
murder_solution(S) :-
    suspects(S),
    motives(M),objects(O),activities(A),
    member((burner,_,cigarette,_),S),
    member((dulles,_,_,walked_past),S),
    member((_,hate,diary,_),S),
    member((_,_,umbrella,left_house),S),
    member((Person,promotion,_,argued),S),
        man(Person),
    associate(S,M,O,A),
    member((curious,MC,OC,AC),S),
        MC \= sacked, OC \= letter,
        OC \= pistol, MC \= hate,
    member((_,sacked,OS,_),S),
        OS \= letter,
    member((ablaze,harassed,OA,AA),S),
        OA \= letter, AA \= commit_murder.

associate([],[],[],[]).
associate([(Name,M,O,A)|Rest],Ms,Os,As) :-
    select(M,Ms,RMs),select(O,Os,ROs),select(A,As,RAs),
    associate(Rest,RMs,ROs,RAs).

select(X,[X|R],R).
select(X,[Y|R],[Y|S]) :- select(X,R,S).

member(X,[X|R]).
member(X,[Y|R]) :- member(X,R).

man(Name) :- member(Name,[burner,evilson]).

suspects([(ablaze,MA,OA,AA),(burner,MB,OB,AB),
          (curious,MC,OC,AC),(dulles,MD,OD,AD),
          (evilson,ME,OE,AE)]).

motives([harassed,abandoned,sacked,promotion,hate]).
objects([pistol,umbrella,cigarette,diary,letter]).
activities([commit_murder,argued,left_house,
            rang_victim,walked_past]).
```

The following query provides an answer to the problem:

```
?- murder_solution(S).
S = [(ablaze, harassed, pistol, rang_victim),(burner,
sacked, cigarette, commit_murder),(curious, abandoned,
umbrella, left_house),(dulles, hate, diary, walked_past),
(evilson, promotion, letter, argued)] ->;

no
```

2.3 Write a Prolog procedure that receives two nonnegative integers X, Y
and returns their greatest common divisor in Z.

Solution:

We apply the property that if $X > Y > 0$, then the greatest common divisor
(gcd) of X, Y is the same as the greatest common divisor of $X \bmod Y$ and
Y. Note also that if $X > 0$, then the gcd of X and 0 is X. So, we have the
following definition:

Z is the gcd of X, Y *if*
    either $X > 0$, $Y = 0$ and $Z = X$
    or $X < Y$ and Z is the gcd of Y and X
    or $X \geq Y$ and Z is the gcd of Y and $X \bmod Y$.

The program:

```
gcd(X,0,X)  :- X > 0.
gcd(X,Y,Z)  :- X < Y, gcd(Y,X,Z).
gcd(X,Y,Z)  :- X >= Y, Y > 0, X1 is X mod Y,
               gcd(Y,X1,Z).
```

2.4 Consider again the *factorial* function defined in Example 2.3 of this
chapter. Redefine the function so that it can be represented by a tail-
recursive procedure.

Solution:

We first recall the mathematical definition of the factorial function, which is
shown below:
$$f(N) = \begin{cases} 1 & \text{if } N = 0 \\ N \times f(N-1) & \text{if } N > 0 \end{cases}$$

It is the operation $N \times f(N-1)$ (which is represented by the goal *combine* in our recursive-reduction scheme of Figure 2.7) that makes the program of Figure 2.5 non-tail-recursive.

Thus, to obtain a tail-recursive formula, we must incorporate the above-mentioned operation into the function itself. So we define a new function of two variables as follows:

$$f(N, T) = \begin{cases} T & \text{if } N = 0 \\ f(N-1, N \times T) & \text{if } N > 0 \end{cases}$$

Now $f(N, T)$ equals T times of factorial of N (denoted by $N!$). In fact, this is obviously true for $N = 0$. Suppose that the equality holds for $N - 1$ ($N > 0$), then we have:

$$\begin{aligned} f(N, T) &= f(N-1, N \times T) \\ &= (N-1)! \times (N \times T) \\ &= N! \, T \end{aligned}$$

Therefore, the factorial of N is precisely $f(N, 1)$. So, we have the following tail-recursive program that defines factorial of N as a restriction of the above function.

```
factorial(N,F) :- fact(N,1,F).

fact(0,T,T).
fact(N,T,F) :-
    N > 0,
    N1 is N-1,
    T1 is N*T,
    fact(N1,T1,F).
```

2.5   The mathematical function Fibonacci is defined as follows:

$$f(n) = f(n-1) + f(n-2) \text{ if } n > 1, \quad f(0) = 0 \text{ and } f(1) = 1.$$

(a) Write a Prolog procedure *fibonacci*(N, F) that receives a non-negative integer N and returns in F the Fibonacci value of N.

(b) Discuss the efficiency of the procedure developed in part (a).

(c) Write another procedure to calculate Fibonacci value of N that is more efficient than the one developed in part (a).

Solution:

(a) The function's definition is expressed as follows:

> F is the Fibonacci value of N *if*
>> *either* $N = 0$ and $F = 0$
>> *or* $N = 1$ and $F = 1$
>> *or* $N > 1$ and $F = F1 + F2$, where
>>> $F1$ is the Fibonacci value of $N - 1$, and
>>> $F2$ is the Fibonacci value of $N - 2$.

Then we have the program:

```
fibonacci(0,0).
fibonacci(1,1).
fibonacci(N,F) :-
    N > 1,
    N1 is N-1, N2 is N-2,
    fibonacci(N1,F1),
    fibonacci(N2,F2),
    F is F1+F2.
```

(b) The above program is elegant, as it is purely declarative. The program is very inefficient, however, because it repeats the calculation of each preceding Fibonacci value several times. In fact, for a given nonnegative integer N, the number of calls $C(N)$ to the procedure in evaluating *fibonacci*(N, F) also follows the Fibonacci pattern. That is,

$$C(N) = C(N - 1) + C(N - 2) + 1 \text{ if } N > 1, \text{ and } C(0) = C(1) = 1.$$

For example, in evaluating *fibonacci*$(20, F)$, the system makes 21,891 calls to the procedure.

(c) To avoid the above-mentioned inefficiency, it is obvious that the program should save the preceding Fibonacci value for use in the next calculation. Thus, the function is redefined as follows:

> $F1, F$ are two last elements in the Fibonacci sequence of N *if*
>> *either* $N = 0$ and $F = 0$, $F1$ undefined
>> *or* $N = 1$ and $F = 1$, $F1 = 0$
>> *or* $N > 1$ and $F = F1 + F2$, where
>>> $F2, F1$ are two last elements in the Fibonacci
>>> sequence of $N - 1$.

Then we have the program:

```
fibonacci(0,_,0).
fibonacci(1,0,1).
fibonacci(N,F1,F) :-
    N > 1, N1 is N-1,
    fibonacci(N1,F2,F1),
    F is F1+F2.
```

For example, consider the query:

```
?- fibonacci(20,_,F).
F = 6765 ->
```

Here, the procedure is called only 20 times.

2.6 Given is a number of facts of the form `direct_travel(A,B)`, each of which represents a fact that there is a way to go directly from city *A* to city *B*. Write a Prolog program to represent the relation that travelling from *A* to *B* is possible (either directly or via other places). Ensure that the program terminates properly.

Solution:

The program has been partly given in Example 2.2. We only need to add the specification that no city will be visited twice. This ensures the planned journey will not be stuck in a cycle. The modified description is given below.

Travelling from *A* to *B* is possible *if*
    either direct-travelling from *A* to *B* is possible
    or   direct-travelling from *A* to some place *C*
           not yet visited is possible, and
           travelling from *C* to *B* is possible.

We use a list to store the names of the cities already visited. Each time a city is chosen, its name is added to the list. The program is as follows.

```
travelling(A,B) :- travel(A,B,[A]).

travel(A,B,_) :- direct_travel(A,B).
travel(A,B,List) :-
    direct_travel(A,C),
    non_visited(C,List),
    travel(C,B,[C|List]).
```

```
non_visited(_,[]).
non_visited(C,[C1|List]) :-
    C \= C1,
    non_visited(C,List).
```

2.7 Given is a list of arcs in the form $[\mathrm{arc}(3,2), \mathrm{arc}(4,1), \ldots]$. Write Prolog programs to perform the following tasks:

(a) Test if the arcs in the given list can be rearranged into a continuous path of the form $[\mathrm{arc}(3,2), \mathrm{arc}(2,4), \mathrm{arc}(4,1), \ldots]$, and if so, return this continuous path.

(b) Test if the arcs in the given list form a *cycle*, that is, a continuous path of which the last arc can be joined to the first one.

(The above problems form a small part of the *Travelling Salesman problem* given in Chapter 7, Problem 7.6.)

Solution:

(a) This problem is a selection problem, which is similar to the selection-sort given in Figure 2.26. For convenience of expression, we use a dummy arc X as the initial arc. The problem is expressed as follows:

> $L1$ is a continuous path made up from L
> to be joined to the arc X *if*
> *either* both $L1$ and L are empty
> *or*   the head H of $L1$ is a selected member of L
> that can be joined to the last arc X, and
> the tail of $L1$ is a continuous path
> made up from the rest to be joined to the arc H.

The program:

```
rearrange(_,[],[]).
rearrange(arc(I,J),L,[arc(J,K)|Tail]) :-
    select(arc(J,K),L,Rest),
    rearrange(arc(J,K),Rest,Tail).

select :- % see Figure 2.16
```

For example:

```
?- rearrange(_,[arc(3,2),arc(4,1),arc(5,4),arc(2,5)],Path).
Path = [arc(3,2),arc(2,5),arc(5,4),arc(4,1)] ->
```

(b) In order to test if a given list of arcs makes a cycle, we rearrange the list into a continuous path exposing its first and last arcs for comparison. Thus, the program *rearrange* developed in part (a) is modified to return the last arc as well. Then we have the program *cycle* as shown below.

```
cycle(L) :- rearrange2(_,L,[arc(I,_)|_],arc(_,I)).

rearrange2(Last,[],[],Last).
rearrange2(arc(I,J),L,[arc(J,K)|Tail],Last) :-
    select(arc(J,K),L,Rest),
    rearrange2(arc(J,K),Rest,Tail,Last).

select :- % see  Figure 2.16
```

For example:

```
?- cycle([arc(3,2),arc(4,1),arc(5,4),arc(2,5),arc(1,3)]).
yes
```

2.8 Consider the following sort programs, where *select* is the procedure given in Figure 2.16.

```
(i)    sort1([],[]).
       sort1([X],[X]).
       sort1(L,[X,Y|R]) :- select(X,L,L1),
                           sort1(L1,[Y|R]),X =< Y.

(ii)   sort2([],[]).
       sort2([X],[X]).
       sort2(L,[X,Y|R]) :- select(X,L,L1),select(Y,L1,L2),
                           X =< Y,sort2([Y|L2],[Y|R]).
```

(a) Use mathematical induction to prove that the two programs are correct (assume the procedure *select* is correct).

(b) Which of the two preceding programs is more efficient?

Solution:

(a) Program *sort1*: For the base cases where list L contains zero or one element, the first two clauses show that *sort1* correctly returns the same list.

Consider the general case (third clause), where list L contains at least two elements and assume that *sort1* is correct for any shorter list. Since X is selected from L leaving the rest in L1, [X|L1] is a permutation of L. Also, since L1 is ordered into [Y|R] and X =< Y, it follows that [X,Y|R] is an ordered permutation of L. That is, L is sorted into [X,Y|R].

Program *sort2*: The base cases are as in *sort1*. Consider the third clause of *sort2* and assume that all subgoals in the body are true. Since X is selected from L leaving the rest in L1, and Y is selected from L1 leaving the rest in L2, [X,Y|L2] is a permutation of L. Furthermore, since X =< Y and [Y|L2] is ordered into [Y|R], it follows that [X,Y|R] is an ordered permutation of L. That is, L is sorted into [X,Y|R].

(b) Program *sort2* is more efficient than *sort1*, because the test X =< Y is placed before the recursive call, allowing the interpreter to abandon any hopeless search path earlier than in *sort1*.

2.9 Part of a database on domestic air flights in Australia is shown below (where ":" is a Prolog built-in functor).

(a) Write a Prolog query to ask for departure time of any Ansett flight from Canberra to Sydney on Wednesday.

(b) Does this database have any disadvantages? If it does, then suggest any changes for improvement.

```
% FLIGHT(DEPART,ARRIVAL,
%        [(DEPTIME,ARRTIME,FLIGHTNUM,AIRLINE,DAYS),...])
flight(canberra,sydney,
        [( 7:45, 8:35, 41,eastwest,[mon,fri]),
         (10:40,11:30,184,ansett,alldays),
         (14:00,14:50, 48,australian,[mon,wed,fri])]).

flight(sydney,brisbane,
        [( 8:45,10:45, 42,eastwest,[mon,tue,thu,fri]),
         (11:50,13:40,186,ansett,alldays),
         (15:10,17:10, 50,australian,[mon,wed,fri])]).
```

```
available(_,alldays).
available(Day,AvailList) :- member(Day,AvailList).
```

Solution:

(a) To find the departure time of an Ansett flight from Canberra to Sydney on Wednesday, we must retrieve the list of flights from Canberra to Sydney, then choose the Ansett flight that is available on Wednesday. More generally, we define the predicate *depart_time* as follows:

```
depart_time(DepTime,Depart,Destination,Airline,Day) :-
    flight(Depart,Destination,FlightList),
    member((DepTime,_,_,Airline,AvailList),FlightList),
    available(Day,AvailList).
```

Then we enter the following query:

```
?- depart_time(Time,canberra,sydney,ansett,wed).
Time = 10:40 ->
```

(b) The first disadvantage of the above database is that in order to find one flight, we have to retrieve the whole list of all flights of the queried route. The second and more serious disadvantage is in its maintenance. If some airline's schedule is changed or cancelled for a particular route, then the whole flight record must be replaced.

To avoid the above-mentioned inefficiency, the relation *flight* needs to be broken down into two separate relations (which are said to be in *first normal form*: Date, 1982) as follows:

```
flight(canberra,sydney,table1).
flight(sydney,brisbane,table2).
    .
    .
    .
schedule(table1, 7:45, 8:35, 41,eastwest,[mon,fri]).
schedule(table1,10:40,11:30,184,ansett,alldays).
schedule(table1,14:00,14:50, 48,australian,[mon,wed,fri]).
schedule(table2, 8:45,10:45, 42,eastwest,[mon,tue,thu,fri]).
schedule(table2,11:50,13:40,186,ansett,alldays).
schedule(table2,15:10,17:10, 50,australian,[mon,wed,fri]).
    .
    .
    .
```

Now, the predicate *depart_time* is redefined as follows:

```
depart_tim2(DepTime,Depart,Destination,Airline,Day) :-
    flight(Depart,Destination,Table),
    schedule(Table,DepTime,_,_,Airline,AvailList),
    available(Day,AvailList).
```

To find the departure time of an Ansett flight from Canberra to Sydney on Wednesday, we enter the query:

```
?- depart_tim2(Time,canberra,sydney,ansett,wed).
Time = 10:40 ->
```

2.10 *The next higher permutation.* A positive integer is represented by a list of decimal digits. Its next higher permutation is defined to be the next greater integer composed of exactly the same digits. For example, the next higher permutation of 123542 is 124235.

The problem of finding the next higher permutation of a given integer is traditionally an algorithmic problem (which is solved in Chapter 3, Problem 3.4). Write a declarative Prolog program that receives a list of decimal digits and returns its next higher permutation. You may use the Prolog built-in predicate *not* for which *not*(*A*) means *A* is not true.

Solution:

The definition of the next higher permutation is expressed as follows:

> *L1* is the next higher permutation of *L* if
> > *L1* is a higher permutation of *L*, and
> > *L1* is not far higher than *L*.

> *L1* is a higher permutation of *L* if
> > *L1* is a permutation of *L*, and
> > *L1* is higher than *L*.

> *L1* is higher than *L* if
> > *either* head of *L1* is greater than head of *L*
> > *or* two heads are equal, and
> > tail of *L1* is higher than tail of *L*.

> *L1* is far higher than *L* if
> > there is a higher permutation *L2* of *L* such that
> > *L1* is higher than *L2*.

Therefore the program is as follows:

```
next_higher_perm(L,L1) :-
    higher_perm(L,L1), not(far_higher(L1,L)).

higher_perm(L,L1) :-
    permutation(L,L1), higher(L1,L).

higher([H1|T1],[H|T]) :- H1 > H.
higher([H|T1], [H|T]) :- higher(T1,T).

far_higher(L1,L) :-
    higher_perm(L,L2), higher(L1,L2).
```

The procedure *permutation* is defined in Figure 2.24. For example, try the query:

```
?- next_higher_perm([1,2,3,5,4,2],N).
N = [1,2,4,2,3,5] ->
```

Obviously, the above program may run slow for long lists. But it is nice that the programmer need not think hard about *how* to solve the problem. The program is merely the problem's definition.

2.11 *Job assignment.* N jobs are to be done using N different machines. The costs of using machine i to do the job j are given in the following table.

		JOBS			
		1	2	3	4
MACHINES	1	6	5	3	6
	2	5	6	8	12
	3	8	6	8	9
	4	3	6	5	8

Write a declarative Prolog program to determine which jobs should be assigned to which machines in order to minimise the total cost. (A procedural solution to this problem is given in Chapter 6, Problem 6.5.)

Solution:

Suppose that both the machines and jobs are numbered from 1 to N. Then, a solution to the job assignment problem can be represented by a list *JobList* of machine-job pairs of the form $[(1, J_1), \ldots, (N, J_N)]$. This list is defined as follows.

> *JobList* is a solution to the N machine-jobs assignment problem
> with corresponding cost *Cost* if
>> *Macs* is the list of machine numbers from 1 to N,
>> *JobList* is a list of job assignments to machines *Macs*
>>> with corresponding cost *Cost*, such that
>> *Cost* is the minimum cost of using machines *Macs*.

> *JobList* is a list of job assignments to machines *Macs*
> with corresponding cost *Cost* if
>> *Jobs* is a permutation of *Macs*,
>> *JobList* is the list of corresponding pairs of *Macs* and *Jobs*
>>> with *Cost* being the total cost.

> *Cost* is the minimum cost of using machines *Macs* if
>> there is not any job assignment with cost less than *Cost*.

The above definition is translated into the following program:

```
assign_jobs(N,JobList,Cost) :-
    list(1,N,Macs),
    assignment(Macs,JobList,Cost),
    minimum_cost(Macs,Cost).

assignment(Macs,JobList,Cost) :-
    permutation(Macs,Jobs),
    pairs(Macs,Jobs,JobList,Cost).

minimum_cost(Macs,Cost) :-
    not((assignment(Macs,_,Cost2),Cost2 < Cost)).

pairs([],[],[],0).
pairs([M|Ms],[J|Js],[(M,J)|L],Cost) :-
    pairs(Ms,Js,L,C),table(M,J,C1),
    Cost is C + C1.

permutation :- % see Figure 2.24
```

```
list(I,N,[]) :- I > N.
list(I,N,[I|L]) :-
    I =< N, I1 is I+1,list(I1,N,L).

table(1,1,6).          table(3,1,8).
table(1,2,5).          table(3,2,6).
table(1,3,3).          table(3,3,8).
table(1,4,6).          table(3,4,9).
table(2,1,5).          table(4,1,3).
table(2,2,6).          table(4,2,6).
table(2,3,8).          table(4,3,5).
table(2,4,12).         table(4,4,8).
```

The following query shows an answer to the given job assignment problem:

```
?- assign_jobs(4,JobList,Cost).

JobList = [(1,3),(2,2),(3,4),(4,1)]
Cost = 21 ->
```

We note again that the above declarative program runs very slow for a large number of machines and jobs. To have a more efficient program, we must use some well-defined algorithm to solve the problem, and that is the subject of Problem 6.5 of Chapter 6.

Supplementary problems

2.12 The Pizza-House chalkboard that lists various types of pizza with their ingredients and prices was wiped out by the rain. You are asked to rewrite the board using the following information. There are five types of pizza with completely different toppings and prices. Each type of pizza has two toppings: one from the list of *ham*, *mussels*, *prawns*, *salami*, and *tuna*; the other from the list of *avocado*, *corn*, *olive*, *pineapple*, and *tomato*. Five prices are $5.00, $6.50, $7.00, $8.50, and $10.00. Other clues are given below.

Hawaiian pizza has mussels and costs over $6.50. *Marco-Polo* has tomato, but no ham, which is on the pizza that costs $8.50. *Pepperoni* costs $7.00 and *Super-Supreme* has no pineapple. The price of the pizza that has tuna and corn is not $6.50, and the pizza that costs $5.00 has olive but no salami. The price of the pizza that has pineapple

is not $10.00. The last type of pizza is called *Ninja-pizza*.
You need to determine which pizzas have what toppings and prices.

2.13 Consider the function f defined as follows:

$$f(x) = x - 10 \text{ if } x > 100,$$
$$f(x) = f(f(x + 11)) \text{ if } x \leq 100.$$

(a) Write a Prolog procedure $f(X, Y)$ that defines Y as the value of the above-given function for any integer X.

(b) What will be the output for the query ?- $f(95, Y)$.

2.14 *The tower of Hanoi.* This legend was first told in a Hanoi monastery more than 200 years ago. A group of overproud monks was assigned by God a task to perform, which was to move 100 golden disks from one peg to another with the help of a third peg. There were two rules: only one disk could be moved at a time, and a larger disk could never be placed on top of a smaller disk. Initially, the disks were all on peg 1, with the largest at the bottom and the smallest at the top.

(a) Write a Prolog program to find a sequence of moves to complete God's task.

(b) What is the total number of moves generated by the program?

2.15 Let L and *L1* denote two lists of terms. Write Prolog procedures to realise the following:

(a) Delete all occurrences of an element X in L, giving the result in *L1*.

(b) Replace the first occurrence of X in L with Y, giving the result in *L1*.

(c) Delete the Nth element in L, leaving the rest in *L1*.

2.16 Let L denote a list of integers.

(a) Write a Prolog procedure $sum(L, S)$ that defines S to be the sum of all elements in L.

(b) Write a procedure $mean(L, X)$ that defines X to be the mean value of elements in L, by referring to the already developed procedures *sum* and *length* (Figure 2.18).

(c) Write a procedure that performs the same function as the one in part (b) without explicitly referring to *sum* and *length*.

2.17 Let *L1, L2*, and *L* denote lists of terms. Write Prolog programs to realise the following.

(a) Interleave alternate elements of *L1* and *L2* into *L*. For example, if $L1 = [a, b, c]$ and $L2 = [1, 2]$, then $L = [a, 1, b, 2, c]$. Are the input-output roles of variables in your answer program reversible?

(b) Transpose *L1, L2* into *L*. That is, if $L1 = [a, b, c]$ and $L2 = [1, 2, 3]$, then $L = [(a, 1), (b, 2), (c, 3)]$. Again, are the input-output roles of variables in your answer program reversible?

(c) Suppose that *L1* and *L2* are lists of numeric values. Write a procedure *inner_prod(L1,L2,X)* that defines *X* to be the inner-product of two vectors *L1, L2*. Are the input-output roles of variables in your program reversible?

2.18 Let *L* be a list of terms. Write Prolog programs for the following definitions.

(a) *cutlast(L,L1)* defines *L1* to be obtained from *L* with the last element removed.

(b) *trim(N,L,L1)* defines *L1* to be obtained from *L* with the first *N* elements removed.

(c) *trimlast(N,L,L1)* defines *L1* to be obtained from *L* with the last *N* elements removed.

2.19 Explain what the following Prolog programs define. Here, *atomic* is a Prolog built-in predicate: *atomic(X)* is true if *X* contains a constant such as 1, 2.6, [], john, or 'John'.

```
(a)   mystery([],1).
      mystery(X,0) :- X \= [], atomic(X).
      mystery([X|Y],N) :- mystery(X,Q),mystery(Y,P),
                          Q1 is Q+1, max(P,Q1,N).

      max(A,B,A) :- A >= B.
```

```
        max(A,B,B) :- A < B.
```

(b)   `strange(X,X) :- atomic(X).`
      `strange([H|T],[H1|T1]) :- strange(H,H1),`
      `                          strange(T,T1).`

2.20   Suppose that each member of a club is associated with a record of information. For example:

> Name : Henry Law
> Sex : male
> Height (in metres) : 1.78
> Weight (in kilograms) : 75
> Hobbies : jogging, skiing, singing.

Write a Prolog database containing data on the club's members to facilitate retrieval of the following information:

(a) Given a name, find height, or weight, or hobbies.
(b) Find someone with a particular hobby.

2.21   Data on each employee of a company consist of the following: name, department in which he or she works, his or her position in the department, number of years of service, and current salary. Write a Prolog database containing the employees' information to facilitate the following queries:

(a) Find the department in which some particular person works.
(b) Find out who is the manager of a particular person.
(c) Give some idea on the salary of a manager.
(d) Add the information that those employees with more than 5 years of service are given a bonus of $2000.

2.22   Write Prolog clauses to express the following sentences. Use Prolog built-in predicate *not* to express that something is not true.

> *X* should plead not guilty of *Y* *if*
> > *X* is accused of *Y*, and
> > *X* has good defence for *Y*.

X should plead guilty of *Y* *if*
    X is accused of *Y*, and
    X does not have good defence for *Y*, and
    penalty for *Y* is light.

X should plead guilty of *Y* *if*
    X is accused of *Y*, and
    X committed *Z*, and
    X is not accused of *Z*, and
    X does not have good defence for *Z*, and
    penalty for *Y* is light, and
    penalty for *Z* is heavy.

2.23 *The Travelling Salesman.* The job of a travelling salesman is to visit every city in his plan and return to his original city. The costs of travelling between cities are given in the following table (here, for convenience, cities are numbered, but city names may be used instead).

CITIES

		1	2	3	4	5	6
	1	0	27	43	16	30	26
	2	7	0	16	1	30	25
CITIES	3	20	13	0	35	5	0
	4	21	16	25	0	18	18
	5	12	46	27	48	0	5
	6	23	5	5	9	5	0

Write a declarative Prolog program to determine the (cyclic) path that the salesman should take to minimise the total travelling cost. (A procedural solution to this problem is given in Chapter 7, Problem 7.6.)

Chapter 3

Procedural
Prolog programming

3.1   Procedural reading of Prolog programs

Consider a Prolog clause of the form

$$A \;\; \text{:-} \;\; B_1, \ldots, B_n.$$

Declaratively, the clause is read "A if B_1 and ... and B_n". But from the operational point of view, the above clause is regarded as the declaration of a procedure, which is read as follows:

$$\text{To do} \;\; A, \;\; \text{do} \;\; B_1 \;\; \text{then} \;\; \ldots \;\; \text{then} \;\; B_n.$$

In general, a Prolog procedure is a set of clauses of the following form, where $T_1, \ldots, T_k$ are lists of terms:

$$A(T_1) \ :- \ B_1, \ldots, B_{n_1}.$$
$$A(T_2) \ :- \ C_1, \ldots, C_{n_2}.$$
$$\vdots$$
$$A(T_k) \ :- \ D_1, \ldots, D_{n_k}.$$

The above clauses can be read procedurally as follows, where the symbol "=" is to be read "unifies with" (or more commonly, "has the form of"):

To do $A(X)$ do
  if $X = T_1$ then do B_1 then ... then B_{n_1};
  if $X = T_2$ then do C_1 then ... then C_{n_2};
  $\vdots$
  if $X = T_k$ then do D_1 then ... then D_{n_k}.

In particular, when $k = 2$ and T_1, T_2 are complementary, the procedure's reading can be expressed in the "if-then-else" form. Note immediately that some of the subgoals $B_1, C_1, \ldots, D_1$ may be just test procedures that return "true" or "false". In such cases, the clause should be read, say

  if $X = T_1$ and B_1 then do B_2 then ... then B_{n_1}.

For example, let us reexamine some simple programs that we have developed in the preceding chapter.

EXAMPLE 3.1

```
length([],0).
length([H|T],N) :- length(T,M),N is M+1.
```

One procedural reading of this program is as follows:

To find the length N of a list L do
  if L is empty then let $N = 0$
  else find the length M of the tail of L,
        then add 1 to M giving N.

We said that the above is *one* reading of the program, because the program can be read in the opposite direction, that is,

To find a list L of length N do
    if $N = 0$ then let L be the empty list
    else find a list T of length M such that N is $M + 1$,
         then add an element H in front of T giving L.

The above two different readings of the same program *length* correspond to two kinds of queries presented in Chapter 2 (page 34).

EXAMPLE 3.2

```
factorial(N,F) :- fact(N,1,F).

fact(0,T,T).
fact(N,T,F) :-
    N > 0,
    N1 is N-1,
    T1 is T*N,
    fact(N1,T1,F).
```

Since the test $N > 0$ requires that N must have a value, the second clause of procedure *fact* can only be called with N as input. Therefore, the only practical procedural reading of the above program is as follows:

To find factorial F of N do
    derive factorial F from N, 1.

To derive factorial F from N, T do
    if $N = 0$ then let $F = T$;
    if $N > 0$ then derive factorial F from $N - 1$, $T \times N$.

From Examples 3.1 and 3.2, we have the following preliminary notes.

Notes

1. The procedural reading of a Prolog program makes significant the order of clauses and order of subgoals in each clause. These are the orders in which the procedures are executed by the Prolog system. (Details on this matter will be discussed in Section 3.5.)

2. When a Prolog program is read procedurally, the input-output roles of variables are explicitly indicated. Thus, a procedural Prolog program loses some flexibility for the benefit of efficiency.

3.2   Writing a procedural Prolog program

The task of writing a procedural program in Prolog is almost the same as in any conventional programming language (except in some aspects that we shall point out later), that is, to follow the three normal stages of program development, namely

- design data structures to represent input and output;
- devise an algorithm to solve the problem;
- translate the algorithm into a Prolog program.

For example, let us consider how to solve the following classic problem.

EXAMPLE 3.3 N queens are to be placed on an $N \times N$ chessboard so that no queens can attack any other queens. Find a solution for the problem.

Here, the input is merely an integer N. The output is a chessboard with N queens' positions to be specified. We represent the output by a list of length N, each position of which represents a column of the chessboard, and each element of the list is an integer representing the row position of a queen. For instance, the chessboard of Figure 3.1 is represented by the list shown below it.

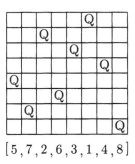

$$[5,7,2,6,3,1,4,8]$$

FIGURE 3.1   A solution for the 8-queens problem.

The following is an algorithm to solve the problem.

> To find a solution S for the N queens problem do
>> make a list L of integers from N down to 1, then
>> move the elements of L, one by one, to an empty list
>>> to produce the required safe list S.

To make a list L of integers from N down to 1 do
> if $N = 0$ then let L be the empty list;
> if $N > 0$ then let N be the head of L, and make the tail of L
>   a list of integers from $N - 1$ down to 1.

To move the elements of L to a list Qs to produce the safe list S do
> if L is empty then let $S = Qs$
> else select an element Q in L, saving the rest in R,
>   such that Q is safe from all queens in Qs, then
>   add Q to the list Qs, and then
>   continue to move elements of R to (Q, Qs) to produce S.

A queen in row Q is safe from all queens in Qs *if*
> *either* Qs is empty
> *or*   there are no queens in Qs on the diagonals of Q
>   (that is, for each distance $D = 1, 2, \ldots$, no queens in
> Qs appear in rows $Q \pm D$; see Figure 3.3).

```
queens(N,S) :-
    make_list(N,L), move_safe(L,[],S).

make_list(0,[]).
make_list(N,[N|T]) :-
    N > 0, M is N-1, make_list(M,T).

move_safe([],S,S).
move_safe(L,Qs,S) :-
    select(Q,L,R), safe(Q,1,Qs),
    move_safe(R,[Q|Qs],S).

select(X,[X|T],T).
select(X,[H|T],[H|T1]) :- select(X,T,T1).

safe(_,_,[]).
safe(Q,D,[Q1|Qs]) :-
    Q+D =\= Q1, Q-D =\= Q1,
    D1 is D+1, safe(Q,D1,Qs).
```

FIGURE 3.2 A program to solve the N-queens problem.

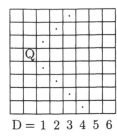
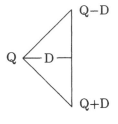

D = 1 2 3 4 5 6

FIGURE 3.3 A queen's attacking range.

The algorithm is translated into the program of Figure 3.2. A query can then be put to Prolog asking for a solution to the problem.

```
?- queens(8,S).
S = [5,7,2,6,3,1,4,8] ->
```

If we repeatedly press the semicolon key to ask for alternative solutions, this program will provide 92 different answers (which are actually symmetries and rotations of 12 basic answers). From Example 3.3 we have the following observations.

Notes

1. The algorithm to solve the *N*-queens problem presented above has been developed in a hierarchical top-down style. Each subalgorithm is directly translated into a Prolog procedure.

2. The program contains no explicit constructs for branching and looping. Instead, branching is realised via alternative clauses, and looping is performed by recursion.

3. There is also no data declaration or assignment in a Prolog program. In fact, all tasks of data manipulation such as data construction, variable assignment, and parameter passing are performed by the unification process. We shall discuss this important feature of Prolog in Section 3.4.

Although the representation of a chessboard as a list of integers is neat and convenient, the display of a solution in this form may be hard to apprehend. So, let us consider how to print out a solution in the form of a chessboard.

EXAMPLE 3.4   Assume the program *queens* has been developed. We write a program to print out a solution in the form of a square chessboard, using two simple built-in predicates: *write* to write a term, and *nl* to move to new line. The algorithm of top-level control and the printing task are as follows.

> To solve the *N*-queens problem do
>> find a solution *S* for the *N*-queens problem, then
>> print the solution *S* from row 1 to row *N*.

> To print *S* from row *M* to row *N* do
>> *if* $M > N$ then return
>> *else* print row *M* of *S*, then
>>> continue to print *S* from row $M + 1$ to row *N*.

> To print row *M* of *S* do
>> *if*   end of row then move to new line
>> *else* *if* *M* is the queen's row in the current column
>>> *then* print a letter 'Q'
>>> *else* print a dot mark,
>> and continue to print row *M* of the remaining columns of *S*.

The program is given below, and a sample output is shown in Figure 3.5.

```
solve_queens(N) :-
    queens(N,S),print_sol(S,1,N).

print_sol(S,M,N) :- M > N.
print_sol(S,M,N) :- M =< N,
    print_row(M,S),
    M1 is M+1,
    print_sol(S,M1,N).

print_row(_,[]) :- nl.
print_row(M,[Q|Qs]) :-
    (M = Q,write('Q'); M \= Q,write('.')),
    print_row(M,Qs).
```

FIGURE 3.4 Program to print a solution of *N*-queens problem.

```
. . . . . Q . .
. . Q . . . . .
. . . . Q . . .
. . . . . . Q .
Q . . . . . . .
. . . Q . . . .
. Q . . . . . .
. . . . . . . Q
```

FIGURE 3.5 Display of solution $[5, 7, 2, 6, 3, 1, 4, 8]$.

3.3   Program execution: unification and resolution

Let us now examine how Prolog answers a query. Generally, the course of a query's execution can be conjectured through the procedural reading of the related clauses in the program. To have an insight into this process, let us first consider the following example.

EXAMPLE 3.5   Suppose that we have the program of Figure 3.2 and we want to find a solution for the 4-queens problem. We enter the following query:

```
?- queens(4,X).
```

Invoked by the above query, the Prolog system performs the following steps of evaluation.

Beginning with the goal:

```
queens(4,X).
```

1. To evaluate this goal, the system finds the procedure *queens* and takes (a copy of) the clause

```
queens(N,S) :- make_list(N,L),move_safe(L,[],S)
```

(with all variables renamed by names not used before) such that the goal $queens(4, X)$ can be unified with the head $queens(N, S)$ of the clause. Here, the unifier is the substitution ($N = 4$, $X = S$). The goal is then replaced with the body of the clause and all variables are instantiated by the obtained substitution to give a new goal. So, we have the new goal:

```
make_list(4,L),move_safe(L,[],S).
```

2. Now, to evaluate this new goal, the system finds the procedure *make_list* and takes (a copy of) the clause

```
make_list(N1,[N1|T]) :- N1 > 0,M is N1-1,make_list(M,T).
```

(with all variables renamed by names not used before) such that the first subgoal $make\_list(4, L)$ can be unified with the head $make\_list$ $(N1, [N1|T])$ of the clause. Here, the unifier is the substitution $(N1 = 4, L = [4|T])$. This subgoal is then replaced with the body of the clause and all variables are instantiated by the obtained substitution to give the new goal:

```
4 > 0, M is 4-1,make_list(M,T),move_safe([4|T],[],S).
```

3. In realising that the predicate ">" is a predefined predicate, the system performs the test $4 > 0$ directly and returns the value "true". Likewise, the next subgoal M *is* $4 - 1$ is evaluated directly and the value $M = 3$ is returned. So, we have a new goal:

```
make_list(3,T),move_safe([4|T],[],S).
```

The above process continues until one of the following situations occurs:

- The last new goal is the empty goal, as a result of the preceding goal being unified with a *fact* in the program. In this case, the goal evaluation *succeeds* and the system composes all the unifiers obtained on the way to return the answer.

- The last new goal is not unifiable with the head of any clause in the program. In this case, the system goes back to the immediately preceding goal to find an alternative way of execution. The whole process is then repeated until either a *success* or a total *failure* (i.e., no clauses to unify and no preceding goals to turn back) occurs.

The procedure used in each step of the above-described process is called (*clause*) *resolution* and the whole process is called *deduction by resolution*.

Thus, in Prolog programming,

> ⋄ *Resolution* is the process of receiving a goal and a clause and producing a new goal. The resolving process is as follows: given the goal $A_1, A_2, \ldots, A_n$ and the clause $A \; :- \; B_1, \ldots, B_m$ such that A_1 is unified with A by the unifier θ; the new goal is $(B_1, \ldots, B_m, A_2, \ldots, A_n)\theta$, where the affix of θ means that all variables in the goal are instantiated by the substitution θ.

No doubt, the process of evaluating a query is complex and tedious. Fortunately, this is the work of the Prolog interpreter, and the user need not be too much concerned with that. In some cases, however, the knowledge of how Prolog works does help to detect errors in a program. To have a complete view of how Prolog works, let us consider a smaller but as representative program.

EXAMPLE 3.6   The program that describes the world of Ann and Sue (Example 1.1) is a small program, but it is a typical one for the purpose of examining Prolog's execution. Here, the program's clauses are numbered for easy reference.

```
likes(ann,X) :- toy(X),plays(ann,X).    % 1
likes(sue,X) :- likes(ann,X).            % 2
toy(doll).                               % 3
toy(snoopy).                             % 4
plays(ann,snoopy).                       % 5
```

When the query ?- likes(sue,X). is entered, Prolog performs the following steps to evaluate the goal.

Begin with the goal:

```
likes(sue,X).
```

1. Make a copy of clause 2 with variables renamed by names not used before:

```
likes(sue,X1) :- likes(ann,X1).
```

Unify the initial goal with the head of the above clause using the unifier $X = X1$. Then replace the goal with the body of the clause to give a new goal:

```
likes(ann,X1).
```

2. Make a copy of clause 1 with variables renamed by names not used before:

```
likes(ann,X2) :- toy(X2),plays(ann,X2).
```

Unify the new goal of step 1 with the head of this clause using the unifier $X1 = X2$. Then replace the goal with the body of the clause to give the new goal:

```
toy(X2),plays(ann,X2).
```

3. Make a copy of clause 3 (which is bodyless and contains no variables):

```
toy(doll).
```

Unify the first subgoal of the new goal in step 2 with the head of the above clause using the unifier $X2 = doll$. Then discard this subgoal (i.e., replacing it with empty) to give the new goal:

```
plays(ann,doll).
```

4. This goal cannot unify with the head of any clause in the program. So undo $X2$ and go back to step 3.

5. Make a copy of clause 4, which is next to clause 3 (and which is also bodyless and contains no variables):

```
toy(snoopy).
```

Unify the first subgoal of the new goal in step 2 with the head of the above clause using the unifier $X2 = snoopy$. Then discard this subgoal to obtain the new goal:

```
plays(ann,snoopy).
```

6. Make a copy of clause 5 (which is also bodyless and contains no variables):

```
plays(ann,snoopy).
```

Unify the new goal of step 5 with the head of this clause. Since the goal has no remaining subgoals and the clause is bodyless, the result is an *empty goal*.

So the evaluation process succeeds and an answer is obtained by the composition of the substitutions: $X = X1$, $X1 = X2$, $X2 = snoopy$.

In practice, to facilitate the perception of the above-described deduction process, we use a tree-picture, called the *resolution tree*, to show the steps of deduction as shown in Figure 3.6, where the numbers on the left side of the vertical bars refer to clause numbers in the program of Example 3.6.

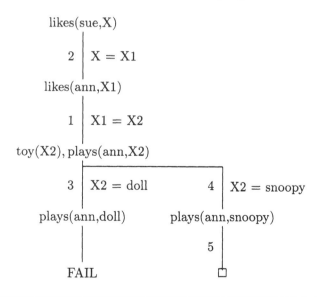

FIGURE 3.6 A resolution tree.

In this section, we have given a description of the process performed by Prolog in evaluating queries. For more details on unification and resolution, the reader is provided with a unification algorithm together with the formal definition of resolution in Appendix A. A pure Prolog interpreter is also given in Appendix B.

As we have mentioned before, the process of evaluating a query is tedious and should not be a grave concern to the user. For practical programming, however, it is essential to acquire a good knowledge of the following questions:

- How parameters are passed between procedures and how variables are instantiated;

- How the orders of clauses and subgoals affect a program's execution;

- How backtracking is performed.

These important issues are discussed in detail in the next sections.

3.4   Parameter passing

In Prolog, parameter passing is realised via unification. It is by unification that variables are assigned values or linked to each other. This process can be repeatedly done to build up complex data structures.

To illustrate the way in which parameters are passed between procedures, consider a typical goal A_1, A_2, where A_1 unifies with the head of a clause $A :\text{-} B_1, B_2$. The diagram of Figure 3.7 shows how data are passed through parameters. Here, T is a term, and X, Y, U, V are variables; the downward arrows represent the input flow, and the upward arrows represent output.

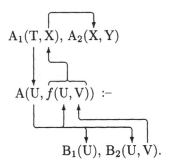

FIGURE 3.7 Parameter passing.

From the diagram, we see that the term T is passed to the variable U, which is immediately passed to U of $f(U, V)$ to be returned, and is also passed to

U in $B_1(U)$ and $B_2(U,V)$. After the successful execution of $B_2(U,V)$, the value of V is returned to V in $f(U,V)$ to fill up the data structure, which is returned to X in $A_1(T,X)$, and is then passed as input to X in $A_2(X,Y)$.

EXAMPLE 3.7   Consider the program *length* of Example 3.1. The data flow during execution of the query ?- *length*$([a,b,c],X)$ is shown in Figure 3.8. Again, the downward arrows represent the input flow, and the upward arrows represent output.

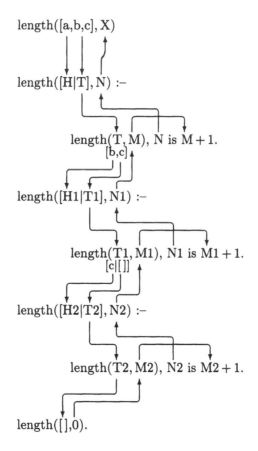

FIGURE 3.8   Data flow in the execution of *length*$([a,b,c],X)$.

Here, the data flow can be divided into two phases: input and output. At the beginning of the input phase, the head a of list $[a,b,c]$ is passed to H, and the tail $[b,c]$ is passed to T. H is not used, but the value of T is passed to T in the subgoal *length*(T,M) of the same clause. Then the head b of T

is passed to *H1*, and the tail [c] is passed to *T1*. Again, *H1* is not used, while the value of *T1* is passed to *T1* in the subgoal *length(T1, M1)*. From here, the head c of *T1* is passed to *H2*, and the tail [] is passed to *T2*. *H2* is not used, but the value of *T2* is passed to *T2* in the subgoal *length(T2, M2)*, which is then unified with list [] in the unit clause *length([], 0)*. This terminates the input phase, and the output phase begins. Now, the value 0 is returned to *M2*, which is then passed to *M2* in the goal *N2 is M2 + 1*. This gives *N2* the value 1, which is passed back to *N2* in the clause head. This value is then returned to *M1*, which is passed to *M1* in the goal *N1 is M1 + 1*. Thus, *N1* has value 2, which is passed back to *N1* in the clause head, to be returned to *M* and then passed to *M* in the goal *N is M + 1*. So *N* has value 3, which is passed back to *N* in the head clause and is finally returned to *X* in the query.

EXAMPLE 3.8   Consider the program *queens* of Figure 3.2. For the query ?- *queens(4, X)*, we have part of the data-flow diagram shown in Figure 3.9. As before, the downward arrows represent the input flow, and the upward arrows represent output.

From the preceding examples, we note the following important points on variable instantiation in Prolog.

Notes

1. Variables can only be instantiated via unification. There is no construct for variable assignment in Prolog.

2. The predicate "is" is frequently used to give values to variables, but it is not an assignment predicate. In fact, the goal *X is T* should be read "*X is unified with the value of T*". Thus, a goal such as *X is X + 1* always fails because, irrespective of whether *X* is instantiated or not, *X* cannot be unified with the value of $X + 1$.

3. More generally, if a variable already has a value, then it cannot be instantiated to another value. This is called the property of *referential uniqueness*, which is a distinguished feature of Prolog that makes it superior to conventional imperative languages in respect of programs' readability and verifiability.

In summary, we have the following compendium:

> ◇ In a Prolog program, data construction, variable assignment, and parameter passing are realised via unification.

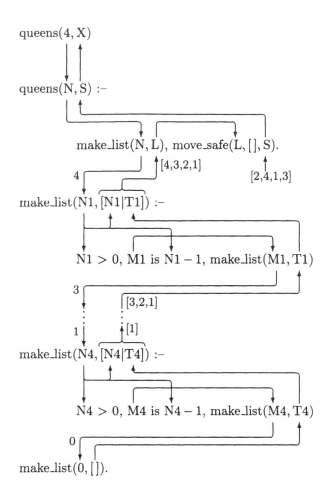

FIGURE 3.9 Part of the data flow in execution of *queens*(4, X).

3.5   Order of goals and clauses

It should be clear by now that in a procedural Prolog program, the orders of goals and clauses are crucial. In fact, the order of goals is the one in which procedures are executed, and the order of clauses is the order according to which control branching is directed. The following are some examples that show the effect of goals and clauses ordering.

EXAMPLE 3.9   Figure 3.10 shows two programs that print out the elements of a list. The first one writes the head of the list before writing its tail. As a result, it prints the list in the normal order. Whereas, the second program writes the tail of the list before writing its head. Thus, it prints the list in the reverse order.

```
write_list([]).                    write_list([]).
write_list([H|T]) :-               write_list([H|T]) :-
    write(H),                          write_list(T),
    write_list(T).                     write(H).

?- write_list([a,b,c]).            ?- write_list([a,b,c]).
abc                                cba
```

FIGURE 3.10 Effect of goals order.

Note that in both programs of Figure 3.10, the order of clauses is insignificant, provided that the query contains no variables (as expected in the procedural reading of the programs). The following is a simple example that shows the effect of clauses order in a Prolog program.

EXAMPLE 3.10   Compare the two programs of Figure 3.11 that differ only in the order of clauses. These two programs are logically equivalent, though, their operational effects are different. For the query ?- $integer\_num(2)$, the first program provides the answer "yes", whereas the second one causes the system to be trapped in an infinite loop, because it keeps using the program's first clause.

```
integer_num(0).                    integer_num(N) :-
integer_num(N) :-                      integer_num(M),
    integer_num(M),                    N is M+1.
    N is M+1.                      integer_num(0).

?- integer_num(2).                 ?- integer_num(2).
yes
```

FIGURE 3.11 Effect of clauses order.

So, to ensure the correctness of a procedural Prolog program, observe the following memento:

In a procedural Prolog program:
⋄ The order of goals determines the sequence in which goals are executed, and the order of clauses dictates control branching.

3.6   Backtracking

Besides the property of *referential uniqueness*, Prolog has another distinguished property, that is, its backtracking ability in program execution. In conventional programming, if a procedure's execution fails, then the whole task is aborted. In Prolog, when a goal fails, the system *backtracks* to the previous goal to find an alternative way of execution.

To illustrate Prolog's backtracking process, consider a typical goal A_1, A_2, A_3. Assume that A_1 has been successfully executed and that A_2 is being executed. Suppose that A_2 unifies with the head of clause $A :\text{-} B_1, B_2, B_3$. So, B_1, B_2, B_3 are executed next, in that order. If B_3 fails, then the system backtracks to execute B_2 again (using the next available clause for unification). If B_2 also fails, then the system backtracks further to execute B_1. Now if B_1 also fails, then the system backtracks to A_2 to find the next available clause for resolution, and so on. This process is described in the diagram of Figure 3.12, where the dotted lines represent the unification process.

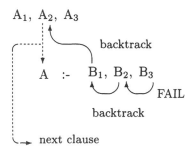

FIGURE 3.12 Backtracking process.

EXAMPLE 3.11   Consider the program *queens* of Figure 3.2. Suppose we wish to find a solution for the 4-queens problem. We have shown in Example 3.8 how the list $[4, 3, 2, 1]$ is generated. Let us now examine how the elements of this list are moved to an empty list to produce a solution. Initially, the goal *move_safe*$([4, 3, 2, 1], [], X)$ is unified with the head of the second clause of procedure *move_safe* as shown in Figure 3.13. Then, the body of this clause is executed, and we have

> *select*$(Q, [4, 3, 2, 1], R)$ succeeds with $Q = 4$ and $R = [3, 2, 1]$, then
>
> *safe*$(4, 1, [])$ succeeds, but
>
> *move_safe*$([3, 2, 1], [4], S)$ fails.

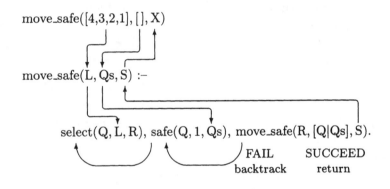

FIGURE 3.13   Backtracking execution.

So, the system backtracks to *safe*$(4, 1, [])$, which also fails, as it does not unify with the second clause of procedure *safe*. Hence, the system backtracks further to execute *select*$(Q, [4, 3, 2, 1], R)$, and we have

> *select*$(Q, [4, 3, 2, 1], R)$ succeeds with $Q = 3$ and $R = [4, 2, 1]$, then
>
> *safe*$(3, 1, [])$ succeeds, and also
>
> *move_safe*$([4, 2, 1], [3], S)$ succeeds with $S = [2, 4, 1, 3]$.

Therefore, the answer $[2, 4, 1, 3]$ is passed to S in the clause head, which is then returned to X.

In summary, we reemphasize the two principal forms of execution control in Prolog:

> In a procedural Prolog program:
> ◇ Control branching is realised via backtracking through alternative clauses;
> ◇ Control looping is performed by recursion.

3.7   Efficient list sorting

In Chapter 2 (Section 2.4), we have given some declarative list sorting programs and commented that they are elegant but inefficient. In this section, we present a number of efficient sort programs that are based on sophisticated algorithms. Again, the lists are assumed to contain only numbers, which are to be sorted into ascending order.

The first sorting algorithm to be considered is called *insertion-sort*. By this algorithm, to sort a list we sort its tail first, then add its head into the result at the right place. The algorithm is expressed as follows:

To sort the list L into $L1$ do
     if L is empty then let $L1$ be empty
   else sort the tail of L into $L2$, then
            insert the head of L into $L2$ to give $L1$.

To insert an element X into a list L giving $L1$ do
    if L is empty then let $L1$ contain X only;
    if $X \leq$ head of L then add X in front of L to give $L1$;
    if $X >$ head of L then take head of L as head of $L1$
            then insert X into tail of L to give tail of $L1$.

This algorithm is translated into the program of Figure 3.14.

```
insertion_sort([],[]).
insertion_sort([H|T],L1) :-
    insertion_sort(T,L2),insert(H,L2,L1).

insert(X,[],[X]).
insert(X,[H|T],[X,H|T]) :- X =< H.
insert(X,[H|T],[H|T1]) :-  X > H,insert(X,T,T1).
```

FIGURE 3.14 Program *insertion_sort*.

The next sorting algorithm is called *bubble-sort*. Here, the list is repeatedly scanned and adjacent elements that are not in order are swapped, until all elements are in order. (It is called bubble-sort because after each round of scanning and swapping, the list's next largest element is flushed to the right like a bubble.) The algorithm is expressed as follows:

To sort the list L into $L1$ do
 scan L and swap any adjacent elements that
 are not in order to obtain the list $L2$;
 if any swapping occurred then
  continue to sort $L2$ into $L1$
 else copy L to $L1$.

To scan L and swap any adjacent elements that
 are not in order to obtain the list $L2$ do
 if the first two elements of L are in order, then
  copy the head of L to head of $L2$, and
  continue to scan and swap tail of L into tail of $L2$;
 if the first two elements of L are not in order, then
  copy the second element of L to head of $L2$, and
  continue to scan and swap the rest of L into tail of $L2$;
 if L has only one element, then copy it to $L2$.

The only difficulty here is, how do we make the system realise that no swapping had occurred? A traditional solution to this problem is to use a signal that is initially set to 0 (or "off"). Whenever two adjacent elements are swapped, the signal is set to 1 (or "on"). Thus, if the signal remains 0 at the end of a scanning round, then the list is entirely ordered. The above algorithm is translated into the program of Figure 3.15.

```
bubble_sort(L,L1) :- swap(L,L2,0),
                     bubble_sort(L2,L1).
bubble_sort(L,L).

swap([X,Y|R],[X|T],S) :- X =< Y,swap([Y|R],T,S).
swap([X,Y|R],[Y|T],S) :- X > Y, swap([X|R],T,1).
swap([X],[X],1).
```

FIGURE 3.15 Program *bubble_sort*.

Observe that if the original list L contains fewer than two elements, then the goal *swap*(L, L2, 0) fails immediately, and so the list L is simply copied to L1. We shall see in the next chapter (Example 4.4) that the effect of using a signal in program *bubble-sort* of Figure 3.15 can be realised by means of Prolog's built-in control predicate *cut* (!).

Finally, let us consider an interesting classic sorting algorithm, namely *quick-sort* (the version presented here is attributed to Warren). Here, to sort a list L into the list $L1$, we use an intermediary list R that is initially empty. The list L is split into two lists Lt and Gt, where all elements of Lt are less than those in Gt. We then sort Gt and push it to the left of R, and sort Lt and push it to the left of the above result. This splitting process is repeated until the lists become trivial to handle. The algorithm is given below and the program is shown in Figure 3.16.

> To sort the list L into $L1$ do
> > sort L through an empty list to produce $L1$.

> To sort L through R to produce $L1$ do
> > *if* L is empty then copy R to $L1$
> > *else* partition L into three parts:
> > > > the head H of L,
> > > > a list Lt of elements of $L \leq H$,
> > > > a list Gt of elements of $L > H$,
> > > sort Gt through R to produce $GtsR$, then
> > > sort Lt through $(H, GtsR)$ to produce $L1$.

To partition L into $Lt \leq X$ and $Gt > X$ do

    if L is empty then let both Lt and Gt be empty;

    if   head of $L \leq X$ then copy it to head of Lt, then

            partition tail of L into tail of Lt and Gt

    if   head of $L > X$ then copy it to head of Gt, then

            partition tail of L into Lt and tail of Gt.

```
sort_list(L,L1) :- quick_sort(L,[],L1).

quick_sort([],R,R).
quick_sort([H|T],R,L1) :-
    partition(T,Lt,H,Gt),
    quick_sort(Gt,R,GtsR),
    quick_sort(Lt,[H|GtsR],L1).

partition([],[],_,[]).
partition([H|T],[H|TLt],X,Gt) :-
    H =< X,partition(T,TLt,X,Gt).
partition([H|T],Lt,X,[H|TGt]) :-
    H > X, partition(T,Lt,X,TGt).
```

FIGURE 3.16 Program *quick_sort*.

3.8 Fundamental techniques of procedural Prolog programming

We conclude this chapter with a summary of the fundamental techniques used in the previous sections in developing procedural Prolog programs. Given a problem or a task to be done, the following steps of program development are to be followed.

1. Design data structures to represent input, output, and any intermediary data as required.

2. Devise algorithms to perform the task, using only two forms of control: *selection* and *recursion*. The algorithms should be developed in a hierarchical top-down manner, and terminate at the levels where all subtasks are elementary.

3. Translate the algorithms of step 2 into a Prolog program. Each sub-algorithm is translated into a Prolog procedure, using the following rules:

- The algorithm's heading is converted into the procedure's head predicate;
- Each unconditional statement is translated into a goal in the body;
- Each conditional statement is translated into a clause, in which conditions are expressed in two ways: equalities are explicitly represented by unification within the clause's head; other conditions are expressed as testing goals (also called *guards*) in the clause's body.

Note that each variable may be used as input or output, but not both. That is, data passing is only one-way, and variable overwriting is not allowed.

4. Establish the correctness of the program by checking the correctness of each procedure. Program testing should be carried out bottom-up. That is, start to test the procedures at the lowest level first, then move up to test higher-level procedures. (More details on program validation are given in Chapter 5, Section 5.5.)

5. Finally, add side-effect features such as input-output to the program as necessary. This topic will be discussed with more details in the next chapter.

In short, procedural Prolog programming aims to achieve efficiency at the cost of generality. In fact, writing procedural programs requires the programmer to have full knowledge of *how* to solve the problem. This is usually difficult for problems in artificial intelligence.

Generally, for large applications, neither of the declarative nor procedural approaches is adequate. But a combination of the two approaches provides a unique and powerful technique of programming, which we shall explore further in Chapter 5 and subsequent chapters.

Solved problems

3.1 Consider the procedure *append* developed in Chapter 2:

```
append([],L,L).
append([H|T],L,[H|R]) :- append(T,L,R).
```

Give all possible procedural readings of the procedure.

Solution:

We have six different readings corresponding to the cases where either two or one of the arguments in *append*($L1, L2, L$) is input and the rest are output.

Case 1: Input $L1, L2$; Output L.

> To append $L1$ to $L2$ to produce L do
>> *if* $L1$ is empty then copy $L2$ to L
>> *else* copy head of $L1$ to head of L, then
>>> append tail of $L1$ to $L2$ to produce tail of L.

```
?- append([a,b,c],[1,2],L).
L = [a,b,c,1,2] ->
```

Case 2: Input $L1, L$; Output $L2$.

> To check and delete prefix $L1$ from L to produce $L2$ do
>> *if* $L1$ is empty then copy L to $L2$
>> *else if* head of $L1$ is the same as head of L
>>> then (discard them and) check and delete tail of $L1$
>>>> as a prefix of tail of L to produce $L2$.

```
?- append([a,b,c],L2,[a,b,c,1,2]).
L2 = [1,2] ->
```

Case 3: Input $L2, L$; Output $L1$.

> To check and delete suffix $L2$ from L to produce $L1$ do
>> *if* $L2 = L$ then return $L1 = [\,]$
>> *else* copy head of L to head of $L1$, then
>>> check and delete suffix $L2$ from tail of L to produce tail of $L1$.

```
?- append(L1,[1,2],[a,b,c,1,2]).
L1 = [a,b,c] ->
```

Case 4: Input L; Output $L1, L2$.

> To split L into $L1$ and $L2$ do
>> *either* make $L1$ empty and copy L to $L2$
>> *or*   copy head of L to head of $L1$, then
>>> split tail of L into tail of $L1$ and $L2$.

```
?- append(L1,L2,[a,b,c,1,2]).
L1 = []
L2 = [a,b,c,1,2] ->;
```

```
L1 = [a]
L2 = [b,c,1,2] ->;

L1 = [a,b]
L2 = [c,1,2] ->;

L1 = [a,b,c]
L2 = [1,2] ->;

L1 = [a,b,c,1]
L2 = [2] ->;

L1 = [a,b,c,1,2]
L2 = [] ->
```

Case 5: Input *L1*; Output *L2, L*.

To save *L1* as a prefix of *L* and identify *L2* with the rest of *L* do
  if   *L1* is empty then return *L = L2* uninstantiated
  else copy head of *L1* to head of *L*, then
            save tail of *L1* as a prefix of tail of *L* and identify *L2*
              with the rest of *L*.

```
?- append([a,b,c],L2,L).
L2 = _0085
L = [a,b,c|_0085] ->;
no
```

Case 6: Input *L2*; Output *L1, L*.

To save *L2* as a suffix of *L* and identify *L1* with the rest of *L* do
  either make *L1* empty and copy *L2* to *L*
  or   identify head of *L1* with head of *L*, then
             save *L2* as a suffix of tail of *L* and identify tail of *L1*
               with the rest of *L*.

```
?- append(L1,[1,2],L).
L1 = []
L = [1,2] ->;

L1 = [_013D]
L = [_013D,1,2] ->;
  .
  .
  .
```

3.2 Write a procedural Prolog program to reverse a list L into a list $L1$, using an intermediary list R that is initially empty.

Solution:

Algorithm:

> To reverse list L into R to produce final list $L1$ do
> > *if* L is empty then simply copy R to $L1$
> > *else* copy head of L and add it in front of R to give a new list,
> > then reverse tail of L into this new list to produce $L1$.

The program:

```
reverse([],R,R).
reverse([H|T],R,L1) :- reverse(T,[H|R],L1).
```

3.3 *In-order binary tree.* A list can also be sorted into an in-order binary tree. Write a Prolog program that sorts a list L of integers into a binary tree T. (For representation of a binary tree, see Chapter 2, Section 2.5.)

Solution:

We begin with an empty tree, and we insert the elements of L, one by one, into it to produce the sorted tree T.

Algorithm:

> To sort the list L into a binary tree T do
> > insert elements of L into an empty tree to produce T.
>
> To insert elements of list L into tree S to produce tree T do
> > *if* L is empty then copy S to T
> > *else* insert head of L into S to produce tree $S1$, then
> > insert elements of tail of L into $S1$ to produce tree T.
>
> To insert element X into tree S to produce tree T do
> > *if* S is empty then T has a single node containing X
> > *else if* $X <$ root of T then
> > > insert X into left branch of S to produce left branch
> > > of T, and copy root and right branch of S to those of T
> > > *else* insert X into right branch of S to produce right branch
> > > of T, and copy root and left branch of S to those of T.

The program is shown as follows:

```
sort_tree(L,T) :- insert_tree(L,nil,T).

insert_tree([],T,T).
insert_tree([X|R],S,T) :-
    insert_elemt(X,S,S1),insert_tree(R,S1,T).

insert_elemt(X,nil,bt(nil,X,nil)).
insert_elemt(X,bt(Left,Y,Right),bt(Left1,Y,Right)) :-
    X < Y, insert_elemt(X,Left,Left1).
insert_elemt(X,bt(Left,Y,Right),bt(Left,Y,Right1)) :-
    X >= Y,insert_elemt(X,Right,Right1).
```

For example:

```
?- sort_tree([4,2,5,1,3],T).
T = bt(bt(bt(nil,1,nil),2,bt(nil,3,nil)),4,bt(nil,5,nil))
```

3.4 *Next-higher permutation.* The problem of finding the next-higher permutation of a given list of decimal digits has been solved declaratively in the preceding chapter (Problem 2.10). Now write a procedural Prolog program to solve the problem of next-higher permutation efficiently.

Solution:

Given is a list L of decimal digits. We want to find a permutation $L1$ of L that represents the least integer greater than the one represented by L. Let us call "low digits" those from the right-hand end of the list. To move a digit within the list causing minimum increase to the number, we choose the lowest digit Y that is smaller than some digits on its right. For example, if $L = [1, 2, 3, 5, 4, 2]$, then choose $Y = 3$. We then choose from the right-hand side of Y, the least digit U that is greater than Y. For the given example, $U = 4$. Now, by swapping Y and U, we make an increase to the number that is the least possible by any pair swapping. For the above example, the list becomes $[1, 2, 4, 5, 3, 2]$. Now, since the low digits are in decreasing order, we simply reverse them to obtain the next-higher permutation. In this case, the answer is $[1, 2, 4, 2, 3, 5]$. So we have the following algorithm:

> To find the next-higher permutation $L1$ of L do
>> scan list L from right
>> to find the first digit $Y <$ its right-neighbour digit X, then
>> scan list L from right again
>> to find the first digit $U > Y$, then
>> swap Y and U, and
>> reverse the digits on U's right.

The program:

```
next_higher_perm(L,L1) :-
    reverse(L,[],L2),
    append(A,[X,Y|B],L2),X > Y,
    append(A,[X],C),
    append(A1,[U|B1],C), U > Y,
    append(A1,[Y|B1],B2),
    reverse([U|B],B2,L1).
```

The procedures *append* and *reverse* are given in Problems 3.1 and 3.2. For example:

```
?- next_higher_perm([1,2,3,5,4,2],L).
L = [1,2,4,2,3,5] ->
```

We note that the above program runs much faster than the declarative program given in Problem 2.10.

3.5 *The cryptarithmetic problem.* Write a Prolog program to assign a unique digit from 0 to 9, to each letter of the following equation, where $S > 0$ and $M > 0$, such that the equation holds.

$$SEND + MORE = MONEY.$$

Solution:
The given equation is equivalent to the following system of equations, where *C1, C2, C3* are carryovers.

C3	C2	C1		$D + E$	$=$	$Y + 10\,C1$
	S	E	N	D		
	N + R + C1	$=$	$E + 10\,C2$			

$$\begin{array}{ccccc}
C3 & C2 & C1 \\
 & S & E & N & D \\
+ & M & O & R & E \\
\hline
M & O & N & E & Y
\end{array}
\qquad
\begin{array}{rcl}
D + E & = & Y + 10\,C1 \\
N + R + C1 & = & E + 10\,C2 \\
E + O + C2 & = & N + 10\,C3 \\
S + M + C3 & = & O + 10\,M
\end{array}$$

Since $M > 0$, we must have $M = 1$. To find values for the remaining letters, we begin with the last equation that has the least number of unknowns. So:

To solve the SEND + MORE = MONEY problem do
let $M = 1$ and $L = [0, 2, 3, 4, 5, 6, 7, 8, 9]$,
select a positive digit for S from L, leaving the rest in *L1*,
choose $C3 = 0$ or 1,
obtain the value of O using the last equation,
eliminate the value of O from *L1*, leaving the rest in *L2*,

select a digit for E from $L2$, leaving the rest in $L3$,
choose $C2 = 0$ or 1,
obtain the value of N using the third equation,
eliminate the value of N from $L3$, leaving the rest in $L4$,
choose $C1 = 0$ or 1,
obtain the value of R using the second equation,
eliminate the value of R from $L4$, leaving the rest in $L5$,
select a digit for D from $L5$, leaving the rest in $L6$,
obtain the value of Y using the first equation,
check to ensure that Y is in $L6$.

The program is shown below, where the procedure *select* is defined in Figure 2.16:

```
solve([S,E,N,D],[M,O,R,E],[M,O,N,E,Y]) :-
    M = 1, L = [0,2,3,4,5,6,7,8,9],
    select(S,L,L1), S > 0, (C3 = 0; C3 = 1),
    O is S+M+C3-10*M, select(O,L1,L2),
    select(E,L2,L3), (C2 = 0; C2 = 1),
    N is E+O+C2-10*C3, select(N,L3,L4),
    (C1 = 0; C1 = 1),
    R is E+10*C2-(N+C1), select(R,L4,L5),
    select(D,L5,L6),
    Y is D+E-10*C1, select(Y,L6,_).
```

3.6 *The analogy problem* (Evans, 1963). Consider the task of solving geometric analogy problems, typically used in intelligence tests. A list of figures is given. Three figures A, B, C are singled out and the candidate is asked: "If figure A is related to figure B, then what figure is C related to?".

(a) Write a Prolog program to solve this problem.

(b) Test the program on the following sets of figures.

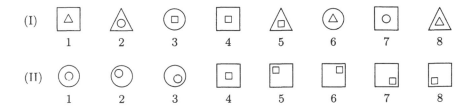

Solution:

We represent each figure with a fact describing the relationship between its components. For example, figure 1 of set (I) is represented by the fact

```
figure(1,middle(triangle,square)).
```

Suppose that the question is expressed as: "If figure number A is related to figure number B, then what figure is figure number C related to?". The algorithm to answer this query is as follows:

> To find the number X of a figure that is related to figure C
> in the same way as figure B related to figure A do
>   retrieve figures FA, FB, FC numbered A, B, C, then
>   find a rule that relates FA to FB, then
>   apply this rule to FC to obtain a figure FX, and then
>   scan the existing figures to find the number X of FX.

The program:

```
analogy((A,B),(C,X)) :-
    figure(A,FA),figure(B,FB),figure(C,FC),
    relate(FA,FB,Rule),
    relate(FC,FX,Rule),
    figure(X,FX).

relate(middle(F1,F2),middle(F2,F1),invert).
relate(middle(F1,F2),left_top(F1,F2),shift_left_top).
relate(middle(F1,F2),right_top(F1,F2),shift_right_top).
```

For example:

```
?- analogy((1,5),(3,X)).
X = 7 ->
```

To run the program with several different sets of figures, we may include in *figure* and *analogy* an additional argument representing the index of the specified set of figures.

Supplementary problems

3.7 Give all possible procedural readings of the procedures *member* and *select* (Chapter 2, Figures 2.13 and 2.16).

3.8 Consider again the *N*-queens problem of Example 3.3. Write a Prolog program to solve this problem by first generating a list of *N* variables and then filling the list with appropriate integers. (Hint: use procedure *length* of Figure 2.18 to generate the initial list.)

3.9 *Merge-sort* is another classic technique of list sorting. In merge-sort, the list is divided into two almost equal sublists, which are separately sorted and then merged back together. Write a Prolog procedure to sort a list *L* of integers into a list *L1* using the technique of merge-sort.

3.10 Given a binary tree of the form *bt(Left, X, Right)*. Write a Prolog procedure that receives a binary tree and produces a list of node values of the tree in in-order.

3.11 Consider the following program:

```
fill(X,N,L) :- length(L,N),append([X],L1,L),
               append(L2,[X],L), L1 = L2.
```

(a) If the input *X* is a term and input *N* is a positive integer, then what will be the output *L*?

(b) Write a procedure that does not call any other procedures and performs the same function as procedure *fill* given above. Compare the execution times of the two versions for various values of *N*.

3.12 Write a Prolog program to assign a unique digit from 0 to 9, to each letter of the following equation, where *C* and *R* are positive, such that the equation holds.

$$CROSS + ROAD = DANGER.$$

3.13 *The assembling problem.* Nine parts of an electronic board have square shape, the same size, and each edge of every part is marked with a letter and a plus or minus sign. The parts are to be assembled into a complete board as shown in the right figure below, such that the common edges have the same letter and opposite signs.

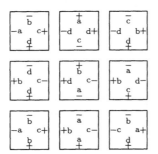 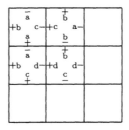

Write a Prolog program to determine how to assemble the parts, that is, to determine the locations and positions of the parts (with respect to their present positions) so that they fit together to make the complete board.

3.14 *The shop bagger* (Winston, 1984). A robot is used in a supermarket to bag customers' goods. At the checkout counter, after the items are checked for payment, a list of items is passed to the robot's memory to be used in the bagging task. Write a Prolog program *bagger* to receive the above-mentioned list of items and instruct the robot to put the items in bags according to the following rules:

- Large items must be placed in bags first, then the medium-size items, and finally the small items.
- Items have size 1, 3, or 5, and all bags are of the same size 19.
- An item must be put into one of the current bags if there is room for it.
- If no current bags have enough room for the item at hand, then a new bag is used.

The program should contain a database on sizes of various items in the shop and produce a list of bags, each of which consists of a list of items in the order from top to bottom of the bag. For example, if the list of items is [coke, cake, mug, mug, choc, cigarette, coke, bread, tissuebox, soap, biscuit, lettuce, coke], then the output could be:

bag 1:	soap	bag 2:	biscuit	bag 3:	bread
	cigarette		cake		coke
	choc		coke		coke
	mug		tissuebox		
	mug				
	lettuce				

Chapter 4

Control and side-effect features of Prolog

4.1 Control of program execution

In the preceding chapter, we have shown how the order of goals and clauses in a Prolog program affects the execution of the program. Thus, the ordering of goals and clauses can be used to control a program's execution.

The general rule of ordering goals and clauses in a Prolog program to improve the program's efficiency is to arrange the clauses top-down in descending order of satisfiability and to place the subgoals of each clause left-to-right in ascending order of satisfiability. This arrangement allows any goal to succeed or fail as early as possible. Thus, the time of searching for an answer could be reduced.

The ordering of goals and clauses is only an implicit form of control, however. Prolog provides a number of built-in predicates for the special purpose of explicit control of execution. For most procedural Prolog programs, the use of control predicates is necessary to ensure the program's correctness as well as to improve its efficiency.

In another aspect, practical programming requires facilities for environment manipulation such as input-output, data updating, and file handling. In Prolog, the system predicates provided for the purpose of environment manipulation are classified as the side-effect features of the language, because they cause changes outside their arguments' variables.

This chapter is devoted to the study of Prolog's built-in predicates that are frequently used in controlling programs' execution and in producing side effects. A full list of all Prolog's built-in predicates is given in Appendix C.

4.2   Prevention of backtracking: the cut predicate

When a Prolog system evaluates a goal, it usually spends a large proportion of time in performing backtracking. Normally, backtracking is very useful, but in some cases it may be unnecessary or even undesirable.

EXAMPLE 4.1   Consider the program *insert* that was developed in Chapter 3 (Figure 3.14).

```
insert(X,[],[X]).                             %1
insert(X,[H|T],[X,H|T]) :- X =< H.            %2
insert(X,[H|T],[H|T1]) :- X > H, insert(X,T,T1).   %3
```

Following is a simple query and the system's response :

```
?- insert(1,[2],L).
L = [1,2] ->;
no
```

The evaluation of the above query is summarised in the resolution tree shown on the next page. The system first unifies the goal $insert(1, [2], L)$ with the head of clause 2 to generate the next goal $1 \leq 2$, which succeeds to produce the answer $L = [1, 2]$. When one presses the semicolon key to request alternative answers, the system backtracks to the goal $insert(1, [2], L)$ and unifies it with the head of clause 3 to generate the next goal $1 > 2, insert(1, [], T1)$, which immediately fails.

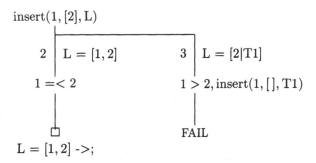

Observably, the above-described backtracking work is a waste of time, because once clause 2 succeeds, clause 3 will predictably lead to a failure. In fact, the three clauses of the program *insert* are mutually exclusive. So, for any given goal, if one clause has been used successfully, then the others need not be considered. This determination can be realised by using the predicate *cut*, which is to be described shortly.

EXAMPLE 4.2   Consider the program *bubble_sort* that was developed in Chapter 3 (Figure 3.15).

```
bubble_sort(L,L1) :- swap(L,L2,0),
                     bubble_sort(L2,L1).
bubble_sort(L,L).

swap([X,Y|R],[X|T],S) :- X =< Y,swap([Y|R],T,S).
swap([X,Y|R],[Y|T],S) :- X > Y, swap([X|R],T,1).
swap([X],[X],1).
```

Observe the following query and the system's responses:

```
?- bubble_sort([3,1,2],L).
L = [1,2,3] ->;
L = [3,1,2] ->;
no
```

Here, the second answer is obviously wrong. This error is due to the system's uncontrolled backtracking. After producing the first answer, the system backtracks to the initial goal *bubble_sort*([3, 1, 2], L) (it is recommended that the reader draws a resolution tree for the given goal to verify the backtracking course) and unifies it with the fact *bubble_sort*(L, L) to produce the incorrect answer L = [3, 1, 2]. This backtracking is certainly unintended.

To prevent unwanted backtracking, Prolog provides the control predicate *cut*, denoted by the symbol "!", the operational meaning of which is given below.

⋄ Cut (!) is a goal that always succeeds, but if backtracking encounters a cut, then the goal containing the cut immediately fails, and the goal most recently calling this goal also fails.

Figure 4.1 shows the change of backtracking course when a goal contains a cut. The right-hand picture shows that if B_3 fails, then the system backtracks to the cut. So the goal $(B_1, B_2, !, B_3)$ fails and A_2 also fails. Therefore, the system backtracks directly to A_1 (ignoring any alternative paths for B_2, B_1, and A_2).

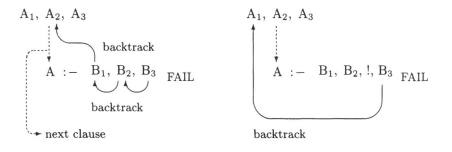

FIGURE 4.1 Effect of *cut* on backtracking.

Let us now see how the *cut* can be used to prevent unwanted backtracking. The following examples typify the cases of correct use of cut, misuse of cut, and softening the effect of cut.

4.2.1 Correct use of cut

Consider first the use of cut to prevent unnecessary backtracking in the program of Example 4.1.

EXAMPLE 4.3   In order to indicate to the Prolog system that the three clauses of the procedure *insert* are mutually exclusive, a cut is placed after the test goal in each clause. Since the first clause has no explicit test goal (the test is implicitly contained in the unification of the input list with the empty list), the cut is the only subgoal in the clause's body. The obtained deterministic program is shown in Figure 4.2.

```
insert(X,[],[X]) :- !.
insert(X,[H|T],[X,H|T]) :- X =< H,!.
insert(X,[H|T],[H|T1]) :- X > H,!,insert(X,T,T1).
```

FIGURE 4.2 The deterministic program *insert*.

Observe that the cut in the third clause of the above program is not really needed, because the clause is the last one in the procedure. Its presence causes absolutely no harm, however. Therefore, it is usually added merely for completeness.

Consider next the use of cut to prevent undesirable backtracking in the program of Example 4.2.

EXAMPLE 4.4   In the program *bubble_sort* of Example 4.2, the goal $swap(L, L2, 0)$ is used as a test: if it succeeds, then control returns to the first clause, otherwise the second clause is used. So, to prevent the system from backtracking after having produced the first answer (which should be the only one), a cut is placed after the goal $swap(L, L2, 0)$. Also, to improve the efficiency of the procedure *swap*, a cut is placed after the test goal in each clause. The modified program is shown in Figure 4.3.

```
bubble_sort(L,L1) :- swap(L,L2,0),!,
                     bubble_sort(L2,L1).
bubble_sort(L,L).

swap([X,Y|R],[X|T],S) :- X =< Y,!,swap([Y|R],T,S).
swap([X,Y|R],[Y|T],S) :- X > Y,!,swap([X|R],T,1).
swap([X],[X],1).
```

FIGURE 4.3 The deterministic program *bubble_sort*.

Note also that in the procedure *swap* of Figure 4.3, the signal 1 is used to indicate that swapping had occurred. This can be realised by the use of cut instead. Thus, the program *bubble_sort* is rewritten as follows.

```
bubble_sort(L,L1) :- swap(L,L2),!,
                     bubble_sort(L2,L1).
bubble_sort(L,L).

swap([X,Y|R],[X|T]) :- X =< Y,!,swap([Y|R],T).
swap([X,Y|R],[Y|T]) :- X > Y,(swap([X|R],T),!; T = [X|R]).
```

FIGURE 4.4 The program *bubble_sort* using cut.

From Examples 4.3 and 4.4 we have the following notes.

Notes

1. The use of cut in the program *insert* of Figure 4.2 (also in the procedure *swap* of Figure 4.3) only improves the program's efficiency and does not change the behaviour of the program. A cut used in this way is called a *green cut*.

2. In the program *bubble_sort* of Figure 4.3, the addition of the cut after the goal *swap*($L, L2, 0$) changes the behaviour of the program. A cut used in this way is called a *red cut*. The use of red cuts requires special caution and should be limited to suppressing undesirable backtracking. The reader is advised to refrain from using the cut as a substitute for alternative test goals, because this is a common cause of program errors.

3. There are other aspects of program *bubble_sort* concerning typical program style and efficiency, but we defer this discussion until after we have discussed the execution of negated goals in Section 4.4.

4.2.2 Incorrect use of cut

Following are two examples of typical erroneous programs due to the misuse of cut.

EXAMPLE 4.5 Consider again the program *insert* of Figure 4.2. One might attempt to improve the program's efficiency further by combining its first two clauses into a single clause and making the third clause the first one. The program could be written as follows:

```
insert(X,[H|T],[H|T1]) :- X > H,!,insert(X,T,T1).
insert(X,L,[X|L]).
```

This program is incorrect, however. To show its error, consider the following query:

```
?- insert(2,[1],[2,1]).
yes
```

The answer is obviously wrong, because inserting 2 into the list [1] should produce the list [1, 2], not [2, 1]. This error is due to the omission of the two crucial tests: $X \leq H$ and input list $= [\,]$.

Let us now compare the erroneous program *insert* of Example 4.5 with the program *bubble_sort* of Figure 4.4. These two programs appear to have the same style, yet program *bubble_sort* does not have the problem incurred in program *insert*. This is because any goal *bubble_sort*(X, Y) can unify with the head of the first clause of program *bubble_sort* and allow the guard *swap*$(L, L2)$ to be tested. Program *insert* of Example 4.5 does not guarantee this. For example, the goal *insert*$(2, [1], [2, 1])$ does not unify with the head of the program's first clause (thus missing the guard $X > H$), and yet it unifies with the second clause to produce the wrong answer. So, the error is caused by the fact that the program's guard is not allowed to perform its role. A simple way to prevent this from happening is to arrange it so that the head of the second clause is an instance of that of the first clause, as in the case of program *bubble_sort*, but this is not always possible. A more general rule to ensure the correct use of *cut* is given in Section 4.4.

EXAMPLE 4.6   The following program contains another common mistake in using cut. The program is intended to assign a grade to each student's mark, according to a specified scale. Here, the cuts are used to replace the specifications of upper bounds such as $Mark < 95$, and $Mark < 80$.

```
grade(Mark,'HD') :- Mark >= 95,!.   % High-distinction
grade(Mark,'DI') :- Mark >= 80,!.   % Distinction
grade(Mark,'CR') :- Mark >= 65,!.   % Credit
grade(Mark,'P')  :- Mark >= 50,!.   % Pass
grade(Mark,'F').                    % Fail
```

The program works fine with queries that find a grade for a given mark. But if we ask, for example: Is mark 60 graded as 'fail'?, then the answer is incorrect.

```
?- grade(60,'F').
yes
```

To correct this misbehaviour of the program, we need only add the test goal *Mark* < 50 to the last clause of the program. Note, however, that in the above program, the mark bounds can be more useful than they currently are. In fact, they can be used to test the marks' range as well as whether *Mark* is instantiated.

Thus, we can rewrite the program so that it is able to return a grade for a given mark, or a mark-range for a given grade. The program is given in Figure 4.5.

```
grade(Mark,'HD') :- range(Mark,95,100).
grade(Mark,'DI') :- range(Mark,80,94).
grade(Mark,'CR') :- range(Mark,65,79).
grade(Mark,'P')  :- range(Mark,50,64).
grade(Mark,'F')  :- range(Mark,0,49).

range(A-B, A,B) :- !.
range(Mark,A,B) :- A =< Mark, Mark =< B.
```

FIGURE 4.5 The program for mark-grade relation.

Some sample queries to the program of Figure 4.5 are shown below.

```
?- grade(98,Grade).
Grade = 'HD' ->

?- grade(65,Grade).
Grade = 'CR' ->

?- grade(45,Grade).
Grade = 'F' ->

?- grade(Mark,'HD').
Mark = 95 - 100 ->
```

```
?- grade(Mark,'CR').
Mark = 65 - 79 ->

?- grade(Mark,'P').
Mark = 50 - 64 ->
```

What is more interesting is that we can find the whole grading scheme by leaving both arguments of the query to be uninstantiated as shown below.

```
?- grade(Mark,Grade).
Mark = 95 - 100
Grade = 'HD' ->;

Mark = 80 - 94
Grade = 'DI' ->;

Mark = 65 - 79
Grade = 'CR' ->;

Mark = 50 - 64
Grade = 'P' ->;

Mark = 0 - 49
Grade = 'F' ->;

no
```

4.2.3   The once predicate

Let us now consider a problem in which the addition of a cut requires some special arrangement.

EXAMPLE 4.7   The purpose of the following program is to find the names of overseas students who have passed an English test (which was done by all students) for admission to a certain course.

```
admit(Name) :- overseas_student(Name),
               english_test(Name,Mark),
               Mark >= 50.
```

```
overseas_student('Sumi Akimoto').
overseas_student('Hans Cozreck').
    .
    .
    .
english_test('Sumi Akimoto',60).
english_test('John Burns',70).
english_test('Hans Cozreck',65).
    .
    .
    .
?- admit(X).
X = Sumi Akimoto ->;
X = Hans Cozreck ->;
    .
    .
    .
```

This program suffers some inefficiency, because each time the semicolon is pressed, the system backtracks to the goal *english_test(Name,Mark)* and attempts to unify it with other facts in the list of English test marks. These attempts are predictably fruitless because each name corresponds to only one mark.

Let us now explore several ways of using the cut to prevent the above-mentioned unnecessary backtracking. The first possible attempt is to place a cut after the goal *english_test(Name,Mark)* in the first clause. Thus, the first clause becomes as shown below and we enter an appropriate query to test the program's reponse.

```
admit(Name) :- overseas_student(Name),
               english_test(Name,Mark),!,
               Mark >= 50.

?- admit(X).
X = Sumi Akimoto ->;
no
```

Here, the query retrieves only one overseas student. The reason is that the cut, at its current place, not only prevents unnecessary backtracking to the goal *english_test(Name,Mark)*, but also prevents useful backtracking to the goal *overseas_student(Name)*.

So, it is necessary to restrict the effect of the cut to the goal *english_test(Name,Mark)* only. In order to do that, we leave the first clause unchanged and place a cut at the end of each clause in the procedure *english_test*. Thus, we have

```
english_test('Sumi Akimoto',60) :- !.
english_test('John Burns',70) :- !.
english_test('Hans Cozreck',65) :- !.
      .
      .
      .
?- admit(X).
X = Sumi Akimoto ->;
X = Hans Cozreck ->;
      .
      .
      .
```

Now the answer is correct and the program no longer generates the above-mentioned unnecessary backtracking. However, another problem arises. If we want to obtain a list of students and test marks, then the cut used as above prevents needed backtracking, and the system provides only one pair of student and test mark.

```
?- english_test(Name,Mark).
Name = Sumi Akimoto
Mark = 60 ->;
no
```

Our final attempt, which is the correct one, is to define a new predicate *once* and to modify the procedure *admit* as follows:

```
once(P) :- P,!.
admit(Name) :- overseas_student(Name),
               once(english_test(Name,Mark)),
               Mark >= 50.

?- admit(X).
X = Sumi Akimoto ->;
X = Hans Cozreck ->;
      .
      .
      .
```

Here, the procedure *once* restricts the effect of the cut to the subgoal *english_test(Name,Mark)* only.

Following are more examples that demonstrate the usefulness of the predicate *once*.

EXAMPLE 4.8   Let us recall the program *factorial* of Figure 2.6 (Chapter 2) that can be used to compute the factorial of a given nonnegative integer, or to find a number whose factorial value is given. A weakness of the program is that after giving an answer (which should be the only one for the nontrivial case), if the program is forced to backtrack, it would be stuck in an infinite loop. To prevent this from happening, we redefine the program, using the predicate *once*, as follows:

```
factorial(N,F) :-
    once(fact(N,F)).

fact(0,1).
fact(N,F) :-
    fact(N1,F1),
    N is N1+1,
    F is N*F1.

once(P)  :- P,!.
```

FIGURE 4.6   The program *factorial* using *once*.

EXAMPLE 4.9   Consider again the program *length* of Figure 2.18 (Chapter 2), which can be used to find the length of a given list, or to construct a list of a given number of variables. To ensure that the program will not be stuck in an infinite loop due to (unnecessary) backtracking, we redefine the program using the predicate *once* as shown in Figure 4.7.

The predicate *once* defined above is called a *meta-predicate*, that is, a predicate whose arguments are goals or clauses instead of terms. Another important meta-predicate in Prolog is the *not* predicate, which is to be studied in Section 4.4. The full technique of meta-programming is presented in Chapter 8.

```
length(L,N) :-
    once(len(L,N)).

len([],0).
len([H|T],N) :-
    len(T,M),
    N is M+1.

once(P) :- P,!.
```

FIGURE 4.7 The program *length* using *once*.

4.3   Forcing of backtracking: the fail predicate

Recall that in Prolog when the evaluation of a goal fails, the system back-tracks to the previous goal to find alternative ways of execution. Therefore, for the purpose of forcing backtracking, Prolog provides the built-in predicate *fail* that represents a goal which always fails. It should be noted that any predicate that is used without having been defined will have the same effect as the predicate *fail* (except in those Prolog systems that require every predicate used to be defined). However, we still choose to use the predicate *fail* for its purpose due to tradition, and also because its meaning is clear.

Following are two common ways of using the *fail* predicate.

1. The *fail* predicate can be used to evoke repetition. The general scheme of a looping procedure using *fail* is as follows:

```
loop :- Goal, fail.
loop.
```

When *loop* is called, the goal *Goal* is executed repeatedly, through a different path each time, until all alternative paths for *Goal* have been explored. The loop then terminates with success.

EXAMPLE 4.10   Suppose that we have a database containing a large number of customer records of the form *customer(ID,Name,Address)*, and for each customer there may be a number of transaction records of the form *transaction(ID,Date,Trans)*. Let us write a Prolog program to process the customers' transactions. In practice, this process could produce account statements to be sent to the customers. For simplicity, however, let us assume that we only need to print out each customer's details, together with a list of his or her transactions, if there are any. The program is given below:

```
process_customer :-
    customer(ID,Name,Address),
    process_trans(ID,Name,Address),
    fail.
process_customer.

process_trans(ID,Name,Address) :- nl,nl,
    write(ID),nl,write(Name),nl,write(Address),nl,
    transaction(ID,Date,Trans),
    write(Date),write(': '),write(Trans),nl.
```

Observe that the above program contains two nested loops that are controlled by the same goal *fail*. The outer loop scans over all customers, and the inner loop processes all transactions for each customer.

Note that the general procedure *loop* defined above is effective only if *Goal* is backtrackable (i.e., it can provide alternative solutions). In the case where *Goal* is nonbacktrackable (e.g., input-output and comparison predicates are nonbacktrackable), in order to force the execution of *Goal* to be repeated, one must precede *Goal* with the control predicate *repeat*, which is to be defined in Section 4.5.

2. The *fail* predicate can be used in conjunction with *cut* to terminate the execution of a goal with failure. The general form of a *cut-fail* combination is as follows:

```
process :- Goal,!,fail.
```

When *process* is called, if *Goal* succeeds (just once), then *process* immediately fails.

EXAMPLE 4.11   Any immigrant is eligible for citizenship if he or she is a child or the spouse of a citizen, or has been a resident for at least three years, except those who have committed certain crimes for which their names have been recorded. A program to determine citizenship eligibility is given below.

```
eligible_citizenship(X) :- commit_crime(X,Y),!,fail.
eligible_citizenship(X) :- child(X,Y),citizen(Y).
eligible_citizenship(X) :- spouse(X,Y),citizen(Y).
eligible_citizenship(X) :- resident(X,Years),Years >= 3.
```

According to the above program, if an immigrant X committed some crime Y, then X is immediately denied citizenship, and no other facts need to be considered. We shall see in the next section that in Prolog the *cut-fail* combination is used to implement a form of negation called *negation-as-failure*.

From Examples 4.10 and 4.11, we have the following observations.

Notes

1. So far, we have known two kinds of loops in Prolog: recursion and fail-driven loops. Their basic differences are summarised below.

   - Recursive programs are based on forward invocation, whereas fail-driven loops are based on backtracking;
   - Recursive programs work on the structure of data, whereas fail-driven loops process the alternative answers of certain given goals.

   So, recursive programs should be used to manipulate data that have recursive structure, while fail-driven loops are used to handle alternative answers of given goals.

2. If the definition of a procedure contains a clause ending with a cut-fail combination, then the procedure can only be called as a test goal and not as a finding goal. For example, consider the program of Example 4.11. To find the names of those applicants who are eligible for citizenship, we must use the query:

   ```
   ?- applicant(X),eligible_citizenship(X).
   ```

   Here, the goal *applicant(X)* is used to find an applicant X, and the goal *eligible_citizenship(X)* serves as a test goal. Without the finding goal *applicant(X)*, Prolog may give the incorrect answer "no" (meaning that no one is eligible for citizenship) if it found someone who had committed a crime.

4.4   Negation-as-failure: the not predicate

In the preceding section, we have discussed the effect of the *cut-fail* combination. In Prolog, the *cut-fail* combination is used to implement a form of negation called *negation-as-failure*. The predicate representing negation-as-failure is denoted by *"not"* (or *"\+"* in many Prolog systems) and is (internally) defined as follows.

```
not(G) :- G,!,fail.
not(G).
```

This program gives *not(G)* the following operational meaning:

> If *G* succeeds then *not(G)* fails;
> If *G* fails then *not(G)* succeeds.

Thus, in any case, *not(G)* does not return any values other than a confirming answer "yes" or "no". Therefore, *not(G)* can only be used as a test goal, and not as a finding goal.

Notes

1. The definition of the predicate *not* clearly shows that the execution of a negated goal *not(G)* may take a long while, because the success of *not(G)* can only be established after all possible paths of executing *G* have been explored and its total failure is confirmed.

2. Having defined the predicate *not*, we can now return to the program *bubble_sort* of Figure 4.4 (see Note 3 below the figure). One might attempt to safeguard the program (unnecessarily in this case) by adding a guard to its second clause in the following way:

```
bubble_sort(L,L1) :- swap(L,L2),!,bubble_sort(L2,L1).
bubble_sort(L,L)  :- not(swap(L,L2)).
```

But this would make the program very inefficient, because at the end, it requires the execution of *not(swap(L,L2))*, while *swap(L,L2)* already failed before. So, this addition is a total waste. Should any guard be added to the program's second clause, it could be a test goal *list(L)*, where the predicate *list* is defined by two clauses *list([])* and *list([_|T]) :- list(T)*. This is again unnecessary if we assume that anything, other than lists, is sorted into itself.

We can now give a general rule as a guide for proper use of cut in writing correct and efficient Prolog programs.

Consider the following algorithm, where A, B, C, D are processes, X is a list of distinct variables, and S, T are lists of terms.

> To do $A(X)$ do
> > *if* B then let $X = S$ and do C
> > *else* let $X = T$ and do D.

◇ In general, this algorithm is translated into the following Prolog program:

```
A(X) :- B,!,X = S, C.
A(T) :- D.
```

◇ If B is a simple test goal that will *terminate* quickly, then the program can be written in the following declarative form:

```
A(S) :- B,!,C.
A(T) :- not(B),D.
```

◇ If either (i) B and $(X = T)$ are mutually exclusive, or (ii) in the environment of the program, it is certain that no goal can unify with $A(T)$ without being unifiable with $A(S)$ (in particular, if T is an instance of S), then the above program can be rewritten as follows:

```
A(S) :- B,!,C.
A(T) :- D.
```

◇ In particular, if $S = T$ (and the subgoals B, C, D are not too long), then the program can be written in the following condensed form:

```
A(S) :- (B,!,C; D).
```

Some Prolog systems provide a built-in predicate *ifthenelse* for which the goal *ifthenelse*(B, C, D) has the same effect as $(B, !, C; D)$. The author does not recommend the use of this predicate, as its programming benefit is insignificant, while its appearance makes the program look clumsy.

We now give some examples to demonstrate the correct use of *not* and to illustrate a common misuse of it. We begin with two typical examples of the correct use of *not*.

4.4.1   Correct use of not

EXAMPLE 4.12   The situation of a hotel is described below.

> Hotel is full if there are no vacant rooms.
> Room 13 is vacant.
> Room 113 is vacant.

Note first that the sentence "There are *no* vacant rooms" is logically equivalent to "*All* rooms are not vacant". So, the above sentences are translated into the following program:

```
hotel_full :- not(vacant_room(X)).
vacant_room(13).
vacant_room(113).
```

To test this program, consider the following queries:

```
?- hotel_full.
no

?- not(hotel_full).
yes

?- vacant_room(X).
X = 13 ->;
X = 113 ->;
no
```

It is very important to note that this program does not allow a query such as "Which rooms are *not* vacant?", because it is a negated finding query. To represent negative queries of this kind, we need a new predicate "*non*", which is to be introduced in Chapter 8 (Section 8.4).

EXAMPLE 4.13   The following are some rules in considering the applications for citizenship.

> X is approved of citizenship *if*
> X applies for it,
> X has not committed *any* crimes, and
> X is qualified to be a citizen.

X is qualified to be a citizen *if*
   either   *X* is the child of a citizen
   or   *X* is the spouse of a citizen
   or   *X* has been a permanent resident for at least 3 years.

These rules are translated into the following Prolog clauses.

```
citizenship_approved(X) :-
    applicant(X),
    not(commit_crime(X,Y)),
    citizenship_qualified(X).

citizenship_qualified(X) :- child(X,Y),citizen(Y).
citizenship_qualified(X) :- spouse(X,Y),citizen(Y).
citizenship_qualified(X) :- resident(X,Y), Y >= 3.
```

Note that if *citizenship_approved(X)* is called as a finding goal, then the goal *applicant(X)* is used to find *X* and the goal *not(commit_crime(X,Y))* only serves as a test goal. Again, this program does not allow a query such as "Who has *not* committed a crime?", because it is a negated finding query. (Again, to represent this kind of negative query we use a new predicate "*non*" that is defined in Chapter 8, Section 8.4.)

4.4.2   Incorrect use of not

The common misuse of *not* is to allow a negated goal to be called as a finding goal (possibly unintentionally). Operationally, this means allowing a negated goal to contain variables when it is evaluated.

EXAMPLE 4.14   The following description is about the members of Sue's family.

   X is at home *if* *X* is not out.
   Sue is out.
   John is Sue's husband.

The above description is likely to be translated into the following program.

```
home(X) :- not(out(X)).
out(sue).
husband(john,sue).
```

This program is logically sound. But when it is run by a standard Prolog system, it may provide contradictory responses. For example, if we ask: "Is John at home?", then Prolog's answer is "yes". But if we ask: "Is there anyone at home?", the answer is "no".

```
?- home(john).
yes

?- home(X).
no
```

The above error is operational. It is due to the fact that Prolog reduces the finding goal *home(X)* to the goal *not(out(X))*, which is interpreted by Prolog's negation-as-failure rule as "Is everyone not out?". This interpretation obviously does not comply with the declarative reading of the first clause.

In conclusion, the reader is cautioned that Prolog's negation-as-failure is not logical negation and its use requires special care. To ensure the correctness of a program that contains negated goals, we should observe the following rules:

◇ In Prolog, negated goals can only be used as test goals, and not as finding goals.

◇ If G is a ground goal (i.e., it has no variables), then the success of $not(G)$ means G is not true.

◇ If G has variables $X_1, \ldots, X_n$, then the success of $not(G)$ means for all values of $X_1, \ldots, X_n$, G is not true.

To overcome the weakness of Prolog's negation, we present in Chapter 8 (Section 8.4) a simple but effective form of logical negation.

4.5   Repetition: the repeat predicate

We have mentioned in Section 4.3 that a fail-driven loop is effective only if the main goal is backtrackable. For a nonbacktrackable goal G, in order to force the execution of G to be repeated, one may precede G with a goal *repeat*, which is (internally) defined as follows:

```
repeat.
repeat :- repeat.
```

By this definition, the goal *repeat* is always backtrackable. Thus, when backtracking encounters a goal *repeat*, control is turned back to work forward again.

The predicate *repeat* can be used to implement *repeat-until* loops in Prolog. The general scheme for a repeat-loop is as follows.

```
loop :- repeat,
        Goal, % normally nonbacktrackable
        Condition.
```

When *loop* is called, the goal *Goal* is executed repeatedly until *Condition* is true. The loop then terminates with success.

EXAMPLE 4.15   Consider again the task of processing customers' transactions given in Example 4.10. Assume, however, that the file of customer records is too large to be brought into the memory. Thus, customer records must be read directly from the file. On the other hand, the transaction file is small enough to be loaded into the memory. The following procedure reads customer records from the input file and, for each customer, prints out the customer's details and the list of his or her transactions. The process terminates when end-of-file is encountered. In Prolog, the end-of-file marker is identified by the constant symbol *end_of_file*.

```
process_customer :-
    repeat,
        read(Record),
        process_trans(Record),
    Record = end_of_file.

process_trans(customer(ID,Name,Address)) :- nl,nl,
    write(ID),nl,write(Name),nl,write(Address),nl,
    transaction(ID,Date,Trans),
    write(Date),write(': '),write(Trans),nl.
process_trans(_).
```

4.6 Input-Output predicates

In the previously given examples, we have occasionally used Prolog's built-in predicates *read* and *write*. The effect of these predicates is now formally described below.

> *read(X)* : reads the next term, which is terminated by a period, from the current input stream and unifies it with X.

> *write(X)* : writes the term X to the current output stream.

Recall that a term is either a *constant*, or a *variable*, or a *list*, or a *compound term* (see Section 2.5 of Chapter 2). In Prolog, a constant can be one of the following:

A number (integer or real): e.g., -2, 14, 0.5, $6.4E2$.
A constant symbol: e.g., *john*, *my_cat*, *end_of_file*.
A string of characters: e.g., 'John Smith', 'Infile.dat'.

EXAMPLE 4.16   The following are typical examples of legal read queries.

```
?- read(X).                    ?- read(X).
john.                          John.
X = john ->                    X = _0085 ->

?- read(X).                    ?- read(tom).
'John Smith'.                  john.
X = 'John Smith' ->            no

?- read(Hour:Min).             ?- read(A+B).
10:45.                         wall_st+mona_ave.
Hour = 10                      A = wall_st
Min = 45 ->                    B = mona_ave ->

?- read(X).
"John Smith".
X = [74,111,104,110,32,83,109,105,116,104] ->
```

The last query above shows that in Prolog a double-quoted string of characters is represented by the list of ASCII-codes of the characters in the string.

So, the reader should distinguish between 'John Smith' and "John Smith". The former is a constant, while the latter is a list of integers. Prolog provides the built-in predicate *name* that transforms between these two forms. For example:

```
?- name(john,X).
X = [106,111,104,110] ->

?- name(X,[106,111,104,110]).
X = john ->
```

EXAMPLE 4.17   Following are some examples on the *write* statements.

```
?- write(father(john,tom)).        ?- write([a,b,c]).
father(john,tom)                   [a,b,c]

?- write('How are you?').          ?- write(Alan).
How are you?                       _0085
                                   Alan = _0085 ->

?- write("How are you?").
[72,111,119,32,97,114,101,32,121,111,117,63]
```

Prolog also allows input and output of individual characters. Following are the built-in predicates provided for those purposes.

get0 (X): inputs the next character from the current input stream, and unifies its ASCII code with X.

get(X) : inputs the next printable character from the current input stream, skipping any nonprintable characters (including the spaces), and unifies its ASCII code with X.

put(X) : outputs the character whose ASCII code is X, to the current output stream.

nl   : outputs a newline character to the current output stream.

For examples:

```
?- get0(X).           ?- get(X).           ?- get(121).
!                     a                    y
X = 33 ->             X = 97 ->            yes


?- put(65).           ?- get(X),put(X).
A                     aa
                      X = 97 ->
```

Many Prolog systems accept characters preceded by backquote in lieu of their ASCII codes. For example, get('y) is equivalent to get(121). Input-output predicates are mainly used in processing user interaction. This topic will be studied in the next chapter. Here, we give two procedures for reading text into lists of characters or lists of words.

The procedure *readline* reads a line of text from the current input stream and stores the characters' ASCII codes in a list. The input characters' codes are initially stored in the reverse order of reading so that the last character can be discarded when a backspace (ASCII code 8) is read. The process terminates when an end-of-line character (ASCII code 13) has been read. The procedure is shown in Figure 4.8.

```
readline(L) :-
    get0(C),
    read_chars(C,[],L1),
    reverse(L1,[],L).

read_chars(13,L,L) :- !.
read_chars(8,[C|L],L1) :- !,
    put(32),put(8),
    get0(C1),
    read_chars(C1,L,L1).
read_chars(C,L,L1) :-
    get0(C1),
    read_chars(C1,[C|L],L1).

reverse([],L,L).
reverse([H|T],L,L1) :- reverse(T,[H|L],L1).
```

FIGURE 4.8 Read a line of text.

```prolog
read_sentence(L) :- read_sent(32,L).

read_sent(C,L) :- end_sent(C),!,L = [].
read_sent(C,[W|L]) :-
    read_word(W,C1),read_sent(C1,L).

read_word(W,C1) :-
    read_first_char(S,C),
    read_word_chars(S,C,[],L,C1),
    reverse(L,[],L1),name(W,L1).

read_first_char(S,C) :-
    get_char(S),start_word(S,C),!;
    read_first_char(S,C).

read_word_chars(S,C,L,L,C1) :- end_word(S,C,C1),!.
read_word_chars(S,8,[C|L],L1,C1) :- !,
    put(32),put(8),get_char(C2),
    read_word_chars(S,C2,L,L1,C1).
read_word_chars(S,C,L,L1,C1) :-
    legal_char(S,C),get_char(C2),
    read_word_chars(S,C2,[C|L],L1,C1).

get_char(C)       :- get0(C),(C = 13,!,nl; true).
start_word(C,C)   :- valid_char(C),!.
start_word(39,C)  :- get_char(C).  % quotation marks
end_word(39,39,C) :- get_char(C).
end_word(S,C,C)   :- S \= 39,C \= 8,not(valid_char(C)).
end_sent(C)       :- (C = 46;C = 63). % period or ?

legal_char(39,_)  :- !.
legal_char(_,C)   :- valid_char(C).
valid_char(C) :- C = 45; `0 =< C, C =< `9;
    `a =< C, C =< `z;    `A =< C, C =< `Z.

reverse([],L,L).
reverse([H|T],L,L1) :- reverse(T,[H|L],L1).
```

FIGURE 4.9 Read a sentence of text on several lines.

The second procedure, *read_sentence*, reads several lines of text and stores the words in a list. Here, each word is either a sequence of valid characters (that are letters, digits, and the hyphen), or a string of any characters enclosed between two single quotation marks (ASCII code 39). The words are separated from each other by nonvalid characters (other than the backspace). The sentence is assumed to be terminated by a period or a question mark that immediately follows the last word (the period or the question mark is not stored in the list of words). The procedure *read_sentence* is shown in Figure 4.9. In this procedure, *read_word_chars* is similar to *read_chars* of procedure *readline*, except that *read_word_chars* takes only the characters that are acceptable to the current word (that is, valid characters for a normal word and any characters for a string), and terminates as soon as the end of the word is detected. Besides returning the list of character codes of a word, the procedure *read_word_chars* also returns the next character that separates the current word with the next one. This character is used by the procedure *read_sent* to detect the end of the sentence.

4.7   Environment manipulating predicates

In Prolog the predicates provided for the purpose of environment manipulation can be classified into three categories:

- File handling predicates;
- Database manipulating predicates;
- System predicates.

These built-in predicates are studied in the following subsections.

4.7.1   File handling predicates

The input-output predicates presented in the preceding section always deal with the *current* input and output streams. By default, the current input stream is from the keyboard and the current output stream is the terminal. To change the input-output streams, Prolog provides the following means.

see(Filename)   :   switches current input stream to *Filename*.

seeing(Name)   :   gives *Name* of the current input stream.

seen   :   closes current input stream and switches back to the default input stream.

tell(Filename) :   switches current output stream to *Filename*.

telling(Name) :   gives *Name* of the current output stream.

told :   closes current output stream and switches back to the default output stream.

EXAMPLE 4.18   Suppose that we have a file named *'test.dat'* containing students' records of the form *student(ID,Name,Mark)*. We wish to read this file and copy the ID-numbers and names of those students who passed the test (i.e., having Mark $\geq$ 50) to another file named *'result.dat'*. The program is as follows:

```
make_pass_list :-
    see('test.dat'),
    tell('result.dat'),
    copy_records,
    seen,told.

copy_records :-
    read(student(ID,Name,Mark)),!,
    (Mark >= 50,!,
     write(pass_stud(ID,Name)),write('.'),nl;
     true),
    copy_records.
copy_records.
```

Note that after each term *pass_stud(ID,Name)* is written to the output file, a period is added to terminate the term, and a new line is processed. When the *end_of_file* marker in the input file *'test.dat'* is read, it cannot be unified with the term *student(ID,Name,Mark)*. So the process *copy_records* terminates by unifying with the fact *copy_records*. Both files are then closed by the goals *seen* and *told*.

Note

Some Prolog systems (such as Arity/Prolog, Prolog-2, and Quintus Prolog) provide the built-in predicates *open* and *close* for the purpose of opening and closing files, and allow the *read* and *write* predicates to have an extra argument referring to the file of source or destination. These facilities allow several files to be involved in input-output activities without the necessity of changing the current input-output streams.

4.7.2   Database manipulating predicates

In Chapter 1 we have briefly discussed the creation of a Prolog program in the system's database. We now study in detail the facilities provided by Prolog for database manipulation.

Suppose that Prolog's database currently contains the following program:

```
likes(ann,X) :- toy(X),plays(ann,X).
likes(sue,X) :- likes(ann,X).
toy(doll).
toy(snoopy).
plays(ann,snoopy).
```

To inspect some particular procedure of the program, we use the predicate *listing* as shown below.

```
?- listing(toy).
toy(doll).
toy(snoopy).
```

```
yes
```

Several procedures can be listed one after another by enclosing their names between square brackets. For example:

```
?- listing([toy,likes]).
toy(doll).
toy(snoopy).

likes(ann,X) :-
    toy(X),
    plays(ann,X).
likes(sue,X) :-
    likes(ann,X).
```

```
yes
```

In particular, the query ?- *listing*., with no arguments, causes all clauses of the program to be listed.

In order to add new clauses to the database, we use the predicates *asserta* and *assertz*. These predicates cause the new clause to be inserted into the database as the first and the last clause, respectively, of the procedure having the same head predicate. For example:

```
?- asserta(plays(ann,doll)).
yes

?- listing(plays).
plays(ann,doll).
plays(ann,snoopy).

yes

?- assertz(plays(ann,kermit)).
yes

?- listing(plays).
plays(ann,doll).
plays(ann,snoopy).
plays(ann,kermit).

yes
```

In order to remove a clause, the predicate *retract* can be used as follows:

```
?- retract(toy(doll)).
yes

?- toy(doll).
no
```

Retracting a clause containing variables is treated by Prolog as a finding query, but the effect is simply the removal of the clause. For example:

```
?- retract((likes(sue,X) :- likes(ann,X))).
X = _0085 ->;
no

?- likes(sue,X).
no
```

Note that the predicate *retract* can only be used to remove one clause at a time. In order to delete a whole procedure, we can use the goal *abolish(Proc/N)*, where *Proc* is the name of the procedure and *N* is its arity. For example:

```
?- abolish(plays/2).
yes

?- plays(X,Y).
no
```

Finally, to save the current database in a file *Filename*, we can use the following procedure:

```
save(Filename) :- tell(Filename),
                  listing,
                  told.
```

4.7.3   System predicates

Recall that if a Prolog program is currently stored in a file, then it can be loaded into the memory by using the predicate *consult*. For example:

```
?- consult(filename).
yes
```

If there is another file, *filename2*, containing a second program that is to be used together with the current program in memory, then the second program can be loaded by the query:

```
?- reconsult(filename2).
yes
```

The effect of the above query is the insertion of *filename2*'s procedures into the current database, replacing any current procedures of the same predicate.

In practice, a Prolog program may be made up of several programs stored in different files. For convenience, most Prolog systems allow the use of square brackets to replace a sequence of *consult, reconsult*, in which a negative sign preceding a filename indicates the reconsulting of that file.

Thus, the query

```
?- consult(file1),reconsult(file2),reconsult(file3).
```

is equivalent to

```
?- [file1,-file2,-file3].
```

Being within the Prolog environment, if we wish to enter DOS to perform some system activities such as file editing, directory managing, or input-output, then we can use the system predicate *shell* as shown below.

```
?- shell.
C>  .
    .
    .
    DOS-commands
    .
    .
    .

C> exit
yes
?-
```

The *exit* command brings control back to the Prolog environment. If the DOS-commands needed consist of a single command, then it can be included as an argument of the *shell* predicate. In this case, control will return to the Prolog environment immediately after the completion of the DOS-command. For example, we may wish to inspect a file named '*c: filename*' in order to decide whether it should be loaded into memory. The query is as follows:

```
?- shell('type c:filename').
.
.
.
contents of the file
.
.
.

yes
?-
```

Although the operations of *shell* and *exit* are available in most Prolog systems, the command names may vary from system to system. For example, in the Unix-based Prolog systems, we have the predicate *sh* (for *shell*) and *<ctrl> D* (instead of *exit*). With the availability of the predicate *shell*, most operating system functions can be easily implemented in Prolog.

Finally, for the purpose of program debugging, Prolog provides the following built-in predicates:

trace	:	turns the debugger on.
notrace	:	turns the debugger off.
spy(Proc/N)	:	sets spy point at procedure *Proc* that has arity *N*.
nospy(Proc/N)	:	eliminates spy point at procedure *Proc* that has arity *N*.

The Prolog debugger follows the execution of a goal via the following four ports (introduced by Byrd, 1980):

CALL port	:	start the execution of the goal.
FAIL port	:	leave the goal with failure.
EXIT port	:	leave the goal with success.
REDO port	:	backtrack to execute the goal in different path.

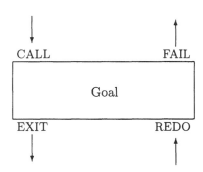

If the debugger is on and a spy-point has been set, then every time the specified procedure is called, tracing messages are displayed. Each message begins with the name of the port where control gets through, followed by the state of the goal having that port. The user may press the key "*c*" (or *<return>*) to *creep* through every state of the execution, until control leaves the initial goal via the EXIT or FAIL port. The user may also break out of the tracing course (to escape an infinite loop, for example), by pressing the key "*b*" instead.

For example, assume that the database currently contains the following program:

```
likes(ann,X) :- toy(X),plays(ann,X).        %1
likes(sue,X) :- likes(ann,X).               %2
toy(doll).                                   %3
toy(snoopy).                                 %4
plays(ann,snoopy).                           %5
```

We now turn on the debugger and set a spy-point as follows:

```
?- trace.
yes
?- spy(likes/2).
yes
```

Then, the following query produces the tracing messages that are shown in Figure 4.10. In these messages, the asterisks (∗∗) indicate that *likes(X, Y)* is a spy-point, and the numbers in parentheses refer to the goal levels.

```
?- likes(sue,X).

**   (0)   CALL :   likes(sue,_0085)  ? > c
**   (1)   CALL :   likes(ann,_0085)  ? > c
     (2)   CALL :   toy(_0085)  ? > c
     (2)   EXIT :   toy(doll)  ? > c
     (3)   CALL :   plays(ann,doll)  ? > c
     (3)   FAIL :   plays(ann,doll)  ? > c
     (2)   REDO :   toy(doll)  ? > c
     (2)   EXIT :   toy(snoopy)  ? > c
     (4)   CALL :   plays(ann,snoopy)  ? > c
     (4)   EXIT :   plays(ann,snoopy)  ? > c
**   (1)   EXIT :   likes(ann,snoopy)  ? > c
**   (0)   EXIT :   likes(sue,snoopy)  ? > c

X = snoopy ->
```

FIGURE 4.10 An example of tracing messages.

The first line shows a call to the goal *likes(sue, X)*. This goal calls the sub-goal *likes(ann, X)* of the second clause in the given program. Then the goal *likes(ann, X)* calls the subgoal *toy(X)* of the first clause, which succeeds with $X = doll$. Next, the goal *plays(ann, doll)* is called and fails. So, the system redoes the subgoal *toy(X)*, which again succeeds with $X = snoopy$. Hence, the system calls the next subgoal *plays(ann, snoopy)*, which succeeds. So, the system exits the goal *plays(ann, snoopy)*, exits the goal *likes(ann, snoopy)*, and finally exits the goal *likes(sue, snoopy)*.

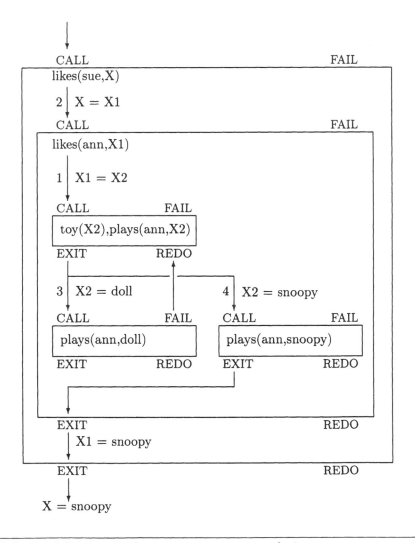

FIGURE 4.11 Mapping tracing messages onto a resolution tree.

The tracing messages given in Figure 4.10 are simply a displayed form of the resolution tree shown in Figure 4.11. Therefore, if the user is familiar with drawing resolution trees for debugging purposes, then the *trace* predicate may not be needed.

Finally, when tracing is finished, the debugger should be turned off (by using *notrace*) and the spy-points must be eliminated (by using the *nospy* predicate).

Solved problems

4.1 Consider the following program:

```
bubble(L,L1) :- append(A,[X,Y|B],L), X > Y,!,
                append(A,[Y,X|B],L2),write(L2),nl,
                bubble(L2,L1).
bubble(L,L).
```

(a) What is the purpose of the cut (!) in the above program?

(b) Is the above cut a green or red cut?

(c) What would happen if the cut is removed from the above program and the query ?- bubble([3,2,1],L) is invoked?

Solution:

(a) The purpose of the cut in the above program is to prevent two courses of backtracking. Firstly, it prevents backtracking to the subgoal *append (A,[X,Y|B],L)* after a pair of elements X > Y has been found. That is, it prevents the system from skipping the first pair X > Y and trying to find another pair X1 > Y1 in an attempt to find alternative solutions.

Secondly, it prevents backtracking to the second clause of the program once a pair X > Y has been found. Thus, the second clause is used only when all elements of the list are in ascending order.

(b) The above cut is a red cut, because its addition changes the behaviour of the program.

(c) Without the cut, the given query would produce the following output. (It is recommended that the reader draws a resolution tree for the query to facilitate tracing of the system's backtracking. The comments in parentheses are our explanations.)

```
?- bubble([3,2,1],L).
```
[2,3,1]	(*append* swaps first pair)
[2,1,3]	(*append* swaps second pair)
[1,2,3]	(*append* swaps first pair again)
L = [1,2,3] ->;	(second clause produces copy of third list)
L = [2,1,3] ->;	(second clause produces copy of second list)
L = [2,3,1] ->;	(second clause produces copy of first list)
[3,1,2]	(*append* skips first pair and swaps second pair)
[1,3,2]	(*append* swaps first pair)
[1,2,3]	(*append* swaps second pair)
L = [1,2,3] ->;	(second clause produces copy of list $[1,2,3]$)
L = [1,3,2] ->;	(second clause produces copy of list $[1,3,2]$)
L = [3,1,2] ->;	(second clause produces copy of list $[3,1,2]$)
L = [3,2,1] ->;	(second clause produces copy of initial list)
no	

The cut in the above program prevents all backtracking work performed after the first ";" is entered.

4.2 Consider the following program, which is intended to define the third argument to be the maximum value of the first two numeric arguments:

```
max(X,Y,X) :- X >= Y,!.
max(X,Y,Y).
```

(a) Provide an appropriate query to show that the above program is incorrect.

(b) Explain the cause of the error and suggest the correction.

Solution:

(a) Consider the following query and the system's response:

```
?- max(3,1,1).
yes
```

The answer is incorrect, because 1 is not the maximum value of 3 and 1.

(b) The cause of the error lies in the misunderstanding that the above program is a translation of the following sentences:

The maximum of X, Y is X if $X \geq Y$,
                        or is Y otherwise.

Actually the given program should be read as follows:

$$\text{The maximum of } X, Y \text{ is } Z \text{ if } X = Z \text{ and } X \geq Y,$$
$$\text{or is } Y \text{ otherwise.}$$

Obviously, this is not the correct definition of the maximum function. Here, the word "otherwise" means either $X \neq Z$ or $X < Y$. Since $3 \neq 1$, the second clause applies, leading to the answer that the maximum of 3 and 1 is 1.

In the given program, the cut is intended to substitute the test $X < Y$ in the second clause by preventing Prolog from using the second clause once the test $X \geq Y$ succeeds. However, the cut was not given a chance, as the goal fails to unify with the head of the first clause.

This error can be easily avoided if we apply the implementing rule given in Section 4.4 to the definition of maximum. By this rule, we have the following program:

```
max(X,Y,Z) :- X >= Y,!, Z = X.
max(X,Y,Y).
```

Here, $X \geq Y$ and $Z = Y$ are not mutually exclusive; also $max(X, Y, Y)$ is not an instance of $max(X, Y, X)$, for $(3, 1, 1)$ is an instance of (X, Y, Y), but not an instance of (X, Y, X). So, by our implementing rule, the clause head $max(X, Y, Z)$ cannot have its argument Z replaced by X.

In this case, as indicated by the rule, either we leave the program in its current form, or we convert it into the following (more elegant, but slightly less efficient) program:

```
max(X,Y,X) :- X >= Y,!.
max(X,Y,Y) :- X < Y.
```

4.3   Consider the following program:

```
insert(X,[H|T],[H|T1]) :- X > H,!,insert(X,T,T1).
insert(X,L,[X|L]).
```

Apply the implementing rule given in Section 4.4 to determine that the above program is incorrect and to provide a correct version for it.

Solution:

This program has been given in Example 4.5, where it was shown to contain an error. The program is probably based on the following algorithm:

To insert X into a list L giving the list $L1$ do
    if $X >$ head of L then
          copy head of L to head of $L1$, and
          insert X into tail of L giving tail of $L1$
    else add X in front of L to give $L1$.

This algorithm is sound and should be translated into the following program:

```
insert(X,[H|T],L1) :- X > H,!, L1 = [H|T1],insert(X,T,T1).
insert(X,[H|T],L1) :- L1 = [X,H|T].
insert(X,[],[X]).
```

Here, X > H and L1 = [X,H|T] are not mutually exclusive; also the goal insert(X,[H|T],[X,H|T]) is not an instance of insert(X,[H|T],[H|T1]). In fact, insert(2,[1],[2,1]) is an instance of the former, but it is not an instance of the latter. Therefore, by our implementing rules, we cannot replace L1 in the first clause by [H|T1] as shown in the question.

Also by the same rule given in Section 4.4, the program can be written as follows:

```
insert(X,[H|T],[H|T1]) :-  X > H,!,insert(X,T,T1).
insert(X,[H|T],[X,H|T]) :- X =< H.
insert(X,[],[X]).
```

4.4 Consider an image represented by a matrix of pixels' brightness as shown in the right-hand side table below. In early image processing, one can detect a particular feature in the image by using a template to represent the feature as shown in the left-hand side table below, and to find the location where the feature best matches the image.

```
0 0 1 1 1 1          0 1 0 1 1 0 0
0 2 0 0 2 0          0 0 0 0 1 1 1
3 3 3 3 0 0          0 1 2 0 1 2 0
                     0 3 3 2 3 3 0
                     0 1 1 0 0 0 1
```

To do this, one calculates, for each point **y** in the image where the template can fit entirely within the image, the *cross-correlation*

$$\sum_{\mathbf{x}} f(\mathbf{x})\, t(\mathbf{x} - \mathbf{y}),$$

where f and t are the image and template's light functions, respectively, and **x** runs over all points in the image. The point with maximum cross-correlation is accepted as the location of the feature in the image. (For more detail, see Ballard and Brown, 1982.)

Write a Prolog program to detect a particular feature in a given image by using the above-described technique.

Solution:

The above-described image-detecting procedure is expressed as follows:

To detect a feature at location XY in the image do
    obtain the size of the image and the template, then
    find the location XY where the template best matches the image.

To find the location where the template best matches the image do
    for each location XY where the template can fit entirely within the image
        calculate the cross-correlation at XY;
    pick the location with maximum cross-correlation.

To calculate the cross-correlation at (X, Y) do
    set the cross-correlation to 0 initially, then
    for each point (I, J) in the template
        add the product $f(X + I, Y + J)\, t(I, J)$ to cross-correlation.

The program is shown below, where the for-loops are controlled by the *fail* predicate.

```
detect_feature(XY) :-
    image_size(IS),
    template_size(TS),
    best_template_match(IS,TS,XY).

best_template_match(IS,TS,_) :-
    location(IS,TS,XY),
    cross_correlation(XY),
    fail.
best_template_match(_,_,XY) :-
    find_max(_,0,XY).

location((IX,IY),(TX,TY),(X,Y)) :-
    image(X,Y,_),
    X + TX =< IX,
    Y + TY =< IY.
```

```
cross_correlation(XY) :-
    assert(cross_value(XY,0)),
    template(I,J,V),
    calculate(XY,(I,J),V),
    fail.
cross_correlation(_).

calculate((X,Y),(I,J),TV) :-
    H is X + I, K is Y + J,
    image(H,K,IV),
    retract(cross_value((X,Y),V)),
    V1 is V + IV*TV,
    assert(cross_value((X,Y),V1)),!.

find_max(_,V,X) :-
    cross_value(X1,V1), V1 > V,!,
    find_max(X1,V1,X).
find_max(X,_,X).
```

Following are the facts representing the given template and image. (Here, the X-axis is from left to right, and the Y-axis is from top to bottom.) The program's response shows the given feature is detected at location $(1, 1)$.

```
template_size((5,2)).       image_size((6,4)).

template(0,0,0).            image(0,0,0).
template(0,1,0).            image(0,1,0).
template(0,2,3).            image(0,2,0).
    .                           .
    .                           .
    .                           .
template(5,0,1).            image(6,2,0).
template(5,1,0).            image(6,3,0).
template(5,2,0).            image(6,4,1).

?- detect_feature(Location).
Location = 1 , 1 ->
```

4.5 Consider the image of an object that has straight-line boundaries. A technique of detecting straight-line boundaries is described below. For any given point (x, y) in the image plane, the straight line passing through this point has equation $y = mx + c$, where m and c may vary within certain ranges. Thus, each point (x, y) in the image plane corresponds to a straight line in the (m, c)-plane (which is called the Hough transformation of (x, y)). Hence, if the image has n points $A_1, \ldots, A_n$ lying on a straight line, then these points correspond to n lines in the (m, c)-plane meeting at a point (m_0, c_0) that represents the line $A_1 A_n$. So, to detect a straight-line boundary in the image, we can do as follows (see, e.g., Ballard and Brown, 1982).

For each point (x, y) in the image plane at which the light contrast is above some predefined threshold, we find the points in the (m, c)-plane satisfying $y = mx + c$ and increment their counters. The point (m, c) with maximum count is taken as the coefficients of a straight-line boundary in the image. The light contrast at a point (x, y) in the image is calculated as the gradient magnitude at that point, which is given by the following formula:

$$s = (\Delta_1^2 + \Delta_2^2)^{\frac{1}{2}},$$

where, $\Delta_1 = f(x+1, y) - f(x-1, y)$ and $\Delta_2 = f(x, y+1) - f(x, y-1)$.

Write a Prolog program to detect a straight-line boundary in an image, using the above-described technique.

Solution:

The straight-line boundary detecting algorithm given above is expressed as follows:

> To detect a straight-line boundary of coefficients (M, C) do
> obtain the predetermined threshold T, then
> for each point (X, Y) in the image with gradient magnitude $> T$
> record the transformations of (X, Y) in the (m, c)-plane;
> finally, pick the point (M, C) with maximum count.

> To record the transformations of (X, Y) in the (m, c)-plane do
> obtain the ranges of M and C, and
> record the transformations of (X, Y) that are in those ranges.

> To record the transformations of (X, Y) in the given ranges do
> for each M and C in their ranges such that $Y = M * X + C$
> increment the counter of (M, C).

The program is given below, where we note that the first for-loop is controlled by the *fail* predicate because it scans the facts representing the image in the database, whereas the second for-loop is implemented as a recursive procedure because it works on the ranges contained in its parameters.

```
detect_line(MC) :-
    threshold(T),
    image(X,Y,G),gradient(X,Y,S), S > T,
    record_transform(X,Y),
    fail.
detect_line(MC) :-
    find_max(_,0,MC).

gradient(u,v,_) :- !,fail.
gradient(X,Y,S) :-
    X1 is X-1, X2 is X+1, Y1 is Y-1, Y2 is Y+1,
    image(X1,Y,G11), image(X2,Y,G12), D1 is G12 - G11,
    image(X,Y1,G21), image(X,Y2,G22), D2 is G22 - G21,
    S is sqrt(D1^2 + D2^2),!.

record_transform(X,Y) :-
    minimum(M1,C1), maximum(M2,C2),
    transform((M1,M2),(C1,C2),(X,Y)),!.

transform((M,M2),(C1,C2),(X,Y)) :-
    M =< M2, C is Y - M*X,
    (C1 =< C, C =< C2,!,increment((M,C)); true),
    N is M+1,
    transform((N,M2),(C1,C2),(X,Y)),!.
transform(_,_,_).

increment(MC) :-
    retract(count(MC,V)),!, V1 is V+1,
    assert(count(MC,V1)).
increment(MC) :-
    assert(count(MC,1)).

find_max(_,V,X) :-
    count(X1,V1), V1 > V,!,
    find_max(X1,V1,X).
find_max(X,_,X).
```

To test the program, we add the following facts about an image and enter the query below. The answer shows that a straight-line boundary is detected to be the line having gradient $m = -1$ and that passes through the point $(0, 4)$.

```
threshold(1).      minimum(-4,0).     maximum(4,20).
image(0,0,2).      image(1,0,1).      image(2,1,5).
image(0,1,2).      image(1,1,4).      image(2,2,6).
```

```
image(0,2,3).     image(1,2,4).     image(3,0,6).
image(0,3,5).     image(1,3,3).     image(3,1,7).
image(0,4,2).     image(2,0,4).     image(4,0,6).
image(_,_,0).

?- detect_line((M,C)).
M = -1
C = 4 ->
```

4.6 Given is a file named '*c: rainfall.dat*' that contains records of the form *rain(State,City,Rain)*. Write a Prolog program to read the rainfall records of state 'CAL' into the memory under the following conditions:

(a) The program uses recursion as its only form of looping.

(b) The program uses repeat to control looping.

Also consider two cases : 1. The rainfall records are not in any order; 2. The records are in alphabetical order of state names.

Solution:

(a) Using recursion.

Case 1: Rainfall records are unordered.

```
read_rain(State) :-
    see('c:rainfall.dat'),     % open file for reading
    read_rec(State),           % read records of State
    seen.                      % close file

read_rec(State) :-
    read(rain(S,C,R)),         % read a record
    (S = State,                % if record has given state
        assertz(rain(S,C,R));  % then store it in memory
     true),                    % otherwise, ignore it and
    read_rec(State).           % continue to read records
read_rec(State).               % If end of file then return.
```

Case 2: Rainfall records are in alphabetical order by state names.

```
read_rain(State) :-
    see('c:rainfall.dat'),      % open file for reading
    skip_rec(State,Record),     % skip records to find State
    read_rec(State,Record),     % store Record, read next rec
    seen.                       % close file.
```

```
skip_rec(S,rain(S,C,R)) :-
    read(rain(S,C,R)),!;        % If found S then return
    skip_rec(S,rain(S,C,R)).    % otherwise skip records

read_rec(S,Rec) :-
    assertz(Rec),               % store Rec in memory
    read(rain(S,C,R)),          % read next record of state S
    read_rec(S,rain(S,C,R)).    % store record, read next rec
read_rec(S,Rec).        % If no more record of state S return
```

(b) Using repeat.

Case 1: Rainfall records are unordered.

```
read_rain(State) :- % the same as in part (a), Case 1.

read_rec(State) :-
    repeat,                     % Repeat
    read(Rec),                  % read a record
    check_state(State,Rec).     % check record's state

check_state(S,rain(S,C,R)) :- !,  % if record has state S
    assertz(rain(S,C,R)),fail.    % then store it and fail
check_state(_,end_of_file).     % Until end of file
```

Case 2: Rainfall records are in alphabetical order by state names.

```
read_rain(State) :-
    see('c:rainfall.dat'),      % open file for reading
    skip_rec(State),            % skip records to find State
    read_rec(State),            % read next records of State
    seen.                       % close file

skip_rec(S) :-
    repeat,                     % repeat
    read(rain(S,C,R)),          % reading until found state S
    assertz(rain(S,C,R)).       % store record in memory

read_rec(S) :-
    repeat,                     % repeat
    read_state(S).              % read record of state S
```

```
read_state(S) :-
    read(rain(S,C,R)),!,        % if record has state S
    assertz(rain(S,C,R)),fail.  %   then store it & fail
read_state(S).                  %   else return
```

4.7 Assume the database currently contains a list of facts of the form *state(StateName)*. Write a Prolog query to guess the name of the state where the user comes from, until the user confirms the guess. (Use backtracking to make a guess.)

Solution:

```
?- state(S),
   write('Are you from '),write(S),write('?'),nl,
   read(yes),
   write('I see! So you come from '),write(S).
```

This query produces the following conversation:

```
Are you from Alaska?
no
Are you from Arizona?
no
  .
  .
  .
Are you from Nevada?
yes
I see! So you come from Nevada
```

4.8 The procedure *readline* of Figure 4.8 reads a line of text into a list of characters. Now write a procedure *tokenize* that receives a list of characters and returns the list of tokens contained in the text. Here, a token is a word, a number, a quoted string of characters, or a separator such as the comma, the (round or square) brackets, and the function symbols. (This procedure is useful in preparing for parsing complex sentences (other than sequences of words as in natural languages), particularly in the case where the procedure *readline* is available, as in many Prolog systems. For example, see Problem 10.5.)

Solution:

This procedure is similar to the procedure *read_sentence* of Figure 4.9, except that the separators such as the comma, the brackets, and any function symbols are also collected as tokens. The program is given below, where, for any given language, the available function symbols should be included in the procedure *separator*. Here, the predicates *member* and *append* have been defined before.

```
tokenize([],[]).
tokenize(CharList,[Token|TList]) :-
    append(_,[C|List],CharList), C \= 32,!,
    get_token([C|List],Token,Rest),
    tokenize(Rest,TList).

get_token(List,Token,Rest) :-
    get_chars(List,Lchars,Rest),
    name(Token,Lchars).

get_chars(L,S,L1) :- separator(L,S,L1),!.
get_chars([C|L],[C|Lc],L1) :-
    check_start(S,C),
    get_word_chars(S,L,Lc,L1).

get_word_chars(S,L,Lc,L1) :-
    check_end(S,L,Lc,L1).
get_word_chars(S,[C|L],[C|Lc],L1) :-
    legal_char(S,C),
    get_word_chars(S,L,Lc,L1).

legal_char(quote,C) :- C \= ''.
legal_char(num,C)   :- digit(C).
legal_char(symb,C)  :- valid_char(C).

check_start(quote,'').
check_start(num, C)  :- digit(C).
check_start(symb,C)  :-
    valid_char(C), not(digit(C)).

check_end(_,[],[],[]) :- !.
check_end(quote,[''|L],[''],L) :- !.
check_end(num, [C|L],[],[C|L]) :- not(digit(C)),!.
check_end(symb,[C|L],[],[C|L]) :- not(valid_char(C)).
```

```
separator([C,D,E|L],[C,D,E],L) :- name(S,[C,D,E]),
    member(S,['=:=','=\=','\==','@=<','@>=','=..','-->']),!.
separator([C,D|L],[C,D],L) :- name(S,[C,D]),
    member(S,
    [(':-'),'\+','->','\=','==','@<','@>','=<','>=','//']),!.
separator([C|L],[C],L) :-
    member(C,[',','(',')',':','[',']','|','+','-','*','/',';','=','<','>','^']).

valid_char(C) :- letter(C); digit(C); C = 95.
letter(C)  :-  'a =< C, C =< 'z; 'A =< C, C =< 'Z.
digit(C)   :-  '0 =< C, C =< '9.
```

Supplementary problems

4.9 Assume that the database currently contains the following facts:

p(a).	q(a,1).	r(1,1).	r(3,5).
p(b).	q(a,2).	r(1,2).	r(3,6).
	q(b,3).	r(2,3).	r(4,7).
	q(b,4).	r(2,4).	r(4,8).

What are the effects of the following queries:

(a)   ?- p(X),q(X,Y),r(Y,Z).
(b)   ?- p(X),!,q(X,Y),r(Y,Z).
(c)   ?- p(X),q(X,Y),!,r(Y,Z).
(d)   ?- p(X),once(q(X,Y)),r(Y,Z).

Here, *once* is the predicate defined in Subsection 4.2.3.

4.10 Translate the following sentences into a Prolog procedure, using the *cut* predicate:

> *X* is entitled
> >   for age-pension   *if* *X*'s age is 65 or over
> *or* for invalid-pension   *if* *X* is invalid
> *or* for unemployment   *if* *X* is unemployed
> *or* for nothing   otherwise

Beware of the common error mentioned in Example 4.6.

4.11 There is an old song that goes as follows:

> 99 bottles of beer on the wall
> 99 bottles of beer
> You take one down and pass it around
> 98 bottles of beer on the wall

and so on, until the last verse

> 1 bottle of beer on the wall
> 1 bottle of beer
> You take one down and pass it around
> No bottles of beer on the wall.

Write a Prolog program *beer* that receives a positive integer and prints the lyrics of the song. The program should print all the verses, and when it gets to the last verse, it must print 1 *bottle*, not 1 bottles and *no bottles* rather than 0 bottles.

4.12 Write a Prolog procedure to perform the following task:

(a) Read a word from the current input stream, by skipping the leading nonletter characters, reading the letters of the word, and stopping when encountering a nonletter character, and then print out the word in reverse. For example, if the input contains `???lived?`, then the output should be `devil`.

(b) Read a line of text from the current input stream and echo the line with a single space between words. For example, if the input line is `What     is    your     problem?`, then the output should be `What is your problem?`

4.13 Given is a file named '*c:customer.dat*' that contains records of the form [CustNum, Name, Address]. Write Prolog programs to perform the following separate tasks:

(a) Read the file and store all records in the database in the form *customer(CustNum,Name,Address)*.

(b) Read from the file only the records having *Name* beginning with "J" and store them in the database in the form described in (a). Consider two different cases: 1) The file records are in ascending order of customer number. 2) The file records are in alphabetical order of names.

Chapter 5

Development of
Prolog programs

5.1 Program development

In Chapters 2 and 3 we have studied the two different techniques of Prolog programming, each of which has both advantages and disadvantages. The declarative technique produces elegant and flexible programs, but they are usually inefficient. On the contrary, the procedural technique aims to achieve efficiency with the loss of transparency, which makes the verification of programs' correctness difficult.

For large and complex problems, it is necessary to combine the declarative and procedural approaches and to make use of the side-effect facilities of Prolog. Thus, a large Prolog program is normally organised hierarchically into several levels, where:

- The top levels take the procedural form;
- The lower levels have the declarative form;
- The bottom levels contain side-effect features such as input-output and database updating (using *assert*, *retract*, etc.).

In general, the development of large applications in Prolog is similar to that in any other programming language. That is, we must go through the following stages:

1. Study the information available and those required, and design data structures to represent them. The choice of data structures is very important, because it has a strong influence on the structure of the program. (For general data structures, we refer to Section 2.5 of Chapter 2. More advanced data structures are presented in Sections 6.3 and 6.4 of Chapter 6.)

2. Identify the immediate subprocesses, their relationship, and their input and output. This identification can be expressed in the form of an algorithm if the process has a procedural nature, or as a definition if the process can be stated declaratively.

   This task is to be repeated at each level until all the processes at the current level are elementary or already defined. A sample process and its subprocesses are depicted in Figure 5.1.

3. Translate the algorithms and definitions of part 2 into Prolog programs. For example, the description of process p as shown in Figure 5.1 is translated into the following program:

```
p(A,B,A1,B1,X) :-
    q(A,A1,U),
    r(B,B1,V),
    s(U,V,X).
```

Here, the goals $q(A,A1,U)$ and $r(B,B1,V)$ are mutually independent and can be executed in parallel if the program is run by a parallel Prolog system.

There are two important points to be noted on the input-output roles of a procedure's arguments in Prolog. First, each argument of a procedure can be used either as input or output, but not both. That is, parameter passing is only one-way, though the direction may vary from one call to another (see Section 3.4 of Chapter 3 for parameter passing). Thus, if an input datum is to be changed and returned, then the changed datum must be returned through an argument other than the input one. Second, a procedure's arguments cannot be declared to be definitely input or output. Hence, they may be used in a way unintended by the programmer. Therefore, the programmer must check all combinations of input-output roles for the program's arguments to ensure the program behaves correctly in all cases.

4. Establish the program's correctness top-down, checking the logic of each procedure. If any problems arise, then we must go back to the previous stages either to correct the translation, or to modify the algorithms and definitions, or to change the data structures.

5. The final stage is program testing. This should be done bottom-up. That is, the procedures at the lowest levels are tested first, and only when they are shown to be satisfactory do we move to the higher levels to continue testing. (More details on program testing are given in Subsection 5.5.2 of this chapter.) Again, if any problems arise, then the tasks of back-checking described in part 4 are to be carried out.

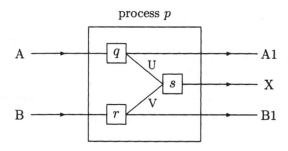

FIGURE 5.1 A sample process and its subprocesses.

5.2 Program style

A good program, besides being correct and efficient, must be *maintainable*. That is, the program must be easy to understand and easy to change.

The purpose of conforming a program to a certain style is to enhance its maintainability. The two basic features of a program's maintainability are its *modularity* and *readability*. Following are some guidelines for realising these two basic features.

1. *Modularity*: A program is said to be *modular* if it is well-divided into subprograms, each of which performs a separate and clearly defined function. Modularity is an intrinsic property that makes a program easy to understand and to change.

To enhance the modularity of a program, the following rules should be observed:

- Program clauses should be short. That is, each clause should contain only a few subgoals.

- Side-effect-producing goals should be isolated. That is, they should be included in separate procedures to be placed at the bottom levels.

2. *Readability*: The appearance of a program also has great effect on its understandability. To enhance a program's readability, the following should be noted:

- Symbols used should be meaningful, but should not be too long. Predicate symbols usually take the form of *verbs*, but when a predicate symbol has the form *is_something*, then a common practice is to omit the word "is" (which is to be read by default). For example, *member(X, Y)* is read "X is a member of Y". In Prolog programming, the use of single-letter variable names is not uncommon (because long variable names tend to make clauses too long), but if the roles of variables are unclear, then comments should be added to indicate their roles.

- Procedure layout should be well-indented. A common practice is to place each subgoal in a separate line, but this should not be taken as a strict rule. For example, a goal such as the output command *write('Customer '), write(CustName),nl* is better placed in a single line.

In general, the top-level control of an application system has the following form:

```
system :-
    initialise,
    activate_system,
    finalise.
```

where the procedure *initialise* normally contains an introduction to the system, creation of initial data, establishment of any global data stuctures, and opening of relevant files. The procedure *finalise* performs final processes, produces reports, and closes files.

The procedure *activate_system* is the main component of the system and normally consists of a loop that can be controlled either by a *repeat* goal or by recursion. Figures 5.2 and 5.3 show two typical forms of this procedure.

```
activate_system :-
    repeat,
        receive_query(Q),
        process_query(Q,X),
        update_global_data(X),
    test_for_termination(Q),!.
```

FIGURE 5.2 A typical top-level control using *repeat.*

The scheme given in Figure 5.2 is normally used to implement the systems that interact with the user in a dialogue pattern (e.g., expert systems and database query-answering systems). Each time the goal *test_for_termination* (Q) fails, the system backtracks to initiate another round of conversation. When the test succeeds, the process *activate_system* terminates with success.

```
activate_system(X) :-
    test_for_termination(X),!.
activate_system(X) :-
    process_data(X,X1),
    update_global_data(X1),
    activate_system(X1).
```

FIGURE 5.3 A typical top-level control using recursion with termination test.

The scheme given in Figure 5.3 is suitable for systems that construct solutions for a given problem (e.g., sort and search procedures, and simulation systems). The effect of the goal *test_for_termination* is similar to that described for the scheme of Figure 5.2. That is, each time the test fails, the system performs a recurrence of the process. (Unlike in the scheme of Figure 5.2, here a test is done right from the beginning.) When the test succeeds, the process *activate_system* terminates with success. Note also that the program of Figure 5.3 carries data from one iteration to the next, whereas the program of Figure 5.2 handles each round of interaction independently, except any possible effect on the global data.

If the goal *test_for_termination*(X) is more complicated than its negation, called *test_for_continuation*(X), then the program of Figure 5.3 can be rewritten as shown in Figure 5.4.

```
activate_system(X) :-
    test_for_continuation(X),
    process_data(X,X1),
    update_global_data(X1),
    activate_system(X1).
activate_system(X).
```

FIGURE 5.4 A typical top-level control using recursion with continuation test.

Here, each time the goal *test_for_continuation*(X) succeeds, the system performs an iteration of the loop. When the test fails, the system terminates with success. Very often, the first process of the system is used as a test for continuation: if this process succeeds, the system continues, otherwise the system terminates.

Returning to the scheme of Figure 5.2, we note that the goal *repeat* is useful only if the system's processes have side effects. If the loop's body has no side effect, then its failure will make the system stick in an infinite loop, because the repetition of its execution will not change the situation. In this case, the goal *repeat* must be removed, and we have the following variant scheme as shown in Figure 5.5.

```
activate_system :-
    receive_information(X),
    solve_the_problem(X,S),
    print_solution(S),
    test_for_termination.
activate_system :-
    finalise.
```

FIGURE 5.5 A typical backtracking-based loop.

Here, if the goal *test_for_termination* fails, the system backtracks to the goal *solve_the_problem*(X, S) to find alternative solutions. If *test_for_termination* succeeds, or if there are no more solutions for the problem, then the system terminates with success. The goal *finalise* can be used to reactivate the system if required.

Notes

1. In many application systems, the tests for termination and continuation take the following form, where 27 is the ASCII code of the <ESC>-key.

```
test_for_termination :-
    write('Press <ESC> to stop, any key to continue'),
    get0(27).

test_for_continuation :-
    write('Press any key to continue, <ESC> to stop'),
    get0(C), C \= 27.
```

2. Some systems require the procedure *activate_system* to loop infinitely (or until being interrupted by another procedure). In this case, the goal *test_for_termination* in the scheme of Figure 5.2 is simply *fail*, the first clause of the scheme in Figure 5.3 is omitted, and the goal *test_for_continuation* of Figure 5.4 is removed together with any alternative clauses.

Following is an example of a simple application that has many features of a large system.

EXAMPLE 5.1   Consider an airport having a single runway (Figure 5.6). Let us write a Prolog program that performs the task of the airport-control system. When an airplane requests permission to land or take off, it is advised to wait and is placed at the end of the landing queue or the taking-off queue. If the runway is clear, then the airplane at the head of the landing queue is allowed to proceed to land. Only when no airplanes are waiting for landing are the airplanes in the taking-off queue processed, also in the first-in-first-out order. The system is intended to work continually through day and night. (The operation of such an airport is simulated in Example 11.1 of Chapter 11.)

For this system, the input are messages from the airplanes requesting permission to land or take off, or reporting on the completion of the services.

FIGURE 5.6 A single-runway airport[1].

These messages are assumed to take the following form:

    AF24   request landing.
    PN06   request taking off.
    QT15   landing completed.
    RF27   taking off completed.

Each message is read into a list of words to be processed for service. The output are simply messages sent to the airplanes advising them to wait or to proceed.

We represent the runway by a fact *runway(Status:Flight)*, where *Status* is either *free* or *busy*, and *Flight* represents the code of the aircraft that occupies the runway if its status is *busy*. The two waiting queues are represented by two lists of facts of the form *landing(Flight)* and *takingoff(Flight)*, where *Flight* contains the flight numbers of the airplanes waiting in the queues. An airplane is added to a queue by using the predicate *assertz*, and is removed from a queue by the predicate *retract*. The outline of the program's development is shown on the next page.

---

[1]This figure is adapted from Figure 5.5 of Kruse, R. L., Programming with data structures, 1989, p. 155. Adapted by permission of Prentice-Hall, Englewood Cliffs, N. J.

Data structures
    Message: ['AF24', request, landing]
    Response: ['AF24', landing, 'request received. Please wait!']

    Queues: landing('AF24').   takingoff('PN06').
               landing('CO16').   takingoff('HK10').
               landing('BA07').   takingoff('AI42').

    Runway: runway(busy:'KL50').

Processes
    Airport control
        receive a message
        process the message
        process the runway
    forever.

    Process the message:
        {Input: message;   Output: nil}
        Check message validity to obtain a response
        Send the responding message.

    Check message to obtain a response
        {Input: message;   Output: response}
        if   message is a request for service then
            return a message asking the airplane to wait
            and add the airplane to appropriate queue;
        if   message is a report of service completion then
            return a message recording the service
            and free the runway;
        otherwise, return an error message.

    Process the runway:
        {Input: nil;   Output: nil}
        if   runway is free then
            access the waiting queues and pick an airplane;
            if   obtain an airplane then
                advise the airplane to proceed and
                record the runway being occupied by this airplane
            else report runway idle.

The lower level development is quite straightforward. The program *airport_control* is given in Figures 5.7 and 5.8. Note that a *repeat-fail* combination would allow the system to run nonstop. In testing this system, we substitute the goal *fail* with a test `terminate([zzzz])` as shown in Figure 5.8.

```
airport_control :-
    repeat,
        receive_message(M),
        process_message(M),
        process_runway,
    terminate(M).

receive_message(M) :- read_sentence(M),nl.

process_message(Message) :-
    check_message(Message,Response),
    respond_message(Response).

check_message(Message,Response) :-
    request_service(Message,Airplane,Response),!,
    add_to_queue(Airplane).
check_message([Flight|Rest],Response) :-
    complete_service([Flight|Rest],_,Response),!,
    change_runway(busy:Flight,free:_).
check_message(_,Response) :- error_message(Response).

request_service([Flight,request,Service],Airplane,
    [Flight,Service,'request received. Please wait!']) :-
    valid(Flight,Service,Airplane).

complete_service([Flight,Service,completed],_,
    [Flight,Service,'completion recorded.']) :-
    valid(Flight,Service,_).

error_message(['Invalid message! Use following format:',nl,
    'FlightNumber request <landing/taking-off>',nl,
    'FlightNumber <landing/taking-off> completed',nl]).
```

FIGURE 5.7 An airport control system.

```
valid(Flight,landing,landing(Flight)).
valid(Flight,'taking-off',takingoff(Flight)).

add_to_queue(Airplane) :- assertz(Airplane).

change_runway(A,B) :-
    retract(runway(A)),!,asserta(runway(B)).
change_runway(_,_) :-
    respond_message(['Invalid flight. Try again.']),
    fail.

process_runway :-
    runway(free:_),
    provide_service(Flight),
    change_runway(_,busy:Flight).
process_runway.

provide_service(Flight) :-
    retract(landing(Flight)),!,
    respond_message([Flight,'may proceed landing now.']).
provide_service(Flight) :-
    retract(takingoff(Flight)),!,
    respond_message([Flight,'may proceed taking off now.']).
provide_service(_) :-
    respond_message(['> Report: No airplane in sight.']),
    nl,fail.

respond_message([]) :- nl,nl.
respond_message([H|T]) :-
    (H = nl, nl,!; write(H),write(' ')),
    respond_message(T).

runway(free:_).
terminate([zzzz]).

read_sentence(L) :- % see Figure 4.9
```

FIGURE 5.8 An airport-control system (continued from Figure 5.7).

5.3   Programming techniques

The techniques used in Prolog programming can be classified into the following basic forms:

- Generate-and-test
- Divide-and-conquer
- Second-order programming
- Search
- Meta-programming

The generate-and-test and divide-and-conquer techniques have been used widely in the previous examples. We now reformulate these techniques and give additional demonstrations. Second-order programming is a more advanced technique that is to be presented in the next chapter. Searching is a special case of generate-and-test and meta-programming is a high-level application of second-order programming. These two techniques are studied in Chapter 7 and Chapter 8, respectively.

5.3.1   Generate-and-test

The generate-and-test technique originated in mathematical definitions, where an entity is defined to be an element of certain class having some special property. For example, the maximum of a list of integers is a member of the list that is greater than or equal to every element of the list. This definition is expressed in Prolog as follows:

```
max(X,L) :- member(X,L),greatest(X,L).
```

When the above-mentioned mathematical concept is brought to the field of computer programming, it becomes an operational means of generating desired objects. The general form of a generate-and-test program is as follows:

```
find(X) :- generate(X),test(X).
```

The procedures that are frequently used as a generator in generate-and-test programs are: *member, select, append, permutation,* and *next_state*. In a program like the above, the generator is repeatedly executed to provide an object, until the desired object is found.

Sometimes the desired object is a transformation of a given object. In this case, the program is called a *change-and-test* program and has the following general form:

```
find(X,X) :- test(X).
find(X,Y) :- change(X,X1),find(X1,Y).
```

Here, the procedure *change* is invoked repeatedly to transform the given object, one bit at a time, until it has the desired property. In particular, the given object may be gradually expanded until it meets the required condition. This form of *expand-and-test* program is the basis of search techniques.

Following is another classic problem for which the generate-and-test technique can be applied.

EXAMPLE 5.2   It has been known for many centuries that one needs only four colours to paint any map so that no two neighbouring states have the same colour. Let us write a Prolog program that receives a map and a list of four colours, and produces a coloured map. We represent a map by a list of states, each of which is composed of a state name and a list of neighbouring states. For example, the maps of Australia and Western Europe (see Figure 5.10) are represented by the following facts:

```
map('Australia',
    [wa : [nt,sa], nt: [wa,sa,qld], qld: [nt,sa,nsw],
     nsw: [qld,sa,vic], vic: [sa,nsw], tas: [],
     sa : [wa,nt,qld,nsw,vic]]).
map('West Europe',
    [portugal : [spain],
     spain    : [portugal,france],
     belgium  : [france,holland,luxembrg,germany],
     holland  : [belgium,germany],
     luxembrg : [france,belgium,germany],
     switzerld: [france,germany,austria,italy],
     italy    : [france,switzerld,austria],
     austria  : [germany,switzerld,italy],
     france   : [spain,belgium,luxembrg,germany,
                 switzerld,italy],
     germany  : [holland,belgium,luxembrg,france,
                 switzerld,austria]]).
```

The coloured map to be output is represented by a list of pairs *S:C*, where *S* is a state name and *C* is a colour chosen for the state *S*. This list is referred to as the list of *chosen colours* (which is initially empty) in the following algorithm:

> To paint a map with a given list of colours do
> > obtain the list of states in the map, then
> > arrange colours for this list of states.

> To arrange colours for a list of states do
> > choose a colour *C* for the first state *S* such that
> > *C* is different from all chosen colours of *S*'s neighbours,
> > add the pair *S* : *C* to the list of chosen colours, and
> > continue to arrange colours for the remaining states in
> > the list (until there are no states left in the list).

The above algorithm is translated into the program of Figure 5.9.

```
paint(MapName,Colours,ColouredMap) :-
    map(MapName,StateList),
    arrange_colours(StateList,Colours,[],ColouredMap).

arrange_colours([S:Nbs|Rest],Colours,ChosenColours,Result) :-
    member(C,Colours),
    different(C,Nbs,ChosenColours),
    arrange_colours(Rest,Colours,[S:C|ChosenColours],Result).
arrange_colours([],_,Result,Result).

different(C,Nbs,[S1:C1|Rest]) :-
    not((member(S1,Nbs), C = C1)),
    different(C,Nbs,Rest).
different(_,_,[]).

member :- % see Figure 2.13
```

FIGURE 5.9 A program to paint a map.

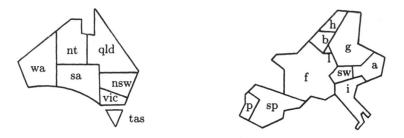

FIGURE 5.10 The maps of Australia and Western Europe.

For example, to find the appropriate colours for the Australian map, we use the following query:

```
?- paint('Australia',[red,blue,yellow,purple],
        Coloured_Map).
Coloured_Map = [sa:yellow, tas:red, vic:red,
        nsw:blue, qld:red, nt:blue, wa:red] ->
```

Predictably, the system provides a large number of answers corresponding to many ways of painting the Australian map with the given four colours.

5.3.2 Divide-and-conquer

In problem-solving the tactic of divide-and-conquer is to break the given problem down to smaller problems of the same nature. This is repeatedly done until the subproblems are trivial enough to be tackled directly.

The general form of a divide-and-conquer program is as follows:

```
find(X,Y) :- trivial(X),!,solve(X,Y).
find(X,Y) :- divide(X,X1,X2),
            find(X1,Y1),find(X2,Y2),
            combine(Y1,Y2,Y).
```

Quick-sort (Figure 3.16) and *merge-sort* (Problem 3.9) are two typical applications of the divide-and-conquer technique. Most problems that deal with binary trees are suitable for the method of divide-and-conquer (for examples, see Figures 2.11 and 2.35). In fact, the task of handling a binary tree can be reduced to handling its left and right subtrees in the same manner. To take the best advantage of the divide-and-conquer technique, however, the two subtrees should be of almost equal size. A special kind of binary tree whose structure allows the best use of the divide-and-conquer technique is called *balanced tree* or AVL-tree (after the names of the inventors, Adelson, Velskii, and Landis).

▷ An AVL-tree is a binary search tree whose subtrees have heights differing by at most 1, and they are also AVL-trees.

The organisation of data into an AVL-tree allows fast searching, while maintenance is relatively easier than using perfectly balanced binary search trees (Wirth, 1976). Maintenance of AVL-trees will be discussed in Chapter 6 (Subsection 6.4.1). The following example shows a method of constructing AVL-trees of given heights with minimum number of nodes (Wirth, 1976).

EXAMPLE 5.3   The binary trees presented below are constructed in the same manner as the Fibonacci numbers and are therefore called the *Fibonacci-trees*. For each integer $h = 0, 1, 2, \ldots$, an AVL-tree T_h of height h is constructed in the following way:

T_0 is the empty tree;
T_1 consists of a single node;
T_h has T_{h-1} as its left subtree and T_{h-2} as its right subtrees.

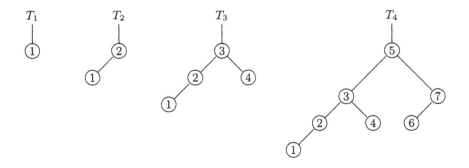

FIGURE 5.11   Fibonacci-trees.

Consequently, the number of nodes in T_h is determined by the following recursive formula:

$$N_0 = 0$$
$$N_1 = 1$$
$$N_h = N_{h-1} + N_{h-2} + 1 \quad (h > 1).$$

Figure 5.11 shows some of the Fibonacci-trees T_h whose nodes contain integer keys from 1 to N_h in in-order. These trees are constructed by the program shown in Figure 5.12, which is very similar to the program constructing the Fibonacci numbers that we have developed in Problem 2.5. Here, in the head predicate

fibonacci_tree(H,N,T)

the argument H represents the height of the tree, N is the number of nodes in the tree, and T is the Fibonacci-tree of height H. The program constructs the tree T by constructing its left subtree *bt(T2,Y,T3)*, noting its number of nodes *N1* and its own left subtree *T2* whose number of nodes is one less than its root key Y (i.e., *N2*+1 = Y). The root key X of T is therefore equal to *N1*+1 and the number of nodes in T is *N1*+Y. Finally, the right subtree of T is *T2* with all its nodes' keys augmented by X.

```
fibonacci_tree(0,0,nil).
fibonacci_tree(1,1,bt(nil,1,nil)).
fibonacci_tree(H,N,bt(bt(T2,Y,T3),X,T2A)) :-
    H > 1, H1 is H-1,
    fibonacci_tree(H1,N1,bt(T2,Y,T3)),
    X is N1+1, N is N1+Y,
    augment(T2,X,T2A).

augment(nil,_,nil).
augment(bt(L,K,R),X,bt(LA,KA,RA)) :-
    KA is K+X,
    augment(L,X,LA),
    augment(R,X,RA).
```

FIGURE 5.12 A program to construct the Fibonacci-trees.

5.4   User interaction

User interface is an important feature of most computer systems. In this section, we study the implementation in Prolog of two basic forms of user interaction, namely *menu* and *dialogue*.

5.4.1   Menu-driven interaction

Menu is probably the most popular form of user interaction in practical programming systems. A menu-driven system helps the user to perform a task by providing a menu that contains a number of options. The user simply chooses an available option, and the system performs the appropriate task or displays the next menu.

For example, a database administration system may display a menu of the following form:

```
DB10 DATABASE ADMINISTRATOR
-------------------------------------------------
We provide the following services :

        1:  Search existing databases
        2:  Update existing databases
        3:  Create new databases
        0:  Exit


Select service required :
```

The user selects an option by typing an appropriate number. Then the database administrator may ask for the database's name and display the next menu. For example, if we choose option 3, then the next menu will be displayed as shown on the next page.

Thus menus are organised in a hierarchical structure as shown in Figure 5.13. In Prolog, menu-handling can be implemented as shown in the program of Figure 5.14. From this program, we note that the procedure *put_menu* displays the options of *MenuName* on the screen and also returns a prompt-sentence and a range of option-numbers. The procedure *accept* prints this prompt-sentence, reads, and checks the user's choice of option until the choice is within the valid range. For example, in the database-administration system shown above, the display of the main menu is produced by the program shown in Figure 5.14.

```
CREATE NEW DATABASE
----------------------------------------------------
Enter database name :  stdaccom
We support the following data structures :

            1:   Sequential data
            2:   AVL-tree
            3:   B-tree
            0:   Return to main menu


Select data structure required :
```

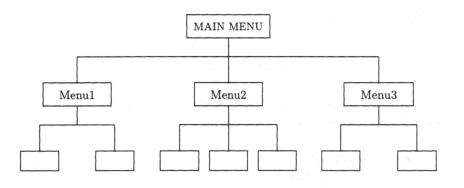

FIGURE 5.13 Menus organisation.

```
put_menu(dbadmin,['Select service required :',0,1,2,3]) :-
    nl,write('DB10 DATABASE ADMINISTRATOR'),
    nl,write('----------------------------------------'),
    write('----------'),
    nl,write('We provide the following services :'),
    nl,nl,write('        1:  Search existing databases'),
      nl,write('        2:  Update existing databases'),
      nl,write('        3:  Create new databases'),
      nl,write('        0:  Exit').
```

```
display_menu(MenuName):-
    put_menu(MenuName,Response),
    accept(Request,Response),
    process(MenuName,Request).

accept(Request,[Prompt|Range]),
    repeat,
        nl,nl,
        write(Prompt),
        read(Request),
    member(Request,Range).
```

FIGURE 5.14 Menu-handling in Prolog.

The procedure *put_menu*(createdb,['Select data structure required :', 0, 1, 2, 3]) that generates the create-new-database menu is similar to the above procedure, except that it contains the following extra subgoals:

```
nl,write('Enter database name :'),
read(DBName),assert(database(DBName)),
```

For each option given in a menu, there is a clause *process(MenuName,Request)* that describes the specific task. For example:

```
process(dbadmin,3) :-
    display_menu(createdb).
```

Menu-driven interaction is simple and can be implemented efficiently. The user is placed under strict guidance and can hardly make any mistake that could jeopardise the system. Some Prolog systems provide built-in predicates for screen-handling such as controlling of the cursor's movement and producing colours and sounds. These facilities make menu-driven interaction more convenient and interesting.

5.4.2   User-system dialogue

In a dialogue sytem, the user is allowed to enter queries in a restricted form of natural language.

For example, to ask for the name and test mark of some particular student whose ID number is given, the user may use a query sentence of the following form:

```
find student name and test mark
where student id is 91-2123 and test id is 91-2123.
```

In the above query, the top line contains the information required and the second line provides the given data. The expected answer is:

```
student name Smith J.R. test mark 40
```

Generally, a dialogue system is controlled by the following top-level procedure:

```
dialogue :-
    repeat,
        read_sentence(Query),
        response(Query,Answer),
        print(Answer),
    Answer = [bye].
```

The procedure *read_sentence* has been given in Chapter 4 (Figure 4.9). This procedure reads the user's query into a list of words, which is to be processed by the procedure *response*. The procedure *response* scans the query to check its grammatical structure, then converts it into a Prolog goal that is executed to produce the answer.

```
response(Query,Answer) :-
    parse(Query,GoalList,Answer),
    convert(GoalList,Goal),
    Goal.
response([bye],[bye]).
```

The structure of the procedure *parse* depends on the grammar of the query language in use. For the simple grammar of the sample query given above, we have a very simple parser shown in Figures 5.15 and 5.16 (more sophisticated parsers are given in Chapter 10).

```
parse([W|WList],Goals,Answer) :-
    valid_command(W),
    split(WList,Query,Data),
    construct(Query,Goals,Answer),
    instantiate(Goals,Data).

split(WList,Query,Data) :-
    append(Query,[where|Data],WList),!.
split(WList,WList,[]).

construct([and|Qs],Goals,Answer) :- !,
    construct(Qs,Goals,Answer).
construct([P,A|Qs],[G|Gs],[P,A,X|Ans]) :-
    match_arg(P,A,G,X),
    construct(Qs,Gs,Ans).
construct([],[],[]).
```

FIGURE 5.15 A simple parser (top level).

Finally, the procedure *convert* transforms a list of goals into a conjunction of goals:

```
convert([G],(G)) :- !.
convert([G|Gs],(G,Ys)) :-
    convert(Gs,Ys).
```

Thus, the sample query given at the beginning of this subsection is converted into the following Prolog goal

```
student(91-2123,X),test(91-2123,Y)
```

which is associated with the list

```
Answer = [student,name,X,test,mark,Y].
```

When the goal is executed, the variables X, Y are instantiated to 'Smith J.R.' and 40, respectively. Thus, the procedure *print* displays the list *Answer* in the form that we have shown.

```
instantiate(Goals,[and|Data]) :- !,
    instantiate(Goals,Data).
instantiate(Goals,[P,A,is,C|Data]) :-
    match_arg(P,A,G,C),
    member(G,Goals),
    instantiate(Goals,Data).
instantiate(_,[]).

match_arg(P,A,G,X) :-
    schema(P,N,Args),functor(G,P,N),
    index(A,Args,I),arg(I,G,X).

index(A,[A|Args],1) :- !.
index(A,[B|Args],I) :-
    index(A,Args,J), I is J+1.

schema(student,2,[id,name]).
schema(test,2,[id,mark]).

valid_command(find).
valid_command(show).
valid_command(give).

member :- % see Figure 2.13
append :- % see Figure 2.21
```

FIGURE 5.16 A simple parser (lower level).

5.5   Program validation

Programs' correctness is always a great concern of programmers in any programming language. In Prolog, however, the task of establishing a program's correctness is relatively easier than that in most conventional programming languages. This is mainly due to the fact that Prolog programs are translated from logical statements, and also because the Prolog language allows programs to be highly modular.

The general rule of verifying a Prolog program is given as follows:

▷ The correctness of a Prolog program is proved top-down and is tested bottom-up.

The proof should start from the top-level procedure and work downward, so that for each procedure, its purpose can be easily determined and the form of its input and output accurately identified. On the other hand, testing must begin with the lowest-level procedures and move upward, so that when a procedure is tested, all of its subgoals are already established to be correct. Thus, if anything goes wrong, we are sure that the errors lie in the current procedure.

Note that the verification of a program's correctness requires both a convincing proof and a satisfactory set of test evidence. A proof alone can establish the program's logical soundness, but may miss minor errors such as the misspelling of procedure names, and the missing of elementary procedures like *member* and *append*. Whereas testing alone is inadequate to establish a program's correctness, as it is well-known that a test can only show the presence of bugs, not their absence.

5.5.1   Proof of a program's correctness

To prove a program's correctness, we start with the top-level procedure and move down to the lower levels once the correctness of all higher-level procedures has been established. At each level and for each procedure, the following steps should be taken:

1. State precisely what the procedure is intended to define or to perform.

2. Identify the expected input and output.

3. Classify the possible input into a (finite) number of cases.

4. For each clause of the procedure, assume that all subgoals are true and show that the clause's head is also true, according to the specification of step 1. (Recall that if the program contains the cut, then the operational meaning of a clause may be different from its separate declarative reading (see Chapter 4, Section 4.2). In this case, the clause must be read (or rewritten if necessary) in a way to reflect its operational meaning. For example, see Problem 5.4(b).)

5. Check that all cases of input have been covered.

If the above-listed five-step process succeeds, then the procedure is established as correct. A program is correct if all of its procedures are correct.

EXAMPLE 5.4   Let us prove the correctness of the program *fibonacci_tree* given in Figure 5.12. This program has only two levels. We begin with level 1 and assume the procedures at the lower level are correct.

Procedure *fibonacci_tree*:

1.   This procedure constructs the Fibonacci-tree T of given height H and returns in N the number of nodes in the tree. More precisely, this procedure defines (N, T) as a function of H with the following properties:

$$\text{if } H = 0 \text{ then } (N, T) = (0, nil)$$
$$\text{if } H = 1 \text{ then } (N, T) = (1, bt(nil, 1, nil))$$
if $H > 1$ then (N, T) is defined as follows

T has the form $bt(L, X, R)$, where

N is the number of nodes in T,

L is a binary tree where $(N1, L)$ is a result of this procedure for $H - 1$,

X $= 1 +$ number of nodes in L,

R is a copy of the left subtree of L with all nodes' keys augmented by X.

2.   Input: H is a nonnegative integer.
     Output: N is a nonnegative integer; T is a binary tree of the form *nil* or $bt(L, X, R)$, where X is an integer, and L, R are binary trees of the same form.

3.   Possible cases of input:
$$H = 0, \quad H = 1 \quad \text{or} \quad H > 1.$$

4.   Proof:
     The first two clauses of the procedure are direct representations of the definition given in step 1 for the cases $H = 0$ and $H = 1$. We need only consider the third clause.
        Suppose that the goal *fibonacci_tree*($H1,N1,bt(T2,Y,T3)$) returns $N1$ and $bt(T2, Y, T3)$, satisfying all the properties listed in step 1, and that the goal *augment*($T2,X,T2A$) creates $T2A$ as a copy of $T2$, with all nodes' keys augmented by the value of X.

Then T has the form $bt(bt(T2, Y, T3), X, T2A)$, and
$$N = N1 + Y$$
$$= N1 + 1 + \text{ number of nodes in } T2$$
$$= N1 + 1 + \text{ number of nodes in } T2A$$
$$= \text{ number of nodes in } T;$$

L, the left subtree of T, is $bt(T2, Y, T3)$, which is
constructed by the procedure for $H1 = H - 1$;
$$X = 1 + N1$$
$$= 1 + \text{ number of nodes in } L;$$

R, the right subtree of T, is $T2A$, which is a copy
of $T2$ (the left subtree of L) with all
nodes' keys augmented by X.

Hence, the third clause is correct for the case $H > 1$.

5. We note that if H is 0 or 1 or uninstantiated, then only the first two clauses are used, and N, T must have the form specified in these clauses. If $H > 1$, then the third clause applies. As this clause has been proved to be correct, the arguments N, T (which may be instantiated or not) must comply with the form specified by this clause.

Since all clauses of the program *fibonacci_tree* are correct and cover all possible cases of input, the program is correct provided that the procedure *augment* (of the second level) is correct. The proof of correctness of the procedure *augment* is straightforward and is left to the reader as an exercise.

5.5.2   Test of a program's correctness

A reasoning proof of a program's correctness is an attempt to demonstrate the logical soundness of the program, but it does not guarantee that the program will run correctly. The following are some common errors that may remain undetected during the phase of program proving:

- Misspelling of procedure names;

- Missing of elementary procedures such as *member* and *append*;

- Mistaking semicolons for commas or vice versa;

- Misplacing or missing of cut;

- Mishandling of recursion.

Note that the above-listed errors are not detected as syntax errors. The first two errors usually cause the program to fail unexpectedly (with a mysterious response "no"). Errors of the third kind also cause the program to behave strangely and to produce unexpected output. A common consequence of missing a cut is the duplication of answers or even wrong answers. Finally, the program may be trapped in an infinite loop as a result of mishandling of recursion. (For termination of recursive programs, see Chapter 2, page 29.)

To test a program, we start with the lowest-level procedures and move up to the higher levels once the procedures at the lower levels have been tested to be correct. At each level and for each procedure the following steps should be taken:

1. Identify the expected input and output.

2. Classify the possible input into a number of cases.

3. Design data to cover all possible cases listed in step 2.

4. Run the procedure with input data designed in step 3.

5. Check the output against expected output described in step 1.

If the input data are complex and are to be used repeatedly, then they should be stored in memory together with the program.

EXAMPLE 5.5   Let us test the program *fibonacci_tree* given in Figure 5.12. To facilitate the perception of a tree, we add the following procedure to display binary trees, where $tmove(X, Y)$ is a built-in procedure (of Arity-Prolog) that moves the cursor to row X and column Y.

```
print_tree(nil,_,_,_).
print_tree(bt(L,K,R),X,Y,D) :-
    tmove(X,Y), write(K),
    D1 is D//2, X1 is X+D1,
    Y1 is Y-D,  Y2 is Y+D,
    print_tree(L,X1,Y1,D1),
    print_tree(R,X1,Y2,D1).
```

We also add the following facts to the program to be used as test data.

```
tree(1,bt(nil,1,nil)).
tree(2,bt(bt(nil,1,nil),2,nil)).
```

```
tree(3,bt(bt(bt(nil,1,nil),2,nil),3,bt(nil,4,nil))).
tree(4,bt(bt(bt(bt(nil,1,nil),2,nil),3,bt(nil,4,nil)),
     5,bt(bt(nil,6,nil),7,nil))).
```

We begin by testing the procedure *augment*. Following are some test results:

```
?- tree(1,T1),augment(T1,2,T2).
T1 = bt(nil,1,nil)
T2 = bt(nil,3,nil) ->

?- tree(2,T1),augment(T1,5,T2).
T1 = bt(bt(nil,1,nil),2,nil)
T2 = bt(bt(nil,6,nil),7,nil) ->

?- tree(3,T1),augment(T1,4,T2).
T1 = bt(bt(bt(nil,1,nil),2,nil),3,bt(nil,4,nil))
T2 = bt(bt(bt(nil,5,nil),6,nil),7,bt(nil,8,nil)) ->

?- tree(4,T1),augment(T1,1,T2).
T1 = bt(bt(bt(bt(nil,1,nil),2,nil),3,bt(nil,4,nil)),
     5,bt(bt(nil,6,nil),7,nil))
T2 = bt(bt(bt(bt(nil,2,nil),3,nil),4,bt(nil,5,nil)),
     6,bt(bt(nil,7,nil),8,nil)) ->
```

Having been satisfied with the correct behaviour of procedure *augment*, we now test the procedure *fibonacci_tree*, and some test results are shown below. The results show that the program works as intended.

```
?- fibonacci_tree(3,N,T),
   cls,print_tree(T,1,6,4),
   nl,nl.

     3

  2       4
1

N = 4
T = bt(bt(bt(nil,1,nil),2,nil),3,bt(nil,4,nil)) ->
```

```
?- fibonacci_tree(4,N,T),
   cls,print_tree(T,1,14,8),
   nl,nl.
```

```
                  5


          3               7

     2       4       6
 1
```

```
N = 7
T = bt(bt(bt(bt(nil,1,nil),2,nil),3,bt(nil,4,nil)),
       5,bt(bt(nil,6,nil),7,nil)) ->
```

```
?- fibonacci_tree(5,N,T),
   cls,print_tree(T,1,30,16),
   nl,nl,nl,nl.
```

```
                              8




            5                               11


        3               7           10              12

     2       4       6           9
 1
```

```
N = 12
T = bt(bt(bt(bt(bt(nil,1,nil),2,nil),3,bt(nil,4,nil)),5,
    bt(bt(nil,6,nil),7,nil)),8,bt(bt(bt(nil,9,nil),10,nil),
    11,bt(nil,12,nil))) ->
```

Solved problems

5.1 *The stable marriage problem* (McVitie & Wilson, 1969). A marriage service agency is asking you to write a Prolog program to solve the following problem. There are N men and N women who want to get married. Each man has a list of all the women in his preferred order, and likewise each woman has a list of men in her preferred order. The problem is to find a set of marriages that is stable. A set of marriages is unstable if there are two married couples of which two members cross-prefer each other. For example, let (A, X) and (B, Y) be two married couples, where A, B are men and X, Y are women. If A prefers Y to X and Y prefers A to B, or B prefers X to Y and X prefers B to A, then the marriages are unstable.

The program should display all solutions at the terminal, one at a time. The program must also allow the user to try different problems without having to exit and reenter the system. Try your program on the following data:

(a) There are three men and three women with their preferences as follows:

> john : annie, suzie, wendy
> mark : wendy, annie, suzie
> tony : wendy, suzie, annie
>
> annie : tony, john, mark
> suzie : mark, john, tony
> wendy : john, mark, tony

(b) Five men and five women with the following preferences:

allan : verra, xania, zonie, wendy, yamie
bobby : zonie, xania, wendy, verra, yamie
chris : verra, wendy, xania, yamie, zonie
danny : yamie, xania, zonie, wendy, verra
ersky : yamie, xania, verra, wendy, zonie

xania : allan, bobby, danny, ersky, chris
yamie : ersky, danny, chris, allan, bobby
zonie : danny, bobby, allan, chris, ersky
verra : bobby, allan, ersky, chris, danny
wendy : chris, bobby, allan, danny, ersky

Solution:

As the given data indicate, it is natural to represent the list of men's preferences in the following form:

$$[M_1 : [W_{11}, \ldots, W_{1N}], \ldots, M_N : [W_{N1}, \ldots, W_{NN}]]$$

where each M_i is a man's name and the W_{ij} are women's names in M_i's preference order. The list of women's preferences is represented likewise.

To solve this problem, we form the couples for marriage, one by one, maintaining the stability of their marriages throughout, until no one is left unengaged. The top-level algorithm for this problem follows the scheme of Figure 5.5 and is expressed as follows.

To form the couples for marriage do
    take one man and select a woman for him
    such that the couple does not jeopardise the stability
    of the already formed couples,
    then continue until no one left unengaged.

A couple P jeopardises the stability of the couples PL *if*
    there is a couple *P1* in *PL* such that
    two members of P and *P1* cross-prefer each other.

Two members of the couples (M, W) and *(M1, W1)*
cross-prefer each other *if*
    either M prefers *W1* to W and *W1* prefers M to *M1*
    or W prefers *M1* to M and *M1* prefers W to *W1*.

The remaining tasks are trivial. The program is given as follows:

```
marriage_solver :-
    read_information(Men,Women),
    solve_marriage(Men,Women,Sol),
    print_solution(_,Sol),
    test_for_termination.
marriage_solver :-
    finalise.

read_information(Men,Women) :- nl,
    write('Enter marrying group number, '),
    write('terminated with a period: '),
    read(N),
    marriage_group(N,Men,Women).

solve_marriage(Men,Women,Sol) :-
    form_couples(Men,Women,[],Sol).

form_couples([],[],Sol,Sol).
form_couples([M|Ms],WL,PairList,Sol) :-
    select(W,WL,WL1),
    not(unstable((M,W),PairList)),
    form_couples(Ms,WL1,[(M,W)|PairList],Sol).

unstable(Pair,PairList) :-
    member(Pair1,PairList),
    cross_prefer(Pair,Pair1).

cross_prefer((M,W),(M1,W1)) :-
    prefer(M,W1,W),prefer(W1,M,M1);
    prefer(W,M1,M),prefer(M1,W,W1).

prefer(P:L,P1:_,P2:_) :-
    append(_,[P1|Rest],L),
    member(P2,Rest).

print_solution(0,[]) :- !,nl.
print_solution(K1,[(M:_,W:_)|Rest]) :-
    print_solution(K,Rest),
    K1 is K+1,
    nl,write('Couple '),write(K1:M+W).

test_for_termination :- nl,nl,
    write('Press any key for more solution,<ESC> to stop'),
    get0(27).
```

```
finalise :- nl,
    write('No more solutions!'),nl,
    write('Another marriage problem? <y/n> '),
    get0(C), (C = 'y,!, marriage_solver; true).

member :- % see Figure 2.13
select :- % see Figure 2.16
append :- % see Figure 2.21
```

With the given data stored in the database in the following form, we have the answers to the first problem shown below. The data for the second problem are stored in the same form, and the solutions are obtained in the same way.

```
marriage_group(1,
    [john:[annie,suzie,wendy],
     mark:[wendy,annie,suzie],
     tony:[wendy,suzie,annie]],
    [annie:[tony,john,mark],
     suzie:[mark,john,tony],
     wendy:[john,mark,tony]]).

?- marriage_solver.
Enter marrying group number, terminated with a period: 1.

Couple 1 : john + annie
Couple 2 : mark + wendy
Couple 3 : tony + suzie

Press any key for more solution,<ESC> to stop

Couple 1 : john + suzie
Couple 2 : mark + wendy
Couple 3 : tony + annie

Press any key for more solution,<ESC> to stop

Couple 1 : john + wendy
Couple 2 : mark + suzie
Couple 3 : tony + annie

Press any key for more solution,<ESC> to stop
No more solutions!
Another marriage problem ? <y/n>
```

5.2 *The knight-tour.* Given a chessboard of size $N \times N$, a knight is placed in a square of coordinates (X, Y) and is allowed to move according to the rules of chess. The problem is to find a sequence of moves for the knight so that every square of the board is visited by the knight exactly once.

Write a Prolog program that reads the board's size N and the knight's initial location (X, Y), and produces the chessboard with traces of the knight's moves to cover the board.

Solution:

We use this problem to present a simple implementation of two-dimensional arrays in Prolog. Here, an $N \times N$ array is represented by a list of lists in the following form:

$$[[1, (1, X_{11}), \ldots, (N, X_{1N})], \ldots, [N, (1, X_{N1}), \ldots, (N, X_{NN})]]$$

We shall see in the next chapter (Subsection 6.3.3) that multidimensional arrays represented in the above-given form can be easily created and manipulated by using the meta-predicate *setof*.

In this problem, we represent the chessboard as an $N \times N$ array, the elements of which are to be filled with positive integers that indicate the sequence of the knight's moves. The top-level procedures are quite standard and are shown below.

```
knight_tour :-
    read_information(N,X,Y),
    find_knight_tour(N,X,Y,Board),
    print_board(Board).

read_information(N,X,Y) :-
    nl,write('Enter board size <n.>: '),
    read(N),
    nl,write('Enter knight position <X + Y.> : '),
    read(X+Y).

find_knight_tour(N,X,Y,Board) :-
    make_array(0,N,Board),
    array_entry(Board,X,Y,1),
    find_moves(1,N,X,Y,Board).
```

```
make_array(N,N,[]) :- !.
make_array(I,N,[[I1|R]|Rs]) :-
    I < N, I1 is I+1,
    make_row(0,N,R),
    make_array(I1,N,Rs).

make_row(N,N,[]) :- !.
make_row(I,N,[(I1,X)|Rest]) :-
    I < N, I1 is I+1,
    make_row(I1,N,Rest).

array_entry(A,I,J,X) :- !,
    member([I|Row],A),
    member((J,X),Row).
```

The algorithm of the procedure *find_moves* is as follows:

To find the knight's moves from the Kth location (X, Y) do
>*if* $K = N^2$ then stop
>*else* let *K1* be $K + 1$,
>>find next location *(X1,Y1)* that can be moved from *(X, Y)*,
>>store *K1* in square *(X1,Y1)*, then
>>continue to find the knight's moves from the *K1*th
>>>location *(X1,Y1)*.

From any location in the chessboard, the knight can have at most eight possible moves, which are determined by the combinations (up,down) × (left,right) × (1,2). For example, *move*$(-1, 2)$ means going up 1 step then right 2 steps, and *move*$(2, -1)$ means going down 2 steps then left 1 step, etc. These moves are restricted by the size of the chessboard. So the procedure *find_moves* is given below.

```
find_moves(K,N,X,Y,Board) :- K =:= N*N,!.
find_moves(K,N,X,Y,Board) :-
    print_board(Board),
    K1 is K+1, next_move(X,Y,X1,Y1,N),
    array_entry(Board,X1,Y1,K1),
    find_moves(K1,N,X1,Y1,Board).

next_move(X,Y,X1,Y1,N) :-
    move(A,B), X1 is X+A, Y1 is Y+B,
    legal(X1,Y1,N).
```

```
legal(X,Y,N) :-
    1 =< X, X =< N, 1 =< Y, Y =< N.

move(-1,2).          move(-2,1).
move(-2,-1).         move(-1,-2).
move(1,-2).          move(2,-1).
move(2,1).           move(1,2).
```

The procedure *print_board* is also simple.

```
print_board([]) :- !,nl.
print_board([[_|Row]|Rest]) :-
    print_row(Row),
    print_board(Rest).

print_row([]) :- nl.
print_row([H|T]) :-
    print_move(H),print_row(T).

print_move((_,M)) :-
    var(M),!,write('.   ');
    write(M),write(' '),
    (M < 10,write(' '),!;true).

member(X,[X|_]).
member(X,[_|T]) :- member(X,T).
```

Following are two answers to the problem:

```
 1  4  9  18 21        25 14 3  8  19
10 17 20 3  8          4  9  18 13 2
 5  2  13 22 19        15 24 1  20 7
16 11 24 7  14         10 5  22 17 12
25 6  15 12 23         23 16 11 6  21
```

The reader is warned that it takes a long time for the program to find a solution, due to the enormous amount of backtracking work.

5.3 *Eliza* (Weizenbaum, 1966). Eliza is a dialogue system that simulates conversations between a user and the system. Eliza does not have a parser to parse the user's query for grammatical structure; rather it converts the query directly into an answer using a list of predefined query-answer patterns. For example:

User :	I feel terrible.
Eliza :	Why do you feel terrible?
User :	I failed the exam.
Eliza :	I see. Please continue
User :	I come to see you for advices.
Eliza :	What makes you come to see me for advices?
User :	I trust you.
Eliza :	What makes you trust me?
User :	You are a nice machine.
Eliza :	I see. Please continue
User :	I tell you about an incredible lady.
Eliza :	What makes you tell me about an incredible lady?
User :	Do you really want to know?
Eliza :	Yes, I really want to know
User :	She is driving me crazy.
Eliza :	I see. Please continue
User :	Can you help?
Eliza :	Yes, I help

The above pairs of query-answer are stored in the following form:

```
pair(['I',feel,1], ['Why',do,you,feel,1,?]).
pair(['I',1,you,2], ['What',makes,you,1,me,2,?]).
pair([1,you,2], ['Yes,','I',2]).
pair(_, ['I','see.', 'Please',continue]).
```

Write a procedure *response*(*Query,Answer*) (refer to the program *dialogue* of Subsection 5.4.2) that converts the list of words *Query* into the list *Answer* according to the patterns given above.

Solution:

We use a list to store the references in the query. For example, the first query given above matches the first query-pattern where the number 1 refers to the word "terrible". So we store away the pair (1 : [terrible]), which will be used to fill the answer-pattern. The algorithm of the procedure *response* is given below and the complete program is shown on the next page.

To find a response *Answer* for *Query* do
  if *Query* is [bye] then *Answer* is [bye]
  else find a pair of *Question-Response* such that
      Query matches *Question* giving a list of *References*,
      then use these references to fill *Response* giving *Answer*.

```
eliza :-
    repeat,
        receive_query(Query),
        response(Query,Answer),
        print_answer(Answer),
    Answer = [bye].

response([bye],[bye]) :- !.
response(Query,Answer) :-
    pair(Question,Response),
    match(Query,Question,References),
    match(Answer,Response,References),!.

match([W|L1],[W|L2],Ref) :-
    atom(W),match(L1,L2,Ref).
match(L1,[N|L2],Ref) :-
    integer(N),
    member(N:Lw,Ref),!,
    append(Lw,Rest,L1),
    match(Rest,L2,Ref).
match([],[],Ref).

print_answer(Answer) :-
    nl,write('Eliza: '),
    print_line(Answer).

print_line([]) :- !,nl.
print_line([H|T]) :-
    write(H),write(' '),
    print_line(T).

receive_query(L) :-
    nl,write('User : '),
    read_sentence(L).
```

In the above program, the procedure *read_sentence* has been given in Figure 4.9 of Chapter 4, the procedures *member* and *append* can be found in Figures 2.13 and 2.21 of Chapter 2, and the facts *pair(Question,Response)* are given in the question.

Observe that since in both procedures *member* and *append*, the input-output roles of their arguments are reversible; hence, the procedure *match* has the same property. That is, in a goal *match(X,Y,Z)*, it is possible that X and Y are input and Z is output, or Y and Z are input and X is output.

5.4 Consider the following programs that appear to have the same style, yet one is correct and the other is not.

(a)   ```
       max(X,Y,X) :- X >= Y,!.
       max(X,Y,Y).
       ```

(b)    ```
       bubble_sort(L,L1) :- swap(L,L2),!,
                           bubble_sort(L2,L1).
       bubble_sort(L,L).
       ```

Use the method of program validation given in Section 5.5 to detect the error of the incorrect program and to establish the correctness of the other one. (For procedure *swap*, see Figure 4.4 of Chapter 4.)

Solution:

We note first that when a program contains the cut, the operational meaning of each clause may be different from its separate procedural reading. Therefore, we must first rewrite the clauses to reflect their operational meaning before considering their correctness.

(a) For the program of part (a), the cut indicates that the second clause is used to evaluate a goal $max(X, Y, Z)$ only when either (X, Y, Z) does not have the form (X, Y, X), or it does not satisfy the condition $X \geq Y$. Thus, the program's reading is the same as that of the following program:

```
max(X,Y,X) :- X >= Y,!.
max(X,Y,Y) :- X \= Y; X < Y.
```

This reveals that the second clause is incorrect, because (X \= Y; X < Y) does not imply that maximum of X and Y is Y. Therefore the program is incorrect. A test run will confirm that the program's answer "yes" to the query $max(3, 1, 1)$ is wrong.

(b) For the second program, since (L, L) is an instance of $(L, L1)$, control will never go to the second clause unless the goal $swap(L, L2)$ fails. Hence, the program's procedural reading is the same as for the following program:

```
bubble_sort(L,L1) :- swap(L,L2),!,
                    bubble_sort(L2,L1).
bubble_sort(L,L) :- not(swap(L,L2)).
```

We can now consider the truth of the above clauses. For the first clause, assume that $swap(L,L2)$ holds and that $bubble\_sort(L2,L1)$ correctly sorts

L2 into *L1*. Then, it follows immediately that *L1* is a sorted list of *L*. For the second clause, it is obvious that if *swap*(*L,L2*) is false, then the elements of *L* are ordered.

Supplementary problems

5.5 In a tribal language, a poem can have any number of verses, each of which takes the following form:

A	B	B	C
D	E	E	C
F	F	G	
H	I	I	C

where the same letter represents rhymed words. For example:

> anun kura tama su
> unuri bimo co kuru
> sonen ariten sicom
> kana te shime xanadu.

Design a database to store a number of tribal words and write a program to produce a poem of a given number of verses.

5.6 Guessing game is a simple game in which one is given a type, such as *animal, thing, country, song,* or *movie,* and is allowed to ask a fixed number of questions about the shape, size, colour, and other characteristics of the object so that he or she can make a guess on what the hidden object is.

Write a Prolog program to play guessing games in which the system can be either the host or the guesser. The system should have a database containing a number of objects with their types and attributes.

5.7 Write a Prolog program to simulate a keyboard typing instructor whose routine task is as follows. The system writes a sentence to the screen and asks the typist to repeat the sentence through the keyboard without using the backspace key. When the typist completes the sentence, the system reads the sentence, word by word. The system then advises the typist on the number and types of mistakes found. There are basically four types of mistakes: missing a letter, adding an extra letter, transposing two adjacent letters, and typing a wrong letter. The process is to be repeated until either the typist makes no more mistakes or he or she decides to give up.

5.8 Write a menu-driven system that simulates the operation of an automated-teller machine. The system should perform the following tasks:

- Receive an ID and a PIN and checks for validity of the user.

- Guide the user to do required transactions such as withdrawal or deposit of cash, or transferring of cash between different accounts.

- Perform all the accounting tasks such as updating the balances and calculating the appropriate numbers of notes of $50, 20, 10$, and 5 dollars for a given amount to be issued.

5.9 Write a Prolog program to convert an English sentence expressing an integer number (less than 2000, say) into a French sentence expressing the same number. For example:

one thousand nine hundred ninety three

is translated into

mille neuf cent quatre-vingt-treize.

5.10 Use the method of program validation given in Section 5.5 to determine if the following programs are correct. If any program is incorrect, give the cause of the error.

(a) `integer(X) :- integer(Y), X is Y+1.`
    `integer(0).`

(b) `insert(X,[H|T],[H|T1]) :- X > H,!, insert(X,T,T1).`
    `insert(X,L,[X|L]).`

(Hint: program (a) is logically sound, but its second clause is operationally invisible. Program (b) is incorrect.)

Chapter 6

Advanced
programming techniques
and data structures

6.1   Nondeterministic programming

A system is said to be nondeterministic if it is able to make a choice when faced with many alternatives. Prolog is regarded as a nondeterministic system, because of its search and backtracking ability. Most Prolog programs contain some degree of nondeterminism, but since the way Prolog makes decisions is well-known to programmers, there is a tendency toward thinking in the way Prolog operates.

We demonstrate in this section that thinking nondeterministically is conducive and that nondeterministic programming (that is, writing nondeterministic programs) is a powerful technique for problem-solving, particularly in the case of complex problems where a full study of various possibilities is tedious and difficult.

196

We shall also show in Chapter 11 that a combination of Prolog's non-deterministic mechanisms with the object-oriented modelling approach results in a powerful technique for system simulation.

6.1.1   Nondeterministic thinking

Abstraction is a powerful method that is used in Mathematics and other fields to represent problems. Nondeterministic thinking can be regarded as a step further from declarative thinking, in the direction of abstracting problems in computer programming. By thinking nondeterministically, one can avoid the tedious details of arranging for appropriate actions if something happens. Rather one thinks of a problem as a union of other problems, and the question of which one should be tackled first is left to the machine to decide. Following is a simple example of nondeterministic programs.

EXAMPLE 6.1   Given a nonempty (nonsorted) binary tree of the form $bt(L, K, R)$, where K represents the root-node's key, and L, R are subtrees of the same structure, a node in the tree is said to be at level H if the path connecting the root to that node contains H nodes. We want to write a program to determine the level of a node containing a given key X.

Obviously, if X matches the root's key, then its level $H = 1$. Otherwise, one would normally think that if the key X is found in the left subtree then its level is 1 plus the level of X in the left subtree, etc. But this would require a test if X is in the left subtree before its level could be determined. A more effective approach to this problem is to specify that the level of X is determined in either subtree. This specification is expressed as follows:

> The level H of a node X in the binary tree $bt(L, K, R)$ is
> defined as follows:
> > *if* $X = K$ then $H = 1$
> > *else either* H is the level of X in L plus 1
> >   *or* H is the level of X in R plus 1.

```
level(X,bt(_,X,_),1).
level(X,bt(L,_,_),H) :-
    level(X,L,HL), H is HL + 1.
level(X,bt(_,_,R),H) :-
    level(X,R,HR), H is HR + 1.
```

FIGURE 6.1 A nondeterministic program.

Figure 6.1 shows the Prolog program that is translated from the above specification. Here, it is unimportant to us which of the last two clauses of the program will be executed, or even which level will be returned should the key X occur at several levels.

6.1.2   Nondeterministic finite automata

A special kind of nondeterministic system that has a wide range of applications and that is easy to implement in Prolog is the class of nondeterministic finite automata.

> ▷ A finite automaton is an abstract machine that can be in a finite number of states and that accepts input signals to change its state accordingly.

A finite automaton is said to be *deterministic* if, for each input signal, it can change from any current state to at most one other state. Otherwise, it is called a *nondeterministic* finite automaton.

A finite automaton is commonly described by a directed graph in which the nodes represent the states and the directed edges are labelled with input signals. Figure 6.2 shows a nondeterministic finite automaton.

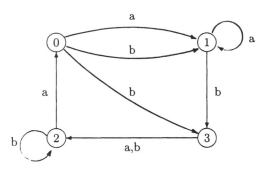

FIGURE 6.2 A nondeterministic finite automaton.

In Prolog, a finite automaton can be represented by a list of facts each of which describes a transition between states. For example, the finite automaton of Figure 6.2 is represented by the following facts:

$fa(0, a, 1).$ $fa(2, a, 0).$
$fa(0, b, 1).$ $fa(2, b, 2).$

$$fa(0, b, 3).$$
$$fa(1, a, 1).$$
$$fa(1, b, 3).$$

$$fa(3, a, 2).$$
$$fa(3, b, 2).$$

The following example shows a useful application of finite automata in text processing.

EXAMPLE 6.2   *A string matching machine.* Given a set of keywords and a text string, we want to build a machine that can scan the text string and locate all occurrences of the given keywords in the text. For example, given the keywords "he, she, his, hers" and the text string "ushers", the machine would produce the following output:

    4   he she
    6   hers

which means that the system found at location 4 two keywords "he, she" and at location 6 one keyword "hers".

Aho and Corasick (1975) constructed a machine that includes a deterministic finite automaton (which they call a *goto* function) representing the state of the machine. For example, for the given keywords "he, she, his, hers", the finite automaton is depicted in Figure 6.3. This figure shows that if the machine is currently in state 0 and the input character is h, then the machine changes to state 1. If the next input character is i, then it changes to state 6, and so on. When the machine is in one of the states $2, 5, 7, 9$, some of the given keywords have been found. Here, the numbers chosen to represent the states are immaterial as long as they are distinct.

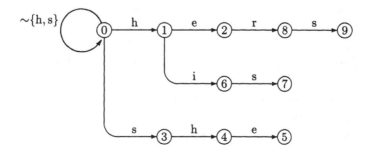

FIGURE 6.3 A deterministic finite automaton in Aho-Corasick machine.

We convert the deterministic finite automaton of Figure 6.3 into a non-deterministic one, which is shown in Figure 6.4. Here, the additional paths are obtained in the following way. For example, with state 3 and the input character h, an alternative to moving to state 4 is to move to state 1, where another match is possible. Likewise, with state 4 and input character e, an alternative to moving to state 5 is to move to state 2. With state 6 and input character s, one can move to state 3 instead of state 7; the same reason applies to state 8 and input character s. Finally, from states 1 and 2, there are no alternatives but moving back to state 0.

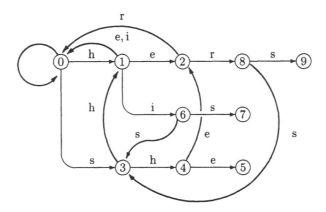

FIGURE 6.4 A nondeterministic finite automaton in Aho-Corasick machine.

The nondeterministic finite automaton of Figure 6.4 is represented by the Prolog procedure *change_state*, which is shown in Figure 6.5.

```
change_state(0,'h,1).          change_state(0,'s,3).
change_state(1,'e,2).          change_state(1,'i,6).
change_state(1,'e,0).          change_state(1,'i,0).
change_state(2,'r,8).          change_state(2,'r,0).
change_state(3,'h,4).          change_state(3,'h,1).
change_state(4,'e,5).          change_state(4,'e,2).
change_state(6,'s,7).          change_state(6,'s,3).
change_state(8,'s,9).          change_state(8,'s,3).
change_state(0,_,0).
```

FIGURE 6.5 State transition of a string matching machine.

The machine states that correspond to the given keywords are listed below.

```
keyword(2,he).
keyword(5,he).
keyword(5,she).
keyword(7,his).
keyword(9,hers).
```

An algorithm that manipulates the matching machine to search a string for the given keywords is given below.

> To find the given keywords in a string do
> > activate the matching machine to scan the string
> > from state 0 and the first character in the string;
> > when the machine completes, print out the keywords found.

> To activate the matching machine do
> > take the machine to its next state,
> > check and store any keywords found,
> > then continue running the machine
> > until the string is exhausted.

The program is given in Figure 6.6, where the lower-level procedures are just routines. To test the program, we use the finite automaton represented in Figure 6.5 and enter the following query:

```
?- find_keywords("she threw herself into the ushers").
3 he she
12 he
14 hers
26 he
31 he she
33 hers

yes
```

Observe from the program of Figure 6.6 that each time a keyword is found, it is stored in the database by procedure *check_keywords*. In the end, the meta-predicate *setof* is used to collect the stored keywords (more details on this useful built-in predicate are given in Subsection 6.2.1).

```
find_keywords(L) :-
    activate_machine(0,L,1),
    print_keywords.

activate_machine(S,[C|L],I) :-
    change_state(S,C,S1),
    check_keywords(I,S1),
    I1 is I+1,
    activate_machine(S1,L,I1).
activate_machine(_,[],_).

check_keywords(I,S) :-
    keyword(S,W),not(store(I,W)),
    assert(store(I,W)),fail.
check_keywords(_,_).

print_keywords :-
    setof(I:W,store(I,W),L),
    print_word(0,L),
    abolish(store/2).
print_keywords.

print_word(_,[]) :- !,nl.
print_word(I,[J:W|Rest]) :-
    (I < J,!,nl,write(J);true),
    write(' '),write(W),
    print_word(J,Rest).
```

FIGURE 6.6 Operation of a string matching machine.

We also note from Figure 6.4 that the alternative paths that we added to the original finite automaton represent the machine's second-best choice of state transition. For example, with state 4 and the input character e, if the machine changes to state 5, the keyword "she" will be found, while moving to state 2 reveals a shorter keyword "he". This choice ranking is reflected in the ordering of the facts shown in Figure 6.5. The machine works very efficiently by this arrangement, but its intended nondeterminism is diminished. To give the machine more flexibility, allowing it to work with any ordering of its state transitions, we must remove the clause `activate_machine(_,[],_).` The missing of this clause forces the machine to enter every possible state and to make every attempt at matching. We also need a second clause `find_keywords(_) :- print_keywords.` to print out the obtained keywords when `activate_machine` completes (with failure). The price of this full nondeterminism is that the machine takes much longer to complete its task.

6.2 Second-order programming

Pure Prolog is based on first-order logic in which variables represent terms only. Second-order logic allows variables to represent predicate and function symbols as well. This gives the language a lot more expressing power, particularly in meta-programming (i.e., writing programs to manipulate other programs, see Chapter 8). Therefore, most Prolog systems provide a number of built-in predicates for the purpose of second-order programming.

In this section, we study some commonly used second-order predicates and their application.

6.2.1 Collection of data: the set-predicates

There are two built-in predicates that can be used in collecting data, namely *bagof* and *setof*. Their definitions are given below:

bagof(X,G,L) : L is the list of all terms X obtained from the solutions of the goal G.

setof(X,G,L) : L is the *ordered* list of *distinct* terms X obtained from the solutions of the goal G.

Thus, the effect of *setof* is similar to that of *bagof*, except that duplicated solutions are eliminated and the elements of the list are in ascending order if they are numbers, or in lexicographical order, otherwise. (The standard order is as follows: lowest are the variables, in order of their generation, followed by numbers, then uppercase letters, and finally lowercase letters.) In practice, the predicate *setof* is more frequently used than *bagof*.

There are two things that should be noted when using the predicates *setof* and *bagof*:

(i) If the goal G is composed of several simple goals, then it must be enclosed between parentheses; otherwise, there would be arity-incompatibility.

(ii) If the goal G has no solutions, then the goal *setof(X,G,L)* or *bagof(X,G,L)* fails. So, in this case, if we wish the answer $L = []$ to be returned, then this must be explicitly expressed in the program.

In general, a procedure using the *setof* (or *bagof*) predicate has the following form:

```
collect(G,L) :- setof(X,G,L),!.
collect(G,[]).
```

EXAMPLE 6.3   Given two lists, their *intersection* is defined to be the set of their common elements and their *difference* is the set of elements in the first list that are not in the second one. These sets can be defined by means of the *setof* predicate as shown in Figure 6.7. (On the other hand, the union of two lists can be obtained by using the procedure *append* of Figure 2.21.)

```
intersection(L1,L2,L) :-
     setof(X,(member(X,L1),member(X,L2)),L),!.
intersection(_,_,[]).

difference(L1,L2,L) :-
     setof(X,(member(X,L1), not(member(X,L2))),L),!.
difference(_,_,[]).
```

FIGURE 6.7 Intersection and difference of sets.

For example:

```
?- intersection([1,2,3,4],[2,4,6],L).
L = [2,4] ->

?- difference([1,2,3,4],[2,4,6],L).
L = [1,3] ->
```

A useful application of the predicate *setof* is to incorporate the three tasks of collecting data, constructing new data, and sorting data into a single goal.

EXAMPLE 6.4   Assume the database currently contains two lists of facts of the forms *student(ID,Name)* and *test(ID,Mark)*. The following procedure produces a list of facts of the form *stud_mark(Name,ID,Mark)*, which are in alphabetical order of student names.

```
test_result(L) :-
    setof(stud_mark(Name,ID,Mark),
          (student(ID,Name),test(ID,Mark)), L).

student(78-2123,'Smith J.R.').
student(84-2201,'Adams P.').
student(90-3150,'Burns M.I.').
    .
    .
    .
test(78-2123,40).
test(84-2201,65).
test(90-3150,56).
    .
    .
    .
```

FIGURE 6.8 Collection of test results using *setof.*

An appropriate query is as follows:

```
?- test_result(L).
L = [stud_mark('Adams P.',84-2201,65),
     stud_mark('Burns M.I',90-3150,56),...]
```

Note from Examples 6.3 and 6.4 that in the goal *setof(X,G,L)*, all the variables of G appear in the term X. We say that the variables of G are all *bound*. In the case where G has an unbound variable Y, say, the effect of *setof(X,G,L)* is the return of several sets L, one after another, each of which corresponds to a different value of Y obtained from the solutions of G.

EXAMPLE 6.5 Assume we have the same database as in Example 6.4. However, the procedure *test_result* is modified as follows:

```
test_result(L) :-
    setof(stud_mark(Name,Mark),
          (student(ID,Name),test(ID,Mark)), L).
```

Now observe the system's response to the following query:

```
?- test_result(L).
L = [stud_mark('Smith J.R.',40)]->;
L = [stud_mark('Adams P.',65)]->;
    .
    .
    .
```

The first answer corresponds to ID = 78-2123; the second answer corresponds to ID = 84-2201, etc.

In order to collect all the above answers into a single list, it is necessary to *quantify* the variable ID. That is, the procedure *test_result* is rewritten as follows (note that the space after ID^ may be necessary in some Prolog systems):

```
test_result(L) :-
    setof(stud_mark(Name,Mark),
          ID^ (student(ID,Name),test(ID,Mark)), L).
```

Now, for the same query, we have:

```
?- test_result(L).
L = [stud_mark('Adams P.',65),
     stud_mark('Burns M.I.',56),...]
```

In general, a *setof* goal has the following forms:

> *setof(t(X),g(X,Y),L)*   :   find Y and L such that L is the ordered list of all distinct terms $t(X)$ where X runs over the answers of $g(X,Y)$.
>
> *setof(t(X), Y^g(X,Y),L)*: L is the ordered list of all distinct terms $t(X)$ such that $g(X,Y)$ succeeds for some value of Y.

The effect of *bagof* is similar, except that the resulting list is unordered and may contain duplicated elements. Most Prolog systems also provide a predicate *findall*, the effect of which is similar to that of *bagof*, except that any free variable is assumed to be existentially quantified.

The following example demonstrates the power of the predicate *setof* in collecting and sorting data.

EXAMPLE 6.6   Suppose that we have a number of cities to be linked into a telecommunication network, such that any two cities can communicate to each other either directly or via other cities within the network. The problem is to determine the links in order to minimise the total linking cost.

For simplicity, we assume that the linking cost between two cities is proportional to their distance. The general algorithm to solve the problem is given below and the program is shown in Figure 6.9.

> To determine the *Links* and *Cost* for a network do
> > collect all nodes into a set of unconnected nodes,
> > take any node to start with, and
> > connect the rest to this node to establish *Links* and *Cost*.

> To connect the unconnected nodes to a network do
> > find the unconnected node that has least distance to the network,
> > link this node to the network and add cost to total cost,
> > then continue to connect the remaining unconnected nodes
> > to the network (until no more left).

```
network(Links,Cost) :-
    setof(X,(Y,D)^distance(X,Y,D),[I|Rest]),
    connect(Rest,[I],Links,0,Cost).

connect([],_,[],TC,TC) :- !.
connect(Uncon,Network,[(A,B)|Links],TC,TC1) :-
    setof((D,X,Y,Rest),(select(X,Uncon,Rest),
            member(Y,Network),distance(X,Y,D)),
            [(C,A,B,Remain)|_]),
    TC2 is TC + C,
    connect(Remain,[A|Network],Links,TC2,TC1).

member :- % see Figure 2.13
select :- % see Figure 2.16
```

FIGURE 6.9 Program for network setting.

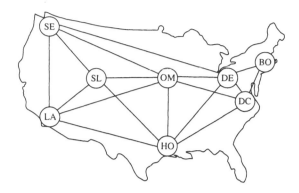

FIGURE 6.10   A telecommunication network[1].

For example, consider a number of cities in the United States as shown in Figure 6.10. The distances between the cities are given below.

```
distance(X,Y,D) :- dist(X,Y,D).
distance(X,Y,D) :- dist(Y,X,D).

dist(se,de,2000).        dist(om,de,780).
dist(se,om,1400).        dist(om,dc,1000).
dist(se,sl,750).         dist(om,ho,800).
dist(se,la,1000).        dist(de,bo,650).
dist(la,sl,500).         dist(de,dc,450).
dist(la,om,1100).        dist(de,ho,1000).
dist(la,ho,1100).        dist(ho,dc,1200).
dist(sl,om,800).         dist(dc,bo,400).
dist(sl,ho,1000).
```

The following query provides an optimal answer to the linking problem:

```
?- network(Links,Cost).

Links = [(dc,bo),(de,dc),(om,de),(ho,om),(sl,om),(la,sl),
(se,sl)]
Cost = 4480 ->
```

---

[1]This figure is adapted from Figure 6.11 of Taha, H. A., Operations Research, An Introduction, 4th ed., 1987, p. 226. Adapted by permission of Macmillan Publishing Co., N. Y.

We shall see in Subsection 6.3.3 that the predicate *setof* is most useful in handling matrices in linear programming problems.

6.2.2   Conversion of data: the =.. predicate

The built-in predicate =.. (called *univ*) provides a means of converting data from list form to general term or vice versa. The general form of conversion is as follows:

```
Term =.. List
```

where the left-hand side is a general term (which could be a compound term or a constant) of the form $f(T_1, \ldots, T_n)$ and the right-hand side is the list $[f, T_1, \ldots, T_n]$. For example:

```
?- father(john,X) =.. L.
L = [father,john,_0085] ->

?- T =.. [landing,'AF24'].
T = landing('AF24') ->

?- T =.. ['+',1,2].
T = 1 + 2 ->

?- T =.. [john].
T = john ->
```

The predicate =.. is very useful in dynamic construction of data and can be used to implement many functional predicates.

EXAMPLE 6.7   Let us write a Prolog procedure *apply(F,L,V)* that receives a functor F, a list of arguments L, and returns in V the value obtained by applying F to the elements of L. We distinguish two cases: F may be a predefined arithmetic function symbol or a user-defined function symbol. In the latter case, we assume the user-defined function returns its value in its last argument. The procedure is shown in Figure 6.11. To test the procedure, we use the built-in functions '+', *mod*, and the function *gcd* (greatest common divisor) that was defined in Problem 2.3.

```
apply(F,L,V) :-
    arithmetic(F),!,
    T =.. [F|L], V is T.

apply(F,L,V) :-
    append(L,[V],L1),
    G =.. [F|L1], G.

arithmetic(F) :-
    member(F, ['+','-','*','/','//','^',
               mod, abs, exp, ln,...]).
```

FIGURE 6.11 The functional procedure *apply*.

Note from the procedure *apply* of Figure 6.11 that some Prolog systems may require the goal G to be expressed in the form *call(G)*, where *call* is a built-in predicate. Following are some examples of using the predicate *apply*:

```
?- apply('+',[1,2],X).
X = 3 ->

?- apply(mod,[5,2],X).
X = 1 ->

?- apply(gcd,[18,24],X).
X = 6 ->
```

EXAMPLE 6.8   Consider the following two typical functions of functional programming.

(1) The function *mapcar* receives a unary function symbol f and a list of elements $[X_1,\ldots,X_n]$, and returns the list of values $[f(X_1),\ldots,f(X_n)]$.

(2) The function *reduce* receives a binary function symbol f, a list of elements $[X_1,\ldots,X_n]$, and an extra element A, and returns the single value $f(X_1,f(\ldots,f(X_n,A)\ldots))$.

The above functions are implemented in Prolog as shown in Figure 6.12.

```
mapcar(_,[],[]).
mapcar(F,[X|L],[Y|L1]) :-
    apply(F,[X],Y),
    mapcar(F,L,L1).

reduce(F,[X],A,V) :- !,
    apply(F,[X,A],V).
reduce(F,[X|L],A,V) :-
    reduce(F,L,A,V1),
    apply(F,[X,V1],V).
```

FIGURE 6.12 Functional procedures *mapcar* and *reduce*.

For example:

```
?- mapcar(abs,[-1,2,-3],L).
L = [1,2,3] ->

?- reduce('+',[1,2,3,4],0,X).
X = 10 ->
```

Here, for the function *abs* we have $L = [\text{abs}(-1), \text{abs}(2), \text{abs}(-3)] = [1, 2, 3]$, and for the *addition*, $X = +(1, +(2, +(3, +(4, 0)))) = 10$.

An interesting application of the *reduce* predicate is in concatenating several lists into a big list. The predicate *concatenate* is defined as follows:

```
concatenate(Lists,BigList) :-
    reduce(append,Lists,[],BigList).
```

For example:

```
?- concatenate([[1,2],[3,4],[5,6,7]],L).
L = [1,2,3,4,5,6,7] ->
```

6.2.3   Inspection of data: the functor and arg predicates

Sometimes it suffices to have partial knowledge of a data structure. For example, we may need to know only the functor or the arity or certain argument of a given term. Prolog provides the built-in predicates *functor* and *arg* for those purposes. Their general form are given below:

> *functor(Term,F,N)* :   *Term* has functor F and arity N.
>
> *arg(N,Term,A)*   :   The Nth argument of *Term* is A.

For examples:

```
?- functor(father(john,X),F,N).
F = father
N = 2 ->

?- arg(2,gcd(18,24,X),A).
A = 24 ->
```

As in the predicate $=..$, the arguments of *functor* and *arg* have reversible input-output roles. That is, one can use the goal *functor(Term,F,N)* to construct *Term* with a given functor F and arity N. The obtained term has uninstantiated arguments. On the other hand, given a term with some uninstantiated argument, the goal *arg(N,Term,Value)* can be used to instantiate the Nth argument of *Term*. For example:

```
?- functor(T,stud_mark,2),
   arg(1,T,'Smith J.R.'),
   arg(2,T,65).

T = stud_mark('Smith J.R.',65) ->
```

Here, the effect of *functor(T,stud_mark,2)* is the creation of a term $T = stud\_mark(X,Y)$. Then the two *arg* goals cause X and Y to be unified with 'Smith J.R.' and 65, respectively.

Some Prolog systems also provide the predicate *argrep* that allows the replacement of certain argument in a given term by a new value. In general, we have

> *argrep(Term,N,Value,NewTerm).*

The effect of the above goal is the creation of *NewTerm*, which is a copy of *Term* with its *N*th argument being replaced by *Value*. For example:

```
?- argrep(stud_mark('Smith J.R.',65),2,45,T).
T = stud_mark('Smith J.R.',45) ->
```

We shall see in the next section that the predicate *argrep* is useful in implementing array operations. If this predicate is not available, it can be easily defined as shown in Figure 6.13.

```
argrep(Term,N,Value,NewTerm) :-
    Term =.. [F|L],
    replace(N,L,Value,L1),
    NewTerm =.. [F|L1].

replace(1,[X|L],Y,[Y|L]) :- !.
replace(N,[X|L],Y,[X|L1]) :-
    N > 1, N1 is N-1,
    replace(N1,L,Y,L1).
```

FIGURE 6.13 Replacing an argument of a given term.

6.2.4   Classification of data: type-predicates

Recall that in Prolog, a *term* can be a variable, a constant, a list, or a compound term. Constants are sometimes referred to as *atomic terms* (to be distinguished from *atomic formulas*; the word "atomic" means indivisible) and include mnemonic symbols, numbers (integer or real), and the empty-list symbol.

Following are some built-in predicates that can be used to detect the type of a given term.

var(X)	:	X is a variable
nonvar(X)	:	X is not a variable
atomic(X)	:	X is a constant
atom(X)	:	X is a mnemonic symbol
integer(X)	:	X is an integer
float(X)	:	X is a floating-point number
number(X)	:	X is an integer or a floating-point number.

Most Prolog systems provide the above-listed type-predicates as predefined predicates. Otherwise, they can be easily defined using the already available predicates. For example:

```
var(X) :- setof(X,(X = 1; X = 2),[1,2]).
nonvar(X) :- not(var(X)).
atom(X) :- functor(X,F,0).
```

Type-predicates are very useful in meta-programming, which is the subject of Chapter 8. The following example shows that the predicates *var* and *nonvar* can be used to determine the input and output arguments of a goal.

EXAMPLE 6.9   Let us write a Prolog program that can find the sum of two given integers or return two integers, the sum of which is given. The program is given in Figure 6.14.

```
sum(X,Y,S) :-
    var(S), S is X+Y;
    nonvar(S),add(X,Y,S).

add(0,S,S).
add(X,Y,S) :-
    add(X1,Y1,S),
    X is X1+1, Y is Y1-1.
```

FIGURE 6.14 Invertible procedure *sum*.

6.2.5   Definition of new functors: the op predicate

Prolog allows functions and predicates to be treated as operators and defined explicitly. The means provided for this purpose is the built-in predicate *op*, which can be used in the following form:

```
:- op(Prec,Type,Func).
```

Here, *Func* is the function symbol being defined; *Prec* is an integer from 1 to 1200 (or from 0 to 255 in C-Prolog) that represents the precedence given to the function (the larger the number is, the lower precedence the function has); and *Type* has the form shown on the next page. Figure 6.15 shows built-in operators with their types and precedences (the full list is given in Appendix E).

Type notation	Meaning
xfx	Infix nonassociative
xfy	Infix right-associative
yfx	Infix left-associative
fx	Prefix nonassociative
fy	Prefix right-associative
xf	Postfix nonassociative
yf	Postfix left-associative

Operator	Type	Precedence
:-	$xfx,\ fx$	1200
?-	fx	1200
;	xfy	1100
,	xfy	1000
not	fy	900
is, =.., and all comparing predicates	xfx	700
+ -	$yfx,\ fx$	500
:	xfy	500
* /	yfx	400
mod	xfx	300
^	xfy	200

FIGURE 6.15 Type and precedence of some built-in operators.

Note that the types and precedences of functions determine how an expression is evaluated. For example, since the functor "−" had type yfx, we have $5 - 3 - 2$ equivalent to $(5 - 3) - 2$, and not $5 - (3 - 2)$; but $5 - 3 * 2$ means $5 - (3 * 2)$, not $(5 - 3) * 2$, because "∗" has higher precedence than "−".

Following are some examples on the use of the *op* predicate.

EXAMPLE 6.10 Let us define an operator "!" to represent the factorial relation that has been defined in Chapter 2 (Figure 2.5). This operator should be nonassociative and should have a precedence higher than those of the predicates ",", *not*, "=..". So, we define:

```
:- op(500,xfx,!).
N ! F :- factorial(N,F).
```

Having given the previous declarations and assuming the program *factorial* exists, we can ask questions such as the following:

```
?- 5!  Answer.
Answer = 120 ->
```

The predicate *op* can also be used to change the syntax of an entire program as shown in the following example.

EXAMPLE 6.11   Consider the Prolog program that describes the world of Ann and Sue developed in Chapter 1 (Figure 1.1). We wish to rewrite this program so that it has a form closer to ordinary English. First of all, some operators are defined using the *op* predicate.

```
:- op(1200,xfx,if).
:- op(1100, fx,:).
:- op(1000,xfy,and).
:- op(500,xf,is_atoy).
:- op(500,xfx,likes).
:- op(500,xfx,plays_with).
```

Observe that several operators can be defined to have the same type and precedence. Here, the operators ":", "if", and "and" are defined by the following rules:

```
: A :- (A if B),(: B).
: A :- A.
A and B :- A,B.
```

The program of Figure 1.1 can now be rewritten as shown in Figure 6.16.

```
sue likes X if ann likes X.
ann likes X if X is_atoy and ann plays_with X.
doll is_atoy.
snoopy is_atoy.
ann plays_with snoopy.
```

FIGURE 6.16 A Prolog program in modified syntax.

Then we can ask the following questions:

```
?- : sue likes What.
What = snoopy ->

?- : snoopy is_atoy.
yes

?- : What is_atoy.
What = doll ->;
What = snoopy ->
```

Note that the use of the colon is essential in the first query, but is optional in the last two queries. The reason is left to the reader as a challenging question.

The following interesting example[1] shows that the syntax of Prolog can be changed to imitate another programming language.

EXAMPLE 6.12   Consider the following Pascal program:

```
for I := 1 to 4 do
    begin
        X := I*I;
        writeln(X);
    end.
```

Let us define the appropriate operators to make the Prolog system recognise the above program as a legal Prolog query and perform the task specified by the program. We first attempt to identify the precedences of the operators in the program by adding parentheses at appropriate places.

```
(for ((I := 1) to 4)) do
    (begin
        ((X := (I*I));
            writeln(X);
            end)).
```

In any expression, the operators' precedences increase from inside out. Thus,

---

[1]This example is adapted from Amble, T., Logic Programming and Knowledge Engineering, 1987, p. 111. Adapted by permission of Addison-Wesley, Reading, Mass.

in the above expression, the operator "*" has highest precedence; next is ":=", which should be followed by ";" and "*to*", then "*for*", and "*begin*". The operator "*do*" has lowest precedence in the above expression, but it should be higher than that of "?-". So, these operators' types and precedences are specified as shown below:

```
:- op(1150,xfx,do).
:- op(1140,fx,for).
:- op(1140,fx,begin).
:- op(1100,xfx,to).
:- op(600,xfx,':=').
```

We now define the predicates as follows:

```
for I := M to N do G :-  for(I,M,N), G, fail; true.

begin X;Y :-  X,(begin Y).
begin end.

X := Y   :- X is Y.
writeln(X) :- write(X),nl.

for(I,I,N) :- I =< N.
for(I,M,N) :- M < N, M1 is M+1, for(I,M1,N).
```

The given Pascal program is now recognised by the Prolog system as a legal Prolog query. In fact, we have:

```
?- for I := 1 to 4 do
        begin
            X := I*I;
            writeln(X);
        end.


1
4
9
16
```

We see that the output produced by the above Prolog query is precisely what is expected from the given Pascal program.

6.3   Representation of queues, frames, and arrays

In Prolog, *term* is the only form of data representation. For convenience, terms are classified into three categories: constants, lists, and compound terms. These various forms of terms can be used to represent any data structures, including:

queue	AVL-tree
frame	B-tree
array	

This section studies the representation of queues, frames, and arrays, and in the next section, we consider the representation of some advanced tree structures.

6.3.1   Queues

A queue is a sequence of items in which insertion is performed at one end, while deletion is made at the other end.

There are two ways to implement a queue in Prolog.

- A *dynamic queue* is represented by a pair of lists $Q - Qt$, where Qt is a trailing part of Q, called the *tail* of Q, and is normally uninstantiated.

The pair $Q - Qt$ is usually called a *difference list*. Note, however, that here the *minus* symbol is used merely to construct the data structure, and it can be replaced with any other binary operator. For example, a queue containing the elements a, b, c, where a is the head of the queue and c is the end, is represented as

```
[a,b,c|Qt]-Qt
```

The advantage of this representation is that a new item is added to the queue by being inserted at the front of the tail of the queue. On the other hand, an item can be easily extracted from the head of the queue. The procedures *addtoq* and *getfromq* are shown below:

```
addtoq(X,Q-[X|Qt1],Q-Qt1).   % Add X to Q-Qt giving Q-Qt1
getfromq(X,[X|Q1]-Qt,Q1-Qt).% Get X from Q-Qt giving Q1-Qt
```

Note that in the first clause above, since Qt is the tail of Q, the insertion of the item X into Qt automatically causes its insertion into Q. For example:

```
?- addtoq(d,[a,b,c|Qt]-Qt,NewQ).
NewQ = [a,b,c,d|_004D]-_004D ->

?- getfromq(X,[a,b,c|Qt]-Qt,NewQ).
X = a
NewQ = [b,c|_007E]-_007E ->
```

Another advantage of representing a queue as a pair of lists is the ease in concatenating two queues. In fact, to append two queues $A - B$ and $D - C$, it suffices to unify B with D and obtain the result $A - C$ as shown in the procedure *appendq* below:

```
appendq(A-B,B-C,A-C).
```

For example:

```
?- appendq([a,b,c|P]-P,[1,2|Q]-Q,NewQ).
NewQ = [a,b,c,1,2|_004F]-_004F ->
```

The effect of the above query is as follows. When the entered goal unifies with the fact *appendq(A−B, B−C, A−C)*, we have (the symbol "=" should be read "unifies with") $A = [a, b, c \mid P]$ and $P = B = [1, 2 \mid Q]$. Hence $A = [a, b, c, 1, 2 \mid Q]$, and on the other hand, $C = Q$. Therefore $NewQ = A - C = [a, b, c, 1, 2 \mid Q] - Q$.

As we have seen above, the definitions of the procedures *addtoq, get-fromq*, and *appendq* are very simple. These procedures are rarely referred to, however, because their tasks are so straightforward that they are usually explicitly expressed in the programs wherever they are needed.

The following procedures are also useful. The procedure *qmember* involves the membership of a queue, and the procedure *list_to_queue* converts a list into a queue.

```
qmember(X,[Y|Q]-Qt) :-
    nonvar(Y),
    (X = Y; qmember(X,Q-Qt)).

list_to_queue(L,Q-Qt) :-
    append(L,Qt,Q).
```

The following example shows a useful application of dynamic queues.

EXAMPLE 6.13   *Topological sort.* Consider an acyclic graph that represents the prerequisite requirement of the units in a university course (Figure 6.17). A topological order of the graph is a listing of its nodes such that all the predecessors of a node appear before it does.

Let us write a procedure *topo_sort(Graph,List)* that receives a graph and returns the list of its nodes in topological order.

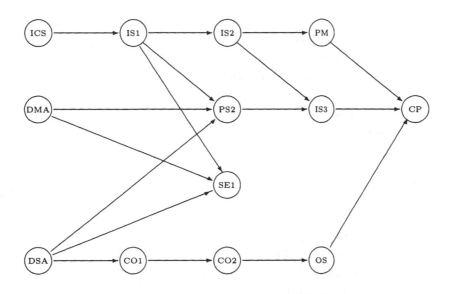

FIGURE 6.17 The prerequisite structure of the BA in Computer Studies.

We represent an acyclic graph as a list of pairs of the form $A : B$, where A is a predecessor of B. Thus, the graph of Figure 6.17 is represented by the list

[ics : is1, dma : ps2, dma : se1, . . . , os : cp].

An algorithm for the topological sort is as follows.

To sort a *Graph* into a *List* of topological order do
    create a *Queue* containing the nodes with no predecessors, then
    sort the *Graph* into *List* using *Queue.*

To sort *Graph* into *List* using *Queue* do
> move the head *X* of *Queue* to head of *List*,
> find *X*'s own successors and append them to *Queue*,
> removing from *Graph* all nodes having *X* as a predecessor,
> then continue to sort the remaining graph into the rest of *List*
> using the new queue (until the queue is empty).

Here, by *X*'s own successors we mean the successors of *X* that have no other predecessors. The program is shown in Figure 6.18.

```
topo_sort(Graph,List) :-
    createq(Graph,Queue),
    t_sort(Graph,Queue,List).

createq(G,Q-Qt) :-
    setof(X,minimal(X,G),L),
    append(L,Qt,Q).

minimal(X,G) :-
    member(X:Y,G),not(member(A:X,G)).

t_sort([],[]-[],[]) :- !.
t_sort(G,[X|Q]-Qt,[X|L]) :-
    find_successors(X,G,G1,Qt-Qs),
    t_sort(G1,Q-Qs,L).

find_successors(X,G,G1,Q-Qt) :-
    select(X:Y,G,G2),!,
    (member(A:Y,G2),!, Q = Q1; Q = [Y|Q1]),
    find_successors(X,G2,G1,Q1-Qt).
find_successors(_,G,G,Q-Q).

member :- % see Figure 2.13
select :- % see Figure 2.16
append :- % see Figure 2.21
```

FIGURE 6.18 The program of *topological sort*.

To test the program of Figure 6.18, we use the graph shown in Figure 6.17.

```
graph([ics:is1,dma:ps2,dma:se1,dsa:ps2,dsa:se1,
    dsa:co1,is1:is2,is1:ps2,is1:se1,co1:co2,is2:pm,
    is2:is3,ps2:is3,co2:os,pm:cp,is3:cp,os:cp]).

?- graph(G),topo_sort(G,L).
L = [dma,dsa,ics,co1,is1,co2,is2,ps2,se1,os,pm,is3,cp] ->
```

- A queue can also be represented by a list of facts in the database. In this case, items are added to the queue by using the predicate *assertz*, and extracted from the queue by using the predicate *retract*.

Examples of queues implemented as lists of facts are the landing and taking-off queues used in the airport-control problem in Example 5.1 of Chapter 5.

6.3.2   Frames

A frame is a collection of *slot-filler* pairs used to store a block of information. In Prolog, a frame can be represented as a list of pairs of the form $A:B$, where A is a slot name and B is a filler. Initially, the fillers are normally uninstantiated. They are filled up with given information when the frame is used.

EXAMPLE 6.14   To automate the task of creating news stories for the media, the following frames are established. Here, the operators "*has*" and "*isa*" are defined to be infix operators (for definition of *op*, see Subsection 6.2.5).

```
:-op(500,xfx,has).
:-op(500,xfx,isa).
```

```
% EVENT                 FRAME
event has               [place: P, day: D, time: T].
disaster_event has      [killed: K, injured: I, damage: D].
political_event has     [who: W, what: H].
sport_event has         [sport: S, winner: W, score: C].
earthquake has          [magnitude: M].

disaster_event isa event.
political_event isa event.
sport_event isa event.
earthquake isa disaster_event.
```

```
create_frame(Event,Frame) :-
    bagof(Slot,collect_slot(Event,Slot),Frame),
    fillup(Frame).

collect_slot(Event,Slot) :-
    Event isa Event1, collect_slot(Event1,Slot).
collect_slot(Event,Slot) :-
    Event has Frame, member(Slot,Frame).

fillup([]) :- nl.
fillup([Slot:Filler|Rest]) :-
    write(Slot),write(' : '),
    read(Filler),
    fillup(Rest).

member :- % see Figure 2.13
```

FIGURE 6.19 The program to create a frame.

A frame is created by the procedure *create_frame* shown in Figure 6.19. For example, a news reporter can create a frame for a report on the earthquake in Newcastle by using the following query:

```
?- create_frame(earthquake,Frame).
place : newcastle.
day : today.
time : 5-am.
killed : 8.
injured : X.
damage : 2-million.
magnitude : 6.5.

Frame = [place : newcastle, day : today, time : 5-am,
         killed : 8, injured : _004F, damage : 2-million,
         magnitude : 6.5] ->
```

When a frame is sent to the headquarters, it is automatically converted into a news story by a procedure *news*, which is partially shown in Figure 6.20.

```
news(earthquake,[place:P, day:D, time:T, killed:K,
                 injured:I, damage:Da, magnitude:M],
  ['An',earthquake,occurred,in,P,D,at,T,nl,measured,at,M,
  on,the,'Richter',scale,'.','There',were,K,killed,',',nl,
  I,injured,and,damage,estimated,at,'$',Da,'.']).

print_news([]) :- nl.
print_news([W|Rest]) :-
    (var(W), write('unknown ');
     nonvar(W),(W = nl,!,nl; write(W),write(' '))),
    print_news(Rest).
```

FIGURE 6.20 Conversion of a frame into a news story.

The procedure *news* has clauses similar to the one shown in Figure 6.20 for other events, such as *war, election,* and *royal_wedding.* For example, the following query will generate and display the news on the earthquake that occurred in Newcastle.

```
?- create_frame(earthquake,Frame),
   news(earthquake,Frame,News),
   print_news(News).
```

```
An earthquake occurred in newcastle today at 5-am
measured at 6.5 on the Richter scale. There were 8 killed,
unknown injured, and damage estimated at $2-million.
```

Here, the procedure *print_news* displays the news, word by word, except for any uninstantiated variables, the word "unknown" is printed instead.

6.3.3 Arrays

An array is a fixed-length sequence of items, each of which can be accessed directly.

- A *one-dimensional array* of length n can be represented by a term $A = a(X_1, \ldots, X_n)$. This array is generated by the following procedure:

```
make_array1(N,A) :- functor(A,a,N).
```

To access to the Ith element of an array A (for either retrieval or storing), we can use the goal *arg(I,A,X)*. If the Ith element is already instantiated and we wish to replace its value with a new item X, then we can use the goal *argrep(A,I,X,NewA)*.

- A *two-dimensional array* of size $m \times n$ is represented by a term of the following form:

$$A = a(r(X_{11}, \ldots, X_{1n}), \ldots, r(X_{m1}, \ldots, X_{mn}))$$

which can be generated by the following procedure

```
make_array2(M,N,A) :-
    functor(A,a,M),make_rows(M,N,A).

make_rows(0,_,A) :- !.
make_rows(I,N,A) :-
    functor(R,r,N), arg(I,A,R),
    I1 is I-1, make_rows(I1,N,A).
```

To access to the (I, J)-element of a two-dimensional array A represented in the above form, we use the following goals:

```
arg(I,A,R),arg(J,R,X).
```

The following is an example in which array appears to be the only appropriate data structure.

EXAMPLE 6.15 *Heap-sort.* A heap is defined to be a complete binary tree in which the key at the root is greatest and both of its subtrees are also heaps. The traditional heap-sort algorithm is as follows:

> To sort an array A of length N into ascending order do
> > make the array into a heap whose root is $A[1]$ and
> > > for each node $A[I]$, its left child is in $A[2 * I]$
> > > > and its right child is in $A[2 * I + 1]$; then
> > adjust the heap into the sorted array.

> To make an array A of length N into a heap do
> > start I from N down to 1 do
> > > adjust the array $A[I..N]$ into a heap.

To adjust a heap A of N nodes into a sorted array do
    start J from N down to 2 do
        swap $A[1]$ with $A[J]$, then
        adjust the array $A[1..J-1]$ into a heap again.

To adjust the array $A[I..J]$ into a heap do
    find the index K of the larger child of $A[I]$,
    if $A[I] < A[K]$ then
        swap $A[I]$ with $A[K]$, and
        adjust the array $A[K..J]$ into a heap.

The procedure *heap_sort(A,N,A1)* that receives an array A of N integers, say, and sorts it into an ascending array *A1* is shown in Figure 6.21. Following is an example to test the program.

```
?- heap_sort(a(7,3,5,1,8,6,2,4),8,X).
X = a(1,2,3,4,5,6,7,8) ->
```

The representation of arrays by compound terms as shown above allows fast access to the arrays' elements by using the built-in predicates *arg* and *argrep*. This representation, however, has two major disadvantages. First, the array is assumed to be indexed by successive positive integers. Second, it is difficult to transpose the array, that is, to exchange its rows and columns.

In linear programming, for example, access to both row and column elements is commonly required and array indices are often discontinuous or even nonnumeric. In this case, it is more suitable to represent a two-dimensional array by a list of lists as shown below.

- A *two-dimensional array* of size $m \times n$ (with arbitrary indices) is represented by a list of the following form:

$$[\,[e(I_1, J_1, X_{11}), \ldots, e(I_1, J_n, X_{1n})],$$
$$\vdots$$
$$[e(I_m, J_1, X_{m1}), \ldots, e(I_m, J_n, X_{mn})]\,].$$

```
heap_sort(A,N,A1) :-
    build_heap(A,N,N,A2),
    adjust_heap(A2,N,A1).

build_heap(A,I,N,A1) :-
    I > 0,!, adjust(A,I,N,A2),
    I1 is I-1,
    build_heap(A2,I1,N,A1).
build_heap(A,0,_,A).

adjust_heap(A,J,A1) :-
    J > 1,!, swap(A,1,J,A2),
    J1 is J-1, adjust(A2,1,J1,A3),
    adjust_heap(A3,J1,A1).
adjust_heap(A,1,A).

adjust(A,I,J,A1) :-
    find_larger_child(A,I,J,K,Y),
    arg(I,A,X),
    X < Y,!,swap(A,I,K,A2),adjust(A2,K,J,A1).
adjust(A,_,_,A).

find_larger_child(A,I,J,K,Y) :-
    L is 2*I, R is 2*I+1,
    L =< J, arg(L,A,LC),
    (R =< J,arg(R,A,RC), RC > LC,!,
    K is R, Y is RC; K is L, Y is LC).

swap(A,I,J,A1) :-
    arg(I,A,X),arg(J,A,Y),
    argrep(A,I,Y,A2),argrep(A2,J,X,A1).
```

FIGURE 6.21 Program *heap_sort*.

An array in the above list-form can be generated by the following procedure, where the row and column indices (which may be nonnumeric) are to be supplied by the user (the procedure *member* is defined in Figure 2.13). Here, the array is established as a set of rows, each of which is a set of elements.

```
make_array2(Array) :-
    row_indices(IList),
    col_indices(JList),
    setof(Row, I^ (member(I,IList),
                setof(e(I,J,X),member(J,JList),Row)),
            Array).
```

To access the (I, J)-element of a two-dimensional array A represented in the above list-form, we use the following procedure:

```
array_entry(A,I,J,X) :-
    member(Row,A),member(e(I,J,X),Row).
```

Note that the procedure *array_entry* can be used in many ways. In fact, it can be used to retrieve an element at a specified location (I, J), or to store an element at that location, or to find the location (I, J) of a given value.

A more common case is when we are given a table of data in the form of a list of facts in the memory, and we want to set up a two-dimensional array to store the data of the table. The procedure that performs this task is shown in Figure 6.22. This procedure is the same as the procedure *make_array2* given above except that the indices are obtained directly from the table.

```
make_table(Table) :-
    setof(Row,
        H^setof(e(I,J,X),(table(H,J,X),I = H),Row),
        Table).

table(can,syd,200).
table(can,mel,300).
    .
    .
    .
```

FIGURE 6.22 Program *make_table*.

Another basic operation on arrays is the transposition between rows and columns. The procedure *transpose* is given in Figure 6.23, where we use the procedure *nth_member* (in addition to the usual procedure *member*) to detect the end of a row (here, N is the number of columns in the table).

```
transpose(N,Table,Table1) :-
    setof(Col,(M,X,Row)^
              (nth_member(M,X,Row),
               (M > N,!,fail;
                setof(X,Row^member(Row,Table),Col))),
          Table1).

nth_member(1,X,[X|T]).
nth_member(N,X,[Y|T]) :- nth_member(M,X,T), N is M+1.
```

FIGURE 6.23 Program to transpose a matrix.

We shall need the above two procedures, *make_table* and *transpose*, in the job assignment problem in this chapter (Problem 6.5) and the Travelling Salesman problem of Chapter 7 (Problem 7.6).

6.4   Advanced tree structures

In this section, we consider two advanced structures of trees that are commonly used in database systems, namely AVL-trees (named after Adelson, Velskii, and Landis) and B-trees.

6.4.1   AVL-trees

An AVL-tree is a binary search tree whose subtrees have heights differing by at most 1 and they are also AVL-trees. An AVL-tree is associated with a *balance indicator* that has value 0 if the two subtrees have equal heights, 1 if the left subtree is taller than the right one, and 2 if the other way is true.

The purpose of organising data into an AVL-tree is to make searching effective, while maintenance is relatively easy in comparison with complete binary search tree. In Prolog, an AVL-tree can be represented by a compound term of the form:

   bt(Left,Node,Right) - I

where I represents the tree's balance indicator whose value is 0, 1, or 2. In particular, the empty tree is represented by the term *nil-z*. Figure 6.24 shows two examples of the AVL-tree, where the number above each node is the balance indicator of the tree rooted at that node.

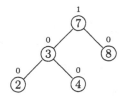
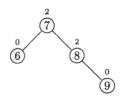

```
bt(bt(bt(nil-z,2,nil-z)-0,          bt(bt(nil-z,6,nil-z)-0,
       3,                                  7,
       bt(nil-z,4,nil-z)-0)-0,             bt(nil-z,
    7,                                        8,
    bt(nil-z,8,nil-z)-0)-1               bt(nil-z,9,nil-z)-0)-2)-2
```

FIGURE 6.24 Prolog representation of AVL-trees.

We now consider the *insertion* of a new item into an AVL-tree. The algorithm is given below.

> To insert an item X into an AVL-tree do
> > *if*   the tree is empty then
> > > the new tree contains X as its only node
> >
> > *else* *if* $X \le$ the key in the root node then
> > > insert X into the left subtree, and
> > > consider if the new tree needs to be rebalanced
> > >
> > > *else* (i.e., $X >$ the key in the root node)
> > > > insert X into the right subtree, and
> > > > consider if the new tree needs to be rebalanced.

To consider if the new tree needs to be rebalanced do
Case 1: No rebalance is required:
> > *if*   the inserted subtree does not grow taller (i.e., either its
> > balance indicator does not change or it changes from 1
> > or 2 to 0) then the tree need not be rebalanced and
> > its balance indicator is the same as the old one
> >
> > *else* *if* the tree's old balance indicator is 0, then
> > > the tree need not be rebalanced but its balance
> > > indicator must be changed to 1 or 2 depending
> > > on the grown subtree is on its left or right
> > >
> > > *else* *if* the grown subtree was the shorter one,
> > > > then the tree need not be rebalanced but its
> > > > balance indicator must be changed to 0.

Case 2: Rebalance by right rotation:

(Call the tree's root node A and its left-child B. See Figure 6.25, where the numbers under the nodes represent old values of balance indicators and the numbers above the nodes represent their new values.)

if   the new node goes to the left subtree of B, then take
the right subtree of B and make it the left subtree of A, then
make A the right-child of B with balance indicator 0, and
take B as the root of the new tree with balance indicator 0.

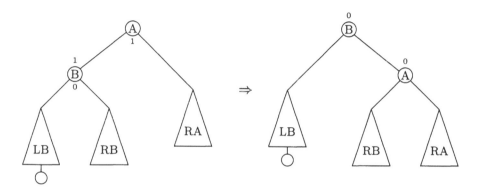

FIGURE 6.25 Rebalance by right rotation.

Case 3: Rebalance by left-right rotation:

(Call the tree's root node A, its left-child B, and B's right-child C.
See Figure 6.26.)

if   the new node goes to the right subtree of B, then take
the left subtree of C and make it the right subtree of B, and
take the right subtree of C and make it the left subtree of A,
then make B the left-child of C, and A the right-child of C;
the balance indicator of the new tree rooted at C is 0;
the balance indicators at A and B are 0 and 1 if the
A-subtree contains the new node, or 2 and 0 if the B-subtree
contains the new node, or both 0 if C itself is the new node

Case 4, 5: Rebalance by left rotation or right-left rotation:

The same as in Cases 2, 3 where the words *left* and *right* are to be
exchanged, and the balance indicator's values 1 and 2 are swapped.

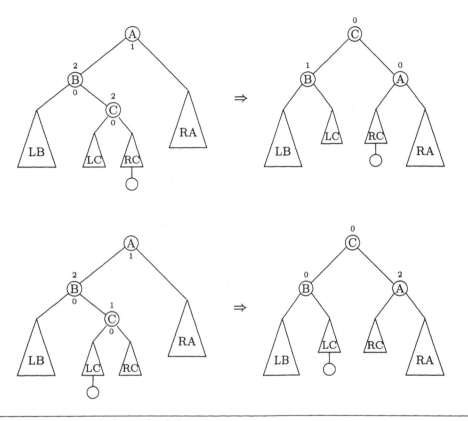

FIGURE 6.26 Rebalance by left-right rotation.

The procedure *insert_avl(X, Old Tree, New Tree)* is shown in Figure 6.27. There are a few things that should be noted from the program of Figure 6.27. First, the special case $I = z$ is included in Case 1 where no rebalance is required. In fact, if $I = z$, then either $IA = 0$ or $IA + S = 3$. Second, if rebalance is required, we must have $S = IA$, because $IA \neq 0$ and $IA + S \neq 3$; also I must be 0 since $I \neq NI$ and $NI \neq 0$ (and insertion cannot change the balance indicator from 1 to 2 or vice versa, after the tree is rebalanced).

To test this program, let us construct an AVL-tree from empty by sequentially inserting the nodes containing the keys $9, 8, 2; 1, 7, 5; 10; 3, 4; 6$. Here, each semicolon indicates a rebalance of the tree is needed. In fact, the insertion of the key 2 causes a right rotation; 5: a left-right rotation; 10: a left rotation; 4: a left-right rotation; and 6: a left rotation. The resulting trees are shown in Figure 6.28.

```
insert_avl(X,nil-z,bt(nil-z,X,nil-z)-0) :- !.
insert_avl(X,bt(L-I,A,R)-IA,NewTree) :-
    X =< A,!,
    insert_avl(X,L-I,NL-NI),
    balance(1,IA,I,NI,bt(NL-NI,A,R),NewTree).
insert_avl(X,bt(L,A,R-I)-IA,NewTree) :-
    X > A,
    insert_avl(X,R-I,NR-NI),
    balance(2,IA,I,NI,bt(L,A,NR-NI),NewTree).

% No rebalance is required
balance(S,IA,I,NI,NewTree,NewTree-NIA) :-
    NI* (NI-I) =:= 0,!, NIA = IA;
    IA =:= 0,!,          NIA = S;
    IA + S =:= 3,!,      NIA = 0.

% Rebalance by right-rotation
balance(1,1,0,1,bt(bt(LB,B,RB)-1,A,RA),
                bt(LB,B,bt(RB,A,RA)-0)-0).

% Rebalance by left-right rotation
balance(1,1,0,2,bt(bt(LB,B,bt(LC,C,RC)-IC)-2,A,RA),
                bt(bt(LB,B,LC)-IB,C,bt(RC,A,RA)-IA)-0) :-
    IC =:= 0,IA = 0,IB = 0,!;
                IA is (IC+1) mod 3,
                IB is (IA+1) mod 3.

% Rebalance by left-rotation
balance(2,2,0,2,bt(LA,A,bt(LB,B,RB)-2),
                bt(bt(LA,A,LB)-0,B,RB)-0).

% Rebalance by right-left rotation
balance(2,2,0,1,bt(LA,A,bt(bt(LC,C,RC)-IC),B,RB)-1,
                bt(bt(LA,A,LC)-IA,C,bt(RC,B,RB)-IB)-0) :-
    IC =:= 0,IA = 0,IB = 0,!;
                IB is (IC+1) mod 3,
                IA is (IB+1) mod 3.
```

FIGURE 6.27 Insertion of an item into an AVL-tree.

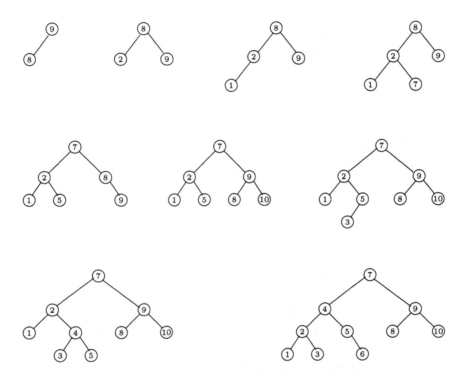

FIGURE 6.28 Insertion of items into an AVL-tree.

We next consider the *deletion* of an item from an AVL-tree. The algorithm is given below.

To delete an item X from an AVL-tree do
> *if* X is in the root and one subtree is empty then
>> return the other subtree as the new tree;
> *if* X is in the root and both subtrees are nonempty then
>> replace X in the root with the data in its successor,
>> delete its successor (which always has empty left subtree),
>> and consider if the new tree needs to be rebalanced;

> *if* $X <$ the key in the root then
>   delete X from the left subtree, and
>   consider if the new tree needs to be rebalanced
> *else* (i.e., $X >$ the key in the root)
>   delete X from the right subtree, and
>   consider if the new tree needs to be rebalanced.

To find the successor of a node, we simply go to its right subtree and follow the left branch until we can go no further, then the last node being visited is the wanted one. The task of rebalancing a tree after deleting a node in one of its subtrees is similar to that in the case of insertion, but is slightly more complex. We shall explain the necessary changes after giving the procedure *delete_avl* below and the modified procedure *balance2* in Figure 6.30.

```
delete_avl(X,bt(L,X,nil-z)-IX,L) :- !.
delete_avl(X,bt(nil-z,X,R)-IX,R) :- !.
delete_avl(X,bt(L,X,R-I)-IX,NewTree) :- !,
    delete_least(Y,R-I,NR-NI),
    balance2(1,IX,NI,I,bt(L,Y,NR-NI),NewTree).

delete_avl(X,bt(L-I,A,R)-IA,NewTree) :-
    X < A,!,
    delete_avl(X,L-I,NL-NI),
    balance2(2,IA,NI,I,bt(NL-NI,A,R),NewTree).

delete_avl(X,bt(L,A,R-I)-IA,NewTree) :-
    X > A,
    delete_avl(X,R-I,NR-NI),
    balance2(1,IA,NI,I,bt(L,A,NR-NI),NewTree).

delete_least(Y,bt(nil-z,Y,R)-IY,R) :- !.
delete_least(Y,bt(L-I,A,R)-IA,NewTree) :-
    delete_least(Y,L-I,NL-NI),
    balance2(2,IA,NI,I,bt(NL-NI,A,R),NewTree).
```

FIGURE 6.29 Deletion of an item from an AVL-tree.

```
% No rebalance is required
balance2(S,IA,NI,I,NewTree,NewTree-NIA) :-
    I* (NI-1)* (NI-2) =:= 0,!, NIA = IA;
    IA =:= 0,!, NIA = S;
    IA + S =:= 3,!, NIA = 0.


% Rebalance by right-rotation
balance2(1,1,_,_,bt(bt(LB,B,RB)-IB,A,RA),
                bt(LB,B,bt(RB,A,RA)-NIA)-NIB) :-
    IB =:= 1,!, NIA = 0, NIB = 0;
    IB =:= 0,!, NIA = 1, NIB = 2.


% Rebalance by left-right rotation
balance2(1,1,_,_,bt(bt(LB,B,bt(LC,C,RC)-IC)-2,A,RA),
                bt(bt(LB,B,LC)-IB,C,bt(RC,A,RA)-IA)-0) :-
    IC =:= 0,!, IA = 0, IB = 0;
                IA is (IC+1) mod 3,
                IB is (IA+1) mod 3.


% Rebalance by left-rotation
balance2(2,2,_,_,bt(LA,A,bt(LB,B,RB)-IB),
                bt(bt(LA,A,LB)-NIA,B,RB)-NIB) :-
    IB =:= 2,!, NIA = 0, NIB = 0;
    IB =:= 0,!, NIA = 2, NIB = 1.


% Rebalance by right-left rotation
balance2(2,2,_,_,bt(LA,A,bt(bt(LC,C,RC)-IC,B,RB)-1),
                bt(bt(LA,A,LC)-IA,C,bt(RC,B,RB)-IB)-0) :-
    IC =:= 0,!, IA = 0, IB = 0;
                IB is (IC+1) mod 3,
                IA is (IB+1) mod 3.
```

FIGURE 6.30 Rebalance of a tree after deletion.

The above program shows that no rebalance is needed if the subtree in which deletion occurs does not become shorter (i.e., its balance indicator I does not change or it changes to $NI = 1$ or 2), or it does become shorter but this does not upset the tree's balance (i.e., the tree's balance indicator IA is either 0 or 2 while deletion occurs in its right subtree ($S = 1$), or 1 while deletion occurs in its left subtree ($S = 2$)). In the case where rebalance is required, if deletion occurs in the right subtree (which is the shorter one), then a *right* or *left-right* rotation is performed, but we must consider all three possible cases where the left subtree's balance indicator *IB* may be 0, 1, or 2 (while in the case of insertion, it can only be 1 or 2). Similar changes apply to the case where deletion occurs in the left subtree.

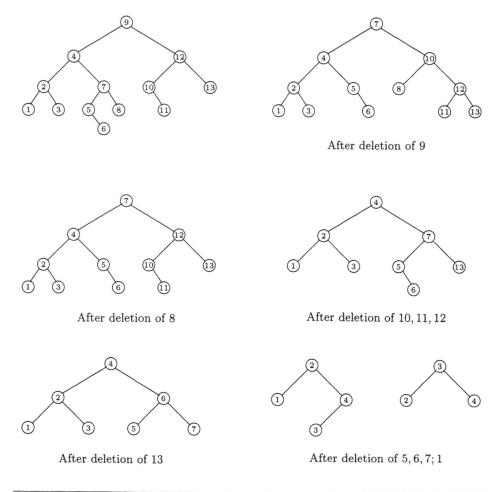

FIGURE 6.31 Deletion of items from an AVL-tree.

To test the program of Figures 6.29 and 6.30, let us demolish the first AVL-tree shown in Figure 6.31 by sequentially deleting the nodes containing the keys 9; 8; 10, 11, 12; 13; 5, 6, 7; 1; 3, 4, 2. Here, each semicolon indicates a rebalance of the tree is needed. The resulting trees are shown in Figure 6.31.

Since the procedures *balance* (Figure 6.27) and *balance2* (Figure 6.30) are very similar, they can be incorporated into a single procedure that covers both cases of insertion and deletion. The common procedure is shown in Problem 6.6.

The AVL-tree structure provides highly efficient search, but as we have seen, its maintenance is rather difficult. A further compromise between effectiveness and maintainability is the structure of B-trees, which is studied in the next subsection.

6.4.2   B-trees

A B-tree of order n is a tree with the following properties:

- Each node contains between n and $2n$ items, except the root, which may contain from 0 to $2n$ items;

- Each node with m items must have $m + 1$ descendants, except the leaf nodes, which have no descendants;

- Each node has its items interleaved with its descendants such that each item is greater than or equal to all the items in the descendant to its left and is less than those in the descendant to its right;

- The items in each node are in ascending order, and all leaf nodes are at the same level.

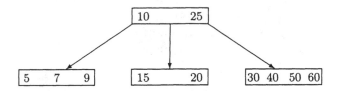

FIGURE 6.32   A B-tree of order 2.

B-tree is the most commonly used data organisation in databases. Conceptually, a B-tree is organised like an indexed sequential file. To search for an item in a B-tree, we first perform a sequential search at the root to find the item or an appropriate path to a node in the lower level, where another sequential search is done, and so on. For example, to search for the key 20 in the B-tree of Figure 6.32, we scan the root node and stop at the key 25, then follow its left path to the lower node, where we scan again to find the desired key 20.

In Prolog, a B-tree can be represented as a list of the form

$$[P_0, \ K_1, \ P_1, \ldots, K_m, \ P_m]$$

where the K_i $(1 \leq i \leq m)$ represent the items and the P_j $(0 \leq j \leq m)$ are B-trees of the same height. For example, the B-tree of Figure 6.32 is represented by the following list:

$$[[5, 7, 9], \ 10, \ [15, 20], \ 25, \ [30, 40, 50, 60]].$$

In practice, each item in a B-tree normally consists of a key and a record of information associated with that key. For example, an item may take the form *(K, record(A,B,C))*, where K is a unique key and A, B, C are data about this key. Assuming this form of representation, we have the procedure *search* shown in Figure 6.33 that searches for information contained in a B-tree about a given key.

```
search(X,BT,Record)  :-
    leaf(BT),!,
    member((X,Record),BT).
search(X,BT,Record)  :-
    append(A,[L,(Y,Rec),R|C],BT),
    (X =< Y,!;  C = []),
    (X = Y,!,  Record = Rec;
     X < Y,!,  search(X,L,Record);
     C = [],   search(X,R,Record)).

leaf([[_|_]|_]) :- !,fail.
leaf(_).

member :- % see Figure 2.13
append :- % see Figure 2.21
```

FIGURE 6.33 Search for information in a B-tree.

We now consider the *insertion* of new items into a B-tree. For simplicity of reference we assume that each node in the tree contains only a key. The generalisation to the case where each item contains a full record is very trivial, however. Let us first consider a simple B-tree of order 2 that contains a single leaf node $[1, 3, 5]$. If we insert the key 2, then we have a full node $[1, 2, 3, 5]$. So, when the key 23 is inserted, the node overflows and it must be adjusted into a tree of two levels $[[1, 2], 3, [5, 23]]$ as shown in Figure 6.34. Now, to insert the key 9, we must enter the right subtree and insert it into the leaf node. If we continue to insert the keys 13, 14, then we have another overflow. So, the overflowing node is adjusted into the tree $[[5, 9], 13, [14, 23]]$, which is installed back to the root node, resulting in the new tree $[[1, 2], 3, [5, 9], 13, [14, 23]]$ (see Figure 6.34).

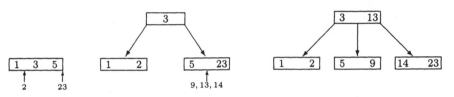

FIGURE 6.34 Examples of insertion into a B-tree.

The general inserting algorithm is given below.

> To insert an item X into a B-tree do
> > *if* the tree is a leaf then
> > > insert X into the leaf, and
> > > adjust it if it overflows
> > *else* (the tree is nonleaf)
> > > find the subtree into which X should be inserted,
> > > insert X into that subtree, then
> > > install the new subtree back to the big tree.

> To install the new subtree back to the big tree do
> > *if* the subtree has grown taller then
> > > break it down to three pieces: the left branch,
> > > the middle item, and the right branch, and
> > > place them at the position of the old subtree, then
> > > adjust the whole tree if it overflows
> > *else* (the subtree's height is unchanged)
> > > simply replace the old subtree with the new one.

To adjust a tree if it overflows do

if the root node overflows then

break it down into three parts: the left and right
branches, each has half length, and the middle node.

A node overflows if

either   it is a leaf and its length $> 2 * \text{order}$

or   it is nonleaf and its length $> 4 * \text{order} + 1$.

Note that a subtree is detected to have grown taller if it contains exactly
three pieces: its left branch, the middle element, and its right branch. Otherwise, a nonleaf subtree always has at least $2n + 1$ elements ($n \geq 2$). The
procedure *insert_bt(X,OldBTree,NewBTree)* is shown in Figures 6.35 and
6.36. Here we assume the tree's order is given by a fact *order(N)*.

```
insert_bt(X,BT,BT1) :-
    leaf(BT),!,
    insert(X,BT,BT2),
    adjust(BT2,BT1).

insert_bt(X,BT,BT1) :-
    append(A,[L,Y,R|C],BT),(X =< Y,!; C = []),
    (X =< Y,!, insert_bt(X,L,L1),
            install(A,[L1,Y,R|C],BT1);
     C = [],    insert_bt(X,R,R1),append(A,[L,Y],A1),
            install(A1,[R1],BT1)).

install(A,[ST|B],BT1) :-
    grown(ST,L,X,R),!,
                append(A,[L,X,R|B],BT2),
                adjust(BT2,BT1);
                append(A,[ST|B],BT1).
```

FIGURE 6.35 Insertion of an item into a B-tree.

To test the program of Figures 6.35 and 6.36, let us construct a B-tree from
nothing by sequentially inserting the keys

1, 3, 5, 2, 23; 9, 13, 14; 10, 12, 15, 16, 17; 18, 19, 20; 21, 22, 24.

```
adjust(BT,[L,X,R]) :-
    overflow(BT,N),
    append(L,[X|R],BT),length(L,N),!.
adjust(BT,BT).

overflow(BT,M) :-
    order(N),length(BT,K),
    (leaf(BT),!, K > 2*N; K > 4*N+1),
    M is K // 2.

grown([[X|Y],Z,[U|V]],[X|Y],Z,[U|V]).

order(2).
leaf :-    % see Figure 6.33
insert :- % see Figure 3.14
append :- % see Figure 2.21
length :- % see Figure 2.18
```

FIGURE 6.36 Insertion of an item into a B-tree (continued).

Here, each semicolon indicates that a tree-break occurs due to overflow. The resulting trees are shown in Figures 6.37. (The insertion of the first two sequences has been shown in Figure 6.34.)

We consider next the *deletion* of items from a B-tree. This task is almost in the reverse order of insertion, but is slightly more complex. Let us consider the first B-tree of order 2 in Figure 6.38. If we delete the item 8, then no difficulty arises. But to delete the key 4, we must replace it with its successor, which is the key 5 in the leaf node to its right, then delete its successor. Now if we continue to delete the key 7, then the node becomes underflow (i.e., having fewer than 2 items). To rebalance this node, we look at its right neighbour and find it has a surplus item. So we pull down the key 9 to fill the underflow node and bring the key 10 up to replace 9 (see Figure 6.38). Now if we continue to delete the key 6, then the node becomes underflow again. This time its right neighbour has no surplus items to be lent, so we look to its left neighbour, which does have extra items. So we pull down the key 5 to fill the underflow node and bring the key 3 up to replace 5.

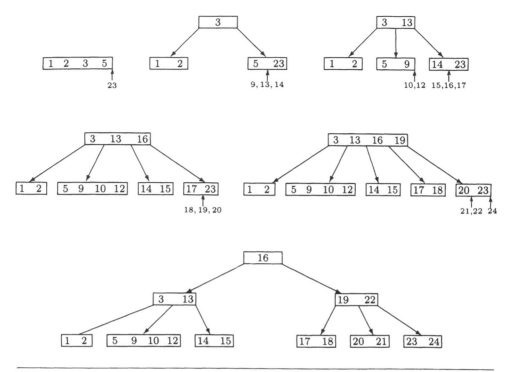

FIGURE 6.37 Insertion of items into a B-tree of order 2.

Finally, if we delete the key 11 then the node containing it becomes underflow, but its only neighbour has no surplus. So the underflow node, its left neighbour and the middle node 10 are collapsed into a single node $[5, 9, 10, 12]$, which is installed back to produce the tree $[[1, 2], 3, [5, 9, 10, 12]]$ as shown in Figure 6.38.

We give below the general algorithm of deletion for B-trees.

To delete an item X from a B-tree do
    if the tree is a leaf then
        simply search to remove X from the tree
    else (the tree is nonleaf)
        scan the root node to locate X,
        if X is in the root node then
            replace X in the root node with its successor
            (which is always in a leaf of its right subtree),
            delete its successor from the right subtree, and
            install the new subtree back to the big tree;

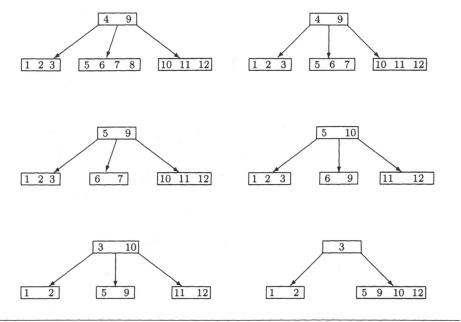

FIGURE 6.38 Examples of deletion from a B-tree.

> *if* $X <$ certain key Y in the root then
> > delete X from the subtree to the left of Y, and
> > install the new subtree back to the big tree;
>
> *if* $X >$ all keys in the root then
> > delete X from the rightmost subtree, and
> > install the new subtree back to the big tree.

To install the new subtree back to the big tree do
> *if* the root of the new subtree is underflow then
> > balance it with one of its neighbours
>
> *else*
> > simply replace the old subtree with the new one.

A node is underflow *if*
> *either* it is a leaf and its length $<$ the order
> *or*   it is nonleaf and its length $< 2 *$ order $+1$

Note that to find the successor of an item X in a node, we simply go to its right subtree and follow the leftmost branches, all the way down to the leaf node; the leftmost element of this leaf is the wanted successor of X.

Following is the algorithm to balance a subtree with its neighbours.

> To balance the new subtree with one of its neighbours do
>> *if*   it has a right neighbour with surplus contents then
>>> balance the new subtree with its right neighbour
>> *else if*   it has a left neighbour then
>>>> *if* this left neighbour has surplus items then
>>>>> balance the new subtree with its left neighbour
>>>> *else* (no neighbours have surplus)
>>>>> merge the new subtree with its left neighbour
>>>>> and the middle element
>>> *else* (there is no left neighbour)
>>>> merge the new subtree with its right neighbour
>>>> and their middle element.

> To balance the new subtree with its right neighbour do
>> *if*   they are leaves then
>>> move the middle element into the new subtree, and
>>> move the first element of the right neighbour into
>>> the middle position
>> *else*
>>> move the middle element and the leftmost branch of
>>> the right neighbour into the new subtree, and
>>> move the first *item* of the right neighbour into
>>> the middle position.

The task of balancing the new subtree with its left neighbour is similar. The procedure *delete_bt* is shown in Figures 6.39 and 6.40.

To test this program, let us take the first B-tree of Figure 6.41 and run the program to delete the keys 8, 4, 7; 6; 11; 24 in that order. Again, the semicolons indicate that rebalancing occurred. The effect of deleting the first five keys has been shown in Figure 6.38. In particular, when the key 11 is deleted, the whole left subtree becomes underflow, so it is balanced with the right subtree to produce the third tree shown in Figure 6.41. Finally, the deletion of the key 24 makes the whole tree collapse into a two-level tree. It is interesting to compare Figure 6.41 with Figure 6.37, and it is recommended that the reader suggests further deletions to reduce the tree step by step as shown in Figure 6.37. Note, however, that the deletion sequence would not be exactly the opposite of the insertion sequence.

```
delete_bt(X,BT,BT1) :-
    leaf(BT),!,
    select(X,BT,BT1).
delete_bt(X,BT,BT1) :-
    append(A,[L,Y,R|C],BT),(X =< Y,!; C = []),
    (X = Y,!, delete_succ(Z,R,R1),append(A,[L,Z],A1),
            install2(A1,[R1|C],BT1);
     X < Y,!, delete_bt(X,L,L1),
            install2(A,[L1,Y,R|C],BT1);
     C = [],   delete_bt(X,R,R1),append(A,[L,Y],A1),
            install2(A1,[R1],BT1)).

delete_succ(Z,[Z|R],R) :- atomic(Z),!.
delete_succ(Z,[L|R],BT) :-
    delete_succ(Z,L,L1),
    install2([],[L1|R],BT).

install2(A,[ST|B],BT) :-
    underflow(ST),!,
        balance(A,[ST|B],BT);
        append(A,[ST|B],BT).

underflow(BT) :-
    order(N), length(BT,K),
    (leaf(BT),!, K < N; K < 2*N+1).

balance(A,[L,X,R|C],BT) :-
    surplus(right,R,Y,Z,_,R2),!,
    balance_right(A,L,X,Y,Z,R2,C,BT).
balance(A,[R|C],BT) :-
    append(A1,[L,X],A),!,
    (surplus(left,L,Y,Z,L1,L2),!,
        balance_left(A1,L1,L2,Y,Z,X,R,C,BT);
        merge(A1,L,[X|R],C,BT2),adjust(BT2,BT)).
balance(A,[L,X,R|C],BT) :-
    merge(A,L,[X|R],C,BT2),adjust(BT2,BT).
```

FIGURE 6.39 Deletion of an item from a B-tree.

```
balance_right(A,L,X,Y,Z,R,C,BT) :-
    atomic(Y),!,
        merge(A,L,[X],[Y,[Z|R]|C],BT);
        merge(A,L,[X,Y],[Z,R|C],BT).
balance_left(A,L1,L2,Y,Z,X,R,C,BT) :-
    atomic(Z),!,
        append(A,[L1,Z,[X|R]|C],BT);
        append(A,[L2,Y,[Z,X|R]|C],BT).

merge(A,L,R,C,BT) :-
    append(L,R,L1),append(A,[L1|C],BT).

adjust([[X|Y]],[X|Y]) :- !.
adjust(BT,BT).

surplus(right,[Y,Z|R],Y,Z,_,R) :-
    have_extra([Y,Z|R]).
surplus(left,L,Y,Z,L1,L2) :-
    have_extra(L),
    append(L1,[Z],L),append(L2,[Y,Z],L).

have_extra(BT) :-
    order(N), length(BT,K),
    (leaf(BT),!, K > N; K > 2*N+1).

order(2).
leaf :-   % see Figure 6.33
select :- % see Figure 2.16
append :- % see Figure 2.21
length :- % see Figure 2.18
```

FIGURE 6.40 Deletion of an item from a B-tree (continued).

6.5   An example of program validation

In Chapter 5, Section 5.5, we have presented the basic techniques of program
validation, including the process of reasoning on a program's correctness and
testing the program's behaviour. In this section, we demonstrate how the
given techniques are applied to relatively large and complex Prolog programs.

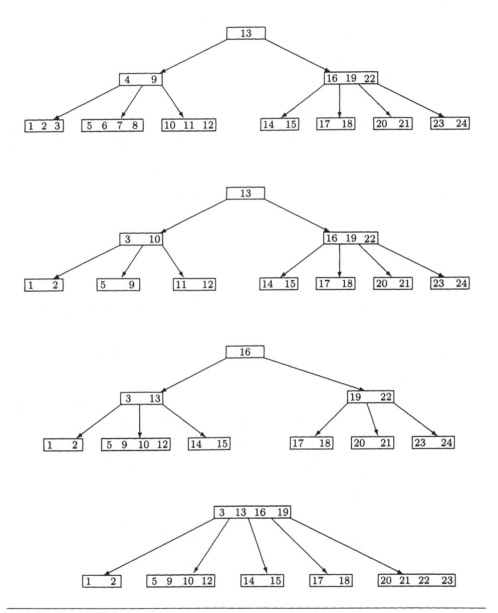

FIGURE 6.41 Deletion of items from a B-tree of order 2.

EXAMPLE 6.16   Let us prove the correctness of the program *delete_bt*, which is shown in Figures 6.39 and 6.40. We begin at the top level and move downward to the lower levels. At each level and for each procedure, we assume that the procedures at the lower levels are correct.

Top level

Procedure delete_bt :

1. This procedure defines $BT1$ to be a B-tree that is the result of deleting a key X from a B-tree BT. The procedure should fail if X is not found in BT.

2. Input   : X is an integer; BT is a B-tree in the form of a list
   $[P_0, K_1, P_1, \ldots, K_m, P_m]$.

   Output : $BT1$ is a B-tree obtained from BT with the key X removed.

3. Possible cases of input:

   X : the integer may be found in BT or not;
   BT : the B-tree may be a leaf (including the empty tree [ ]) or a nonleaf node.

4. Proof:

   Clause 1:

   Suppose that BT is a leaf. Then there are two subcases. If X is in BT, then *select(X,BT,BT1)* succeeds in removing X from BT to produce $BT1$. If X is not in BT (including the case $BT = [\,]$), then *select(X,BT,BT1)* fails, so *delete_bt(X,BT,BT1)* fails (due to the effect of the cut !). Therefore, clause 1 is correct.

   Clause 2:

   Suppose that BT is a nonleaf node (as a result of the cut in the first clause). Then the procedure *append* splits BT into two sublists, A and $[L, Y, R \,|\, C]$, with three possibilities:

   If $X = Y$ then

   > the procedure *delete_succ* finds the successor Z of Y in the subtree R and removes Z from R giving $R1$, the procedure *append* adds L, Z to the end of A giving $A1$, and the procedure *install2* assembles $A1, [R1|C]$, possibly with rebalance, to produce $BT1$.

If $X < Y$ then

> the procedure *delete_bt* deletes X from L to give $L1$ (or fails), and the procedure *install2* assembles A, $[L1,Y,R|\ C]$, possibly with rebalance, to produce $BT1$.

If $C = [\ ]$ (i.e., $X >$ all keys in the root node) then

> the procedure *delete_bt* deletes X from R to give $R1$ (or fails), the procedure *append* adds L, Y to the end of A giving $A1$, and the procedure *install2* assembles $A1$ and $[R1]$, possibly with rebalance, to produce $BT1$.

Thus, if X is in BT then, in any case, all the subgoals succeed and $BT1$ is the result of removing X from BT. Otherwise, we are in the last two cases ($X < Y$ or $C = [\ ]$) where *delete_bt* fails to delete X from a subtree (L or R); hence *delete_bt(X,BT,BT1)* fails. Therefore, clause 2 is correct.

Since all clauses of the procedure *delete_bt* are correct and cover all possible cases of input, the procedure *delete_bt* is correct, provided that the procedures at the lower levels are correct.

Second level

Procedure delete_succ :

1. This procedure finds the least key Z of a nonempty B-tree and removes it to produce a new B-tree.

2. Input   : a nonempty B-tree in the second argument.

   Output : a key Z in the first argument, and a new B-tree in the third argument.

3. Possible cases of input:

   The input B-tree is expected to be nonempty, but it could be a leaf or a nonleaf node.

4. Proof:

   Clause 1:

   Suppose that the input B-tree has the form $[Z\ |\ R]$, where Z is atomic. Then the tree is just a leaf and Z is the least key in the tree. So R is the result of removing Z from the tree. Therefore, clause 1 is correct.

Clause 2:

Suppose that the input B-tree is nonleaf (as a result of the cut in the first clause). Then, it has the form $[L \mid R]$, where L is its leftmost subtree, which contains the least key of the tree. The procedure *delete_succ* finds the least key Z of L and removes it from L to produce $L1$. Then, the procedure *install2* assembles $[]$ and $[L1 \mid R]$, possibly with rebalance, to produce BT. Thus BT is the result of removing the least key Z from the input B-tree. Therefore, clause 2 is correct.

Since all clauses of the procedure *delete_succ* are correct and cover all possible cases of input, the procedure *delete_succ* is correct, provided that the procedure *install2* is correct.

Procedure install2 :

1. This procedure assembles two parts A and $[ST \mid B]$ of a tree (where ST is a new subtree), possibly with rebalance, to produce a B-tree BT.

2. Input : A and $[ST \mid B]$ are two parts of a B-tree in which a subtree is replaced with a new subtree ST.

   Output : BT is the resulting B-tree.

3. Possible cases of input:

   The new subtree ST may be underflow (i.e., it contains fewer than the minimum number of items) or not.

4. Proof:

   The only clause :

   If ST is underflow, then the procedure *balance* assembles A and $[ST \mid B]$ and rebalances it to produce the new B-tree BT. Otherwise, the procedure *append* simply rejoins A and $[ST \mid B]$ into BT. Therefore, this clause is correct, provided that the lower level procedures *underflow* and *balance* are correct.

Third level

Procedure underflow :

1. This procedure tests if a B-tree's root node contains fewer than the minimum number of items required.

2. Input is a B-tree BT.

3. Possible cases of input: BT may be leaf or nonleaf.

4. Proof:

The only clause :

Suppose that the minimum number of items required is N and the length of BT is K. If BT is a leaf and $K < N$, then *underflow(BT)* succeeds. If BT is nonleaf and $K < 2N + 1$ (i.e., the node contains fewer than N items plus $N + 1$ subtrees), then *underflow(BT)* also succeeds. Otherwise, *underflow(BT)* fails. Thus, this clause is correct.

Procedure balance :

1. This procedure receives two parts A and $[ST| B]$ of a tree, balances the subtree ST with one of its neighbours, and reassembles them into a B-tree BT.

2. Input : A and $[ST|B]$ are two parts of a B-tree in which a subtree is replaced with an underflow new subtree ST.

   Output : BT is a B-tree.

3. Possible cases of input:

   ST has a right neighbour that contains surplus items;
   ST has a left neighbour that contains surplus items;
   ST has no surplus neighbours but does have a left neighbour;
   ST has no left neighbour but does have a nonsurplus right neighbour.

4. Proof:

Clause 1:

Suppose that $[ST|B]$ has the form $[L, X, R\,|\,C]$. Then the subtree ST $= L$ has a right neighbour R. If *surplus(right,R,Y,Z,_,R2)* succeeds, then R has extra items and has the form $R = [Y, Z\,|\,R2]$, and the procedure *balance_right* performs a right-balance of *(A,L,X,Y,Z,R2,C)* to produce BT.

Clause 2:

Suppose that ST has no surplus right neighbour (as a result of the cut in the first clause). If the procedure *append* succeeds in splitting A into *A1* and $[L, X]$, then $ST = R$ has a left neighbour L. If *surplus(left,L,Y,Z,L1,L2)* succeeds, then L has extra items and has one of the forms *(L1,Z)* or *(L2,Y,Z)*, and the procedure *balance_left* performs a left-balance of *(A1,L1,L2,Y,Z,X,R,C)* to produce *BT*. If *surplus(left,L,Y,Z,L1,L2)* fails, then L has no extra items. Thus, the procedure *merge* collapses L, X, R into a single subtree and places it between $A1$ and C to produce *BT2*, and the procedure *adjust* checks if the whole tree's height is reduced to produce *BT*.

Clause 3:

Suppose that ST has no left neighbour (as a result of the cut in the second clause). Then $[ST \,|\, B]$ must have the form $[L, X, R \,|\, C]$, that is, $ST = L$ has a right neighbour that contains no surplus items (as a result of the cut in the first clause). So the procedure *merge* collapses L, X, R into a single subtree and places it between A and C to produce *BT2*, and the procedure *adjust* checks if the whole tree's height is reduced to produce *BT*.

Since all three clauses of the procedure *balance* perform the specified task and cover all possible cases of input, the procedure *balance* is correct, provided that the procedures at the lower levels are correct.

Fourth level

Procedure balance_right :

1. This procedure performs a right-balance of A, L, X, Y, Z, R, C to produce the B-tree *BT*.

2. Input : L is an underflow node in a B-tree;
   $[Y, Z, R]$ is its right neighbour;
   A is part of the B-tree to the left of L;
   C is part of the B-tree to the right of R;
   X is the item between L and $[Y, Z \,|\, R]$.

   Output : the resulting B-tree *BT*.

3. Possible cases of input: L may be a leaf or a nonleaf node.

4. Proof:

   The only clause :

   If Y is atomic, then both L and $[Y, Z \,|\, R]$ are leaves. Thus, the procedure *merge* joins L and $[X]$ into a single node and places it between

A and $[Y, [Z \mid R] \mid C]$ (the effect is adding X to the end of L and moving Y of the right neighbour up to the position of X) to produce BT. Otherwise, both L and $[Y, Z \mid R]$ are nonleaf. In this case, Y is a subtree of the B-tree. So the procedure *merge* joins L and $[X, Y]$ into a single node and places it between A and $[Z, R \mid C]$ (the effect is adding the key X and the subtree Y to the end of L and moving Z up to the position of X) to produce BT.

Thus, in any case, the middle key X is added to the underflow node and the least key of its right neighbour is moved up to replace X. Therefore, this clause is correct.

The proof of the procedure *balance_left* is similar to that of the procedure *balance_right*, and the procedures *merge*, *adjust*, *surplus*, *leaf*, and *have_extra* are trivial.

Since all procedures of the program *delete_bt* are proved to be correct, the program *delete_bt* is correct.

As we have pointed out in Chapter 5, Section 5.5, the validation of a program requires both a convincing proof and a satisfactory set of test evidence. A proof establishes the program's logical soundness, but may miss the minor errors such as misspelling of procedure names and missing elementary procedures like *member* and *append*. In the following, we show how to apply the procedure set out in Subsection 5.5.2 of Chapter 5 to test the program *delete_bt*, the soundess of which has been established above.

EXAMPLE 6.17 Let us test the program *delete_bt*, which is shown in Figures 6.39 and 6.40. We first add the following facts to the program:

```
btree(0,[[1,2,3],4,[5,6,7,8],9,[10,11,12]]).
btree(1,[[1,2],3,[5,9,10,12]]).
btree(2,[[14,15],16,[17,18],19,[20,21],22,[23,24]]).
btree(3,[[26,27],28,[29,30]]).
btree(4,[[1,2],3,[5,9,10,12],13,[14,15]]).
btree(5,[[17,18],19,[20,21,22,23]]).
```

In what follows, we show only some test results. It is recommended that the reader performs the remaining tests, using the above-mentioned testing scheme, and compare the results with the trees shown in Figures 6.38 and 6.41.

```
?- leaf([]),leaf([1,2,3]).
yes
?- leaf([[1,2],3,[4,5]]).
no

?- have_extra([1,2]).
no
?- have_extra([1,2,3]).
yes
?- btree(4,BT),have_extra(BT).
no
?- btree(2,BT),have_extra(BT).
BT = [[14,15],16,[17,18],19,[20,21],22,[23,24]]) ->
yes

?- surplus(right,[1,2,3],Y,Z,_,R).
Y = 1
Z = 2
R = [3]

?- btree(2,BT),surplus(right,BT,Y,Z,_,R).
BT = [[14,15],16,[17,18],19,[20,21],22,[23,24]]
Y = [14,15],
Z = 16
R = [[17,18],19,[20,21],22,[23,24]]

?- surplus(left,[1,2,3],Y,Z,L1,L2).
Y = 2
Z = 3
L1 = [1,2]
L2 = [1]

?- btree(2,BT),surplus(left,BT,Y,Z,L1,L2).
BT = [[14,15],16,[17,18],19,[20,21],22,[23,24]]
Y = 22
Z = [23,24]
L1 = [[14,15],16,[17,18],19,[20,21],22]
L2 = [[14,15],16,[17,18],19,[20,21]]
```

```
?- merge([[1,2],3],[5,9],[10,12],[13,[14,15]],BT).
BT = [[1,2],3,[5,9,10,12],13,[14,15]]


?- btree(1,L),btree(2,R),surplus(right,R,Y,Z,_,R2),
   merge([],L,[13,Y],[Z,R2],BT).
L = [[1,2],3,[5,9,10,12]]
R = [[14,15],16,[17,18],19,[20,21],22,[23,24]]
Y = [14,15]
Z = 16
R2 = [[17,18],19,[20,21],22,[23,24]]
BT = [[[1,2],3,[5,9,10,12],13,[14,15]],16,
      [[17,18],19,[20,21],22,[23,24]]]


?- merge([],[5,9],[10,12],[],BT2),adjust(BT2,BT).
BT2 = [[5,9,10,12]]
BT = [5,9,10,12]


?- btree(4,L),btree(5,R),
   merge([],L,[16|R],[],BT2),adjust(BT2,BT).
L = [[1,2],3,[5,9,10,12],13,[14,15]]
R = [[17,18],19,[20,21,22,23]]
BT2 = [[[1,2],3,[5,9,10,12],13,[14,15],16,
        [17,18],19,[20,21,22,23]]]
BT = [[1,2],3,[5,9,10,12],13,[14,15],16,
      [17,18],19,[20,21,22,23]]


?- btree(0,L),btree(2,R),
   delete_bt(8,[L,13,R],T1),
   delete_bt(4,T1,T2),
   delete_bt(7,T2,T3),
   delete_bt(6,T3,T4),
   delete_bt(11,T4,T5),
   delete_bt(24,T5,T6).

L = [[1,2,3],4,[5,6,7,8],9,[10,11,12]]
R = [[14,15],16,[17,18],19,[20,21],22,[23,24]]
T1 = [[[1,2,3],4,[5,6,7],9,[10,11,12]],13,
      [[14,15],16,[17,18],19,[20,21],22,[23,24]]]
```

```
T2 = [[[1,2,3],5,[6,7],9,[10,11,12]],13,
      [[14,15],16,[17,18],19,[20,21],22,[23,24]]]
T3 = [[[1,2,3],5,[6,9],10,[11,12]],13,
      [[14,15],16,[17,18],19,[20,21],22,[23,24]]]
T4 = [[[1,2],3,[5,9],10,[11,12]],13,
      [[14,15],16,[17,18],19,[20,21],22,[23,24]]]
T5 = [[[1,2],3,[5,9,10,12],13,[14,15]],16,
      [[17,18],19,[20,21],22,[23,24]]]
T6 = [[1,2],3,[5,9,10,12],13,[14,15],16,
      [17,18],19,[20,21,22,23]]]
```

Solved problems

6.1 Design a database to store information on a computing course at a university. The database should be adequate to provide answers to the following queries:

(a) Given a list of course units chosen by a student, find a list of pairs of units that have timetable clash. If there is no timetable clash, then an empty list is to be returned.

(b) Given a student ID and a list of course units chosen by this student for the current semester, find a sublist of those units that do not meet the prerequisite requirement of the course in which this student is enrolled.

Write Prolog procedures that perform the tasks described above.

Solution:

This database must have at least two tables: the first table contains information on the course units, including prerequisites and timetable for each unit; the second table contains students' records, including the units each student did in past semesters and the units registered for the current semester. The tables are shown below.

```
% UNIT(UNITCODE,CREDITPT,PREREQUISITES,TIMETABLE)
unit(ics,3,[],[(mon,9:30),(tue,9:30),(thu,11:30)]).
unit(dma,3,[],[(tue,8:30),(wed,8:30),(fri,10:30)]).
unit(dsa,3,[],[(mon,10:30),(wed,14:30),(fri,14:30)]).
unit(is1,3,[ics],[(tue,9:30),(wed,9:30),(thu,9:30)]).
```

```
unit(co1,3,[dsa],[(mon,9:30),(tue,9:30),(thu,9:30)]).
unit(se1,3,[dma,dsa,is1],[(mon,14:30),(wed,16:30),(fri,16:30)]).
unit(ps2,3,[dma,dsa,is1],[(mon,14:30),(wed,14:30),(fri,14:30)]).
unit(is2,3,[is1],[(tue,8:30),(thu,9:30),(fri,10:30)]).
   .
   .
   .
% STUDENT(ID,NAME,COURSE,PAST-CREDITS,CURR-PROGRAM)
student(78-2123,'Smith J.R.','Computer Science',
        [(ics,'P'),(dma,'P'),(dsa,'CR'),(is1,'NX')],
        [ps2,co1,is1,se1]).
student(84-2201,'Adams P.','Computer Engineering',
        [(ics,'CR'),(dma,'P'),(dsa,'DI'),(ma1,'DI')],
        [ma2,co1,is1,se1]).
   .
   .
   .
```

(a) The following procedure *check_clash(R,L)* receives a list R of registered units, and returns the list L of pairs of units that have timetable clash.

```
check_clash(R,L) :-
    setof((U,V),(member(U,R),member(V,R),
                 U @< V, clash(U,V)),L),!.
check_clash(_,[]).

clash(U,V) :-
    unit(U,_,_,TU),unit(V,_,_,TV),
    member(T,TU),member(T,TV).
```

(b) The following procedure *check_prereq(ID,R,L)* receives a student ID and a list R of registered units, and returns the list L of those units in R that do not meet the prerequisite requirement.

```
check_prereq(ID,R,L) :-
    student(ID,_,_,Credits,_),
    setof(U,(member(U,R),
             not(meet_prereq(U,Credits))),L),!.
check_prereq(_,_,[]).

meet_prereq(Unit,Credits) :-
    unit(Unit,_,Prerequisites,_),
    satisfy(Prerequisites,Credits).
```

```
satisfy([],_) :- !.
satisfy([U|Us],Credits) :-
    member((U,G),Credits),pass(G),
    satisfy(Us,Credits).

pass(G) :- member(G,['P','CR','DI','HD']).
member(X,[X|T]).
member(X,[H|T]) :- member(X,T).
```

6.2 Some Prolog systems may not provide any built-in predicates for the purpose of data collecting. Write a procedure *find_all* in Prolog, so that *find_all(X,G,L)* returns the list L of all instances of X (which are unordered and may contain duplications) for which the goal G succeeds. Note that any free variable in G is assumed to be existentially quantified.

Solution:

In order to find all answers of a goal G, we use the goal *fail* to force the system backtrack on G. The algorithm of *find_all* is as follows:

> To find the collection L of all X such that G succeeds do
> > let L be empty,
> > repeat
> > > find the next X such that G succeeds,
> > > add X to L
> > until no more answers for G;
> > return L.

Therefore, the program:

```
find_all(X,G,L) :-
    assert(answer([])),
    G,
    once(retract(answer(L1))),
    assert(answer([X|L1])),
    fail.
find_all(_,_,L) :-
    retract(answer(L)).

once(P) :- P,!.
```

For example, consider the following facts and the program's answer to the query given below.

```
student(78-2123,'Smith J.R.').        test(78-2123,40).
student(84-2201,'Adams P.').          test(84-2201,65).
student(90-3150,'Burns M.I.').        test(90-3150,56).

?- find_all(stud_mark(Name,Mark),
            (student(ID,Name),test(ID,Mark)), List).

List =  [stud_mark('Burns M.I.',56),
         stud_mark('Adams P.',65),
         stud_mark('Smith J.R.',40)] ->
```

Observe that in the above query, the variable *ID* is treated as if it is existentially quantified. Note also that the procedure *find_all* defined above returns an empty list if the goal *G* has no answers. If we want the procedure to fail when the goal *G* has no answers, it suffices to add the subgoal L \= [] to the second clause of *find_all*.

6.3 Assume the availability of the built-in predicates *bagof* and *setof*. Write Prolog procedures to perform the following tasks.

(a) Remove duplicated elements in a given list and sort the list into (numeric or alphanumeric) ascending order.

(b) Count the total number of answers to a given goal.

Solution:

(a)   sort_set(L,L1) :-
           setof(X,member(X,L),L1).

(b)   count_answers(G,N) :-
           bagof(a,G^G,L),length(L,N).

6.4 A *palindrome* is a word that reads the same backwards as forwards. For example, "madam" is a palindrome. Write a procedure to determine if a given word is a palindrome.

Solution:

A natural approach to this problem is to fold the given word at certain point and to try to match the characters of the two parts. To do this, an effective way is to use a nondeterministic finite automaton to perform the automatic trials and errors. The word's characters are stored in a stack *L* and are to be moved to a second stack P for matching. Thus the finite automaton has only two states:

State 0 : moving a character from L to P;

State 1 : matching head characters of L and P.

The pair (L, P) serves as input signals to the automaton. An interesting point is that the next input signal is produced by the current state transition. The following graph shows the transitions of states where each arc is labelled above with the current input signal and is labelled below with the next input signal.

Note that, being in state 0, the system may remain in this state or change to state 1. If it remains in state 0, then one character is moved from L to P. If it changes from state 0 to state 1, then either both stacks are unchanged, or one character is popped from stack L. The choice of these state transitions is nondeterministic and is realised by Prolog's backtracking process.

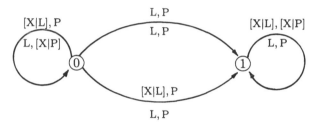

When the system is in state 1, it can only remain in this state, and the head characters of L and P are matched and popped. If this fails, then the system backtracks to the previous choice of state transition. Thus, the system automatically performs a sequence of trial and error to determine if the word is a palindrome. The program is shown below.

```
palindrome(Word) :-
    name(Word,L),palind(0,L,P).

palind(S,L,P) :-
    change_state(S,L,P,S1,L1,P1),
    palind(S1,L1,P1).
palind(1,[],[]).

change_state(0,[X|L],P,0,L,[X|P]).
change_state(0,L,P,1,L,P).
change_state(0,[X|L],P,1,L,P).
change_state(1,[X|L],[X|P],1,L,P).
```

For example:

```
?- palindrome(madam).
yes
?- palindrome('dog a devil deified , deified lived a god').
yes
```

6.5 *Job assignment.* N jobs are to be done using N different machines. The costs of using machine i to do the job j are given in the following table:

JOBS

		1	2	3	4
	1	6	5	3	6
	2	5	6	8	12
MACHINES	3	8	6	8	9
	4	3	6	5	8

Write a Prolog program to determine which jobs should be assigned to which machines in order to minimise the total cost. (This problem has been given in Chapter 2, Problem 2.11, where a simple solution was expected. Here, an efficient solution based on some well-defined algorithm is required.)

Solution:

We note first that for any machine, if the costs of running the jobs are all reduced by the same amount, then the optimal solution will be unchanged. Likewise, for any particular job, if the costs of running it on different machines are all reduced by the same amount, then the optimal solution will also be unchanged. So, we have the following algorithm to solve the problem, which is adopted from Taha (1982).

First, we reduce the elements in each row by their minimum value, and do the same for the columns. The total amount taken away is a *lower bound* for the optimal cost. At this stage, if the table shows an optimal solution, that is, a set of 0-entries in different rows and different columns, then the problem is solved: the list of locations (I, J) of those 0-entries is the optimal solution and the cost lower bound is the minimum cost. Otherwise, we must go on to adjust the table in the following way.

	1	2	3	4
1	3	2	0	3
2	0	1	3	7
3	2	0	2	3
4	0	3	2	5

	1	2	3	4
1	3	2	0	0
2	0	1	3	4
3	2	0	2	0
4	0	3	2	2

- Find a minimum set of horizontal and vertical lines to cross out all the 0-entries.
- Find the least uncrossed element. This element is subtracted from each uncrossed element and added to each element at the lines' intersections.

This process is repeated until an optimal solution is found.

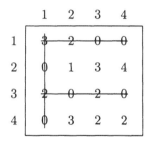

	1	2	3	4
1	4	2	0	0
2	0	0	2	3
3	3	0	2	0
4	0	2	1	1

The above algorithm is expressed in the programming style as follows:

> To find a *Job-Assignment* with *Minimum-Cost* do
>> set up the cost table T,
>> reduce the costs in table T
>>> giving new *Table* and *Cost* lower bound, then
>>
>> optimise *Table* and *Cost*
>>> to obtain *Job-Assignment* and *Minimum-Cost*.

> To reduce the costs in table T giving new *Table*
> and *Cost* lower bound do
>> reduce the rows of T giving $T1$ and first lower bound,
>> reduce the columns of $T1$
>>> giving new *Table* and new *Cost* lower bound.

To reduce the rows of T giving $T1$ and lower bound $V1$ do
>   for each row, check
>>   *if*   it contains 0 then leave it unchanged
>>   *else* find the least element in the row, and
>>   subtract it from every element of the row.

To optimise *Table* and *Cost* to obtain *Job-Assignment*
and *Minimum-Cost* do
>   *if*   *Table* already shows a solution, then
>   return the solution and the cost lower bound
>   as *Minimum-Cost*
>   *else* adjust *Table* to obtain new table and adjusted amount,
>   adjust *Cost* using the adjusted amount, and
>   repeat the process until a solution shows up.

Table contains a solution *if*
>   each row I has a 0-entry in column J_I such that
>   the J_I's are all different;
>   the solution is the list of *Job-Assignments* (I, J_I).

To adjust table T giving new table $T1$ and adjusted amount $C1$ do
>   find a minimum set of zero-lines (rows or columns containing 0),
> $C1$ is the minimum of the elements off those zero-lines,
>   adjust the rows of table T using the amount $C1$ giving $T1$.

To find a set of zero-lines do
>   find a 0-entry not yet crossed out, that is,
>>   not already on any zero-line obtained so far,
>   take either its row or column index to mark a zero-line,
>   then continue until no more 0-entries left uncrossed.

To adjust the rows of table T by amount C giving $T1$ do
>   for each row,
>>   reduce the uncrossed elements by C, and
>>   increase the elements at the lines' intersections by C,
>>   leaving other elements unchanged.

The lower level subalgorithms are straightforward. The program is given below.

```
assign_jobs(JobList,MinCost) :-
    cost_table(N,T),
    reduce_cost(N,T,Table,Cost),
    optimise(N,Table,Cost,JobList,MinCost).
```

```prolog
cost_table(N,Table) :-
    make_table(Table),
    length(Table,N).

reduce_cost(N,T,Table,Cost) :-
    reduce_rows(T,T1,0,V),transpose(N,T1,T2),
    reduce_rows(T2,T3,V,Cost),transpose(N,T3,Table).

reduce_rows([R|Rs],[R1|Rs1],V,V1) :-
    (member(e(_,_,0),R),!, R = R1, V = V2;
     setof(C,(I,J)^member(e(I,J,C),R),[C0|_]),
     setof(e(I,J,C1),
        C^ (member(e(I,J,C),R),C1 is C - C0), R1),
     V2 is V + C0),
    reduce_rows(Rs,Rs1,V2,V1).
reduce_rows([],[],V,V).

optimise(N,T,Cost,JobList,Cost) :-
    solution(T,[],JobList),!.
optimise(N,T,Cost,JobList,MinCost) :-
    adjust_cost(N,T,T1,ACost,M),
    NCost is Cost + ACost*(N-M),
    optimise(N,T1,NCost,JobList,MinCost).

solution([],_,[]) :- !.
solution([R|Rs],List,[(I,J)|IJList]) :-
    member(e(I,J,0),R),not(member(J,List)),
    solution(Rs,[J|List],IJList).

adjust_cost(N,T,T1,C1,ML) :-
    setof((K,L),zero_lines(N,T,[],0,L,K),[(ML,Lines)|_]),
    setof(C,(I,J)^uncrossed(Lines,T,I,J,C),[C1|_]),
    adjust_rows(Lines,C1,T,T1).

zero_lines(N,T,L,K,L1,K1) :-
    uncrossed(L,T,I,J,0),!,K < N, H is K+1,
    (Line = row:I; Line = col:J),
    zero_lines(N,T,[Line|L],H,L1,K1).
zero_lines(_,_,L,K,L,K).

uncrossed(L,T,I,J,C) :-
    member([e(I,K,D)|R],T), not(member(row:I,L)),
    member(e(I,J,C),[e(I,K,D)|R]), not(member(col:J,L)).
```

```
adjust_rows(Lines,C0,[R|Rs],[R1|Rs1]) :-
    setof(e(I,J,C1),
    C^ (member(e(I,J,C),R),adjust(Lines,I,J,C,C0,C1)),R1),
    adjust_rows(Lines,C0,Rs,Rs1).
adjust_rows(_,_,[],[]).

adjust(L,I,J,C,C0,C1) :-
    member(row:I,L),member(col:J,L),!, C1 is C + C0;
    (member(row:I,L);member(col:J,L)),!, C1 is C;
    C1 is C - C0.

member :-      % see Figure 2.13
make_table :-  % see Figure 6.22
transpose :-   % see Figure 6.23

table(1,1,6).          table(3,1,8).
table(1,2,5).          table(3,2,6).
table(1,3,3).          table(3,3,8).
table(1,4,6).          table(3,4,9).
table(2,1,5).          table(4,1,3).
table(2,2,6).          table(4,2,6).
table(2,3,8).          table(4,3,5).
table(2,4,12).         table(4,4,8).
```

Note from procedure *optimise* that if the cost-table has N rows, in which M lines (consisting of R rows and C columns) are crossed out, and if the minimum of the uncrossed elements is $ACost$, then the increase in cost lower bound is $ACost * (N - R) - ACost * C = ACost * (N - M)$.

We can now obtain an optimal solution for the job assignment problem by entering the following query:

```
?- assign_jobs(JobList,Cost).

JobList = [(1,3),(2,2),(3,4),(4,1)]
Cost = 21 ->
```

We also note from procedure *adjust_cost* that, for a large number of jobs, the subgoal

```
setof((K,L),zero_lines(N,T,[],0,L,K),[(ML,Lines)|_])
```

may cause stack overflow. In this case, it is necessary to replace this system goal by a new goal *setof_lines*($N, T, Lines, ML$) (which is slower but more space efficient), where the procedure *setof_lines* is defined as follows:

```
setof_lines(N,T,Lines,ML) :- assert(lines(_,100)),
    zero_lines(N,T,[],0,L,K),lines(L0,K0), K < K0,
    retract(lines(L0,K0)),assert(lines(L,K)),fail.
setof_lines(_,_,Lines,ML) :- retract(lines(Lines,ML)).
```

6.6 In the procedures *insert_avl* and *delete_avl* (Figures 6.27, 6.29, and 6.30), the two subprocedures *balance* and *balance2* are very similar. They only differ in the case where either no rebalance is required or a single (right or left) rotation is needed.

Write a common version of procedure *balance* that incorporates both cases for insertion and deletion.

Solution:

We note first that the procedure *balance* of *insert_avl* deals with a subtree that might have "grown", while the procedure *balance2* of *delete_avl* treats a subtree that might have "shrunk".

So to distinguish the two cases, we introduce an extra argument *Change* for the procedure *balance*, which may contain the value "grown" or "shrunk". Thus, in the procedure *insert_avl*, all calls to *balance* are replaced with *balance(grown,...)*, whereas in the procedure *delete_avl*, all calls to *balance2* are replaced with *balance(shrunk,...)*. Then, the common version of the procedure *balance* is as follows.

```
% No rebalance is required
balance(Change,S,IA,I,NI,NewTree,NewTree-NIA) :-
    subtree_not(Change,I,NI),!, NIA = IA;
    IA =:= 0,!,    NIA = S;
    IA + S =:= 3,!, NIA = 0.

% Rebalance by right-rotation
balance(_,1,1,_,_,bt(bt(LB,B,RB)-IB,A,RA),
                bt(LB,B,bt(RB,A,RA)-NIA)-NIB) :-
    IB =:= 1,!, NIA = 0, NIB = 0;
    IB =:= 0,!, NIA = 1, NIB = 2.

% Rebalance by left-right rotation
balance(_,1,1,_,_,bt(bt(LB,B,bt(LC,C,RC)-IC)-2,A,RA),
                bt(bt(LB,B,LC)-IB,C,bt(RC,A,RA)-IA)-0) :-
    IC =:= 0, IA = 0, IB = 0,!;
            IA is (IC+1) mod 3,
            IB is (IA+1) mod 3.
```

```
% Rebalance by left-rotation
balance(_,2,2,_,_,bt(LA,A,bt(LB,B,RB)-IB),
                 bt(bt(LA,A,LB)-NIA,B,RB)-NIB) :-
   IB =:= 2,!, NIA = 0, NIB = 0;
   IB =:= 0,!, NIA = 2, NIB = 1.

% Rebalance by right-left rotation
balance(_,2,2,_,_,bt(LA,A,bt(bt(LC,C,RC)-IC,B,RB)-1),
                 bt(bt(LA,A,LC)-IA,C,bt(RC,B,RB)-IB)-0) :-
   IC =:= 0, IA = 0,IB = 0,!;
              IB is (IC+1) mod 3,
              IA is (IB+1) mod 3.

subtree_not(grown,I,NI) :-
   NI* (NI-I) =:= 0.
subtree_not(shrunk,NI,I) :-
   I* (NI-1)* (NI-2) =:= 0.
```

Supplementary problems

6.7 (a) Write a procedure *satisfy(P,L)* that receives a unary predicate symbol P and returns the list L of all terms X such that $P(X)$ succeeds.

(b) Given a database that contains two relations: *father(X, Y)* means "X is father of Y", and *male(X)* means "X is male", write a procedure *male_gene(X)* to find a father X whose children are all male.

6.8 (a) Generalise the procedure *mapcar* of Figure 6.12 to handle functions of any arity. That is, *mapcar(F,A,L)* receives a function symbol F of any arity n and a list of arguments $A = (A_1, \ldots, A_n)$, where, for each i, $A_i = [X_{i1}, \ldots, X_{ip}]$, and returns a list $L = [F(X_{11}, \ldots, X_{n1}), \ldots, F(X_{1p}, \ldots, X_{np})]$. For example:

```
?- mapcar('*',([1,2,3],[4,5,6]),L).
L = [4,10,18]
```

(b) Write a procedure *inner_product(X, Y, V)* that receives two vectors X and Y (of the same dimension) and returns the value of their inner product $X \cdot Y$. (Hint: use the procedure *mapcar* defined in part (a) and the procedure *reduce* of Figure 6.12.)

6.9 (a) Provide appropriate definitions for the infix and postfix operators in the following sentences so that the sentences are recognised by Prolog as legal clauses to be stored in memory:

> X admires Y if Y isa_hero.
> X isa_hero if X went_to_war and
> X came_back_alive.
>
> john went_to_war.
> john came_back_alive.
> cathy is_fiancee_of john.

(b) Test your program with the following queries:

```
?- : cathy admires Whom.
?- : john went_to_war.
?- : Who isa_hero.
```

6.10 Consider the game of noughts-and-crosses. The game has two players and a square board of grids. One player uses a nought and the other uses a cross, and they take turns to mark a square on the board. Whichever player has three marks in a line wins the game.

(a) Design data structure to represent a board of the game.

(b) Write a program to simulate a game between a user and the system. (Hint: use the built-in predicates *var* and *nonvar* to inspect the board.)

6.11 (a) Take a Pascal program and design a graph to represent the identifiers used in the program and their referring relationship (i.e., indicate which identifiers are referred to by others).

(b) Run the program *topo_sort* of Figure 6.18 to sort the graph of part (a) into topological order. (This topological order indicates which identifiers should be defined before the others.)

6.12 Write a procedure *derive(E,X,F)* that receives an algebraic term E and a single letter X, and returns a term F that is the derivative of E with respect to X.

For example,

```
?- derive(sin(a*x)+y,x,F).
F = a*cos(a*x)
```

(Hint: represent all derivative rules by a relation *der* and all simplification rules by a relation *simp*. For each function symbol that may appear in E, write a rule for *der* and a rule for *simp*.)

6.13 Write a program to perform the task of a course advisor for students of a computing course at a university. The system should be able to advise on the following matters:

- Given a list of course units chosen by a student, the course advisor should tell if any of those units have timetable clash.

- Given a student ID and a list of course units chosen by this student for the current semester, the course advisor should tell if any of those units are not allowed due to the lack of prerequisites.

- Given a student ID, the course advisor should advise the student what course units need to be taken for the current semester. This advice is based on the course's program and the student's past credit record. The number of units to be taken may range from 2 to 5, depending on the advisor's judgement that the student is a poor, average, good, or excellent student.

6.14 Prove (or disprove) the correctness of the programs *insert_avl*, *delete_avl*, and *insert_bt* (Figures 6.27, 6.29, 6.30, 6.35, and 6.36), using the technique described in Section 5.5 of Chapter 5.

Chapter 7

Search techniques

7.1 Search: a problem-solving technique

In the preceding chapter we have briefly discussed a programming technique called *expand-and-test* in which we start with a primary object and gradually expand it until it meets the requirements of a solution to a given problem. This expand-and-test procedure is the basis of many search methods, which form a powerful technique of problem-solving, particularly in the field of artificial intelligence.

In order to apply search techniques to solve problems, we adopt the view that a problem is a world in a bad state, and to solve a problem is to change the related world from its current state to a desirable state.

Thus, solving a problem using search requires two main tasks:

- Represent the states of a world;

- Find a procedure to change the world's states.

7.1.1   Representation of states

Consider a world that is the object of our investigation. From a certain point of view, the world consists of a number of relevant entities, each of which can be in several different states. The state of the world is composed of the states of its entities.

So a world's state can be represented by a *list of variables*, each of which represents the state of a relevant entity of the world.

EXAMPLE 7.1   The state of a nation's economy can be represented by the following variables:

- National income per person;

- Trade balance (surplus/deficit);

- Foreign debt;

- Inflation rate;

- Interest rate.

A desirable state of the economy is one in which the first two variables have high values and the last three variables have low values.

EXAMPLE 7.2   The state of a motor car is represented by a long list of variables, including the following:

- The starter;

- The radiator;

- The battery; etc.

Each of the above variables may have two or three states: defective, removed, or perfect. A desirable state of the motor car is one in which all of its components are in *perfect* state.

7.1.2 Change of states

As the purpose of solving a search problem is to find a desirable state of the world under study, we must know how to change the world or how the world changes itself from one state to another.

For example, the state of a nation's economy as described in Example 7.1 can be changed by economic measures as shown in Figure 7.1. (Here, the state values are simplified to be rough level-indicators.)

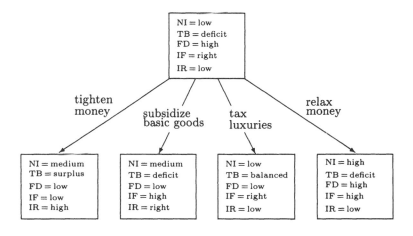

FIGURE 7.1 Change of states of a nation's economy.

Thus, the state transition of a world can be described by a directed graph in which each node represents a state and each directed edge represents a change of states. Searching for a desired state of a world becomes searching the graph for a node that satisfies some specified conditions.

Generally, any acyclic-directed graph can be converted into a tree. The root of the tree represents the *initial state*, and the node being searched for represents the *final state*. Any sequence of successive nodes is called a *path*, and a path connecting the initial state to the final state is called an *answer-path*. Figure 7.2 shows the conversion of an acyclic graph into a tree.

7.2 Search strategies

Most search strategies are based on the following two basic approaches:

- *Depth-first search*;
- *Breadth-first search*.

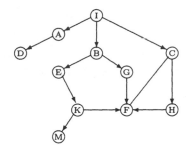 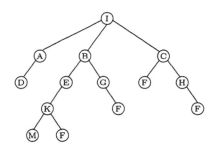

FIGURE 7.2 Conversion of an acyclic graph into a tree.

In traversing a tree, with depth-first search we go to the left as far as possible before branching to the next right branch, whereas with breadth-first search, we visit all nodes of one level before moving to the next level.

Consider the tree of Figure 7.2 in which the root I represents the initial state and the nodes F represent the final desired state. Figure 7.3(a) shows the order of nodes visited by a depth-first search, and Figure 7.3(b) shows those visited by a breadth-first search, in the course of searching for the final state F.

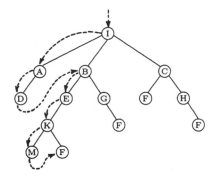 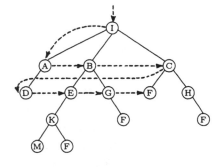

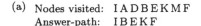

(a) Nodes visited: I A D B E K M F
    Answer-path: I B E K F

(b) Nodes visited: I A B C D E G F
    Answer-path: I C F

FIGURE 7.3 Depth-first and breadth-first traversing of a tree.

The depth-first search is simple, but it may result in an answer-path that is longer than necessary. In some cases, the depth-first search may get stuck in an infinite branch while the desired state is in another branch.

On the other hand, the breadth-first search ensures that the final state is found (if it exists), and the answer-path always contains the minimum number of nodes needed. The breadth-first search is, however, more difficult to implement than the depth-first search as we shall see in the next sections.

The breadth-first search has two variants, namely:

- *Wave search*;
- *Inter-wave search*.

In wave search, we do not visit one node at a time, but we consider all nodes of the same level at once as a *wave*. The wave is expanded one level at a time, until it hits the final desired state (Figure 7.4 (a)).

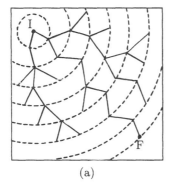   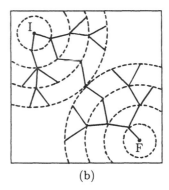

(a)   (b)

FIGURE 7.4 Wave search and inter-wave search.

Thus, wave search is likely to find the final state faster than breadth-first search, but it obviously requires much more space. A way to reduce the amount of required space is to expand the waves from the initial and the final state in parallel. When the waves meet each other, we obtain an answer-path (Figure 7.4 (b)). We call this strategy *inter-wave search* (which is often called the *bidirectional search*).

The above-described search strategies are classified as *nonguided* search. The depth-first search and breadth-first search can be improved by using some guidance in the form of *heuristics* or *evaluation functions*.

> ▷ *Heuristics* are experience-based rules that are used to select the next state in a search.

Following are some examples of heuristics:

- In searching traffic roads, we may have some rough idea about the direction of the destination. So, to move ahead, a rule of thumb is to select the next road intersection that is approximately in the estimated direction.

- In taking economic measures, a government must choose among several options of measure the one that meets its policy of priorities.

- In controlling a robot's activities, it is sensible to advise the robot not to pick up something it just put down, or not to unscrew a bolt which it had just screwed in.

Heuristics are vague and sometimes contradictory. A more accurate guidance for searching is the use of evaluation functions.

▷ An *evaluation function* is a function that gives each state a numeric value, so that in searching for the next state, the one with the least value is to be selected.

Here, the state with the least evaluation function value is considered to be the one that is most promising in leading towards the final state.

Following are some examples of evaluation functions:

- In searching traffic roads, the distance from a road intersection to the destination can be used as an evaluation function. So, the next intersection on the move would be the one that is closest (in bird-flight distance) to the destination.

- In taking economic measures, we can use a mathematically formulated economic function as an evaluation function.

- In controlling a robot's activities, the number of remaining jobs to be done can be used as an evaluation function.

The following are two search procedures that use evaluation functions:

- *Hill-climbing search* = depth-first search + evaluation function;
- *Best-first search* = breadth-first search + evaluation function.

With hill-climbing search, we "climb" from one level of a tree to another using the node having the lowest evaluation function value. For example, consider the tree of Figure 7.5 (a) in which the number above each node is the evaluation function value of that node. We start at node I and climb to node B, which has the least value among A, B, C. From B, we move to G, which is the better of E and G, and finally we arrive at F. So, in this case, the first answer produced by a hill-climbing search is *IBGF*. Observe that with hill-climbing search, we do not move back to the previous level unless we fail to move ahead. So, if the evaluation function is badly chosen, then it may lead us away from rather than closer to the final state.

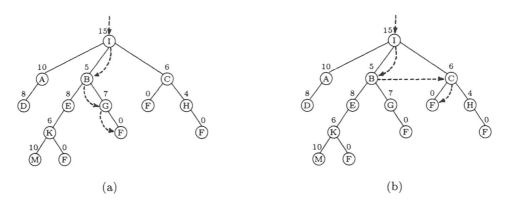

(a)   (b)

FIGURE 7.5 (a) Hill-climbing search.   (b) Best-first search.

With best-first search, we are allowed to compare the best next node with those in the current level to determine if we should move ahead or try another node in the current level. For example, consider the tree of Figure 7.5 (b). We start at node I and move to node B, which is the best among A, B, C. But when we compare the next node G with C, we find that C is the better one, so we move to C instead. Then from C we go directly to F. So, the answer produced by best-first search is *ICF*. (Note that for the given small tree, breadth-first search and best-first search produce the same answer, but this is not necessarily true in general; e.g., see Figure 7.7.)

Search procedures that use evaluation functions are classified as *lookahead* search. Another kind of function that involves the past rather than the future is called *cost function*.

▷ A *cost function* is a function that gives each path (from the initial state) a numeric value. So, in searching for the next state, the one that results in a path with the least cost function value is to be selected.

Here are some examples of cost functions:

• In searching traffic roads, the total road distance from the initial location to a road intersection can be used as a cost function. So the next intersection on the move is the one with the shortest distance from the initial location.

- In taking economic measure, the total loss in trade plus the decrease in national production can be used as a cost function.
- In controlling a robot's activities, the total estimated time for the jobs so far can be used as a cost function.

The following are two search procedures that use cost functions:

- *Best-cost search* = breadth-first search + cost function;
- *Best-path search* = breadth-first search + cost function + evaluation function.

Consider the tree of Figure 7.6 (a) in which the numbers beside the edges are to be used to calculate the cost of the paths. For example, the cost of the path IAD is $9 + 7 = 16$.

With *best-cost search*, we begin from node I and we move to node B since the path IB has least cost among the paths IA, IB, IC. From B we could move to E or G, but these paths have higher cost than the path IC, so we abandon B and take the path IC. From C we could move to F or H, but now these paths have higher cost than the path IBE, so we abandon C and take the path IBE. From E we could move to K, but the cost would be higher than that of the path IA, so we abandon the path IBE to take the path IA. From A we could move to D, but again the cost is higher than that of the path IBG, so we abandon A and take the path IBG. Then, in the same manner, we abandon IBG to take the path ICH, and finally abandon ICH to take the path $IBGF$. So, the answer produced by best-cost search is $IBGF$. (Note that for the given small tree, best-cost search and hill-climbing search happen to produce the same answer, but this is not necessarily true in general.)

Now consider the tree of Figure 7.6 (b), in which the number beneath each node is the sum of the node's evaluation function value (which appears above the node) and the cost of the path from I to that node.

With *best-path search*, we begin from node I and we move to node B since it has the least sum among A, B, C. From B we jump to C, which has least sum among all the nodes we could move to. Then, in the same manner, we move from C to H, and finally from H to F. So, the answer is $ICHF$.

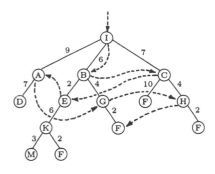

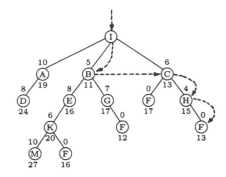

(a) Best-cost search
     Answer-path: I B G F

(b) Best-path search
     Answer-path: I C H F

FIGURE 7.6 Best-cost and best-path search.

Notes

1. The *best-cost search* is also called *branch-and-bound* search, because it jumps around from one state to another (see Figure 7.6 (a)). Note, however, that the best-first search also jumps around within the state tree, though probably not so wildly as in the best-cost search. Therefore, we avoid using the name "branch-and-bound", which is ambiguous.

2. The *best-path search* is also called *A**-search and is the best of all search strategies presented above.

Following is a summary of the results of different search procedures.

- *Depth-first search* finds any answer-path. If the problem states are represented by a tree, then depth-first search produces the leftmost answer-path first.

- *Breadth-first search* (also *wave* and *inter-wave* search) finds the answer-path with the minimum number of intermediary states.

- *Hill-climbing search* finds an answer-path in which each state is the best state in the direction of the final state that is accessible from the previous state.

- *Best-first search* finds the answer-path that is most direct towards the final state.

- *Best-cost search* finds the answer-path with minimum cost.

- *Best-path search* finds the answer-path that is the best compromise of cost and directness towards the final state.

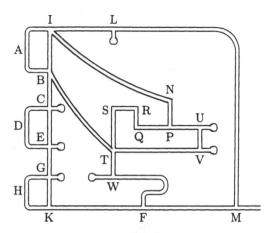

FIGURE 7.7 Different routes from I to F in a road map.

Figure 7.7 shows a small map of city roads where different routes from a place I to another place F can be found by different procedures. Here, the evaluation function is the bird-flight distance from any road intersection to the destination F plus the estimated waiting time at that intersection, and the cost function is the total road distance from the location to the departure point I. The results are listed below (and are to be justified by the programs given in the following sections).

Depth-first search:	$I\,A\,B\,C\,D\,E\,G\,H\,K\,F$
Breadth-first search:	$I\,L\,M\,F$
Hill-climbing search:	$I\,N\,P\,Q\,R\,S\,T\,W\,F$
Best-first search:	$I\,N\,P\,U\,V\,T\,W\,F$
Best-cost search:	$I\,B\,C\,E\,G\,K\,F$
Best-path search:	$I\,B\,T\,W\,F.$

In the next sections, we study the implementation in Prolog of the above-described search procedures.

7.3 Depth-first search

Given a system that represents a certain world, the purpose of a search is to find a sequence of state transitions that brings the system from its initial state to a final desired state.

In general, the system's initial state is known and unique, but its final state may not be unique or it may be even unknown. For example, in a game of chess, we want to find a sequence of moves leading to a winning state without knowing fully what the final state would be. We can, however, recognise the final state once it occurs.

So, to find an answer-path using depth-first search, we start with an initial path consisting of the initial state and we extend this path, step by step, until it reaches a state which is recognised to be the final state.

The algorithm for extending a path in depth-first search is as follows:

To extend a path into an answer-path do
    if the path has reached the final state
        then return it as an answer-path
        else *if* the current path can be extended to a new state
            then save the current state, and
                continue to extend the path from the new state
            else backtrack to extend the path from the previous
                state, in a different direction.

To extend a path to a new state do
        find the next state of the last state in the path
        that does not occur in the path; the state
        found is a new state.

Path	Effect
I	initial
I A	extend
I A D	extend
I B	backtrack
I B E	extend
I B E K	extend
I B E K M	extend
I B E K F	backtrack

FIGURE 7.8 Development of a path in depth-first search.

When the above algorithm of *depth-first search* is applied to the state tree of Figure 7.3 (a), where the root I represents the initial state and the nodes F represent the final desired state, the search path develops as shown in Figure 7.8.

The program *depth_first_search* is shown in Figure 7.9, where the predicates *initial_state*, *final_state*, and *next_state* are to be defined for the particular problem.

```
depth_first_search(AnsPath) :-
    initial_state(Init),
    depth_first([Init],AnsPath).

depth_first([S|Path],[S]) :-
    final_state(S),!.
depth_first([S|Path],[S|AnsPath]) :-
    extend([S|Path],S1),
    depth_first([S1,S|Path],AnsPath).

extend([S|Path],S1) :-
    next_state(S,S1),
    not(member_state(S1,[S|Path])).
```

FIGURE 7.9 Program *depth_first_search*.

For most search problems, an answer-path consisting of a sequence of states is an adequate description of the development of the world under study.

For some problems, however, it may be more convenient to associate with each problem state a term representing the operation (or the action) that changes the world from its previous state to the current state. In this case, a problem state is represented by a pair (M, S) where M represents the operation that results in the world's current state S. Then, the predicate *member_state* used in procedure *extend* of Figure 7.9 is defined as follows:

```
member_state((_,S),[(_,S)|_]).
member_state(X,[_|T]) :- member_state(X,T).
```

In the normal circumstances, the predicate *member_state* is defined in the same way as the predicate *member* of Figure 2.13.

Following is a classic problem that is typically suitable for the depth-first search technique.

EXAMPLE 7.3   A farmer has a wolf, a goat, and a cabbage on the north side of the river, and also a small boat. He wants to bring his property to the south side of the river, but the boat can only carry himself and at most one of the three. So, obviously, he will have to cross the river several times to bring all of his property to the other side. The problem is that if he leaves the wolf with the goat unattended then he will have no more goat; also if the goat is left behind with the cabbage, then the cabbage will be finished. The farmer wants our advice on a way to bring his property safely to the south side.

In this problem, there are four relevant entities: the farmer, the wolf, the goat, and the cabbage (the boat is irrelevant as it is always with the farmer). So, it is natural to represent a problem state by a list of four variables representing the above-mentioned entities:

$$[F, W, G, C].$$

Each of these entities can only have two states: "n" for north, and "s" for south. The initial state is when all the entities are on the north side, and the final state is when they are on the south side.

```
initial_state([n,n,n,n]).
final_state([s,s,s,s]).

next_state(S,S1) :- move(S,S1),safe(S1).

move([F,W,G,C],[F1,W,G,C])   :- cross(F,F1).
move([F,F,G,C],[F1,F1,G,C])  :- cross(F,F1).
move([F,W,F,C],[F1,W,F1,C])  :- cross(F,F1).
move([F,W,G,F],[F1,W,G,F1])  :- cross(F,F1).

safe([F,W,G,C]) :- F = G,!; F = W, F = C.

cross(n,s).
cross(s,n).
```

FIGURE 7.10 Program for the farmer problem.

The world changes from a current state S to a next state $S1$ when the farmer makes a move that changes the state S to $S1$ under the condition that $S1$ is safe. There are only four possible moves: either the farmer crosses the river alone, or with one of his three items. A state is *safe* if either the farmer is with the goat, or he is with both the wolf and the cabbage. Figure 7.10 shows the rules and facts needed to run the depth-first search program of Figure 7.9.

To test the program of Figures 7.9 and 7.10 (remember to add the definition of *member_state*) we enter the following query:

```
?- depth_first_search(AnsPath).
```

```
AnsPath = [[n,n,n,n],[s,n,s,n],[n,n,s,n],[s,s,s,n],
[n,s,n,n],[s,s,n,s],[n,s,n,s],[s,s,s,s]] ->;
```

```
AnsPath = [[n,n,n,n],[s,n,s,n],[n,n,s,n],[s,n,s,s],
[n,n,n,s],[s,s,n,s],[n,s,n,s],[s,s,s,s]] ->;
```

```
no
```

The result shows that there are two answers to the problem. The first answer indicates that the farmer first takes the goat with him to the south side, leaves the goat there and goes back alone; he then takes the wolf to the south side and brings the goat back to the north side, then takes the cabbage to the south side, goes back alone, and finally takes the goat with him to the south side. The second answer can be explained similarly.

7.4   Breadth-first search

With breadth-first search, to be able to visit all states of one level before moving to the next level, we must store all paths developed to the current level. These paths are stored in a queue so that their last states are visited one after another and their extended paths are added to the end of the queue for the next level visit.

So, the algorithm of breadth-first search is as follows:

To search for an answer-path using breadth-first search do
create a queue that contains the only path consisting of
the initial state, and apply breadth-first procedure
to expand this queue until an answer-path is found.

To expand a path-queue in finding an answer-path do
if any path in the queue has reached the final state
then   return the path as an answer-path
else   expand the first path of the queue in all possible ways,
add the extended paths to the end of the queue,
remove the first path from the queue, and
continue to expand the new queue.

To expand a *Path* in all possible ways to obtain a queue of extended
paths do
collect all paths $S + Path$, where S is an extended state from *Path*,
into a list, then convert the list into a queue.

When the above algorithm of *breadth-first search* is applied to the state tree
of Figure 7.3 (b), where the root I represents the initial state and the nodes
F represent the final desired state, the initial queue develops as shown in
Figure 7.11.

```
I  │ I A │     │     │
   │ I B │ I B │     │
   │ I C │ I C │ I C │
   │     │ I A D│ I A D│ I A D
   │     │     │ I B E│ I B E
   │     │     │ I B G│ I B G
   │     │     │     │ I C F  ←  this path reaches
   │     │     │     │ I C H     the final state
```

FIGURE 7.11 Development of a path-queue in breadth-first search.

The program *breadth_first_search* is shown in Figure 7.12, where the predicates *qmember* and *list_to_queue* are defined in Chapter 6 (page 220), the predicate *extend* is defined in Figure 7.9, the predicate *reverse* is given in Problem 3.2, and the predicates *initial_state*, *final_state*, and *next_state* are to be defined for the particular problem.

```
breadth_first_search(AnsPath) :-
    initial_state(Init),
    breadth_first([[Init]|Q]-Q,AnsPath).

breadth_first(Q-Qt,AnsPath) :-
    qmember([S|Path],Q-Qt),final_state(S),!,
    reverse([S|Path],[],AnsPath).
breadth_first([Path|Q]-Qt,AnsPath) :-
    expand(Path,Qt-Qs),
    breadth_first(Q-Qs,AnsPath).

expand(Path,Queue) :-
    setof([S|Path],extend(Path,S),List),!,
    list_to_queue(List,Queue).
expand(Path,Q-Q).
```

FIGURE 7.12 Program *breadth_first_search*.

Notes

1. The program *breadth_first_search* of Figure 7.12 uses a dynamic queue to store the developed paths. For large and complex search problems the use of a dynamic queue may cause stack-overflow. In this case, we could adopt a less stylish approach by employing a static queue and using the built-in predicates *assert* and *retract* to manipulate the queue. This efficient version of the breadth-first search program is given in Problem 7.7.

2. As usual, we assume that the search problem under study does have an answer. If this assurance is not granted, then we must add the following clause:

   ```
   breadth_first([]-[],_) :- !, fail.
   ```

   to the program of Figure 7.12 as the first clause of procedure *breadth_first* in order to prevent its being trapped in an infinite loop.

EXAMPLE 7.4   Consider the map of city roads given in Figure 7.7. Let us find a route from I to F that contains the minimum number of road intersections or corners.

Here, we are only interested in the road intersections (or corners) of the city. So, the problem state is represented by a single variable S whose values are single letters that mark the intersections in the city (in practice a road intersection may be represented by a term such as *wall_st + akuna_ave*).

```
initial_state('I').
final_state('F').

next_state(S,S1) :-
    next_corners(S,Corners),
    member(S1,Corners).

next_corners('I',['A','B','N','L']).
next_corners('A',['B','I']).
next_corners('B',['A','C','T']).
next_corners('C',['D','E']).
next_corners('D',['C','E']).
next_corners('E',['D','G']).
next_corners('G',['H','K']).
next_corners('H',['G','K']).
next_corners('K',['H','F']).
next_corners('F',['K','W','M']).
next_corners('W',['T','F']).
next_corners('T',['B','S','V','W']).
next_corners('S',['T','R']).
next_corners('R',['S','Q']).
next_corners('Q',['R','P']).
next_corners('P',['Q','N','U']).
next_corners('U',['P','V']).
next_corners('V',['T','U']).
next_corners('N',['P','I']).
next_corners('L',['I','M']).
next_corners('M',['L','F']).
```

FIGURE 7.13 A database of city-road intersections.

Figure 7.13 shows the definitions of the predicates *initial_state*, *final_state*, *next_state*, and a database of city-road intersections. (For a larger database, it would be more convenient to represent road intersections by positive integers, each of which refers to a list of names of the roads meeting at the intersection.)

To run the program of Figures 7.12 and 7.13 (remember to add the definitions of predicates *qmember, list_to_queue, extend, member,* and *reverse*), we enter the following query:

```
?- breadth_first_search(AnsPath).
AnsPath = ['I','L','M','F'] ->;
no
```

The result shows that there is only one route from I to F with a minimum number of intersections (in general, there may be more than one such route). Let us compare the above result with the answers produced by depth-first search by running the program of Figure 7.9 using the data of Figure 7.13.

```
?- depth_first_search(AnsPath).
AnsPath = ['I','A','B','C','D','E','G','H','K','F'] ->
```

If we repeatedly press the semicolon key, then we will eventually obtain an answer-path with a minimum number of intersections, possibly without being aware of it.

7.5   Wave search

Wave search is a variant of breadth-first search. In wave search, we expand all paths at once as a wave. So we do not need a queue, but we simply represent the wave as a list of paths. The wave is expanded one level at a time, until it hits the final desired state.

The algorithm of wave search is as follows:

To search for an answer-path using wave search do
        start with an initial wave that contains the only path
        consisting of the initial state, and apply wave procedure
        to expand this wave until it hits the final state.

To expand a wave in finding an answer-path do
    if any path in the wave hits the final state
        then return the path as an answer-path
        else expand the wave by one level into a new wave, and
            continue the expansion with the new wave.

To expand *Wave* into *NewWave* do
  if   *Wave* is empty then *NewWave* is empty
  else expand the first path in *Wave* into N paths, and
        expand the remaining paths in *Wave* into R paths, then
        append these N paths and R paths to give *NewWave*.

When the above algorithm of *wave search* is applied to the state tree of
Figure 7.3 (b), where the root I represents the initial state and the nodes F
represent the final state, the wave develops as shown in Figure 7.14.

$$
I \left|
\begin{array}{l}
IA \\
IB \\
IC
\end{array}
\right|
\begin{array}{l}
IAD \\
IBE \\
IBG \\
ICF \; \leftarrow \; \text{this path hits} \\
 \text{the final state} \\
ICH
\end{array}
$$

FIGURE 7.14 Development of a wave in wave search.

The program *wave_search* is presented in Figure 7.15, where the following
predicates have been defined before: *member* in Figure 2.13, *reverse* in Problem 3.2, *append* in Figure 2.21, and *extend* in Figure 7.9.

It is worth noting that the predicate *expand_wave* of program *wave_search*
(Figure 7.15) can be defined more elegantly as follows:

```
expand_wave(Wave,NewWave) :-
    mapcar(expand,Wave,Lists),
    reduce(append,Lists,[],NewWave).
```

where the predicates *mapcar* and *reduce* are defined in Figure 6.12. However,
this requires the inclusion of procedures *mapcar, reduce,* and *apply* (Figure
6.11), which we think the user may be reluctant to do. Also, this version of
expand_wave is slightly less efficient than the one given in Figure 7.15.

To test the program of Figure 7.15 we use the data given in Figure 7.13
(and add the definitions of *member, reverse, append, extend,* and *member_state*) and enter the following query:

```
?- wave_search(AnsPath).
AnsPath = ['I','L','M','F'] ->
```

```
wave_search(AnsPath) :-
    initial_state(Init),
    wave([[Init]],AnsPath).

wave(Wave,AnsPath) :-
    member([S|Path],Wave),final_state(S),!,
    reverse([S|Path],[],AnsPath).
wave(Wave,AnsPath) :-
    expand_wave(Wave,NewWave),
    wave(NewWave,AnsPath).

expand_wave([],[]) :- !.
expand_wave([Path|Rest],NewWave) :-
    expand(Path,NPaths),
    expand_wave(Rest,RPaths),
    append(NPaths,RPaths,NewWave).

expand(Path,NPaths) :-
    setof([S|Path],extend(Path,S),NPaths),!.
expand(_,[]).
```

FIGURE 7.15 Program *wave_search*.

The result is in accord with that of breadth-first search. We note that for the given small problem, wave search is slightly faster than breadth-first search. For larger and more complex problems, wave search should be much faster than breadth-first search, provided that the machine in use has a large enough memory.

7.6 Inter-wave search

Inter-wave search is another variant of breadth-first search. In inter-wave search, we expand two waves in parallel, one from the initial state and the other from the final state. When the waves meet each other we obtain an answer-path.

It should be pointed out immediately that inter-wave search can be used only if the problem's final state is explicitly representable. Also for simplicity we assume that the representation of the final state is unique. (The case where there is more than one representation of the final state is discussed in Problem 7.3.)

The algorithm of inter-wave search is as follows:

To search for an answer-path using inter-wave search do
start with two initial waves: the first wave contains the only path consisting of the initial state, the second wave contains the only path consisting of the final state, and apply inter-wave procedure to expand the waves until they meet each other.

To expand *Wave1* and *Wave2* in finding an answer-path do
if any path in *Wave1* meets a path in *Wave2*
then return the joined path as an answer-path
else expand *Wave1* by one level into *NewWave1*, change side to *Wave2*'s side, and continue the expansion of *Wave2* and *NewWave1*.

```
inter_wave_search(AnsPath) :-
    initial_state(Init),
    final_state(Final),
    inter_wave(0,[[Init]],[[Final]],AnsPath).

inter_wave(Side,Wave1,Wave2,AnsPath) :-
    member([S|Path1],Wave1),
    member([S|Path2],Wave2),!,
    join(Side,Path1,[S|Path2],AnsPath).
inter_wave(Side,Wave1,Wave2,AnsPath) :-
    expand_wave(Side,Wave1,NewWave1),
    change_side(Side,OppSide),
    inter_wave(OppSide,Wave2,NewWave1,AnsPath).

join(0,Path1,Path2,AnsPath) :- reverse(Path1,Path2,AnsPath).
join(1,Path1,Path2,AnsPath) :- reverse(Path2,Path1,AnsPath).

change_side(I,J)  :- J is 1-I.
```

FIGURE 7.16 Program *inter_wave_search* (top level).

The top-level of program *inter_wave_search* is presented in Figure 7.16. The procedure *expand_wave* of Figure 7.16 is the same as in Figure 7.15, except that it contains a *Side* to indicate the direction of wave expansion. This direction has a crucial effect on the extension of a path. For example, in searching for traffic roads it is possible that we can go from *A* to *B*, but not from *B* to *A* as the road is only one-way. The full definition of procedure *expand_wave* is given in Figure 7.17.

```
expand_wave(_,[],[]) :- !.
expand_wave(Side,[Path|Rest],NewWave) :-
    expand(Side,Path,NPaths),
    expand_wave(Side,Rest,RPaths),
    append(NPaths,RPaths,NewWave).

expand(Side,Path,NPaths) :-
    setof([S|Path],extend(Side,Path,S),NPaths),!.
expand(Side,Path,[]).

extend(Side,[S|Path],S1) :-
    (Side = 0,next_state(S,S1);
     Side = 1,next_state(S1,S)),
    not(member(S1,[S|Path])).
```

FIGURE 7.17 Procedure *expand_wave* of *inter_wave_search*.

To test the program of Figures 7.16 and 7.17 (after adding the definitions of *member, reverse,* and *append*), we use the data of Figure 7.13 and enter the following query:

```
?- inter_wave_search(AnsPath).
AnsPath = ['I','L','M','F'] ->
```

The result is in accord with that of *wave search* and *breadth-first search*. Note that *inter-wave search* is as fast as *wave search* but requires far less memory than wave search.

7.7   Hill-climbing search

Hill-climbing search is depth-first search guided by an evaluation function. In hill-climbing search we move from one state, not to any next state like in depth-first search, but to the next state that gives the best chance of getting closer to the final state. This most promising next state is determined by the evaluation function.

So, the program of hill-climbing search is the same as that of depth-first search, except that the goal *next_state(S,S1)* is replaced with the goal *best_next_state(S,S1)*. The program *hill_climb_search* is shown in Figure 7.18, where the predicates *initial_state*, *final_state*, *next_state*, and *value* are to be defined for individual problems.

```
hill_climb_search(AnsPath) :-
    initial_state(Init),
    hill_climb([Init],AnsPath).

hill_climb([S|Path],[S]) :-
    final_state(S),!.
hill_climb([S|Path],[S|AnsPath]) :-
    extend([S|Path],S1),
    hill_climb([S1,S|Path],AnsPath).

extend([S|Path],S1) :-
    best_next_state(S,S1),
    not(member_state(S1,[S|Path])).

best_next_state(S,S1) :-
    setof((V,NS),(next_state(S,NS),value(NS,V)),List),
    member((V1,S1),List).
```

FIGURE 7.18   Program *hill_climb_search*.

EXAMPLE 7.5   Consider again the road map of Figure 7.7. We wish to find a route from I to F using the technique of hill-climbing search.

We define an evaluation function for this problem as follows. The value of a state representing a road intersection or corner is defined to be the bird-flight distance from the intersection to F plus a number indicating the estimated waiting time at that intersection. It has been recorded that waiting times at intersections are almost the same except at K, where the waiting time is tripled because of the existence of schools and factories in that area.

Figure 7.19 shows the rules and facts that are to be used in calculating the evaluation function values.

```
value(S,V) :-
    coord(S,X,Y),wait_time(S,W),
    final_state(F),coord(F,X1,Y1),
    V is W + sqrt((X-X1)^2 + (Y-Y1)^2).

coord('I',2,17).          coord('T',7,6).
coord('A',0,15).          coord('S',7,10).
coord('B',2,13).          coord('R',9,10).
coord('C',2,9).           coord('Q',9,8).
coord('D',0,7).           coord('P',11,8).
coord('E',2,6).           coord('U',14,8).
coord('G',2,3).           coord('V',14,6).
coord('H',0,1).           coord('N',11,11).
coord('K',2,0).           coord('L',7,17).
coord('F',10,0).          coord('M',18,0).
coord('W',7,3).

wait_time('K',3) :- !.
wait_time(_,1).
```

FIGURE 7.19 Definition of an evaluation function.

We now run the program of Figure 7.18 (after adding the definitions of *member* and *member_state*, which are the same in this case) using the data of Figures 7.13 and 7.19.

```
?- hill_climb_search(AnsPath).
AnsPath = ['I','N','P','Q','R','S','T','W','F'] ->
```

Note from the obtained result that from state Q, the hill-climbing search moves to state R in the wrong direction because it has no other options. We shall see in the next section that the best-first search is smarter in backtracking from Q to move to U.

7.8   Best-first search

Best-first search is breadth-first search guided by an evaluation function. In best-first search we are not required to visit all states of the current level before moving to the next level like in breadth-first search, but we can select the next state in the next level or even in the previous level if it is more promising than the remaining unvisited states in the current level.

So, with best-first search we store the developed paths in a list ranging from the one having the most promising last state, to those with less promising ones. The first path of the list is extended and the extended paths are inserted into the list according to the values of their last states. Thus, we always extend the most promising path at the time, until it hits the final state.

The algorithm of best-first search is as follows.

To search for an answer-path using best-first search do
start with a list that contains the only path consisting of
the initial state and its value, and apply best-first procedure
to expand this list until an answer-path is found.

To expand a path-list in finding an answer-path do
if the first path has reached the final state
then return the path as an answer-path
else expand the first path in all possible ways to obtain
a list of extended paths ordered in increasing value
of last state, then merge this list with the list
of remaining paths to give a new list, and
continue to expand the new list.

When the above algorithm of *best-first search* is applied to the state tree of Figure 7.5 (b), where the root I represents the initial state and the nodes F represent the final state, the list of paths develops as shown in Figure 7.20.

(15, I)	(5, IB)	(6, IC)	(0, ICF)	← first path reaches
	(6, IC)	(7, IBG)	(4, ICH)	the final state
	(10, IA)	(8, IBE)	(7, IBG)	
		(10, IA)	(8, IBE)	
			(10, IA)	

FIGURE 7.20 Development of a path-list in best-first search.

The program *best_first_search* is presented in Figure 7.21, where the predicate *extend* has been defined in Figure 7.9, the predicate *reverse* in Problem 3.2 and the predicates *initial_state*, *final_state*, *next_state*, and *value* are to be defined for the particular problem.

```
best_first_search(AnsPath) :-
    initial_state(Init),value(Init,V),
    best_first([[V,Init]],AnsPath).

best_first([[_,S|Path]|_],AnsPath) :-
    final_state(S),!,
    reverse([S|Path],[],AnsPath).
best_first([Path|Rest],AnsPath) :-
    expand(Path,NPaths),
    merge(NPaths,Rest,NewList),
    best_first(NewList,AnsPath).

expand([_|Path],NPaths) :-
    setof([V,S|Path],
            (extend(Path,S),value(S,V)),NPaths),!.
expand(_,[]).
```

FIGURE 7.21 Program *best_first_search*.

The program *best_first_search* of Figure 7.21 calls the elementary procedure *merge*, which has been previously mentioned in Problem 3.9. For convenience, we give its detailed definition below:

```
merge([],L,L) :- !.
merge(L,[],L) :- !.
```

```
merge([X|P],[Y|Q],[X|R]) :-
    less(X,Y),!,merge(P,[Y|Q],R).
merge(L,[Y|Q],[Y|R]) :-
    merge(L,Q,R).

less([V1|Path1],[V2|Path2]) :- V1 < V2.
```

Notes

1. With best-first search, when an answer-path is found, it always appears at the head of the path-list, because the final state has the least value (which is normally zero).

2. The program *best_first_search* of Figure 7.21 uses a list to store the developed paths. For large and complex search problems, this list may become too large, causing the problem of stack-overflow. In this case, we could adopt a less stylish approach by storing the paths as facts and using the built-in predicates *assert* and *retract* to manipulate them. This version of the program *best_first_search* is given in Problem 7.8.

To test the program of Figure 7.21 (after adding the definitions of *member*, *reverse*, *merge*, *extend* (Figure 7.9), and *member_state*), we use the data of Figures 7.13 and 7.19 and enter the following query:

```
?- best_first_search(AnsPath).
AnsPath = ['I','N','P','U','V','T','W','F'] ->
```

In comparing the above answer with the result previously produced by hill-climbing search, we observe that best-first search finds a better path than hill-climbing search. It is clear, however, that the best-first search program is more complex and requires more memory space than hill-climbing search.

7.9   Best-cost search

Best-cost search is breadth-first search guided by a cost function. With best-cost search, we are concerned with the total cost in selecting the next state. So, the algorithm of best-cost search is almost the same as that of best-first search:

To search for an answer-path using best-cost search do
　　start with a list that contains the only path consisting of
　　the initial state with 0 cost, and apply best-cost procedure
　　to expand this list until the best answer-path is found.

To expand a path-list in finding the best answer-path do
　　if the first path has reached the final state
　　　　then　return the path as the best answer-path
　　　　else　expand the first path in all possible ways to obtain
　　　　　　　　a list of extended paths ordered in increasing cost,
　　　　　　　　then merge this list with the list of remaining
　　　　　　　　paths to give a new list, and
　　　　　　　　continue to expand the new list.

When the above algorithm of *best-cost search* is applied to the state tree of
Figure 7.6 (a), where the root I represents the initial state and the nodes F
represent the final state, the list of paths develops as shown in Figure 7.22.

(0, I)	(6, IB)	(7, IC)	(8, IBE)	(9, IA)	(10, IBG)	(11, ICH)	(12, IBGF)
	(7, IC)	(8, IBE)	(9, IA)	(10, IBG)	(11, ICH)	(12, IBGF)	(13, ICHF)
	(9, IA)	(9, IA)	(10, IBG)	(11, ICH)	(14, IBEK)	(14, IBEK)	(14, IBEK)
		(10, IBG)	(11, ICH)	(14, IBEK)	(16, IAD)	(16, IAD)	(16, IAD)
			(17, ICF)	(17, ICF)	(17, ICF)	(17, ICF)	(17, ICF)

FIGURE 7.22 Development of a path-list in best-cost search.

The program *best_cost_search* is shown in Figure 7.23 where the predicates
merge, extend, and *reverse* have been defined before, and the predicates *initial_state, final_state, next_state*, and *cost* are to be defined for the particular
problem.

Note

　　In best-cost search, a path that has reached the final state is not necessarily
　　the best answer-path if it is not the first path of the list, because it is possible
　　that the first path needs just a little extra cost to reach the final state.

EXAMPLE 7.6   Consider once more the road map of Figure 7.7, and we
wish to find the shortest route from I to F. The road distances between
intersections are given in Figure 7.24.

```
best_cost_search(AnsPath) :-
    initial_state(Init),
    best_cost([[0,Init]],AnsPath).

best_cost([[_,S|Path]|_],AnsPath) :-
    final_state(S),!,
    reverse([S|Path],[],AnsPath).
best_cost([Path|Rest],AnsPath) :-
    expand(Path,NPaths),
    merge(NPaths,Rest,NewList),
    best_cost(NewList,AnsPath).

expand([C,S|Path],NPaths) :-
    setof([C1,S1,S|Path],
          (extend([S|Path],S1),
           costsum(S,C,S1,C1)),NPaths),!.
expand(_,[]).

costsum(S,C,S1,C1) :-
    cost(S,S1,D), C1 is C + D.
```

FIGURE 7.23 Program *best_cost_search*.

To find a shortest route from I to F, we run the program *best_cost_search* of Figure 7.23 (after adding the definitions of the predicates *merge*, *reverse*, *extend* (Figures 7.9 and 7.21), and *member_state*) using the data in Figures 7.13, 7.19, and 7.24:

```
?- best_cost_search(AnsPath).
AnsPath = ['I','B','C','E','G','K','F'] ->
```

7.10   Best-path search

Best-path search is another form of breadth-first search that is guided by the combination of an evaluation function and a cost function. Thus, best-path search offers the best compromise between cost and directness in searching for an answer-path.

```
cost(S,S1,D) :-
    distance(S,NextCorners),
    member(S1:D,NextCorners),!.
cost(S,S1,D) :-
    cost(S1,S,D).

distance('I',['A':3,'B':4,'N':12,'L':5]).
distance('A',['B':3]).
distance('B',['C':4,'T':11]).
distance('C',['D':3,'E':3]).
distance('D',['E':2]).
distance('E',['G':3]).
distance('G',['H':3,'K':3]).
distance('H',['K':2]).
distance('K',['F':8]).
distance('F',['W':8,'M':8]).
distance('W',['T':3]).
distance('T',['S':4,'V':7]).
distance('S',['R':2]).
distance('R',['Q':2]).
distance('Q',['P':2]).
distance('P',['N':3,'U':3]).
distance('U',['V':2]).
distance('L',['M':27]).
```

FIGURE 7.24 Definition of a cost function.

Best-path search can be regarded as best-cost search with its cost function augmented by an evaluation function. So, the algorithm of best-path search is the same as that of best-cost search, except that in calculating the augmented cost for an extended path we must subtract the value of the previous state and add the value of the new state. Therefore, we must store with a path the value of its last state as well as its total cost. The program *best_path_search* is given in Figure 7.25, where again the predicates *merge*, *extend*, and *reverse* have been defined before.

To test the program of Figure 7.25 (after adding the definitions of *merge*, *reverse*, *extend* (Figures 7.9 and 7.21), and *member_state*), we use the data of Figures 7.13, 7.19, and 7.24 and enter the following query:

```
best_path_search(AnsPath) :-
    initial_state(Init),value(Init,V),
    best_path([[V,V,Init]],AnsPath).

best_path([[_,_,S|Path]|_],AnsPath) :-
    final_state(S),!,
    reverse([S|Path],[],AnsPath).
best_path([Path|Rest],AnsPath) :-
    expand(Path,NPaths),
    merge(NPaths,Rest,NewList),
    best_path(NewList,AnsPath).

expand([C,V,S|Path],NPaths) :-
    setof([C1,V1,S1,S|Path],
          (extend([S|Path],S1),
           recost(S,C,V,S1,C1,V1)),NPaths),!.
expand(_,[]).

recost(S,C,V,S1,C1,V1) :-
    value(S1,V1),cost(S,S1,D),
    C1 is C - V + D + V1.
```

FIGURE 7.25 Program *best_path_search*.

```
?- best_path_search(AnsPath).
AnsPath = ['I','B','T','W','F'] ->
```

The result shows that although the path *IBTWF* is not the shortest one, it is the best path if we take into account the waiting time at road intersections. Note, however, that if we include the waiting time at road intersections in the cost function instead of the evaluation function, then the path *IBTWF* is the answer for both best-cost and best-path search.

All the foregoing guided-search procedures employ the strategy of looking just one step ahead. For large and complex search problems, such as in game search, it is necessary to look several steps ahead, taking into account the likelihood of the opponent's reaction, to determine the next state of the current state. This special technique of searching is called *alpha-beta search*, which is based on the *minimax principle* and which is to be studied in Problems 7.9 and 7.10.

7.11 Performance of a search procedure

In Section 7.2 we have discussed in general terms the strong and weak points of various search procedures. We now give a detailed analysis of those search procedures that forms the basis for the selection of a suitable procedure for any given search problem.

Basically, the performance of a search procedure depends on the following two factors:

- The size of the search space;

- The branching factor of the search tree.

These factors are defined as follows.

7.11.1 The search space

Given a search problem, the search space is defined to be the set of all possible states of the world under study. The size of the search space can be found by a simple calculation.

Suppose that the world's state is represented by m variables $X_1, \ldots, X_m$, where each X_i has k_i states. Then the total number of states in the search space is

$$k_1 \times k_2 \times \cdots \times k_m$$

Following are some examples:

1. In the farmer's problem of Example 7.3, the problem state is represented by a list of four variables $[F, W, G, C]$, each of which can have two states ("n" or "s"). So the number of states in the search space is $2^4 = 16$.

2. In the problem of searching the traffic roads of Example 7.4, the problem state consists of a single variable that represents any road intersection on the map. So the number of states in the search space is the number of road intersections within the map, which is 21.

3. In the problem of car repairing, assume that the maximum number of parts involved is 100 and suppose that each part can be in one of three states: defective, removed, or perfect. Then the number of states in the search space is 3^{100}, which is quite a large number.

The size of the search space gives us some rough idea of how difficult the search may be. For example, in the problem of car repairing mentioned above, the pure depth-first search is completely ruled out, as the search space is too large. Knowing the size of the search space is insufficient, however, to decide which search procedure is most suitable. The branching factor, which is defined below, provides more information for the decision.

7.11.2   The branching factor

Given a search problem, the *branching factor* is defined to be the average number of next states of any problem state. For example:

1. In the farmer's problem of Example 7.3, the problem state changes when the farmer makes a move. There are at most four possible moves: either the farmer crosses the river alone, or he takes one of the three items with him. However, in any intermediary state, the farmer can have at the most two items with him, because if he has all items, that's the initial or final state. So, there are at most three possible moves, one of which leads to the previous state and is discounted. Therefore, the branching factor is 2.

2. In the problem of searching the traffic roads of Example 7.4, from any road intersection in the map, we have on average three ways to move to the next intersection. So, the branching factor is 3.

3. In the problem of car repairing, assume that there are 100 parts involved and that at each step only one part is repaired. Then, there are at most 200 ways to change from one state to another (e.g., some part changes from being defective to removed or perfect). Therefore, the branching factor is 200.

The branching factor can be used to estimate the size of the search tree, which enables us to measure the performance of any search procedure.

Generally, the performance of a search procedure (or any procedure) is measured by the following accounts:

- The amount of memory space needed in running the procedure;
- The time consumed in running it.

With any search procedure, the main concern in memory space is the size of the stack needed to store the paths being developed. On the other hand, the running time is proportional to the number of iterations generated by the search process.

To facilitate the measurement, let us call *stack size* the estimated number of states contained in the paths that need to be stored, and *iteration count* the estimated number of iterations generated by the search process.

Let B be the branching factor of a given search problem. Then the search tree has 1 node at level 1, B nodes at level 2, B^2 nodes at level 3, ..., B^{K-1} nodes at level K. Also let N be the estimated length of an answer-path. Then, the stack size and iteration count of a search procedure are calculated as follows.

- *Depth-first search* stores only one path at any time, so the stack size is N. On the other hand, the iteration count is

$$1 + B + B^2 + \cdots + B^{N-1} = \frac{B^N - 1}{B - 1}.$$

For example, in the problem of searching the traffic roads, suppose that the destination is about 10 blocks from the point of departure. Then, the stack size is 10 and the iteration count is

$$\frac{3^{10} - 1}{3 - 1} = 29,524.$$

This means that a depth-first search requires very modest memory space, but may run quite a long while before finding an answer (which may happen to be the rightmost branch of the search tree).

- *Breadth-first search* stores all developed paths, but it extends only one path at a time. Thus, after the first iteration the stack contains B paths of length 2; after the $(1 + B)$-th iteration, B^2 paths of length 3; after the $(1 + B + B^2)$-th iteration, B^3 paths of length 4, and so on.

  So, to find an answer path of estimated length N, the stack size is $B^{N-1} \times N$ and the iteration count is

$$1 + B + B^2 + \cdots + B^{N-2} = \frac{B^{N-1} - 1}{B - 1}.$$

For example, in the problem of searching traffic roads, if the point of departure and the destination are 10 blocks apart, then the stack size is $3^9 \times 10 = 196,830$, and the iteration count is

$$\frac{3^9 - 1}{3 - 1} = 9841.$$

This indicates that a breadth-first search requires much more memory space than a depth-first search, but it can find the answer-path in far fewer iterations.

- *Wave search* also stores all developed paths and extends all paths in each iteration. Thus, after the first iteration the stack contains B paths of length 2; after the second iteration, B^2 paths of length 3; after the third iteration, B^3 paths of length 4, and so on.

  So, to find an answer-path of estimated length N, the stack size is the same as in a breadth-first search, i.e., $B^{N-1} \times N$, and the iteration count is just $N - 1$.

For example, in the problem of searching for traffic roads mentioned above, the stack size required by wave search is also 196,830, but it takes only 9 iterations to find an answer.

- *Inter-wave search* performs two wave searches in parallel. Thus, to find an answer-path of estimated length N, the stack size is

  $$2 \times B^{N/2-1} \times \frac{N}{2} = B^{N/2-1} \times N$$

  and the iteration count is $N - 1$.

For example, in the problem of road search, with inter-wave search the stack size is $3^4 \times 10 = 810$ and the iteration count is $10 - 1 = 9$.

This shows that inter-wave search is a great improvement of both wave search and breadth-first search. Note, however, that inter-wave search can be used only if the problem's final state is represented explicitly.

The above-presented formulas, which are used to measure the performance of nonguided search procedures, can also be used to estimate the performance of guided-search procedures such as hill-climbing, best-first, best-cost, and best-path search with almost the same accuracy.

Solved problems

7.1 Consider the problem of the farmer and his property given in Example 7.3. Suppose that the problem state is represented by a pair of lists (N, S), where N represents the members of the group on the north side of the river and S represents those on the south side. Thus, the initial state is $([f, w, g, c], [])$ and the final state is $([], [f, g, c, w])$, in which the order of the elements in the lists is immaterial. (Note the use of lowercase letters.)

(a) Write the definitions of the predicates *initial_state, final_state*, and *next_state* to be used in a depth-first search.

(b) Define an evaluation function to be used in hill-climbing search.

(c) Run the programs of depth-first search (Figure 7.9) and hill-climbing search (Figure 7.18) and compare the results with that of Example 7.3.

Solution:

(a) The final state is identified by the fact that the north side is empty. So, we define

```
initial_state(([f,c,g,w],[])).
final_state(([],_)).
```

A state is changed when the farmer crosses the river, and he may take nothing or one of the items with him provided that what is left behind is safe. So:

```
next_state(([f|N],S),(N1,[f|S1])) :-
    move(N,S,N1,S1),safe(N1).
next_state((N,[f|S]),([f|N1],S1)) :-
    move(S,N,S1,N1),safe(S1).

move(A,B,A,B).
move(A,B,A1,B1) :-
    select(M,A,A1),insert(M,B,B1).
```

The unattended items are safe if either the goat is not among them or it is there alone.

```
safe([g]).
safe(L) :- not(member(g,L)).
```

(b) We define the evaluation function value for any state to be the number of members on the north side of the river. That is,

```
value((N,S),V)  :- length(N,V).
```

(c) Running the program *depth_first_search* (Figure 7.9) (after adding the definitions of *member_state*, *select*, and *insert*) using the above-defined procedures, we have:

```
?- depth_first_search(AnsPath).

AnsPath = [([f,c,g,w],[]),([c,w],[f,g]),([f,c,w],[g]),
          ([w],[f,c,g]),([f,g,w],[c]),([g],[f,c,w]),
          ([f,g],[c,w]),([],[f,c,g,w])] ->;

AnsPath = [([f,c,g,w],[]),([c,w],[f,g]),([f,c,w],[g]),
          ([c],[f,g,w]),([f,c,g],[w]),([g],[f,c,w]),
          ([f,g],[c,w]),([],[f,c,g,w])] ->;

no
```

The result shows two answers, which are identical to those obtained in Example 7.3. Now if we run the *hill_climb_search* program of Figure 7.18, we have the same answer as above.

7.2 Jimbo is a strong-hand robot whose task is to move heavy blocks from one place to another. There are several places and several blocks.

Write a Prolog program to produce a sequence of moves that brings the blocks from an initial state to a final desired state using the following search procedures:

(a) depth-first search;

(b) depth-first search guided by heuristics.

Run the programs with the example of blocks pictured above and compare the answers. Comment on the possibility of using breadth-first search.

Solution:

(a) We represent a problem state by a term of the form:

```
piles(Pile1,...,Pilen)
```

where, for each $1 \leq i \leq n$, `Pilei` is a list of block names. To facilitate the task of reporting a sequence of moves (rather than a sequence of states) we associate with each state a term `move(I,J)` that represents the action of moving the top block of pile I to the top of pile J. Thus, a problem state is now represented by a pair:

```
(move(I,J), piles(Pile1,...,Pilen)).
```

For example, the initial state and the final state of the blocks pictured above are defined as follows:

```
initial_state((none,piles([b,c],[a],[]))).
final_state((_,piles([],[a,b,c],[]))).
num_of_piles(3).
```

A state is changed when the top block of some pile I is moved to the top of some pile J. So,

```
next_state((_,Piles),(move(I,J),NewPiles)) :-
    choose_indices(I,J),
    move_block(I,J,Piles,NewPiles).

choose_indices(I,J) :-
    num_of_piles(N),
    index(I,N),index(J,N),I \= J.

move_block(I,J,Piles,NewPiles) :-
    arg(I,Piles,[B|IBlocks]),
    arg(J,Piles,JBlocks),
    argrep(Piles,I,IBlocks,IPiles),
    argrep(IPiles,J,[B|JBlocks],NewPiles).

index(1,N).
index(I,N) :-
    index(K,N),
    (K >= N,!,fail; I is K+1).
```

To solve the problem using depth-first search, we run the program of Figure 7.9 (after adding the definition of *member_state*).

```
?- depth_first_search(Answer).
```

```
Answer = [(none,piles([b,c],[a],[])),
(move(1,2),piles([c],[b,a],[])),(move(1,2),piles([],[c,b,a],[])),
(move(2,3),piles([],[b,a],[c])),(move(2,1),piles([b],[a],[c])),
(move(1,3),piles([],[a],[b,c])),(move(2,1),piles([a],[],[b,c])),
(move(3,1),piles([b,a],[],[c])),(move(1,2),piles([a],[b],[c])),
(move(1,2),piles([],[a,b],[c])),(move(2,3),piles([],[b],[a,c])),
(move(2,1),piles([b],[],[a,c])),(move(3,1),piles([a,b],[],[c])),
(move(3,1),piles([c,a,b],[],[])),(move(1,2),piles([a,b],[c],[])),
(move(1,2),piles([b],[a,c],[])),(move(1,2),piles([],[b,a,c],[])),
(move(2,3),piles([],[a,c],[b])),(move(2,1),piles([a],[c],[b])),
(move(1,3),piles([],[c],[a,b])),(move(2,1),piles([c],[],[a,b])),
(move(3,1),piles([a,c],[],[b])),(move(1,2),piles([c],[a],[b])),
(move(1,2),piles([],[c,a],[b])),(move(2,3),piles([],[a],[c,b])),
(move(2,1),piles([a],[],[c,b])),(move(3,1),piles([c,a],[],[b])),
(move(3,1),piles([b,c,a],[],[])),(move(1,2),piles([c,a],[b],[])),
(move(1,2),piles([a],[c,b],[])),(move(1,2),piles([],[a,c,b],[])),
(move(2,3),piles([],[c,b],[a])),(move(2,1),piles([c],[b],[a])),
(move(1,3),piles([],[b],[c,a])),(move(2,1),piles([b],[],[c,a])),
(move(3,1),piles([c,b],[],[a])),(move(1,2),piles([b],[c],[a])),
(move(1,2),piles([],[b,c],[a])),(move(3,1),piles([a],[b,c],[])),
(move(1,2),piles([],[a,b,c],[]))]
```

Observe that blind depth-first search has produced an answer-path consisting of 39 moves to bring the blocks into the final desired positions. Many of these moves are quite unnecessary.

(b) In order to find some heuristics that can improve the effectiveness of the depth-first search used in part (a), let us consider the following examples for gaining some experience.

- If the final state contains a pile of the form $[a, b, c, d, e]$ and the corresponding pile in the current state is $[m, n, d, e]$ (where the common sublist $[d, e]$ may contain zero or more blocks), then the top block of this pile should be moved to some other pile that does not contain the block c.

- If the final state contains a pile of the form $[a, b, c, d, e]$ and the corresponding pile in the current state is $[d, e]$ (where the common sublist $[d, e]$ may contain zero or more blocks), then we should find the pile containing the block c and move its top block either to the pile containing $[d, e]$ if the block is c, or to some other pile if it is not c.

So the procedure *choose_indices* in part (a) is redefined as follows:

```
choose_indices(Piles,I,J) :-
    final_state((_,FPiles)),
    num_of_piles(N),index(K,N),
    arg(K,FPiles,Pile0),arg(K,Piles,Pile1),
    append(P0,[A|Bs],Pile0),
    (append(P1,[B|Bs],Pile1),!; Bs = []),
    ((A \= B,!; P1 \= [],!),
        I is K, index(J,N), J \= I,
        arg(J,Piles,Pile2),not(member(A,Pile2));
     (var(B), C = A,!; append(P00,[C],P0)),
        index(I,N),arg(I,Piles,Pile3),
        member(C,Pile3),
        (Pile3 = [C|_],!,J is K;
        index(J,N), J \= I, J \= K)).
```

If we run the depth-first search program again using the above-defined procedure *choose_indices* (with the addition of the procedures *member, member_state,* and *append*), we have

```
?- depth_first_search(Answer).

Answer = [(none,piles([b,c],[a],[])),
          (move(2,3),piles([b,c],[],[a])),
          (move(1,3),piles([c],[],[b,a])),
          (move(1,2),piles([],[c],[b,a])),
          (move(3,2),piles([],[b,c],[a])),
          (move(3,2),piles([],[a,b,c],[]))]
```

The answer shows that it requires only six moves to bring the blocks into their final desired positions.

We note that the given search problem has a high branching factor. In fact, each problem state can have up to six next states. This makes breadth-first search very expensive. In order to avoid the problem of stack-overflow, we can use the static-queue version of the *breadth_first_search* program given in Problem 7.7, which provides the same answer as the depth-first search using heuristics shown in this part.

7.3 You have two empty glasses of capacities *C1* and *C2*, a tap to fill the glasses with water, and a sink. You are asked to provide a glass with a specified amount of water. The glasses have no grading marks and the only things you can do are fill the glasses from the tap, empty the glasses into the sink, or pour water from one glass to the other.

(a) Which search procedure is most suitable for this problem?

(b) Write a program to search for a sequence of actions needed to obtain a specified quantity of water. Run the program with the following data: $C1 = 7$, $C2 = 5$, and the quantity required is $4, 3, 2, 1$.

(c) Find some heuristics to be included in the procedure *next_state*. Apply depth-first search using those heuristics and compare the result with that of part (a).

Solution:

(a) In this problem, the relevant entities are the two glasses. So, we represent a problem state by a pair of variables $[U, V]$, where the variables represent the amounts of water in the glasses.

Theoretically, the variable U can have any integer value from 0 to $C1$, and the variable V can take any integer value from 0 to $C2$. So, the maximum number of states in the problem's search space is $(C1+1) \times (C2+1)$.

Let us now estimate the branching factor of the search problem. We first prove that every state in the search tree must have one of the forms $[0, V]$, $[C1, V]$, $[U, 0]$, $[U, C2]$. That is, one of the glasses must be either empty or full. This is obviously true for the initial state. Suppose that the claim holds at some state, we show that it also holds at the next state.

In fact, if the current state has the form $[0, V]$, then

- Filling glasses generates either $[C1, V]$ or $[0, C2]$;

- Emptying glasses generates $[0, 0]$;

- Pouring one glass into the other generates $[V, 0]$ if $V \leq C1$, or $[C1, V1]$ if $V > C1$.

If the current state has the form $[C1, V]$, then

- Filling glasses generates $[C1, C2]$;

- Emptying glasses generates either $[0, V]$ or $[C1, 0]$;

- Pouring one glass into the other generates $[U, C2]$ if $C1 \geq C2 - V$, or $[0, V1]$ if $C1 < C2 - V$.

The same reasoning applies to the cases of $[U, 0]$ and $[U, C2]$. Observe that if one glass is empty or full, then there is at most one way of pouring one glass into the other. The above reasoning also reveals that each state in the search tree has at most four successors of which the states [0, 0], [0, *C2*], [*C1, C2*], and [*C1,* 0] are likely to occur before if the path is long enough. Therefore, the branching factor is 2. That is, the search tree is almost a binary tree. This suggests that breadth-first search (or wave search or inter-wave search) is the most suitable search procedure for this problem.

(b)   To facilitate the task of reporting the required sequence of actions, we associate with each state [*U, V*] a term representing the action that results in that state. There are three types of actions:

fill_glass(I) :   fill glass I ;
empty_glass(I) :   empty glass I ;
pour_glass(I, J) :   pour glass I into glass J.

So, with *C1* = 7, *C2* = 5, and the required quantity being 4, we have:

```
initial_state((none,[0,0])).
final_state((_,[4,_])).
final_state((_,[_,4])).

capacity(1,7).
capacity(2,5).

next_state((_,[U,V]),(fill_glass(I),[X,Y])) :-
    capacity(I,C),
    fill_glass(I,C,U,V,X,Y).
next_state((_,[U,V]),(empty_glass(I),[X,Y])) :-
    capacity(I,C),
    empty_glass(I,C,U,V,X,Y).
next_state((_,[U,V]),(pour(I,J),[X,Y])) :-
    capacity(J,C),I is 3-J,
    pour_glass(I,J,C,U,V,X,Y).

fill_glass(1,C,0,V,C,V).
fill_glass(2,C,U,0,U,C).

empty_glass(1,C,C,V,0,V).
empty_glass(2,C,U,C,U,0).

pour_glass(1,2,C,U,V,X,Y) :- pour(C,U,V,X,Y).
pour_glass(2,1,C,U,V,X,Y) :- pour(C,V,U,Y,X).

pour(C,U,V,X,Y) :-
    U > 0, V < C,
    (U+V < C, X is 0, Y is U+V,!;
     U+V >= C, X is U+V-C, Y is C).
```

We can now run the program *breadth_first_search* of Figure 7.12 (after adding the definitions of *qmember*, *list_to_queue*, *reverse*, *member*, and *member_state*) using the above-defined procedures.

```
?- breadth_first_search(Answer).

Answer = [(none,[0,0]),(fill_glass(1),[7,0]),
           (pour(1,2),[2,5]),(empty_glass(2),[2,0]),
           (pour(1,2)[0,2]),(fill_glass(1),[7,2]),
           (pour(1,2),[4,5])] ->
```

(c) We observe that the actions can be organised into a sequence of groups of the following three actions:

1. If glass 1 is empty, then fill it;
2. If glass 2 is full, then empty it;
3. Pour glass 1 into glass 2.

A group of three actions as described above is represented by a pair of variables $[A, B]$, where $A = 1$ if the action 1 takes place and $A = 0$ otherwise; likewise $B = 1$ if the action 2 is carried out and $B = 0$ otherwise. Obviously, action 3 always takes place. Thus, the predicate *next_state* is redefined as follows:

```
next_state((_,[U,V]),([A,B],[X,Y])) :-
    capacity(1,C1),capacity(2,C2),
    (U = 0,!, A = 1, U1 = C1; A = 0, U1 = U),
    (V = C2,!,B = 1, V1 = 0;  B = 0, V1 = V),
    (U1+V1 < C2,!, X = 0, Y is U1+V1;
                   X is U1+V1-C2, Y = C2).
```

By this arrangement, each problem state has exactly one next state. Therefore, depth-first search is now the best choice. To report the sequence of moves, we define a printing procedure as follows:

```
print_answer([]).
print_answer([S|Rest]) :-
    print(S),print_answer(Rest).

print((_,[0,0])) :- !,write(0:0),nl.
print(([A,B],[X,Y])) :-
    (A = 0,!; write('Fill glass 1, ')),
    (B = 0,!; write('Empty glass 2, ')),
    write('Pour glass 1 into glass 2'),nl,
    write(X:Y),nl.
```

To solve the problem with the given sample data we enter the query:

```
?- depth_first_search(Answer),
   print_answer(Answer).

0:0
Fill glass 1, Pour glass 1 into glass 2
2:5
Empty glass 2, Pour glass 1 into glass 2
0:2
Fill glass 1, Pour glass 1 into glass 2
4:5
```

For other required quantities $3, 2, 1$, the results are similar.

7.4 Five couples of husbands and wives are trapped on an island just a few kilometres of water from the mainland. They want to go to the land, but only have a boat that can carry at most three persons. They agree to sail back and forth to help each other, but with one condition. That is, due to jealousy, no woman is allowed to be at the same place (on the boat or at either side of the water) with another man without the presence of her husband (even when that man is accompanied by his wife or somebody else).

(a) Design a data structure to represent a problem state. Give the initial and final states.

(b) Define the procedure *next_state* that receives a problem state and returns one of its next states.

(c) Define an evaluation function to be used in a hill-climbing search. Run the search procedure and explain the result.

Solution:

(a) In this problem the relevant entities are the five couples and the boat. As the number of entities is large enough to be processed recursively, we represent a problem state as a list

```
[B,(M1,W1),...,(M5,W5)]
```

where, B represents the boat which can have value 2 (at the island's shore) or 0 (at the mainland's shore), and each pair of variables (M, W) represents the states of a man and his wife, which can be 2 (on the island), 1 (on the boat), or 0 (on mainland). Here, we use integers to represent state values so that an evaluation function can be easily defined later.

To facilitate the task of reporting the sequence of moves, we associate with each problem state a list [ML, MB, WL, WB] that stores the following counts:

ML : number of men who leave the boat to land;
MB : number of men who get on the boat;
WL : number of women who leave the boat to land;
WB : number of women who get on the boat.

Thus, a problem state is fully represented by a pair:

```
([ML,MB,WL,WB],[B,(M1,W1),...,(M5,W5)])
```

We can now define the initial and final states as follows:

```
initial_state(([],[2,(2,2),(2,2),(2,2),(2,2),(2,2)])).
final_state((_,[_,(0,0),(0,0),(0,0),(0,0),(0,0)])).
```

(b) A problem state is changed when the boat's direction is changed and some people (men or women) leave the boat to land while others may get on the boat, provided that the men are happy and the boat is not overloaded. So, we have:

```
next_state(S,S1) :-
    change(S,S1),
    not(jealous(S1)),
    boat_ok(S1).

change((_,[B|Pairs]),([ML,MB,WL,WB],[NB|NewPairs])) :-
    NB is 2-B,
    transfer(B,Pairs,[],[0,0,0,0],[ML,MB,WL,WB],NewPairs).

transfer(_,[],Pairs,C,C,Pairs).
transfer(B,[P|Pairs],MPairs,K,C,NewPairs) :-
    move_pair(B,K,P,K1,P1),
    insert(P1,MPairs,NPairs),
    transfer(B,Pairs,NPairs,K1,C,NewPairs).

move_pair(D,[ML,MB,WL,WB],(M,W),[ML1,MB1,WL1,WB1],(M1,W1)) :-
    move(D,(M,ML,MB),(M1,ML1,MB1)),
    move(D,(W,WL,WB),(W1,WL1,WB1)).

move(D,(D,ML,MB),(1,ML,MB1)) :- MB1 is MB+1.
move(D,(1,ML,MB),(D,ML1,MB)) :- ML1 is ML+1.
move(D,S,S).
```

```
insert(X,[],[X]) :- !.
insert(X,[Y|T],[X,Y|T]) :- X @=< Y,!.
insert(X,[Y|T],[Y|R]) :- insert(X,T,R).

jealous((_,[_|Pairs])) :-
    member((M,W),Pairs), M \= W,
    member((W,_),Pairs).

boat_ok((_,[_|Pairs])) :-
    number_onboat(Pairs,N),1 =< N, N =< 3,!;
    final_state((_,[_|Pairs])).

number_onboat([],0).
number_onboat([(M,W)|Pairs],N) :-
    number_onboat(Pairs,K),
    N is K+ (M mod 2)+ (W mod 2).
```

Here, the predicate *insert* is already defined in Figure 3.14 (replace "<" with "@<") and the predicate *member* is defined in Figure 2.13. Note also that the predicate *member_state* used in the procedure *extend* of Figure 7.9 should be slightly modified as follows:

```
member_state((_,[_|X]),[(_,[_|X])|_]).
member_state(S,[_|T]) :- member_state(S,T).
```

(c) We define the evaluation function value of a state to be the sum of the numbers representing the states of the ten people involved. Thus, the evaluation function decreases when there are more people on the mainland and on the boat.

```
value((_,[_|Pairs]),Value) :-
    add_up(Pairs,Value).

add_up([],0).
add_up([(M,W)|Pairs],Value) :-
    add_up(Pairs,V),
    Value is V+M+W.
```

We can now run the *hill_climb_search* program of Figure 7.18 (after adding the definitions of *member* and *member_state*) to solve the problem:

```
?- hill_climb_search(Answer).

Answer = [([],[2,(2,2),(2,2),(2,2),(2,2),(2,2)]),
   ([0,0,0,3],[0,(2,1),(2,1),(2,1),(2,2),(2,2)]),
   ([0,0,2,0],[2,(2,0),(2,0),(2,1),(2,2),(2,2)]),
   ([0,0,0,2],[0,(2,0),(2,0),(2,1),(2,1),(2,1)]),
   ([0,0,2,0],[2,(2,0),(2,0),(2,0),(2,0),(2,1)]),
   ([0,2,0,0],[0,(1,0),(1,1),(2,0),(2,0),(2,0)]),
   ([0,0,1,0],[2,(1,0),(1,0),(2,0),(2,0),(2,0)]),
   ([0,1,0,0],[0,(1,0),(1,0),(1,0),(2,0),(2,0)]),
   ([3,0,0,2],[2,(0,0),(0,0),(0,0),(2,1),(2,1)]),
   ([0,2,1,0],[0,(0,0),(0,0),(0,0),(1,1),(1,2)]),
   ([1,0,1,0],[2,(0,0),(0,0),(0,0),(0,0),(1,2)]),
   ([0,0,0,1],[0,(0,0),(0,0),(0,0),(0,0),(1,1)]),
   ([1,0,1,0],[2,(0,0),(0,0),(0,0),(0,0),(0,0)])] ->
```

We can also define a *print_answer* procedure to produce a better display of the answer:

```
print_answer([]).
print_answer([(Move,State)|Rest]) :-
    print_move(Move,State),
    print_answer(Rest).

print_move([],_).
print_move([ML,MB,WL,WB],[Boat|Pairs]) :-
    locate(Boat,Location,Direction),write('>'),
    (ML = 0,!; print([' ',ML,' men land on ',Location])),
    (MB = 0,!; print([' ',MB,' men get on ',boat])),
    (WL = 0,!; print([' ',WL,' women land on ',Location])),
    (WB = 0,!; print([' ',WB,' women get on ',boat])),
    (final_state((_,[_|Pairs])),!;
            print([', the boat sails to ',Direction]),nl).

locate(0,island,mainland).
locate(2,mainland,island).

print([]).
print([X|T]) :- write(X),print(T).
```

Then, we have:

```
?- hill_climb_search(Answer),
   print_answer(Answer).
```

> 3 women get on boat, the boat sails to mainland
> 2 women land on mainland, the boat sails to island
> 2 women get on boat, the boat sails to mainland
> 2 women land on mainland, the boat sails to island
> 2 men get on boat, the boat sails to mainland
> 1 women land on mainland, the boat sails to island
> 1 men get on boat, the boat sails to mainland
> 3 men land on mainland 2 women get on boat, the boat
sails to island
> 2 men get on boat 1 women land on island, the boat
sails to mainland
> 1 men land on mainland 1 women land on mainland, the
boats sails to island
> 1 women get on boat, the boat sails to mainland
> 1 men land on mainland 1 women land on mainland

Observe that the above display does not explicitly show which men or which women take the action (it would be much more complicated to do so and the reader may try by adding an index to each pair (M, W), making it become (I, M, W)), but the constraint on jealousy makes it obvious which ones should take the action.

It is interesting to note that if we do not include the list [ML, MB, WL, WB] to represent a move, the above program produces a better answer that consists of only ten moves to bring all five couples to the mainland. The inclusion of the list [ML, MB, WL, WB] makes the procedure *best_next_state* of the *hill_climb_search* program favour the women in selecting the best next state. In fact, if two states have the same value, then the predicate *setof* always places a move such as $[0, 0, 0, 2]$ in front of $[0, 2, 0, 0]$.

7.5 Robyn is a housekeeping robot whose job is to clean the two-room house every morning, when its owner has left for work. Its job includes dusting the furniture, vacuuming the carpet, and emptying the trash bins in the rooms. Dusting the furniture gets dust onto the carpet and vacuuming the carpet creates dust that goes into the trash bin placed in the same room. To empty the trash bins, Robyn has to pick them up, go to the chute to dispose of the trash, then bring them back to where they were before. Robyn is equipped with built-in duster and vacuum, and is able to carry one or both trash bins.

Write Prolog programs according to the following specifications to find
a sequence of actions for the robot to get everything cleaned. Assume
that initially the robot is in room 2, both rooms' furniture needs dusting, the carpet in room 1 is clean but the carpet in room 2 is not, also
the bin in room 1 has trash but the bin in room 2 is empty. The robot
must finish at either room and not at the trash chute.

(a) Use depth-first search with some heuristics such as:

   Things are dusted or vacuumed only if they are uncleaned;
   Carpets should not be vacuumed when furniture needs dusting;
   The trash bin should be emptied only when the room is al-
   ready cleaned.

(b) Find an evaluation function that gives each state a value which
   represents the distance from that state to the final state. Use this
   evaluation function in the best-first search procedure to find a
   sequence of actions for Robyn, and compare the result with that
   of part (a).

(c) Use the best-cost search procedure with the following energy costs:

   Dusting furniture in a room needs 6 units;
   Vacuuming a single room costs 8 units;
   Picking up a bin requires 3 units;
   Putting a bin down requires only 1 unit;
   Emptying a trash bin needs 5 units;
   Travelling between two rooms requires 4 units;
   Travelling between the trash chute and any room needs 10 units.

(Note: This problem is adapted from Exercise 10.9 of Neil C. Rowe, *Artificial
Intelligence through Prolog*, 1988, p. 253. Adapted by permission of Prentice
Hall, Englewood Cliffs, New Jersey.)

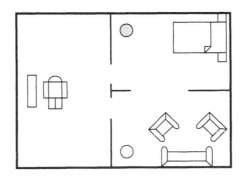

Solution:

In this problem, the relevant entities are the robot and the furniture, the carpet, the trash bins of the two rooms. So, we represent a problem state by a pair:

$$S = (R, [F1, C1, (B1, P1)] - [F2, C2, (B2, P2)]),$$

where R represents the robot's location, which can be 0: at the chute, 1: in room 1, or 2: in room 2; $F1$, $C1$, $B1$, respectively, represents the status of the furniture, the carpet, and the trash bin of room 1 that can have the value 0 for "clean", or 1 for "unclean", whereas $P1$ represents the situation of the bin, which is 0 if the bin is on the floor of room 1 and is 1 if it is carried by the robot; likewise, $F2$, $C2$, $B2$, $P2$ represent the corresponding statuses of the furniture, the carpet, and the bin of room 2.

To facilitate the task of reporting on a sequence of action, we associate with each state S, a term M representing the action that results in state S. Thus, a problem state is fully represented by a pair (M, S), and we have:

```
initial_state((none,(2,[1,0,(1,0)]-[1,1,(0,0)]))).
final_state((_,(R,[0,0,(0,0)]-[0,0,(0,0)]))) :-
    R = 1; R = 2.
```

(a) The problem state changes when the robot performs an action. Typical actions are described below:

- If the robot is in a room, then it can do the following work if appropriate: dusting furniture, vacuuming carpet, picking up trash bin, or putting down empty bin.

- If the robot is at the trash chute, then it can dispose of the trash in the bins it carries.

- If the robot has nothing to do at its current place, then it can move to another place.

So, the procedure *next_state* is defined as follows:

```
next_state((_,(I,States)),(Action,(I,NewStates))) :-
    I \= 0, arg(I,States,RmState),
    work(I,RmState,NewRmState,Action),!,
    argrep(States,I,NewRmState,NewStates).
next_state((_,(0,States)),(Action,(0,NewStates))) :-
    dispose_trash(States,NewStates,Action),!.
next_state((_,(I,States)),(move(I,J),(J,States))) :-
    J is (I+1) mod 3; J is (I+2) mod 3.
```

```
work(I,[1,C,B],[0,1,B],dust_room(I)).
work(I,[0,1,(B,P)],[0,0,(1,P)],vacuum_room(I)).
work(I,[0,0,(1,0)],[0,0,(1,1)],pickup_bin(I)).
work(I,[0,0,(0,1)],[0,0,(0,0)],putdown_bin(I)).

dispose_trash([0,0,(1,1)]-R2,[0,0,(0,1)]-R2,empty_bin(1)).
dispose_trash(R1-[0,0,(1,1)],R1-[0,0,(0,1)],empty_bin(2)).
```

Now we can run the *depth_first_search* program of Figure 7.9 (after adding the definition of *member_state*), and we have:

```
?- depth_first_search(Answer),
   print_answer(Answer).

none,            2 , [1,0,(1,0)] - [1,1,(0,0)]
dust_room(2),    2 , [1,0,(1,0)] - [0,1,(0,0)]
vacuum_room(2),  2 , [1,0,(1,0)] - [0,0,(1,0)]
pickup_bin(2),   2 , [1,0,(1,0)] - [0,0,(1,1)]
move(2,0),       0 , [1,0,(1,0)] - [0,0,(1,1)]
empty_bin(2),    0 , [1,0,(1,0)] - [0,0,(0,1)]
move(0,1),       1 , [1,0,(1,0)] - [0,0,(0,1)]
dust_room(1),    1 , [0,1,(1,0)] - [0,0,(0,1)]
vacuum_room(1),  1 , [0,0,(1,0)] - [0,0,(0,1)]
pickup_bin(1),   1 , [0,0,(1,1)] - [0,0,(0,1)]
move(1,2),       2 , [0,0,(1,1)] - [0,0,(0,1)]
putdown_bin(2),  2 , [0,0,(1,1)] - [0,0,(0,0)]
move(2,0),       0 , [0,0,(1,1)] - [0,0,(0,0)]
empty_bin(1),    0 , [0,0,(0,1)] - [0,0,(0,0)]
move(0,1),       1 , [0,0,(0,1)] - [0,0,(0,0)]
putdown_bin(1),  1 , [0,0,(0,0)] - [0,0,(0,0)]
```

Here, the procedure *print_answer* simply prints out the list *Answer*, one element per line. (Note that the built-in predicate *write* does not print the brackets around a term if no ambiguity may arise.)

Observe that although we have used some heuristics to guide the robot in its activities, the first answer still contains some unnecessary actions. For example, the robot visited the trash chute twice to empty the two trash bins. If we repeatedly press the semicolon key to obtain alternative answers, then we will eventually find the optimal answer. A better way of obtaining the optimal answer is to use *best_first* search as shown in part (b).

(b) We define the evaluation function value of a state to be the sum of two values, each of which is associated with a room's state.

The value of a room's state is calculated as follows. First of all, the following indicators are defined.

In a given state and for a particular room:

- If the robot is away from this room, then TR = 1, otherwise TR = 0;
- If the robot is away from the chute, then TC = 1, otherwise TC = 0;
- If the bin is unclean or not in place, then BD = 1, otherwise BD = 0;
- If the unclean bin is already picked up, then GC = 1, otherwise GC = 0.

The first two indicators signal whether or not a move to the required place is necessary. Besides this possible move, the following are the tasks that may need to be done in the listing order:

1. Dusting the furniture;
2. Vacuuming the carpet;
3. Picking up the bin;
4. Moving to the chute;
5. Emptying the bin;
6. Moving back to room;
7. Putting down the bin.

So, for a room's state [F, C, (B, P)], we have (besides the possible move to the place):

If $F = 1$, then the robot must do the above-listed 7 tasks.
If $F = 0$ and $C = 1$, then it must do the last 6 tasks.
If $F = 0$ and $C = 0$, then
   if $B = 1$ and $P = 0$, then it must do the last 5 tasks;
   if $B = 1$ and $P = 1$, then it can go directly to the chute (task 4) instead of moving to this room, then do the last 3 tasks;
   if $B = 0$ and $P = 1$, then, besides the possible move to this room (task 6), the robot needs only do the last task.

Therefore, the value of [F, C, (B, P)] is defined by the following formula:

```
V = TR + F*7 + (1-F)* (C*6 +
        (1-C)*BD* (3 + 2* (B-P) + GC* (TC-TR))).
```

So the evaluation function is defined as follows:

```
value((_,(I,R1-R2)),Value) :-
    room_value(I,1,R1,V1),
    room_value(I,2,R2,V2),
    Value is V1 + V2 - I.
```

```
room_value(I,J,[F,C,(B,P)],V) :-
    travel_need(I,J,TR),
    travel_need(I,0,TC),
    bin_state(B,P,BD,GC),
    V is TR + F*7 + (1-F)* (C*6 +
        (1-C)*BD* (3 + 2* (B-P) + GC* (TC-TR))).

travel_need(I,I,0) :- !.
travel_need(I,J,1).

bin_state(0,0,0,0).
bin_state(0,1,1,0).
bin_state(1,0,1,0).
bin_state(1,1,1,1).
```

We can now run the best-first search program of Figure 7.21 (after adding the definitions of *merge*, *reverse*, *extend*, *member*, and *member_state*) using the above-defined evaluation function:

```
?- best_first_search(Answer),
    print_answer(Answer).

none,          2 , [1,0,(1,0)] - [1,1,(0,0)]
dust_room(2),  2 , [1,0,(1,0)] - [0,1,(0,0)]
vacuum_room(2),2 , [1,0,(1,0)] - [0,0,(1,0)]
pickup_bin(2), 2 , [1,0,(1,0)] - [0,0,(1,1)]
move(2,1),     1 , [1,0,(1,0)] - [0,0,(1,1)]
dust_room(1),  1 , [0,1,(1,0)] - [0,0,(1,1)]
vacuum_room(1),1 , [0,0,(1,0)] - [0,0,(1,1)]
pickup_bin(1), 1 , [0,0,(1,1)] - [0,0,(1,1)]
move(1,0),     0 , [0,0,(1,1)] - [0,0,(1,1)]
empty_bin(1),  0 , [0,0,(0,1)] - [0,0,(1,1)]
empty_bin(2),  0 , [0,0,(0,1)] - [0,0,(0,1)]
move(0,2),     2 , [0,0,(0,1)] - [0,0,(0,1)]
putdown_bin(2),2 , [0,0,(0,1)] - [0,0,(0,0)]
move(2,1),     1 , [0,0,(0,1)] - [0,0,(0,0)]
putdown_bin(1),1 , [0,0,(0,0)] - [0,0,(0,0)]
```

(c) The cost function is defined in an obvious way:

```
cost(_,(dust_room(I),_),6).
cost(_,(vacuum_room(I),_),8).
```

```
cost(_,(pickup_bin(I),_),3).
cost(_,(putdown_bin(I),_),1).
cost(_,(empty_bin(I),_),5).
cost(_,(move(I,J),_),C) :-
    I+J =:= 3,!, C = 4; C = 10.
```

Running the *best_cost_search* program of Figure 7.23 (after adding the definitions of *merge, reverse, extend, member*, and *member_state*) with the above-defined cost function, we obtain the same result as in part (b).

7.6 *The Travelling Salesman.* The job of a travelling salesman is to visit every city in his plan and return to his original city. The costs of travelling between cities are given in the following table (here, for convenience, cities are numbered, but city names may be used instead).

		CITIES					
		1	2	3	4	5	6
	1	∞	27	43	16	30	26
	2	7	∞	16	1	30	25
	3	20	13	∞	35	5	0
CITIES	4	21	16	25	∞	18	18
	5	12	46	27	48	∞	5
	6	23	5	5	9	5	∞

Write a Prolog program to determine the (cyclic) path that the salesman should take to minimise the total travelling cost. (This problem has been given in Chapter 2, Problem 2.23, where a simple declarative solution was expected. Here, it is suggested to use the best-cost-search technique to solve the problem.)

Solution:

We apply the technique of *best-cost search* to solve this problem, using a classic simple algorithm to guide the search. This algorithm is due to Gomory (1966) and is based on the following observations:

- If the travelling costs from any city to other cities are all reduced by the same amount, then the optimal solution will be unchanged;

- If an arc (joining two cities) is included in the salesman's path, then the cost table's size is reduced by 1.

So, we first reduce the elements in each row of the table by their minimum value, and do the same for the columns. The total amount taken away is a lower bound for the optimal cost. We then choose the 0-entry, the exclusion of which would cause the maximum increase in the cost lower bound.

For example, the given cost table is reduced to the table shown below (with cost lower bound = 48) and the 0-entry at location $(1, 4)$ provides us with the best arc. In fact, if we exclude the arc $(1, 4)$ by placing ∞ at the location $(1,4)$, we will be able to reduce row 1 by 10 and column 4 by 0, giving a total increase of 10 in the cost lower bound, which is larger than all such increases at other 0-entries.

	1	2	3	4	5	6
1	∞	11	27	0	14	10
2	1	∞	15	0	29	24
3	15	13	∞	35	5	0
4	0	0	9	∞	2	2
5	2	41	22	43	∞	0
6	13	0	0	4	0	∞

At this stage, we have two options: either we exclude the arc $(1, 4)$ by placing ∞ at this location (so that this arc will never be selected); or we include the arc $(1, 4)$ by removing the first row and the fourth column from the table (and place ∞ at location $(4, 1)$ to avoid immature loops). This choice of branching together with the cost-lower-bound function provides us with the means for a best-cost-search.

Here, we represent a problem state by a triplet (T, A, V), where T is a cost table, A is an arc in the form *go(I, J)* (for inclusion) or *no(I, J)* (for exclusion), and V is the associated cost-lower-bound increment. The *initial state* contains the cost table after the first reduction, and the *final state* has its table reduced to a 2×2 table from which the choice of routes becomes trivial. Thus, we define:

```
initial_state((Table,nil,Value),Value) :-
    cost_table(N,T),
    reduce_cost(N,T,Table,Value).

final_state(([R1,R2],_,_),go(I,J),go(H,K)) :-
    member(e(I,J,0),R1),member(e(H,K,0),R2),
    I \= H,  J \= K.
```

The procedures *cost_table* and *reduce_cost* have been defined in Problem 6.5 and the procedure *member* is given in Figure 2.13. We now define the procedure *next_state*, using the convenient built-in predicate *setof*, as follows:

```
next_state((T,_,_),(T1,A,V),Path) :-
    best_arc(T,Row,Col),
    branch(T,Row,Col,Path,(T1,A,V)).

best_arc(T,(I0,CI),(J0,CJ)) :-
    setof((C,(I,M),(J,N)),(table_entry(T,I,J,0),
            min_cost(T,(I,M),(J,N)),C is 10000 - M - N),
            [(_,(I0,CI),(J0,CJ))|_]).

min_cost(T,(I,M),(J,N)) :-
    setof(C,(K,C)^ (table_entry(T,I,K,C),K \= J),[M|_]),
    setof(C,(H,C)^ (table_entry(T,H,J,C),H \= I),[N|_]).

table_entry(Table,I,J,C) :-
    member(Row,Table),member(e(I,J,C),Row).

branch(T,(I,CI),(J,CJ),_,(Table,no(I,J),Cost)) :-
    setof(R1,R^ (member(R,T),exclude((I,CI),(J,CJ),R,R1)),
            Table), Cost is CI + CJ.
branch(T,(I,_),(J,_),Path,(Table,go(I,J),Cost)) :-
    setof(R1,R^ (member(R,T),include(I,J,Path,R,R1)),
            Table1), length(Table1,N),
            reduce_cost(N,Table1,Table,Cost).

exclude(Row,Col,R,R1) :-
    setof(e(H,K,C1),C^ (member(e(H,K,C),R),
            adjust(Row,Col,H,K,C,C1)),R1).

adjust((I,_),(J,_),I,J,_,10000) :- !.
adjust((I,CI),_,I,J,C,C1) :- !, C1 is C - CI.
adjust(_,(J,CJ),I,J,C,C1) :- !, C1 is C - CJ.
adjust(_,_,_,_,C,C).
```

```
include(I,J,Path,R,R1) :-
    setof(e(H,K,C1),C^ (member(e(H,K,C),R),H \= I,K \= J,
        change(Path,I,J,H,K,C,C1)),R1).

change(Path,I,J,H,K,0,10000) :-
    rearrange(go(H,K),[go(I,J)|Path],_,go(_,H)),!.
change(_,_,_,_,_,C,C).
```

Before calling the *best_cost_search* procedure, there are a few things to be noted. First, since the answer path is circular, it does not need to be reversed, as in the usual cases; instead, we rearrange the arcs into a successive sequence for easy perception. Second, to save space we store in each path only the last state and its preceding arcs. Therefore, the procedure *best_cost_search* of Figure 7.23 is slightly modified as follows:

```
salesman(Journey,Cost) :-
    best_cost_search([Cost|Journey]).

best_cost_search(AnsPath) :-
    initial_state(Init,V),
    best_cost([[V,Init]],AnsPath).

best_cost([[[C,S|Path]|_],[C|AnsPath]) :-
    final_state(S,A,B),!,
    rearrange(_,[A,B|Path],AnsPath,_).
best_cost([Path|Rest],AnsPath) :-
    expand(Path,NPaths),
    merge(NPaths,Rest,NewList),
    best_cost(NewList,AnsPath).

expand([C,S|Path],NPaths) :-
    setof([C1,(T,A,V),A|Path],
        (extend([S|Path],(T,A,V)),
        C1 is C + V), NPaths),!.
expand(_,[]).

extend([S|Path],(T,A,V)) :-
    next_state(S,(T,A,V),Path),
    not(member(A,Path)).

rearrange(go(I,J),L,[go(J,K)|L1],Last) :-
    select(go(J,K),L,L2),!,rearrange(go(J,K),L2,L1,Last).
rearrange(Last,_,[],Last).
```

The procedure *select* is given in Figure 2.16 and the procedure *merge* can be found on pages 297-298. We can now find an optimal solution for the problem by adding the facts $table(1, 1, 10000)$, $table(1, 2, 27), \ldots$, $table(6, 5, 5)$, $table(6, 6, 10000)$, and entering the following query:

```
?- salesman(Journey,Cost).

Journey = [go(4,3),go(3,5),go(5,6),go(6,2),go(2,1),go(1,4)]
Cost = 63 ->
```

7.7 The program *breadth_first_search* of Figure 7.12 uses a dynamic queue to store the developed paths. For large and complex search problems, this may cause the problem of stack-overflow. In this case, we could adopt a less stylish but more efficient approach by storing the paths as facts of a static queue and using the built-in predicates *assert* and *retract* to manipulate them.

Write a program *breadth_first_search* using the above-suggested data structure.

Solution:

The algorithm of breadth-first search is the same as previously described, but is now reexpresssed as follows to suit the procedural effect of the built-in procedures *assert* and *retract*.

To search for an answer-path using breadth-first search do
    create a queue that contains the only path consisting of
    the initial state, and apply breadth-first procedure to
    expand this queue until an answer-path is found.

To expand a path-queue in finding an answer-path do
    repeat
        copy the first *Path* of the queue,
        repeat
            extend *Path* to a new state, and
            place the extended path at the end of the queue
        until the final state is found or no more new state;
        If the final state is found then return the
            extended path as an answer-path
        else remove *Path* from the queue
    until an answer-path is found (or the queue is empty).

The program is given on the next page.

```
breadth_first_search(AnsPath) :-
    initial_state(Init),
    assert(queue([Init])),
    breadth_first(AnsPath).

breadth_first(AnsPath) :-
    queue(Path),
    extend(Path,NewState),
    final_state(NewState),
    reverse([NewState|Path],[],AnsPath).
breadth_first(AnsPath) :-
    queue(_),breadth_first(AnsPath).

extend([S|Path],S1) :-
    next_state(S,S1),
    not(member_state(S1,[S|Path])),
    assertz(queue([S1,S|Path])).
extend(Path,_) :-
    retract(queue(Path)),
    fail.
```

7.8 The program *best_first_search* of Figure 7.21 also uses a dynamic list to store the developed paths. Write another version of *best_first_search* that stores developed paths as facts and uses the built-in predicates *assert* and *retract* to manipulate them.

Solution:

The algorithm of best-first search is the same as that of breadth-first search except that instead of taking the first path of the list, we pick the best path of the list, that is, the one of which the last state has least value.

> To search for an answer-path using best-first search do
> > store the initial path consisting of the initial state
> > and its value, and apply the best-first procedure
> > to expand this store until an answer-path is found.

> To expand the path-store in finding an answer-path do
> > *repeat*
> > > pick the best *Path* in store,
> > > *repeat*
> > > > extend *Path* to a new state, evaluate it
> > > > and store the evaluated extended path

until the final state is found or no more new state;
If the final state is found then
return the extended path as an answer-path
until an answer-path is found (or the store is empty).

```
best_first_search(AnsPath) :-
    initial_state(Init),value(Init,Value),
    assert(store([Value,Init])),
    best_first(AnsPath).

best_first(AnsPath) :-
    pick_best(Path),
    extend(Path,NewState),
    final_state(NewState),
    reverse([NewState|Path],[],AnsPath).

extend([S|Path],S1) :-
    next_state(S,S1),
    not(member_state(S1,[S|Path])),
    value(S1,V1),
    assert(store([V1,S1,S|Path])).

pick_best(Path) :-
    least_value(V),
    retract(store([V|Path])).
pick_best(Path) :-
    store(_),pick_best(Path).

least_value(V0) :-
    setof(V,Path^store([V|Path]),[V0|Vs]).
```

Observe that the procedure *extend* does not have a second clause as shown in Problem 7.7, because here, the best path is already removed by the procedure *pick_best*.

7.9 *Minimax search.* Game playing is a special kind of search problem. For most interesting games, the search space is very large, therefore the most suitable search procedure is hill-climbing search. However, in game search one must study several moves ahead and take into account the opponent's predicted reactions in order to select the best next state of the current game state.

Suppose that the game involves two players, and that there exists an evaluation function that gives each game state a value which increases with the chance of winning for player 1 (called the *maximiser*), and decreases if the chance of winning for player 2 (called the *minimiser*) increases.

Write a procedure, for any particular player, to select the best next state of a game state so that after N moves, this player will be in a position of having the best chance of winning.

Solution:

Consider a sample game search tree that represents all possible ways of having N moves made by the two players taking their turns.

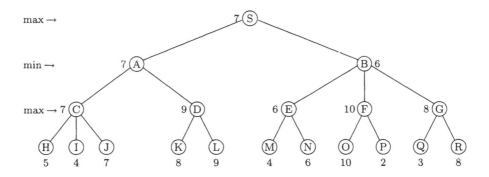

The numbers below the terminal nodes are the evaluation function values of the states represented by those nodes. Suppose that at the second last level, it is the maximiser's turn. So, if the maximiser is at state C, he should choose the next state J to achieve the maximum value; if he is at state D, then he should choose the next state L to secure the maximum value 9, etc.

Now at the second level, it is the minimiser's turn. So, if the minimiser is at state A, then he would certainly choose the next state C to achieve the minimum value 7; if he is at state B, then he would choose the next state E to achieve the minimum value 6.

Therefore, being at state S and having studied three steps ahead, the maximiser should choose the state A as his *best next state* to achieve the maximum value 7. In fact, his opponent would choose the following state C, and he would then choose the terminal state J whose evaluation function value is 7. Observe that no other *minimax* paths (minimising-maximising) lead to any value greater than 7.

The above-described selection procedure is expressed in the following general algorithm:

To find the best next state *S1* of a state *S* do
   determine the depth-of-search *N*, and
   find the *N*-minimax value *(V,S1)* of *S*.

To find the *N*-minimax value *(V,S1)* of a state *S* do
   if $N = 0$ then *V* is the evaluation function value of *S*,
      and *S1* is undefined;
   if $N > 0$ then find the $(N - 1)$-minimax values of all
      next states of *S*, and choose *(V,S1)* to be the next
      state *S1* with minimum or maximum value *V*, depending
      on whether *N* is a minimising or maximising level.

For convenience, let us assume that we are at a minimising level if *N* is even, and we are at a maximising level if *N* is odd. The *minimax* procedure is given below:

```
best_next_state(S,S1) :-
    depth_of_search(N),
    minimax(N,S,V,S1).

minimax(0,S,V,_) :- !,value(S,V).
minimax(N,S,V,S1) :-
    N1 is N-1,
    setof((W,NS,NV,T),
          (next_state(S,NS),
           minimax(N1,NS,NV,T),
           minimaxorder(N,NV,W)),
          [(_,S1,V,_)|Rest]).

minimaxorder(N,V,V) :- (N mod 2) =:= 0,!.
minimaxorder(N,V1,V) :- V is 1000 - V1.
```

7.10 *Alpha-beta search.* The minimax procedure given in Problem 7.9 computes the minimax values of all nodes in a game-search tree, many of which are not needed. For example, in the sample game-search tree of Problem 7.9, the values of states L, F, G are not needed. In fact, we have

$$\text{Value} = \max(\min(7, \max(8, \text{othervalues})), \min(6, \text{othervalues}))$$
$$= \max(7, \min(6, \text{othervalues}))$$
$$= 7.$$

More generally, we have

$$\max(\alpha, \min(V, \text{othervalues})) = \alpha \quad \text{if} \ \ V < \alpha,$$
$$\min(\beta, \max(V, \text{othervalues})) = \beta \quad \text{if} \ \ V > \beta,$$

where "othervalues" need not be computed.

Write a procedure to perform the minimax search using the above-described computation-saving rule (which is called the *alpha-beta* rule).

Solution:

The alpha-beta algorithm of selecting the best next state of a given game state is expressed as follows.

> To find the best next state *S1* of a state *S* do
>> obtain the depth-of-search *N*, and the lower and upper
>> bounds α and β of the evaluation function,
>> then find the (N, α, β)-minimax value *(V,S1)* of *S*.

> To find the (N, α, β)-minimax value *(V,S1)* of a state *S* do
>> *if* $N = 0$ then *V* is the evaluation function value of *S*,
>>> and *S1* is undefined;
>> *if* $N > 0$ then *S1* is the next state of *S* that has the
>>> best $(N - 1, \alpha, \beta)$-minimax value (V, T) among all
>>> next states of *S*.

> To find the state *S1* in a list [*S* | *Rest*] that has the best
> $(N - 1, \alpha, \beta)$-minimax value do
>> find $(V, T) = (N - 1, \alpha, \beta)$-minimax value of *S*, and
>> select the better of (S, V) and the best of the *Rest*.

> To select the better of (S, V) and the best of the *Rest* do
>> *if Rest* is empty then take (S, V)
>> *else if* *N* is a minimising level then
>>> *if* $V < \alpha$ then take (S, V), ignoring the *Rest*
>>> *else if* $V < \beta$ then use *V* as new β;
>>>> find the state *S2* in the *Rest* that has the
>>>> best $(N - 1, \alpha, \beta)$-minimax value *(V2,T2)*, and
>>>> take the one with lower value of (S, V), *(S2, V2)*;
>> *if* *N* is a maximising level then
>>> *if* $V > \beta$ then take (S, V), ignoring the *Rest*
>>> *else if* $V > \alpha$ then use *V* as new α;
>>>> find the state *S2* in the *Rest* that has the
>>>> best $(N - 1, \alpha, \beta)$-minimax value *(V2,T2)*, and
>>>> take the one with higher value of (S, V), *(S2, V2)*.

So we have the program:

```
best_next_state(S,S1) :-
    depth_of_search(N),
    value_bounds(Alpha,Beta),
    alphabeta(N,Alpha,Beta,S,V,S1).

alphabeta(0,_,_,S,V,_) :- !,value(S,V).
alphabeta(N,Alpha,Beta,S,V,S1) :-
    setof(NS,next_state(S,NS),List),
    find_best(N,Alpha,Beta,List,V,S1).

find_best(N,Alpha,Beta,[S|Rest],V1,S1) :-
    N1 is N - 1,
    alphabeta(N1,Alpha,Beta,S,V,T),
    select_better_of(N,Alpha,Beta,S,V,Rest,S1,V1).

select_better_of(_,_,_,S,V,[],S,V) :- !.
select_better_of(N,Alpha,Beta,S,V,List,S1,V1) :-
    minimising(N),
    (V < Alpha,!, (S1,V1) = (S,V);
    (V < Beta,!, Beta1 = V; Beta1 = Beta),
    find_best(N,Alpha,Beta1,List,V2,S2),
    (V < V2,!, (S1,V1) = (S,V); (S1,V1) = (S2,V2))).
select_better_of(N,Alpha,Beta,S,V,List,S1,V1) :-
    maximising(N),
    (V > Beta,!, (S1,V1) = (S,V);
    (V > Alpha,!,Alpha1 = V; Alpha1 = Alpha),
    find_best(N,Alpha1,Beta,List,V2,S2),
    (V > V2,!, (S1,V1) = (S,V); (S1,V1) = (S2,V2))).

minimising(N) :- (N mod 2) =:= 0.
maximising(N) :- (N mod 2) =:= 1.
```

The reader is recommended to use the following sample data and the built-in tracing facilities *trace* and *spy* to follow the search of the above *alpha-beta* procedure.

```
depth_of_search(3).
value_bounds(-100,100).
```

```
next_state(s,a).      next_state(c,j).
next_state(s,b).      next_state(d,k).
next_state(a,c).      next_state(d,l).
next_state(a,d).      next_state(e,m).
next_state(b,e).      next_state(e,n).
next_state(b,f).      next_state(f,o).
next_state(b,g).      next_state(f,p).
next_state(c,h).      next_state(g,q).
next_state(c,i).      next_state(g,r).

value(h,5).           value(n,6).
value(i,4).           value(o,10).
value(j,7).           value(p,2).
value(k,8).           value(q,3).
value(l,9).           value(r,8).
value(m,4).
```

Finally there are two things that should be noted in game search. First, in most games, a game state always has next states, which are normally in a large number. Second, a sequence of game states is allowed to contain duplicated states. By common rules, if a game contains more than a certain number of duplications of some state, then the game is considered a draw.

Supplementary problems

7.11 Three missionaries have persuaded three cannibals to follow them and they are now on the north side of a river. They want to move to the south side, but only have a small boat that can carry at most two people. The problem is that the cannibals are not yet converted, so they should not be allowed to outnumber the missionaries, otherwise they may go back to their habit.

Write a Prolog program to produce a schedule that helps to bring all of the people safely to the south side of the river.

7.12 In a word game you are given two words of the same length and are asked to change the first word, one letter at a time, making it into another meaningful word, until it becomes the second word. For example, given the words "code" and "mark", we have:

code mode more mare mark.

(a) Which search procedure is the most suitable one for this problem?

(b) Write a Prolog program to solve the problem using breadth-first search.

(c) Define an evaluation function that can be used to solve the problem using best-first search.

7.13 A heavy-machine shop has made a terrible mistake by delivering some machines to the wrong customers. The five customers involved are A, B, C, D, and E whose addresses are in the listed order on the delivery line, and the distances between the adjacent locations are almost the same. Machines 1 and 2 are ordered by customer A, but machine 1 is delivered to C and machine 2 is delivered to E. Machine 3 is ordered by B but delivered to D. Machine 4 is ordered by C but delivered to E. Machines 5 and 6 are ordered by D, but machine 5 is delivered to B, while machine 6 is delivered to A. Finally, machines 7 and 8 are ordered by E, but machine 7 is delivered to A, while machine 8 is delivered to B. The shop is in the same district as A, and a truck has to be sent out to pick up and redeliver the machines to the right customers.

Write a Prolog program to advise the truck driver on the most efficient route to pick up and deliver the machines, knowing that the truck can carry at most two machines at a time.

7.14 In the eight-tile puzzle, you are given a board of nine squares, eight of which are occupied by eight tiles numbered from 1 to 8. The task is to find a sequence of moves, shifting one tile at a time, to rearrange the tiles in numerical order with tile 1 in the top-left corner, and with the space in the middle.

2	8	1
4	6	3
7		5

1	2	3
8		4
7	6	5

(a) Find a representation of a state for this problem.

(b) Define an evaluation function that is to be used in the best-first search.

(c) Write a program to solve the problem using best-first search procedure.

7.15 You are given two nickels and two dimes that are initially arranged as shown below. The purpose of the game is to make a sequence of simple moves to bring the coins into the final position shown below.

Initial state   Final state

A coin can be moved by either sliding it to the empty square next to its square, or hopping it over another coin into an empty square. The nickels can only be moved to the right, and the dimes can only be moved to the left, and no backing up is allowed.

Write a Prolog program to find a sequence of legal moves to bring the coins from the given initial state to the final desired state.

7.16 In the problem of harmonising a melody, you are given two notes: an initial note and a terminal note. You are asked to generate a melody that begins with the given initial note, and terminates with the given terminal note, which is taken as the tonic. The notes can be generated as a crotchet, or two quavers, or a triplet. The rule of harmony requires two adjacent notes to be either of the same tone or the second one must be either a second or third up or down. For example:

Write a Prolog program that generates a melody according to the harmonic rule described above.

7.17 A simple fault-tolerant scheme in VLSI-design is described below. The circuit is composed of a grid in which each point represents an electric node. The nodes can communicate along the horizontal and vertical lines. But at any time, there may be some nodes that are at fault. The problem is to find the shortest path through which a node A can send signals to a node B, avoiding any obstacles formed by the faulty nodes.

(a) Which search procedure is the most suitable one for this problem?

(b) Write a program that receives two nodes A and B and produces the shortest path connecting A to B.

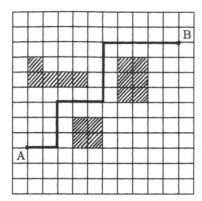

7.18 The traffic in Batehaven is quite busy during the holidays. The tourist bureau of Batehaven is asking you to write a Prolog program to guide tourist car drivers in finding ways of travelling between places in the city.

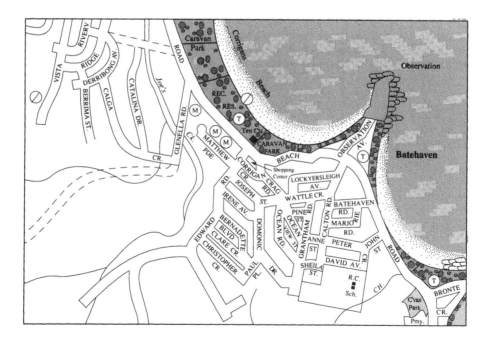

The program receives depart and arrival points, and should produce a list of appropriate moves as shown in the following example:

Where are you now? Enter road intersection
in the form: street1 + street2. > calton + anne.

Where do you want to go? Enter intersection
in the form: street1 + street2. > crag + wattle.

From the intersection of calton + anne
go along anne to the intersection of anne + oceanview
go along oceanview to the intersection of oceanview + pine
⋮

go along ocean to arrive at crag + wattle.

Chapter 8

Meta-programming in Prolog

8.1 Meta-programs

A *meta-program* is a program that manipulates other programs. Examples of meta-programs include program compilers, interpreters, debuggers, and transformers. Many knowledge-based systems also take the form of meta-programs (e.g., TEIRESIAS (Davis, 1980), PRESS (Sterling et al., 1982), NEOMYCIN (Clancey and Bock, 1982), SYLLOG (Walker, 1986), and ESSLN (Le, 1989)).

In Prolog, meta-programming is quite natural, because Prolog programs have the same form as data represented in Prolog. In fact, many programs developed in the preceding chapters involve meta-programming in the form of meta-predicates such as *not, var, setof, arg,* and *functor* (see Section 6.2

of Chapter 6). Those programs, however, perform their activities mainly at the normal level and only occasionally do they have an expression that needs to be evaluated at the meta-level (by the above-mentioned built-in meta-predicates). In this chapter, we study the construction of large meta-programs. In particular, we present the implementation of two typical systems: the first one is LnProlog, a Prolog system with a logical negation evaluator, and the second one is a Prolog debugger.

Conceptually, a meta-program consists of two levels:

- The *object-level* contains the knowledge of an application problem, which is called the domain knowledge. Reasoning within the domain knowledge is performed by an object-level interpreter, which is normally the underlying Prolog system.

- The *meta-level* contains a set of rules on how to use the domain knowledge. These strategic rules form the control-knowledge of the meta-level. The inference at the meta-level is performed by a meta-level interpreter, which can be the same underlying Prolog system.

The structure of a meta-level system is depicted in Figure 8.1

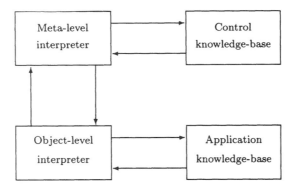

FIGURE 8.1 Structure of a meta-level system.

Note that the underlying Prolog system can be used at both levels. At the meta-level, it is used to select the strategic rule that controls its own behaviour in interpreting the object-level knowledge.

The degree of control of the meta-level on the object-level varies greatly. At one extreme, the control-knowledge may be reduced to the set of the already built-in meta-predicate definitions. In this case, the meta-level interpreter is not needed (because its role is performed by the Prolog system's meta-predicate evaluator), and the meta-program is just an ordinary procedural Prolog program. At the other extreme, the control-knowledge may cover all the inference rules of the object-level interpreter, leaving only the elementary side-effect activities such as input-output and arithmetic computation to be performed at the object-level.

The lifting of object-level inference to the meta-level has the following advantages:

- The control-knowledge becomes explicit and is easier to understand and modify.

- The system can generate explanations of its own behaviour and trace its own activities for debugging.

- The meta-level handles all control aspects of the system, allowing the domain knowledge to be purely declarative.

- The same meta-level structure can be used as a shell for various application problems.

In theory, a meta-level system can be developed into several levels. That is, the system's object-level is controlled by a meta-level, which is in turn controlled by a meta-meta-level, and so on. In practice, however, a two-level organisation is normally adequate for most meta-level systems.

8.2   Meta-programming techniques

In this section, we present some fundamental techniques of meta-programming and we supply a set of meta-programming tools that are useful in developing meta-level systems.

As described in the preceding section, the main component of a meta-level system is its control-knowledge. Syntactically, a control-knowledge has the form of a procedural Prolog program whose procedures, rules, variables are called *meta-procedures, meta-rules, meta-variables*, etc. Semantically, to build a meta-level control-knowledge, the following two important features should be noted:

- A meta-procedure represents a general scheme that specifies how to perform (not a specific task but) a class of tasks. For example, consider the definition of the meta-predicate *not*:

```
not(A) :- A, !, fail.
not(A).
```

These meta-rules apply to the class of formulas of the form $not(A)$ and specify that:

> To evaluate the goal $not(A)$ do
> > evaluate the goal A, and
> > *if* A succeeds then let $not(A)$ fail
> > *else* let $not(A)$ succeed.

- A meta-variable represents a formula, which may contain object-variables within it. Thus, meta-rules and goals may have both meta-variables and object-variables, which should be distinguished from each other. Object-variables represent object-terms, which are constructed from a fixed set of constant and function symbols, whereas meta-variables represent formulas, which are formed by predicate symbols and object-terms. For example, in the goal $setof(X, G, L)$, X and L are object-variables, whereas G is a meta-variable. In writing meta-rules, the reader is advised to take special care to avoid accidental instantiation of object-variables. (For theoretical treatment of meta-variables, we refer to the paper by Lloyd and Hill (1988).)

Having noted the above semantic characteristics of meta-programming, we can now outline a step-by-step process in developing a meta-level control-knowledge.

To build the control-knowledge of a meta-level system, the following steps should be followed:

1. Specify the application problems that are intended to be within the scope of the meta-level system being developed.

2. Classify the various tasks of the application problems into typical classes each of which is represented by a typical formula.

3. For each class of tasks, write a meta-procedure that represents the scheme of performing these tasks.

4. Refine the meta-procedures of step 3 until all subprocedures referred to are either built-in predicates or already developed meta-programming tools.

We shall apply the previously described process to develop a number of useful meta-programming tools, which are to be presented in the following subsections.

As the function of a meta-program is to manipulate other programs, its activities normally involve the following basic tasks:

- Inspecting formulas;
- Modifying formulas;
- Generating new formulas;
- Executing goals.

Following are some typical programs that perform the above-mentioned elementary tasks.

8.2.1   Inspection of formulas

For any given formula, two aspects of interest are its *type* and its *components*. Prolog provides a number of built-in predicates such as *var, nonvar, atom, integer*, and *float* to detect the basic type of a formula. In what follows, we develop programs to extract the components such as *variables, constant symbols*, and *function symbols* from a given formula.

Following is an algorithm that extracts the variables of a formula A and stores them in a list L.

> To extract the variables of a formula A into a list L do
> > collect all variables of A into a queue Q, then
> > eliminate any duplication in Q to obtain L.

> To collect all variables of a formula A into a queue Q do
> > *if* A is a constant then let Q be empty,
> > *if* A is a variable then let Q contain A only,
> > *if* A is an atomic formula of the form $p(A_1, \ldots, A_n)$,
> > > then collect the variables of $A_1, \ldots, A_n$ into Q.

Note that in Prolog, every formula is represented internally as an atomic formula. For example, conjunctions, disjunctions, and implications are represented as follows:

conjunction	A,B	:	','(A,B)
disjunction	A;B	:	';'(A,B)
implication	A :- B	:	':-'(A,B).

Note from the previous algorithm that the extracted variables are initially stored in queues in order to facilitate the task of appending them (see Subsection 6.3.1 of Chapter 6 for queue appending). Note also that this algorithm can be used to detect if a given formula is ground (i.e., having no variables). It is more efficient, however, to check if the formula is ground before attempting to collect its variables. The task of testing a formula's groundness is quite simple: we just make an attempt to change its variables; if the formula does not change, then it is ground. The program to extract the variables of a formula (including a test of the formula's groundness) is given in Figure 8.2.

```
var_list(A,[]) :- ground(A),!.
var_list(A,L) :- collect_var(A,Q-[]),
    setof(X,member(X,Q),L).

collect_var(A,Q-Q) :- constant(A),!.
collect_var(A,[A|Q]-Q) :- var(A), !.
collect_var(A,Q) :- A =.. [P|Args],collect_vars(Args,Q).

collect_vars([],Q-Q) :- !.
collect_vars([A|As],Q-Qt) :-
    collect_var(A,Q-Qs),collect_vars(As,Qs-Qt).

constant(A) :- atom(A); integer(A); float(A).

ground(A) :- copy(A,B), A == B.
copy(A,B) :- assert(zzzz(A)),retract(zzzz(B)).

member :- % see Figure 2.13
```

FIGURE 8.2 Program to extract the variables of a formula.

For example:

```
?- var_list(leq(X,max(X,Y)),L).
X = _0085
Y = _0095
L = [_0085,_0095] ->
```

Once one has got hold of the variables of a given formula, one can instantiate the formula in many ways to inspect its structure. Following are some direct applications of the procedure *var_list* :

- Test if a formula A is an instance of a formula B.
- Test if a formula A is a variant of a formula B, that is, they are the same except that the names of their variables may be different.
- Test if a formula A is a subterm of a formula B.

The programs are shown in Figure 8.3. Here, the procedure *instance* expresses that a formula A is an instance of a formula B if after being instantiated by an arbitrary substitution for its variables, it is still unifiable with B. The definitions of procedures *variant* and *subterm* are obvious.

```
% Test if A is an instance of B:
instance(A,B) :- var_list(A,L),bind_var(L,1),A = B.

bind_var([],_) :- !.
bind_var(['@var'(N)|Xs],N) :- N1 is N+1,bind_var(Xs,N1).

% Test if A is a variant of B:
variant(A,B) :- not(not(instance(A,B))),
                not(not(instance(B,A))).

% Test if A is a subterm of B:
subterm(A,B) :- variant(A,B),!.
subterm(A,[B|Bs]) :- !,(subterm(A,B),!; subterm(A,Bs)).
subterm(A,B) :- B =.. [P|Bs], Bs \= [], subterm(A,Bs).
```

FIGURE 8.3 Applications of *var_list* in inspecting formulas.

For example:

```
?- instance(p(a,f(U)),p(X,Y)).
U = '@var'(1)
X = a
Y = f('@var'(1)) ->
yes
```

```
?- variant(likes(X,Y),likes(U,V)).
X = _0085
Y = _0095
U = _00A5
V = _00B5 ->
yes


?- subterm(f(a,X),[a,b,p(a,f(a,Y))]).
X = _0085
Y = _0095 ->
yes
```

Observe that the procedure *instance* may change the formulas A and B when it binds the variables of A and unifies A and B. To avoid this instantiation we can use $not(not(instance(A, B)))$ as shown in the definition of the procedure *variant*. An alternative way to avoid unwanted instantiation is to perform the test on copies of A and B. That is, we can define:

```
instance_of(A,B) :-
    copy((A,B),(A1,B1)), instance(A1,B1).
```

For example:

```
?- instance_of(p(a,f(U)),p(X,Y)).
U = _0085
X = _0095
Y = _00A5 ->
yes
```

In practice, however, it is more often that we need to test if a formula A is *not* an instance of some other formula B. A typical example is the suppression of duplicated answers to a given problem. This can be realised by the following simple procedure:

```
check_result(A) :-
    not((answer(B),instance(A,B))),
    assert(answer(A)),!.
check_result(A).
```

The next program is to extract constant and function symbols from a given formula. This time, we must distinguish the function symbols from non-functional predicates such as the connectives ",", ";", ":-" and the negating predicates *not* (and *non*, which is to be introduced shortly). Also, to make the symbols globally accessible, we store them as facts of the form:

```
constsymbol(john).              functsymbol(s,1).
constsymbol(sue).               functsymbol(f,2).
   .                               .
   .                               .
   .                               .
```

The program *extract_symbols* is shown in Figure 8.4.

```
extract_symbols((A :- B)) :- !,extract_symbols((A,B)).
extract_symbols((A;B)) :- !,extract_symbols((A,B)).
extract_symbols((A,B)) :- !,extract_symbols(A),
                             extract_symbols(B).
extract_symbols(true) :- !.
extract_symbols(not(A)) :- !,extract_symbols(A).
extract_symbols(non(A)) :- !,extract_symbols(A).
extract_symbols(A) :- A =.. [P|Args],!,extr_symb(Args).
extract_symbols(_).

extr_symb([]) :- !.
extr_symb([A|As]) :- extracts(A),extr_symb(As).

extracts(A) :- var(A),!.
extracts(A) :- constant(A),!,
    (constsymbol(A),!;assert(constsymbol(A))).
extracts(A) :- A =.. [F|Args],functor(A,F,N),
    (functsymbol(F,N),!;assert(functsymbol(F,N))),
    extr_symb(Args).

constant(A) :- atom(A);integer(A);float(A).
```

FIGURE 8.4 Program to extract constant and function symbols from a formula.

The following query extracts constant and function symbols from a clause and stores them in the knowledge-base.

```
?- extract_symbols((p(X) :- not(non(q(X,f(a,b)))))),
   listing([constsymbol,functsymbol]).

constsymbol(a).
constsymbol(b).
functsymbol(f,2).
```

8.2.2   Modification of formulas

The simplest form of modifying a formula is making a copy of it with different variable names. This is realised by the procedure *copy* given in Figure 8.2.

A further step in modifying a formula is to instantiate the formula by using a proper maximally general substitution for its variables. (A substitution is said to be maximally general if there is no other substitution for the same variables that is more general.)

To do this, we extract the variables of the formula into a list L, and we instantiate an arbitrary variable of L with a proper maximally general term constructed from the available constant symbols, function symbols, and the variables in L. A proper maximally general substitution for a variable X in L has one of the following forms:

$X = a$, where a is any available constant symbol;

$X = f(U)$, where f is any available function symbol and U is an appropriate list of new variables;

$X = Y$, where Y is another variable in the list L.

The instantiation program is shown in Figure 8.5.

```
instant_form(A) :- var_list(A,L),instantiate(L).

instantiate([X|Xs]) :- get_term(X,Xs).
instantiate([X|Xs]) :- instantiate(Xs).

get_term(X,Xs) :- constsymbol(X).
get_term(X,Xs) :- functsymbol(F,N),functor(X,F,N).
get_term(X,Xs) :- get_var(X,Xs).

get_var(X,[X|Xs]).
get_var(X,[Y|Xs]) :- get_var(X,Xs).
```

FIGURE 8.5 Instantiation of a formula.

For example, assume that the database currently contains the following only facts of the *constsymbol* and *functsymbol* relations:

```
constsymbol(0).
functsymbol(s,1).
```

Then, we have:

```
?- instantiate([X,Y]).
X = 0
Y = _0095 ->;

X = s(_01E5)
Y = _0095 ->;

X = _0085
Y = _0085 ->;

X = _0085
Y = 0 ->;

X = _0085
Y = s(_0235) ->;
no
```

We shall see in the next sections that the procedure *instantiate* defined above is very useful in implementing a form of logical negation for Prolog.

Another form of changing formulas is to *freeze* the object-variables within the formulas before performing a meta-level operation, and then *melt* them afterwards in order to avoid accidental instantiation. This technique will be discussed in Subsection 8.2.4.

8.2.3   Generation of new formulas

The task of generating new formulas, which is required in many expert system shells, comprises mainly the generation of new predicate and function symbols. To do this, we use a common character (or string of characters) and maintain a global counter to index the generated symbols. The algorithm is given below and the program is shown in Figure 8.6.

To generate a symbol *Symb* do
>   get the common symbol *P* and the global index *I*,
>   convert the integer *I* + 1 into a list *L* of characters,
>   join *P* and *L* to give the new symbol *Symb*,
>   save the value *I* + 1 as new global index.

```
generate_symbol(Symb) :-
    common_symbol(P),
    retract(symbol_index(I)),I1 is I+1,
    int_to_chars(I1,[],L),
    name(Symb,[P|L]),
    assert(symbol_index(I1)).

int_to_chars(0,L,L) :- !.
int_to_chars(I,L,L1) :-
    C is 48 + (I mod 10),
    I1 is I//10,
    int_to_chars(I1,[C|L],L1).

common_symbol(112).
symbol_index(24).
```

FIGURE 8.6 Generation of a new symbol.

For example:

```
?- generate_symbol(Symb).
Symb = p25 ->
```

Some Prolog systems (such as Arity-Prolog and Turbo-Prolog) provide built-in predicates that perform the task of the procedure *int_to_chars* defined above.

8.2.4 Execution of goals

A great power of meta-programming in Prolog is its capability of generating new formulas that can be executed later. For the purpose of handling the execution of goals, Prolog provides the built-in predicates *call* and *clause*.

The goal *call*(*A*), which is equivalent to *A* in most Prolog systems, invokes the execution of the goal *A*, and the goal *clause*(*A, B*) provides a clause whose head unifies with *A* and whose body unifies with *B*.

Meta-programming also provides the potential of changing the course of Prolog's execution, thus, giving much more flexibility to the application system. For example, we can change the order of execution of subgoals in a given goal, or the order of clauses chosen for unification. However, in order to avoid accidental instantiation of object-variables within the goals, it may be necessary to *freeze* them before rearranging the goals, and then *melt* them afterwards.

To *freeze* a goal, we simply substitute its variables with special constant symbols that represent object-variables at the meta-level. These symbols are replaced with the corresponding variables when the goal is *melted*. The programs *freeze* and *melt* are shown in Figure 8.7, where the predicates *var_list*, *copy*, and *constant* have been defined in the preceding subsections.

```
freeze(G,L,G1) :-
    var_list(G,L),copy((G,L),(G1,L1)),
    bind_var(L1,1).

bind_var([],_) :- !.
bind_var(['@var'(N)|L],N) :-
    N1 is N+1,bind_var(L,N1).

melt(A,L,A) :- constant(A),!.
melt('@var'(N),L,V) :- !,nth_var(N,L,V).
melt(A,L,A1) :- A =.. [P|Args],
    melt_list(Args,L,Args1),A1 =.. [P|Args1].

melt_list([],_,[]) :- !.
melt_list([A|As],L,[B|Bs]) :-
    melt(A,L,B),melt_list(As,L,Bs).

nth_var(1,[X|L],X) :- !.
nth_var(N,[_|L],X) :- N1 is N-1, nth_var(N1,L,X).
```

FIGURE 8.7 *Freeze* and *melt* object-variables.

By using *freeze* and *melt*, we can now develop a program that rearranges the subgoals of a given goal so that any subgoals that have some common variables are close to one another. This is for the purpose of efficiency and also for the possibility of parallel evaluation. The program is given below.

```
rearrange(Goal,NewGoal) :- freeze(Goal,L,FGoal),
    arrange([],FGoal,FGoal1), melt(FGoal1,L,NewGoal).

arrange(GL,G,(A,As)) :-
    occurs('@var'(N),GL), subgoal(A,G,G1),
    occurs('@var'(N),A),!,arrange([A|GL],G1,As).
arrange(GL,(A,As),(A,Bs)) :- !,arrange([A],As,Bs).
arrange(_,A,A).

subgoal(A,(A,As),As).
subgoal(A,(B,As),(B,Bs)) :- subgoal(A,As,Bs).
subgoal(A,(B,A),(B)) :- A \= (C,D).

occurs(X,X).
occurs(X,[A|As]) :- !,(occurs(X,A); occurs(X,As)).
occurs(X,Term) :- Term =.. [P|Args], Args \= [],
    occurs(X,Args).
```

FIGURE 8.8 Rearrangement of subgoals in a given goal.

For example:

```
?- rearrange((p(X,Y),q(Z),r(X),s(Z),t(Y)),G).
X = _0085
Y = _0095
Z = _00A5
G = p(_0085,_0095),r(_0085),t(_0095),q(_00A5),s(_00A5) ->
```

Observe from the above program that a goal is unaffected by the procedure *rearrange* if it has fewer than three subgoals. Note also that the predicates *freeze* and *occurs* can be used to check if a variable occurs in a given term. The procedure *occur_check* is defined as follows:

```
occur_check(X,Term) :-
    freeze((X,Term),_,(X1,Term1)),occurs(X1,Term1).
```

The construction of a program that selects the clauses for unification in some specific way is the subject of Problem 8.7. Some Prolog systems, such as the one developed by Gallaire and Lasserre (1982), provide the built-in predicates that allow changing the course of Prolog's execution.

8.3   The problem of the meta-predicate not

Prolog provides, via the meta-predicate *not*, a very simple and efficient form of negation, namely negation-by-failure (see Section 4.4 of Chapter 4). This form of negation has a serious problem, however, as it requires negated goals to be ground at the time of evaluation, otherwise the answers may be incorrect. For example, consider the following simple programs.

EXAMPLE 8.1   The following program describes the situation in John and Sue's home.

```
home(X) :- not(out(X)).
out(sue).
husband(john,sue).
```

With the above program, if we ask "Is John at home?", Prolog's answer is "yes". But when we ask "Is there anyone at home?", the answer is "no".

```
?- home(john).
yes

?- home(X).
no
```

Normally, one would try to overcome this problem by adding a type-goal *person*(X), say, in front of the negated goal. This is not a satisfactory solution, however, for the following two reasons. First, since the program's intended universe contains only "people", we may have in the program the following fact:

```
person(X).
```

which states that everything in this world is a person. Then the addition of the goal *person*(X) would not help at all (anyway, Prolog is a nontype language, so variables are not required to be typed). Second, the issue here is not about how to write programs that fit the system (the question of making good use of the predicate *not* has been discussed in Section 4.4 of Chapter 4), but about how to make the system interpret programs correctly. The program of Example 8.1 is logically correct, so it should be interpreted consistently. The cause of the above-mentioned inconsistency will be pointed out shortly.

EXAMPLE 8.2   The following program defines *even* and *odd* integers using the only constant symbol 0 and a function symbol s (for "successor").

```
even(0).
even(s(s(X))) :- even(X).

odd(X) :- not(even(X)).
```

Again, if we ask "Is $s(0)$ odd ?", Prolog's answer is "yes". But if we ask "Is there anything odd ?", then the answer is "no".

```
?- odd(s(0)).
yes

?- odd(X).
no
```

The above-observed inconsistency is due to Prolog interpreting positive and negative goals in different ways. A positive query ?- $p(X)$ is interpreted as a request for a proof of $\exists X\, p(X)$ (which is read "there exists X such that $p(X)$ is true"), while a negative query ?- $not(p(X))$ is interpreted as a request to prove $\forall X \sim p(X)$ (which is read "for all X, $p(X)$ is false"). This inconsistency is highlighted by the instance that when the variable X is instantiated to a constant a, say, then $not(p(X))$ becomes $not(p(a))$. Thus, a variable in a negated goal may be treated as being bound (by the quantifier $\forall$) at one time, and unbound at other times. Consequently, the goal $not(not(p(X)))$ has no logical meaning.

Several attempts have been made to solve this problem (Sakai and Miyachi (1985), Gabbay and Sergot (1986), Poole and Goebel (1986), Vasey (1986), Sergot and Vasey (1986), Wallace (1987), Chan (1988), and Chan and Wallace (1988)). These authors' suggested systems are effective, but have two common disadvantages. First, the complexity of the negating algorithms used in those systems is comparable to those of many theorem provers, which makes those algorithms difficult to implement efficiently. Second, the answer to a negated goal is normally in the form of inequalities or qualified answers, which are not very useful. For example, if we ask "Which nodes in an integrated circuit are at fault", then an answer such as $X \neq a$, $X \neq b, \ldots$ is certainly unsatisfactory, particularly when only a few nodes are at fault, and the large majority are normal.

In the next section, we present a simple logical negation evaluator, which is used in our LnProlog system and which adds significant power to standard Prolog with little cost. The system has many features that demonstrate the techniques of meta-programming discussed in the preceding section.

8.4   LnProlog's negation evaluator

LnProlog is standard Prolog augmented with a logical negation evaluator. LnProlog extracts the constant and function symbols in a program at the time the clauses are stored in memory.

In LnProlog, negation of an atomic formula A is written as $non(A)$. Evaluation of positive and negative goals in LnProlog is performed in the same manner. That is, in evaluating a positive goal A, the system finds a maximally general substitution for the variables of A such that A succeeds. Similarly, to evaluate a negative goal $non(A)$, the system searches for a maximally general substitution for the variables of A such that A fails.

The meta-procedure that evaluates $non(A)$ is shown in Figure 8.9, in which most predicates have already been defined in Section 8.2. In this procedure, the first clause indicates that in order to evaluate a goal $non(A)$, the system first extracts the variables of A into a list L, and then attempts to instantiate L in evaluating $non(A)$. The next three clauses represent the three typical cases. Two base cases are: if A fails, then $non(A)$ succeeds with no instantiation; if A succeeds with L uninstantiated (i.e., L remains variable-pure with no restriction), then $non(A)$ fails. Otherwise, L is instantiated by a proper maximally general substitution before *eval_non* is called recursively.

The examples that follow the program of Figure 8.9 demonstrate the system's behaviour in evaluating negative goals. (For a proof of the system's correctness, we refer to the paper by Le (1990).)

```
non(A) :- var_list(A,L),eval_non(A,L).

eval_non(A,L) :- not(A),!.
eval_non(A,L) :- eval(A),uninstantiated(L),!,fail.
eval_non(A,L) :- instantiate(L),
                 re_var_list(L,VL),eval_non(A,VL).

eval(A) :- A,!.
uninstantiated(L) :- var_pure(L),unrestricted(L,0).

var_pure([]) :- !.
var_pure([X|Xs]) :- var(X),var_pure(Xs).

unrestricted([],_) :- !.
unrestricted([N|Xs],N) :- N1 is N+1,unrestricted(Xs,N1).

re_var_list(A,L) :- var_list(A,L1),shift_var(L1,L).

shift_var([],[]) :- !.
shift_var([X|L],L1) :- append(L,[X],L1).

var_list :-    % see Figure 8.2
instantiate :- % see Figure 8.5
```

FIGURE 8.9 LnProlog's negation evaluator.

EXAMPLE 8.3   The program that describes the world of John and Sue is now rewritten as follows:

```
home(X) :- non(out(X)).
out(sue).
husband(john,sue).
```

When the above program is entered, LnProlog recognises the constant symbols "sue" and "john" as the only constants that exist in the world described by the program. These constants are automatically stored as facts:

```
constsymbol(sue).
constsymbol(john).
```

The above facts form a part of the system's meta-knowledge and are used by the negation evaluator in evaluating negated goals. In fact, we have:

```
?- home(john).              ?- home(X).
yes                         X = john ->;
                            no


?- non(home(X)).            ?- non(non(home(X))).
X = sue ->;                 X = john ->;
no                          no


?- not(non(home(X))).
no
```

Note that the second query is equivalent to the fourth one, which shows that the meta-predicate *non* is a logical negator. The last query given above is a quantified query which asks "Is everyone at home ?"; the answer is "no", as the response to the third query shows Sue is not at home. More details on the representation of quantified goals in LnProlog are discussed in Section 8.6.

In order to explain the internal process of evaluating a negated goal, let us consider a more general program that contains both constant and function symbols. The program is given in the next example.

EXAMPLE 8.4   Consider the following program:

```
even(0).
even(s(s(X))) :- even(X).

odd(X) :- non(even(X)).
```

When the above program is entered, LnProlog recognises the constant symbol '0' and the function symbol 's' as the only constant and function symbols that exist in the world described by the program (i.e., the world of the natural integers). These symbols are automatically stored as facts:

```
constsymbol(0).
functsymbol(s,1).
```

that form a part of the system's meta-knowledge and are used by the negation evaluator in evaluating negated goals.

So, we have the following results:

```
?- odd(s(0)).              ?- odd(X).
yes                        X = s(0) ->;
                           X = s(s(s(0))) ->;
                           X = s(s(s(s(s(0))))) ->;
```

If we repeatedly press the semicolon key, the system would provide all *odd numbers* in the form $s^{2n+1}(0)$, where $n = 0, 1, 2, \ldots$. Internally, the evaluation of the goal $odd(X)$ proceeds as follows.

To evaluate $odd(X)$, the system evaluates $non(even(X))$. To do this, the system first attempts $not(even(X))$, which fails since $even(X)$ succeeds. Then the system tries to evaluate $even(X), uninstantiated([X])$, which also fails, as X is instantiated to 0. So, the system attempts to instantiate X with a maximally general term, which is either 0 or $s(Y)$.

With $X = 0$, $eval\_non(even(0), [])$ fails because $even(0), uninstantiated([])$ succeeds. With $X = s(Y)$, again both goals $not(even(s(Y)))$ and $even(s(Y))$, $uninstantiated([Y])$ fail. So, the system attempts to instantiate Y with a maximally general term, which is again 0 or $s(Z)$.

With $Y = 0$, $eval\_non(even(s(0)), [])$ succeeds as $not(even(s(0)))$ succeeds. Therefore, the system returns the first answer $X = s(0)$. If we press the semicolon key to request alternative answers, then the system backtracks to instantiate Y to $s(Z)$, and the whole evaluating process described above is repeated until an answer $X = s(s(s(0)))$ is found, and so on.

EXAMPLE 8.5   The following program describes faulty nodes in an integrated circuit. A node is faulty if it does not respond to some other nodes.

```
fault(X) :- non(respond(X,Y)), X \== Y.

respond(a,b).
respond(a,c).
respond(b,a).
```

When the above program is entered, LnProlog recognises the constant symbols a, b, c and they are stored in the following facts:

```
constsymbol(a).
constsymbol(b).
constsymbol(c).
```

The relation *respond* represents a report recorded by an automated checking device. The list covers all nodes in the circuit (which is assumed, in this example, to have only three nodes). The queries and responses are shown below:

```
?- fault(a).                    ?- fault(b).
no                              yes

?- fault(c).                    ?- fault(X).
yes                             X = b ->;
                                X = c ->;
                                no

?- non(fault(X)).               ?- non(non(fault(X))).
X = a ->;                       X = b ->;
no                              X = c ->;
                                no

?- not(non(fault(X))).
no
```

Here, node *a* is not faulty, as it responds to both nodes *b* and *c*; this is reflected in the answers to the first and the fifth queries. Nodes *b* and *c* are faulty, as *b* does not respond to *c* and *c* does not respond at all; this is reflected in the answers to the second, the third, and the fourth queries. Note again that the fourth and the sixth queries are equivalent since the meta-predicate *non* is a logical negator. Finally, the last query means "Is every node faulty?"; the answer is "no" because node *a* is not faulty.

EXAMPLE 8.6 The following example is not really practical, but it provides an insight into the system's behaviour. The program defines the length of a list, and we can ask if there is anything whose length is either undefined or not equal to a given number N. The answers show that the system's behaviour is quite logical.

```
length([],0).
length([H|T],N) :-
    length(T,M),(N is M+1; N < M+1,!,fail).
```

```
?- non(length(L,0)).           ?- non(length(L,1)).
L = 0 ->;                      L = [] ->;
L = 1 ->;                      L = 0 ->;
L = [_2AB5|_2AB9] ->;          L = 1 ->;
L = _2AC1 + _2AC5 ->;          L = [_2AB5|0] ->;
no                             L = [_2AB5|1] ->;
                               L = [_2AB5,_39E1|_39E5] ->;
                               L = [_2AB5|_39ED + _39F1] ->
```

Observe that the system does not realise that the function length should apply to lists only and that in a list $[X\,|\,Y]$, the second argument Y must be a list. The reason is that this information is not given to the system. More precisely, since Prolog is a nontype language, the domain of any function is universal, that is, the function can be applied to any kind of arguments. This relaxed behaviour, though logical, is undesirable. We shall see in the next chapter that when predicates and functions are typed, the system's behaviour becomes quite rational.

8.5   LnProlog's meta-preprocessor

The preprocessor of LnProlog performs the following tasks:

1. Read the user's query and convert it into a Prolog query.

2. Process the query according to the following rules:

   - If the query is a clause, then extract the constant and function symbols from the clause, and store the clause in the object knowledge-base.

   - If the query is a *consult* or *reconsult* goal, then inspect the specified file to extract all constant and function symbols in the file before loading the file into the object knowledge-base.

   - If the query is a goal of the form *assert, asserta*, or *assertz*, then extract the constant and function symbols from its argument before storing it in the object knowledge-base.

   - If the query is an ordinary goal, then perform the process of evaluating the goal and report the result.

LnProlog's preprocessor and negation evaluator form the system's control-knowledge, which is to be placed in the system's meta-level. Any application knowledge is stored in a separate object-level.

```
lnprolog :-
    initialise,
    repeat,
        receive_query(S,G),
        process_query(S,G),
    fail.

initialise :-
    introduction,
    create_world(objworld),
    code_world(_,objworld).

introduction :-
    cls,nl,
    nl,write('===================LNPROLOG===================='),
    nl,write('== is standard Prolog plus a logical negator. =='),
    nl,write('==In LNPROLOG, the negating predicate is "non"=='),
    nl,write('== and the success of non(A) provides values  =='),
    nl,write('== for the variables of A so that A is false. =='),
    nl,write('==============================================').

receive_query(S,G) :-
    nl,nl,write('?:'),write(' '),
    read_query($ $,S),
    convert_query(S,G).

read_query(S0,S) :-
    read_string(100,S1),concat(S0,S1,S2),nl,
    (end_query(S1),!,S = S2; read_query(S2,S)).

end_query(S) :-
    string_length(S,K),N is K-1,nth_char(N,S,46).

convert_query(S,G) :- string_term(S,G),!.
convert_query(S,G) :- nl,write('syntax error'),!,fail.
```

FIGURE 8.10 LnProlog's preprocessor(top levels).

```
process_query(S,(A :- B)) :- !,process_clause((A :- B)).
process_query(S,G) :- G =.. [P|Args],
    (member(P,[consult,reconsult]),!,process_file(Args);
     member(P,[assert,asserta,assertz]),!,
         process_assert(Args); true),
    process_goal(S,G).

process_clause(Clause) :-
    extract_symbols(Clause),
    assert(Clause),nl,write(stored).

process_file([Filename]) :-
    see(Filename), readfile, seen.

readfile :-
    repeat,
        read(Clause),
        (Clause = end_of_file,!;
        extract_symbols(Clause),fail).

process_assert([Clause]) :-
    extract_symbols(Clause).

extract_symbols :- % see Figure 8.4
process_goal :-    % see Figure 8.12
```

FIGURE 8.11 LnProlog's processing of clauses, files, and assert-goals.

For the role of the meta-level interpreter, we can choose either Arity-Prolog, Turbo Prolog, Prolog-2, or any other Prolog system that provides the means to divide the database into separate levels. Without such facilities, we must find some other way (e.g., prefixing the meta-predicates with special characters and rewriting the database-manipulating predicates such as *listing, retract,* and *abolish*) to prevent the user from arbitrary access to the system's control-knowledge.

In the version of LnProlog's meta-preprocessor given in Figures 8.10 and 8.11, we use some special predicates provided by Arity-Prolog for database management and string handling, which are explained below.

`create_world(objworld)` : create a world called 'objworld'.

`code_world(_,objworld)` : make 'objworld' the current object-level, which is the only world accessible to the built-in predicates *listing, assert, asserta, assertz, retract, abolish*, and *clause*. Note, however, that the default world (which is called *"api"* in Arity-Prolog 4.0), where the control-knowledge is stored, is accessible to the meta-level interpreter from anywhere. (Surprisingly, this convenient access is not allowed in Arity-Prolog 5.1. In that case, we place LnProlog in the same place as any user's program by replacing the goal *initialise* in Figure 8.10 with the goal *introduction*.)

`read_string(100,S1)` : read a string of up to 100 characters from the current input device into *S1*.

`concat(S0,S1,S2)` : concatenate the strings *S0, S1* giving *S2*.

`string_length(S,K)` : the length of string *S* is *K*.

`nth_char(N,S,46)` : the *N*th character of string *S* is the period.

`string_term(S,G)` : convert string *S* into a Prolog goal *G*.

We now consider how LnProlog processes a goal and reports the result. The system first extracts a list of variable symbols from the string representing the goal to maintain alongside the goal's list of (internally represented) variables. Then, the system performs the evaluation of the goal, which, if successful, instantiates the above-mentioned variables. The system then matches the list of variable symbols with the list of variables' values to report the result.

To avoid reporting duplicate answers, LnProlog saves all found answers. If the next answer is an instance of some already found answer, then it is simply ignored. At the end of a goal's evaluating process, all answers are discarded. The goal processing procedure is shown in Figure 8.12.

Figure 8.13 shows the procedure that extracts variable symbols from a string of characters. First of all, the string is converted into a list of characters (by using the built-in predicate *list_text*). Then, the system scans the list (using *append*), skipping any substrings enclosed between matching quotation marks, to find the variable symbols that start with a capital letter or an underscore and are terminated by an invalid character. If the variable symbol found has occurred before and is not the underscore, then it is discarded, otherwise it is collected. Here, the procedure *quote_found* is used to detect the next quotation mark (which could be a single quote (ASCII code 39), a double quote (34), or a dollar sign (36)), and the procedure *var_found* is called to recognise the start of a variable symbol.

```
process_goal(S,Goal) :-
    var_symbols(S,VS),
    var_list(Goal,VL),
    evaluate(Goal,VS,VL),
    remove(answer(X)).

evaluate(Goal,VS,VL) :-
    prove(Goal,_,_),process_result(VS,VL),!.
evaluate(_,_,_) :- nl,write('no').

prove(Goal,_,_) :- call(Goal).

process_result([],[]) :- !,nl,write('yes').
process_result(VS,VL) :- duplicated_answer(VL),!,fail.
process_result(VS,VL) :- print_answer(VS,VL,VL1),
    assert(answer(VL1)), process_response.

print_answer(['_'|Xs],[V|VL],[_|VL1]) :- !,
    print_answer(Xs,VL,VL1).
print_answer([X|Xs],[V|VL],[V|VL1]) :-
    nl,write(X),write(' = '),write(V),
    print_answer(Xs,VL,VL1).
print_answer([],[],[]).

process_response :- write(' ->'),
    (get0(59),!,fail;nl,write('yes')).

duplicated_answer(A) :-
    answer(B),instance(A,B).

remove(A) :- retract(A),fail; true.

instance :-      % see Figure 8.3
var_list :-      % see Figure 8.2
var_symbols :- % see Figure 8.13
```

FIGURE 8.12 LnProlog's goal evaluating procedure.

```
var_symbols(S,VS) :- list_text(L,S),
    list_var_symbols(L,0,[],VS).

list_var_symbols(L,Q,VT,VS) :-
    append(A,[B,C|D],L),
    (quote_found(Q,B,Q1),!,
        list_var_symbols([C|D],Q1,VT,VS);
     var_found(Q,B,C),!,
        append(A1,[C1|D1],[C|D]),not(valid(C1)),!,
        name(V,A1),
        (member(V,VT),V \= '_', VS = VS1,!; VS = [V|VS1]),
        list_var_symbols([C1|D1],0,[V|VT],VS1)).
list_var_symbols(_,_,_,[]).

quote_found(0,B,B) :- member(B,[34,36,39]),!.
quote_found(Q,Q,0).

var_found(0,B,C) :- not(valid(B)),var_start(C).

var_start(C) :- (65 =< C, C =< 90); C = 95.
valid(C) :- (65 =< C, C =< 90);    % A - Z
            (97 =< C, C =< 122);   % a - z
            (48 =< C, C =< 57);    % 0 - 9
            C = 95.                % underscore

member :- % see Figure 2.13
append :- % see Figure 2.21
```

FIGURE 8.13 LnProlog's variable symbols extracting procedure.

Finally, at the end of an application session, the object-level knowledge
should be removed by using the following procedure:

```
clear_objbase :-
    delete_world(objworld),
    create_world(objworld),
    code_world(_,objworld),!.
```

The built-in predicate *delete_world* cleans out the world 'objworld' and cancels its name as well. So, we have to recreate the world and make it the current object-level again for the next round of application.

8.6   Representation of quantified goals in LnProlog

The availability of the built-in predicates *not* and *non* (defined in Section 8.4) allows quantified goals to be represented with ease in LnProlog. Following is a list of typical quantified goals and their representation in LnProlog.

Quantified goal	Representation in LnProlog
$\forall X\, p(X)$	`not(non(p(X)))`
$\forall X \sim p(X)$	`not(p(X))`
$\exists X\, \forall Y\, p(X,Y)$	`p(X,_),not(non(p(X,_)))`
$\exists X\, \forall Y \sim p(X,Y)$	`non(p(X,_)),not(p(X,_))`

The operational meanings of the above-listed goals are elucidated as follows:

1. The goal $not(non(p(X)))$ succeeds if and only if $non(p(X))$ fails. That is, there are no values for X such that $p(X)$ is false. Equivalently, $p(X)$ is true for every value of X.

2. The goal $not(p(X))$ succeeds if and only if $p(X)$ fails. That is, there are no values for X such that $p(X)$ is true. Equivalently, $p(X)$ is false for every value of X.

3. The goal $p(X,\_),not(non(p(X,\_)))$ succeeds with an answer $X = S$ if and only if $p(X,Z)$ succeeds with an answer $X = S$, $Z = T$, and $not(non(p(S,Y)))$ succeeds. This means $p(S,Y)$ is true for every value of Y.

4. The goal $non(p(X,\_)),not(p(X,\_))$ succeeds if and only if $non(p(X,Z))$ succeeds with an answer $X = S$, $Z = T$, and $not(p(S,Y))$ succeeds. This means $p(S,Y)$ is false for every value of Y.

EXAMPLE 8.7   Let us consider the program of Example 8.5 again. In this version, the last fact expresses that the node c responds to all nodes.

```
fault(X) :- non(respond(X,Y)), X \== Y.

respond(a,a).              respond(b,a).
respond(a,b).              respond(b,b).
respond(a,c).              respond(c,X).
respond(a,d).
```

```
?- not(non(fault(X))).     % Are all nodes faulty ?
no
```

```
?- not(fault(X)).          % Are all nodes not faulty ?
no
```

% Which node responds to all nodes ?
```
?- respond(X,_),not(non(respond(X,_))).
X = a ->;
X = c ->;
no
```

% Which node doesn't respond to any node ?
```
?- non(respond(X,_)),not(respond(X,_)).
X = d ->;
no
```

The above representation of quantified goals has several advantages over the traditional representation using combinations of type predicates and the *not* predicate. To justify this claim, we make the following query again:

Which node responds to all nodes ?

As we have shown, this query is represented in LnProlog as follows:

```
?- respond(X,_),not(non(respond(X,_))).                    (1)
```

Traditionally, it can be represented in the following form:

```
?- node(X),not((node(Y),not(respond(X,Y)))).               (2)
```

The first obvious advantage of the goal (1) over goal (2) is that it contains only one user-defined predicate and one explicit variable. This makes it easier for the first form to be translated back to a user language than the second one. (This advantage becomes more significant when we deal with multitype systems such as expert systems, as we shall see in the next chapter.)

The second advantage involves efficiency. Suppose that the knowledge-base contains the following single fact for the relation *respond*:

```
respond(X,Y).
```

which states that "every node responds to all nodes". Then goal (1) succeeds immediately (with no instantiation), whereas goal (2) may take a long while to scan all nodes, yet it can only be able to return one node name at a time, and this does not express that "every node responds to all nodes".

In LnProlog, we also introduce a built-in predicate *all*, which is defined by the following clauses in the system's control-knowledge:

```
all(G) :- G \= (A,B), not(non(G)).
all(L,G) :-  copy((L,G),(L1,G1)), L = L1,
             G1,not(non(G)).


non(non(G)) :- !,G.
```

The first two clauses given above simplify the representation of the quantified goals listed at the beginning of this section. The last clause is not logically necessary (as $non(non(G))$ has been shown (in Le(90)) to be logically equivalent to G), but it enhances the system's efficiency by avoiding unnecessary work. Thus, the following pairs of goals are equivalent:

Quantified goal in LnProlog	Representation using *all*
not(non(p(X)))	all(p(X))
not(p(X))	all(non(p(X)))
p(X,_),not(non(p(X,_)))	all([X],p(X,_))
non(p(X,_)),not(p(X,_))	all([X],non(p(X,_)))

EXAMPLE 8.8   The queries given in Example 8.7 can be expressed in the simplified form using the predicate *all* as shown below.

```
?- all(fault(X)).        % Are all nodes faulty ?
no

?- all(non(fault(X))).   % Are all nodes not faulty ?
no
```

```
% Which node responds to all nodes ?
?- all([X],respond(X,_)).
X = a ->;
X = c ->;
no
```

```
% Which node doesn't respond to any node ?
?- all([X],non(respond(X,_))).
X = d ->;
no
```

For applications that involve user languages, however, it is advisable to translate user queries directly to the *not-non* form to avoid unnecessary extra work for the system's interpreter and explanation generator.

8.7   Simulation of a Prolog interpreter for debugging

In this section, we present the construction of a meta-level system that simulates a Prolog interpreter for the purpose of program debugging.

As the system's objective is to operate like a Prolog interpreter and to record the results and activities during the course of proving a goal, the system must satisfy the following primary requirements:

- The system must handle failure properly to prevent loss of information due to failure.

- The system must detect the situation where there is the possibility of nontermination to avoid being trapped in an infinite loop.

Thus, for any goal, the search tree is finite and every search branch is terminated with a goal that causes one of the following situations:

- A *successful termination* that results from the current goal being unified with a fact.

- A *failed termination* that results from the current goal not being resolved with any clause.

- A *forced termination* that results from the system's detection that the current search branch has reached the maximum allowable depth.

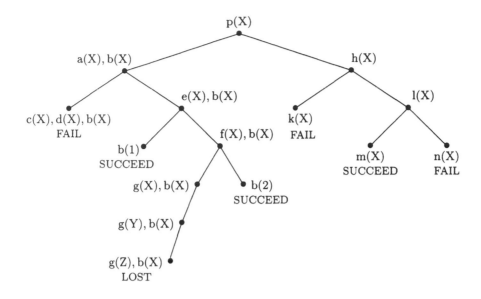

FIGURE 8.14 A finite search tree.

Figure 8.14 shows an example of a finite search tree. This search tree describes the execution of the goal $p(X)$ using the program of Example 8.9.

EXAMPLE 8.9

```
p(X) :- a(X),b(X).          a(X) :- c(X),d(X)
p(X) :- h(X).               a(X) :- e(X).

b(1).                       e(1).
b(2).                       e(X) :- f(X).

f(X) :- g(X).               g(X) :- g(Y).
f(2).                       h(X) :- k(X); l(X).

l(X) :- m(X); n(X).
m(3).
```

To copy the behaviour of a Prolog interpreter in proving the goal $p(X)$, we require the simulating system to operate in the manner described in the following list.

1. Follow the leftmost search branch to the end. In realising that the goal
   $c(X)$ does not resolve with any clause, the system records a *branch failure proof*:

   ```
   p(X) :- (a(X) :- (c(X) :- noclause), (d(X) : nottried)),
           (b(X) : nottried).
   ```

2. Backtrack to follow the next leftmost search branch to the end. Now,
   realising that this is a successful termination, the system reports to
   the user a successful result and the *success proof*:

   ```
   p(1) :- (a(1) :- (e(1) :- fact)), (b(1) :- fact).
   ```

   Then the system waits for the user's request of alternative proof or
   termination.

3. If the user requests an alternative proof, then the system backtracks
   to follow the next leftmost search branch. In realising that this search
   branch has reached the maximum allowable depth, the system stops
   and records an *assumed failure proof*:

   ```
   p(X) :- (a(X) :- (e(X) :- (f(X) :- (g(X) :- (g(Y) :-
           (g(Z) :- toofar)))))), (b(X) : nottried).
   ```

4. Backtrack to follow the next leftmost search branch to the end. This is
   a successful termination, so the system reports the current successful
   result and the success proof:

   ```
   p(2) :- (a(2) :- (e(2) :- (f(2) :- fact))), (b(2) :- fact).
   ```

   Then, it waits for the user's request.

5. If the user requests another alternative proof, then the system backtracks to follow the next leftmost search branch, which terminates with
   a failed goal. So, the system records another branch failure proof:

   ```
   p(X) :- (h(X) :- (k(X) :- noclause)).
   ```

6. Backtrack to follow the next leftmost search branch, which terminates with a success. So, the system reports the successful result and the success proof:

```
p(3) :- (h(3) :- (l(3) :- (m(3) :- fact)))
```

and waits for the user's request.

7. If the user requests more alternative proofs, then the system backtracks to follow the next leftmost search branch, which terminates with a failure and which is also the last branch. So, the system reports a *failure* and presents the list of all *branch failure proofs*.

Thus, if a goal has no answers at all, then all search branches fail, and the goal's failure proof is a list that is made up of all branch failure proofs.

The foregoing-described step-by-step process is generalised into the following top-level algorithm of the *meta-interpreter*.

To prove a goal up to a specified depth and return the result
and the goal's proof do
        follow the next leftmost search branch to its terminal goal
            to collect a branch proof, and
        check the result to see:
            if it is a success then
                return a success result and a success proof, and
                wait for the user's request
            else record the branch (actual or assumed) failure, and
                backtrack to search the next leftmost branch.
        If there are no more search branches
            then collect the failure proofs.

Now, to search for a *branch proof*, the system must handle the following different classes of goals.

General cases :

If the goal has the form

$(A; B)$: then first try to find a proof of A;
            if unsuccessful, then find a proof of B.

(A, B) : then first try to find a proof of A;
            if successful then
                find a proof of B, and combine the two proofs to give
                a proof of (A, B)
            else B need not be tried.

A : a system goal, then call the object-level interpreter to execute A.
         The proof of A is returned in the form A :- *system* : *result*.

A : an atomic formula that is not a system goal.
         Find a clause $A1$:- B such that A unifies with $A1$. Then find a
         proof of B (with the allowable depth decremented by 1).
         The proof of A is returned in the form A :- *proof of B*.
         If there are no clauses that could be resolved with A, then
         terminate with failure. The failure proof of A is returned in the
         form A :- *noclause*.

Special cases :

Depth = 0 : The branch has reached the maximum allowable depth. The
        result should indicate that the system has lost track of the proof, and
        it is *assumed* to be a *failure*.

The goal may also have the following special form:

true : The proof terminates successfully with a *fact*.

not(A) : The system must find a proof of A, then inverts it to obtain a
        proof of *not*(A). That is, if A succeeds then *not*(A) fails and its failure
        proof has the form *fails*(*success proof of A*); conversely, if A fails then
        not(A) succeeds and its success proof has the form *succeeds*(*failure
        proof of A*).

setof(X, G, L) : The system first collects all the proofs of G. If G fails then
        L is empty and the failure proof of *setof*(X, G, L) is returned in the
        form *setnull*(*failure proof of G*). If G succeeds then for each answer,
        the corresponding value of X (with no duplication) is placed in L and
        the corresponding proof is stored in a list of proofs of G. The proof of
        the goal *setof*(X, G, L) is returned in the form *setfull*(*proofs of G*).

The program that performs the above-described meta-level activities is shown
in Figures 8.15 and 8.16.

```
prove(Goal,Depth,Result,Proof) :-
    prove_branch(Goal,Depth,Result,Proof),
    check_result(Goal,Depth,Result,Proof).
prove(Goal,Depth,no,FailProof) :-
    collect_failbranches(Goal,FailProof).


prove_branch(true,D,yes,fact) :- !.
prove_branch(A,0,lost,toofar) :- !.
prove_branch(not(A),D,NegResult,NegProof) :-
    prove(A,D,Result,Proof),!,
    invert(A,Result,NegResult,Proof,NegProof).
prove_branch(setof(X,G,L),D,Result,(setof(X,G,L) :- Proof)) :-
    !, setof(p(X,D,R,P),prove(G,D,R,P),ListProof),
    filter_proof(ListProof,Result,L,Proof).
prove_branch((A;B),D,Result,Proof) :- !,
    (prove_branch(A,D,Result,Proof);
     prove_branch(B,D,Result,Proof)).
prove_branch((A,B),D,Result,(ProofA,ProofB)) :- !,
    prove_branch(A,D,ResultA,ProofA),
    prove_conj(ResultA,B,D,Result,ProofB).
prove_branch(A,D,Result,(A :- system:Result)) :-
    syst(A),!,(A,!,Result = yes; Result = no).
prove_branch(A,D,no,(A :- noclause)) :-
    not(clause(A,B)),!.
prove_branch(A,D,Result,(A :- Proof)) :-
    clause(A,B),D1 is D-1,
    prove_branch(B,D1,Result,Proof).
```

FIGURE 8.15 A Prolog meta-interpreter (part 1).

The Prolog meta-interpreter shown in Figures 8.15 and 8.16 does not cater for the *cut*. In fact, the cut is treated simply as a system goal that always succeeds, and thus it has absolutely no effect on the system's operation.

Simulating the effect of the *cut* is easy if we have the availability of a built-in referential cut predicate, such as *cut(Label)* in IBM-Prolog or *cut(Ancester)* in Waterloo-Prolog (see Problem 8.1). Standard Prolog does not provide such facilities, however. So, the system must detect the occurrence of the cut well in advance, in order to arrange for its effect.

```
invert(A,yes,no,SuccProof,(not(A) :- fails(SuccProof))).
invert(A,no,yes,FailProof,(not(A) :- succeeds(FailProof))).

prove_conj(yes,B,D,Result,Proof) :- !,
    prove_branch(B,D,Result,Proof).
prove_conj(RA, B,D,RA,B:nottried).

check_result(G,D,yes,_) :- !,
    (maxdepth(D),!; collect_failbranches(G,_)).
check_result(G,_,_,Proof) :-
    assert(failproof(G:Proof)),!,fail.

collect_failbranches(G,[FailBranch|Rest]) :-
    copy(G,G1),retract(failproof(G1:FailBranch)),!,
    collect_failbranches(G,Rest).
collect_failbranches(_,[]).

syst(A) :- functor(A,F,N),system(F/N).

filter_proof([p(X,D,no,P)],no,[],setnull(P)) :- !.
filter_proof(ListProof,yes,L,setfull(LProof)) :-
    filter(ListProof,[],L,LProof).

filter([],_,[],[]) :- !.
filter([p(X,_,R,_)|Rest],L1,L,LProof) :-
    (R = no; member(X,L1)),!,filter(Rest,L1,L,LProof).
filter([p(X,_,yes,P)|Rest],L1,[X|Xs],[P|Ps]) :-
    filter(Rest,[X|L1],Xs,Ps).

member(X,[X|_]).
member(X,[_|T]) :- member(X,T).

copy(A,B) :- assert(zzzz(A)),retract(zzzz(B)).
maxdepth(20).
```

FIGURE 8.16 A Prolog meta-interpreter (part 2).

The arrangement to simulate the cut's effect is described as follows.

To find a branch proof for a single goal A, we find a clause $(A1 :- B)$ such that A unifies with $A1$. If B contains the cut, then it is split into two parts: $B1$ consists of the subgoals to the left of the cut, including the cut, and $B2$ consists of the subgoals to the right of the cut (if there are none, then let $B2$ be *true*). Then we find a branch proof for $B1$. If it is a failure proof, then we simply add $B2$ untried to it to give a branch failure proof of A. If it is a success proof, then we cut all alternatives before finding a branch proof for $B2$, which is to be added to the branch proof of $B1$ to give a branch (success or failure) proof of A.

So, the last clause of the program shown in Figure 8.15 is to be replaced by a new clause, which is presented in Figure 8.17.

```
prove_branch(A,D,Result,(A :- Proof)) :-
    clause(A,B),D1 is D-1,
    detect_cut(B,B1,B2,Cut),
    (Cut = yes,prove_branch(B1,D1,R1,Proof1),
      (R1 \= yes,Result = R1,return_proof(Proof1,B2,Proof);
       R1 = yes,!,prove_branch(B2,D1,Result,Proof2),
                conjunct(Proof1,Proof2,Proof));
     Cut = no,prove_branch(B,D1,Result,Proof)).

detect_cut(B,B1,B2,yes) :- cutin(B,B1,B2),!.
detect_cut(_,_,_,no).

cutin(!,!,true) :- !.
cutin((!,B),!,B) :- !.
cutin((A,!),(A,!),true) :- !.
cutin((A,B),(A,As),Bs) :- cutin(B,As,Bs).

return_proof(Proof1,B,Proof) :-
    B = true,!, Proof1 = Proof;
    conjunct(Proof1,(B : nottried),Proof).

conjunct(A,fact,A) :- !.
conjunct((A,As),L,(A,Bs)) :- !,conjunct(As,L,Bs).
conjunct((A),L,(A,L)).
```

FIGURE 8.17 Simulation of the cut in standard Prolog.

Let us now perform a number of tests on the Prolog meta-interpreter shown in Figures 8.15, 8.16, and 8.17. Taking again the program of Example 8.9, we have:

```
?- prove(p(X),20,Result,Proof).

X = 1
Result = yes
Proof = p(1) :- (a(1) :- (e(1) :- fact)), (b(1) :- fact) ->;

X = 2
Result = yes
Proof = p(2) :- (a(2) :- (e(2) :- (f(2) :- fact))),
(b(2) :- fact) ->;

X = 3
Result = yes
Proof = p(3) :- (h(3) :- (1(3) :- (m(3) :- fact))) ->;

X = _0085
Result = no
Proof = [(p(_032D) :- (a(_032D) :- (c(_032D) :- noclause),
d(_032D) : nottried), b(_032D) : nottried),
(p(_0745) :- (a(_0745) :- (e(_0745) :- (f(_0745) :-
(g(_0745) :- (g(_099D) :- (g(_09B1) :- (g(_09C5) :-
(g(_09D9) :- (g(_09ED) :- (g(_0A01) :- (g(_0A15) :-
(g(_0A29) :- (g(_0A3D) :- (g(_0A51) :- (g(_0A65) :-
(g(_0A79) :- (g(_0A8D) :- (g(_0AA1) :- (g(_0AB5) :-
toofar)))))))))))))))))), b(_0745) : nottried),
(p(_0C91) :- (h(_0C91) :- (k(_0C91) :- noclause))),
(p(_1069) :- (h(_1069) :- (1(_1069) :- (n(_1069) :-
noclause))))] ->
```

Consider next the proofs of some special goals.

```
?- prove(not(a(4)),20,Result,Proof).

Result = yes
Proof = not(a(4)) :- succeeds([(a(4) :- (c(4) :- noclause),
(d(4) : nottried)), (a(4) :- (e(4) :- (f(4) :- (g(4) :-
```

```
(g(_0A2D) :- (g(_0A41) :- (g(_0A55) :- (g(_0A69) :-
(g(_0A7D) :- (g(_0A91) :- (g(_0AA5) :- (g(_0AB9) :-
(g(_0ACD) :- (g(_0AE1) :- (g(_0AF5) :- (g(_0B09) :-
(g(_0B1D) :- (g(_0B31) :- (g(_0B45) :- (g(_0B59) :-
toofar)))))))))))))))))))])) ->
```

```
?- prove(setof(X,p(X),L),20,Result,Proof).
```

```
X = _0085
L = [1,2,3]
Result = yes
Proof = setof(_0085,p(_0085),[1,2,3]) :- setfull([(p(1) :-
(a(1) :- (e(1) :- fact)), (b(1) :- fact)),
(p(2) :- (a(2) :- (e(2) :- (f(2) :- fact))), (b(2) :- fact)),
(p(3) :- (h(3) :- (l(3) :- (m(3) :- fact))))]) ->;
```

```
no
```

We now test the effect of the cut by using the following program:

```
p(X) :- a(X),!,b(X).
p(X) :- c(X).
```

```
a(1).          b(X).
a(2).          c(4).
a(3).
```

```
?- prove(p(X),20,Result,Proof).
```

```
X = 1
Result = yes
Proof = p(1) :- (a(1) :- fact), (! :- system : yes),
(b(1) :- fact) ->;
```

```
X = _0085
Result = no
Proof = [] ->;
no
```

8.8   A Prolog debugger

Having constructed a Prolog meta-interpreter that provides proofs for any given goal, we can now build a Prolog debugger that locates the erroneous clauses in a program if some answer to a given goal is incorrect.

We distinguish two types of errors:

- The system gives an answer that is realised to be incorrect. We call this *type-0* error.

- The system gives a "no" response while the goal is expected to have some answers. We call this *type-1* error.

Let us consider first the *type-0* errors. Given a success proof of a goal (which may be a single goal or a conjunction of goals), we want to find the erroneous clause that is used in the proof and that led to the incorrect success. Consider the following cases:

1. If the goal is a single goal, then its success proof has the form $A :\text{-} B$, and the erroneous clause is within this proof.

2. If the goal is a conjunction of goals, then its success proof has the form $((A :\text{-} B), (C :\text{-} D), \ldots, (P :\text{-} Q))$, and the erroneous clause could be in $(A :\text{-} B)$ or in $(C :\text{-} D), \ldots, (P :\text{-} Q)$.

3. If the goal has the form $not(A)$, then its success proof has the form $succeeds(FailProof)$, and the erroneous clause is the cause of a type-1 error in *FailProof*.

4. If the goal has the form $setof(X, G, L)$, then its success proof has the form $setfull(SetProof)$, and the erroneous clause is within *SetProof*.

Now to find the erroneous clause within a success proof $A :\text{-} B$, we do as follows:

First we check with the user if A is true.
If the user confirms that A is true then the proof is fine.
If the user indicates that A is false then
    we try to find the erroneous clause in B;
      if nothing is wrong with B, then the erroneous clause
        must be the very first clause $A :\text{-} B_1, \ldots, B_n$.

```
find_error(0,(A :- B),Clause) :- !,
    find_errclause(0,(A :- B),Clause).
find_error(0,((A :- B),Rest),Clause) :- !,
    (find_errclause(0,(A :- B),Clause),!;
     find_error(0,Rest,Clause)).
find_error(0,succeeds(FailProof),Clause) :- !,
    find_error(1,FailProof,Clause).
find_error(0,setfull(SetProof),Clause) :-
    convert(SetProof,ConjProof),
    find_error(0,ConjProof,Clause).

find_errclause(R,(A :- B),Clause) :-
    ask_user(A,R),!,
    (find_error(R,B,Clause),!;
     recollect_body(B,Body),Clause = (A :- Body)).

ask_user(A,R) :-
    nl,write('Do you expect the goal '),
    write(A),write(' to be true? (y/n): '),
    get0(C),
    (C =:= 110+R*11,!; C =:= 110+11* (1-R),!,fail;
     ask_user(A,R)).

recollect_body(fact,true) :- !.
recollect_body(noclause,nofact) :- !.
recollect_body(toofar,nonterminate) :- !.
recollect_body((B : nottried),B) :- !.
recollect_body((B :- C),B) :- !.
recollect_body(((B :- C),Rest),(B,Bs)) :-
    recollect_body(Rest,Bs).

convert([A|T],(A,S)) :- convert(T,S).
convert([A],(A)).
```

FIGURE 8.18 A Prolog debugger (part 1: incorrect success).

The first part of the debugger is shown in Figure 8.18. There are a few things in the program of Figure 8.18 that may need further explanation.

First of all, it is necessary to convert a *SetProof*, which is a list of proofs, into a conjunction of proofs, *ConjProof*, so that the procedure *find_error* can be called to find the erroneous clause within *ConjProof*. Secondly, when the user is asked whether a goal A is true, if the answer is "n", then $C = 110$ $(R = 0)$ and the goal *ask_user*(A, R) succeeds, so *find_error* is called to find the erroneous clause in B; but if the answer is "y", then $C = 121$ $(R = 0)$ and the goal *ask_user*(A, R) fails, hence *find_errclause* is abandoned. If the answer is anything other than "y" or "n", then the question is repeated.

The procedures *find_errclause* and *ask_user* are designed to be reused in the second part (finding type-1 error) of the debugger. Note that if $R = 1$, then in the above-given explanation, the references to "n" and "y" on the one hand, and 110 and 121 on the other hand, are to be exchanged.

Now, to find the erroneous clause in a failure proof we consider the following cases:

1. If the failure proof is a list of branch failure proofs, then the error can be in any of those branch failure proofs.

2. If the failure proof is a branch failure proof of the form

$$((A :\text{-} B), \ldots, (C :\text{-} D), (E : \text{nottried}), \ldots)$$

   then the erroneous clause is certainly within the proof $(C :\text{-} D)$. In the case there is no proof of the form $(E : \text{nottried})$, then the error is in the last proof of the conjunction.

3. If the failure proof has the form *fails*(*SuccProof*), then the erroneous clause is the cause of a type-0 error in *SuccProof*.

4. If the failure proof has the form *setnull*(*SetProof*), then the error is within *SetProof*.

The process of finding a type-1 erroneous clause in a branch failure proof of the form $A :\text{-} B$ is similar to that for type-0 error. That is:

We first check with the user if A is true.
If the user asserts that A is false then the proof is fine.
If the user indicates that A is true then
  we try to find the erroneous clause in B;
    if nothing is wrong with B, then the erroneous clause
      must be the very first clause $A :\text{-} B_1, \ldots, B_n$.

```
find_error(1,[Proof|Rest],Clause) :-
    find_error(1,Proof,Clause);
    find_error(1,Rest,Clause).

find_error(1,(A :- B),Clause) :- !,
    find_errclause(1,(A :- B),Clause).
find_error(1,Proof,Clause) :-
    convert(ListProof,Proof),
    append(Left,[(A :- B)|C],ListProof),
    (C = [(D : nottried)|_]; C = []),!,
    find_errclause(1,(A :- B),Clause).
find_error(1,fails(SuccProof),Clause) :- !,
    find_error(0,SuccProof,Clause).
find_error(1,setnull(SetProof),Clause) :-
    find_error(1,SetProof,Clause).

append([],L,L).
append([X|T],L,[X|R]) :- append(T,L,R).
```

FIGURE 8.19 A Prolog debugger (part 2: incorrect failure).

The debugger's second part is shown in Figure 8.19. Let us now perform some tests on the debugger.

EXAMPLE 8.10 Consider the following program, which is intended to define the greatest common divisor of two given positive integers.

```
gcd(X,0,X) :- X > 0.
gcd(X,Y,Z) :- X < Y, gcd(Y,X,Z).
gcd(X,Y,Y) :- X >= Y, Y > 0, X1 is X mod Y, gcd(Y,X1,Z).
```

However, when the following query is entered, the answer is incorrect:

```
?- gcd(14,35,Z).
Z = 14 ->
```

So, we use our Prolog meta-interpreter and debugger to find out what is wrong with the program.

```
?- prove(gcd(14,35,Z),20,Result,Proof),
   find_error(0,Proof,ErrorClause).

Do you expect the goal gcd(14,35,14) to be true? (y/n): n
Do you expect the goal 14 < 35 to be true? (y/n): y
Do you expect the goal gcd(35,14,14) to be true? (y/n): n
Do you expect the goal 35 >= 14 to be true? (y/n): y
Do you expect the goal 14 > 0 to be true? (y/n): y
Do you expect the goal 7 is 35 mod 14 to be true? (y/n): y
Do you expect the goal gcd(14,7,7) to be true? (y/n): y

Z = 14
Result = yes
Proof = gcd(14,35,14) :- (14 < 35 :- system : yes),
(gcd(35,14,14) :- (35 >= 14 :- system : yes),
(14 > 0 :- system : yes), (7 is 35 mod 14 :- system : yes),
gcd(14,7,7) :- (14 >= 7 :- system : yes), (7 > 0 :-
system : yes), (0 is 14 mod 7 :- system : yes),(gcd(7,0,7) :-
(7 > 0 :- system : yes))))

ErrorClause = gcd(35,14,14) :- 35 >= 14, 14 > 0,
7 is 35 mod 14, gcd(14,7,7) ->
```

The result indicates that the last clause of the program is wrong, because there is an instance where its head is false while all the subgoals in its body are true. In fact, the clause's head should be corrected to be $gcd(X, Y, Z)$.

EXAMPLE 8.11   The following program is intended to find the least number in a given list.

```
least_num(X,[H|T]) :-
    least_num(Y,T),
    (H =< Y, X = H; H > Y, X = Y).
```

But when we try the following query, the program fails to provide an answer, which does exist.

```
?- least_num(X,[4,2,1,3]).
no
```

So, we call the Prolog meta-interpreter and the debugger to locate the error in the program.

```
?- prove(least_num(X,[4,2,1,3]),20,Result,Proof),
   find_error(1,Proof,ErrorClause).
```

```
Do you expect the goal least_num(_03C9,[4,2,1,3])
to be true? (y/n) : y
Do you expect the goal least_num(_0621,[2,1,3])
to be true? (y/n) : y
Do you expect the goal least_num(_0645,[1,3])
to be true? (y/n) : y
Do you expect the goal least_num(_0669,[3])
to be true? (y/n) : y
Do you expect the goal least_num(_068D,[])
to be true? (y/n) : n
X = _0085
Result = no
Proof = [(least_num(_03C9,[4,2,1,3]) :-
(least_num(_0621,[2,1,3]) :- (least_num(_0645,[1,3]) :-
(least_num(_0669,[3]) :- (least_num(_068D,[]) :- noclause),
(3 =< _068D, _0669 = 3; 3 > _068D, _0669 = _068D):nottried),
(1 =< _0669, _0645 = 1; 1 > _0669, _0645 = _0669):nottried),
(2 =< _0645, _0621 = 2; 2 > _0645, _0621 = _0645):nottried),
(4 =< _0621, _03C9 = 4; 4 > _0621, _03C9 = _0621):nottried)]
```

```
ErrorClause = least_num(_0669,[3]) :- least_num(_068D,[]),
(3 =< _068D, _0669 = 3; 3 > _068D, _0669 = _068D) ->
```

The result shows that the program's only clause is incorrect when the given list consists of a single element. In fact, the following fact should be added to the program:

```
least_num(X,[X]).
```

Note

The Prolog meta-interpreter shown in Figures 8.15, 8.16, and 8.17, and the debugger shown in Figures 8.18 and 8.19 are ready to be used in any standard Prolog system. The incorporation of these tools into an existing Prolog system such as LnProlog is discussed in Problems 8.2, 8.3, and 8.4.

Solved problems

8.1 IBM-Prolog provides a built-in referential cut predicate that is not available in standard Prolog. In IBM-Prolog, the goal *cut(mark)* cancels all alternatives between the execution of the current goal and the immediately preceding execution of *label(mark)*; any alternatives of the goal that calls this *label(mark)* are also cancelled.

By using a combination of *label(mark)* and *cut(mark)*, rewrite the program of Figure 8.17 to realise the effect of the standard cut that may appear in a Prolog program.

Solution:

```
prove_branch(!,D,yes,(! :- system:yes)) :- cut(mark).
prove_branch(A,D,Result,(A :- Proof)) :-
    label(mark),
    clause(A,B),D1 is D-1,
    prove_branch(B,D1,Result,Proof).
```

Suppose that after the execution of *label(mark)*, the goal *clause(A, B)* succeeds with B being unified with a goal of the form *B1,!,B2*. If *B1* fails, then *prove_branch* returns a branch failure proof and backtracks as usual. But as soon as *B1* succeeds, the goal *prove_branch(!,...)* calls *cut(mark)*, which cancels all alternatives between the current goal and the execution of the last *label(mark)*, effectively preventing any further backtracking to *B1* and *clause(A, B)*.

8.2 Write a meta-program to simulate the tracer of Prolog (see Subsection 4.7.3 of Chapter 4). That is, the system should report to the user every time it crosses one of the four ports *call, exit, redo,* or *fail,* in evaluating a goal. For the form of display, copy the format of Prolog's tracer, a sample of which is shown in Figure 4.10.

Solution:

The tasks performed by a Prolog tracer are quite simple. When the system starts evaluating a simple goal, it reports a *call* to the user. If the goal succeeds, then the system reports *exiting* the goal. If the goal fails, then the system reports a *failure* before backtracking to the previous goal. On re-entering a (previous) goal, the system reports a *redo* of this goal. To keep track of the level of the current goal, the system maintains a depth indicator that is incremented each time the search branch is extended. The program is given below.

```
trace(true,D) :- !.
trace((A;B),D) :- !,(trace(A,D); trace(B,D)).
trace((A,B),D) :- !, trace(A,D), trace(B,D).

trace(A,D) :-
    report(D,'CALL',A),
    trace_goal(A,D),
    report(D,'EXIT',A).
trace(A,D) :-
    report(D,'FAIL',A),fail.

trace_goal(A,D) :- syst(A),!,A.
trace_goal(A,D) :- find_clause(A,B,D),D1 is D+1,
    detect_cut(B,B1,B2,Cut),
    (Cut = yes,trace(B1,D1),!,trace(B2,D1);
     Cut = no, trace(B,D1)).

find_clause(A,B,D) :-
    clause(A,B), report_redo(A,D).

report_redo(A,D).
report_redo(A,D) :- report(D,'REDO',A),fail.

report(Depth,Port,Goal) :-
    nl,write([Depth]),write(' '),write(Port),write(': '),
    write(Goal), write(' ? >'), (get0(99),!; nl,abort).

syst(A) :- functor(A,F,N),system(F/N).
detect_cut :- % see Figure 8.17
```

8.3 LnProlog evaluates a goal simply by calling the object-level interpreter to do the task (see procedure *evaluate* of Figure 8.12). In order to incorporate the debugger developed in Section 8.8 into LnProlog, it is necessary to make the procedure *evaluate* return a proof of the evaluated goal, which is to be used by the debugger.

(a) Rewrite the procedures *evaluate* and *process_result* of LnProlog to incorporate the meta-interpreter and the debugger developed in Sections 8.7 and 8.8, respectively.

(b) What changes are required for the meta-interpreter to work in the special environment in which LnProlog is placed?

Solution:

(a) The procedures *evaluate* and *process_result* are rewritten as follows:

```
evaluate(Goal,VS,VL) :-
    prove(Goal,20,Result,Proof),
    process_result(VS,VL,Result),
    process_response(Result,Proof),!.
evaluate(_,_,_).

process_result(_,_,no) :- !,nl,write('no').
process_result([],[],yes) :- !,nl,write('yes').
process_result(VS,VL,yes) :- duplicated_answer(VL),!,fail.
process_result(VS,VL,yes) :- print_answer(VS,VL,VL1),
    assert(answer(VL1)).

process_response(Result,Proof) :- write(' ->'),get0(C),
    (C = 59, !, fail; % 59 is ';' and 119 is 'w'
     C = 119,!, error_type(Result,R),
                find_error(R,Proof,ErrorClause),
                print_error(ErrorClause); true).

error_type(yes,0).
error_type(no,1).
print_error(ErrorClause) :-
    nl,nl,write('Error Clause: '),write(ErrorClause).
```

(b) Recall that LnProlog's control knowledge, including its logical negator, is stored at the meta-level, and any application knowledge it possesses is stored at the object-level. For application programs that do not contain the *non* predicate, the meta-interpreter works fine, as the goal *clause*(A, B) only needs access to the object-level. If an application program contains the *non* predicate, then there are two cases:

- If we are not interested in having proofs for the negated goals of the form *non*(A), then we can simply declare *non* to be a system predicate by changing the definition of *syst*:

  ```
  syst(A) :- functor(A,F,N),(system(F/N); F = non).
  ```

- If we do want proofs for negated goals *non*(A), then we must allow the meta-interpreter to access the definition of the *non* predicate. To do this, we replace the goal *clause*(A, B) with *find_clause*(A, B), which is defined as follows:

  ```
  find_clause(A,B) :- clause(A,B).
  find_clause(A,B) :- code_world(X,api),
          clause(A,B), code_world(_,X).
  ```

The good thing about the built-in predicate *code_world* of Arity-Prolog is that it changes the current world from one level to another, but if it is encountered during backtracking, then the current world is changed back to the previous level. Thus, the predicate *code_world* can be used as a door that stands between the object-level and the meta-level.

Here, the system initially works at the object-level. So, when *find_clause* (A, B) is called, the goal *clause*(A, B) searches the object-knowledge base for clauses that can unify with A. When the object-knowledge is exhausted, the system backtracks to execute the second clause of *find_clause*(A, B), which calls *code_world*(X, api) to enter the meta-level (which is the default world of Arity-Prolog and is called *api*), where the goal *clause*(A, B) continues to search the meta-knowledge for clauses that can unify with A. Every time it succeeds, *code_world*$(\_, X)$ changes the current world back to the object-level. When the system backtracks to find alternative clauses, it passes the goal *code_world*$(\_, X)$ to get into the meta-level again, where *clause*(A, B) searches for alternative clauses, and so on.

Note that it is obviously simpler to place LnProlog in the environment of standard Prolog, where there is no division between the object-level and the meta-level. This, however, risks possible damages to the system's control-knowledge by accidental execution of the predicates *abolish, assert, retract,* etc., in the application program.

8.4   Assume that LnProlog (or any Prolog system) already has the meta-interpreter (Figures 8.15 and 8.16), the debugger (Figures 8.18 and 8.19), and the tracer (developed in Problem 8.2) in its control-knowledge. We now study how to give the user the choice of running LnProlog with the debugger or the tracer on or off.

(a) Write an extra clause for the procedure *process_query* of Figure 8.11 that recognises special queries such as *debug, nodebug, trace, notrace* and turns the relevant tool on or off accordingly.

(b) Rewrite the procedure *evaluate* so that the system calls the debugger or the tracer only when their indicators are on, otherwise the system simply calls the object-interpreter to evaluate the goal.

(c) What changes to the procedure *find_clause* of the tracer developed in Problem 8.2 are necessary to make it work in the environment of LnProlog (which separates the object-level from the meta-level)?

Solution:

(a) The following clause should be added at the beginning of procedure *process_query* :

```
process_query(S,G) :- special_query(G),!,G.
```

The special queries are defined as follows:

```
special_query(G) :-
    member(G,[debug,nodebug,trace,notrace,clear_objbase]),!.

debug :- assert(debugger(on)),
    nl,write('Display proof ? (y/n): '),
    (get0(121),!,assert(displayproof(on)); true),nl.

nodebug :- retract(debugger(on)),
           retract(displayproof(on)).

trace :-   assert(tracer(on)).
notrace :- retract(tracer(on)).
clear_objbase :- % see page 367.
```

(b) The procedure *evaluate* must now test if the debugger or the tracer has been turned on.

If the debugger is on, then the system calls the meta-interpreter to evaluate a goal so that a proof is returned together with the answer (which may be positive or negative). After displaying the answer, the system prompts for the user's response. If the user is satisfied with the answer, then the user simply presses any key other than the semicolon and "w", and the evaluation terminates. If the user presses the semicolon key (in the case of a positive answer), then the system backtracks to find alternative answers. If the user judges that the answer is incorrect, then she presses "w" (meaning "wrong"), and the system calls the debugger to locate the erroneous clause in the proof.

If the debugger is off and the tracer is on, then the system calls the tracer to evaluate the goal. Each time the tracer crosses one of the ports *call, exit, redo, fail*, it reports the goal to the user; the user presses "c" to continue or any other key to terminate.

The debugger gives more specific help to the user, but runs much slower than the tracer. The procedure *evaluate* is rewritten as follows:

```
evaluate(Goal,VS,VL) :-
    (debugger(on),!, prove_goal(Goal,VS,VL);
     tracer(on),!,  trace(Goal,0);
                    call_goal(Goal,VS,VL)),!.
```

```
evaluate(_,_,_) :- remove(failproof).

prove_goal(Goal,VS,VL) :-
    prove(Goal,20,Result,Proof),
    process_result(VS,VL,Result),
    process_response(Result,Proof),!.

call_goal(Goal,VS,VL) :-
    call(Goal), process_result(VS,VL,yes),
    (VS = [],!; process_response(yes,_)),!.
call_goal(_,_,_) :- nl,write('no').

process_response(Result,Proof) :-
    write(' ->'),get0(C),
    (C = 59, !, fail;  % 59 is ';' and 119 is 'w'
     C = 119,!, (debugger(on),!,error_type(Result,R),
                 find_error(R,Proof,ErrorClause),
                 print_error(Proof,ErrorClause);
                 nl,write('Debugger is not on !'));
     true).

print_error(Proof,ErrorClause) :-
    (displayproof(on),!,nl,nl,write(Proof); true),
    nl,nl,write('Error Clause: '),write(ErrorClause).

error_type(yes,0).
error_type(no,1).

remove(P) :- A =..[P,X],retract(A),!,remove(P).
remove(P).
```

Note that, we can remove the unnecessary details in a goal's proof by declaring some predicates to be system predicates. For example, in evaluating a negative goal of the form $non(A)$, we may not wish to know how the system extracts the variables from a goal and how the variables are instantiated, etc. So, we can redefine the predicate *syst* as follows:

```
syst(A) :- functor(A,F,N),
           (system(F/N);
            member(F,[var_list,eval,uninstantiated,
                      instantiate, re_var_list]).
```

Then, we remove the second *cut* in the *prove_branch* clause that handles system goals to allow backtracking on the predicates declared above.

That is, the clause becomes:

```
prove_branch(A,D,Result,(A :- system : Result)) :-
    syst(A),!,(A, Result = yes; Result = no).
```

(c) To allow the tracer to access the definition of the predicate *non*, which is placed at the meta-level in LnProlog, the procedure *find_clause*(A, B, D) is changed as follows:

```
find_clause(A,B,D) :-
    clause(A,B),report_redo(A,D).
find_clause(A,B,D) :-
    code_world(X,api),
    clause(A,B),
    code_world(_,X),
    report_redo(A,D).
```

8.5 A simple way to provide proofs of goals is to store the proof of every atomic formula of an application program as an extra argument of the formula, so that when the goal is evaluated, its proof is returned immediately.

(a) Explain how the above-suggested method applies to the following program, and how a proof of the goal $p(X)$ is obtained:

```
p(X) :- a(X),b(X).
a(X) :- c(X),d(X).
b(X) :- e(X).
c(1).
c(2).
d(X).
e(1).
```

(b) Write a meta-program that transforms standard Prolog clauses into clauses of the form suggested above.

(c) What are the advantages and disadvantages of the suggested method?

Solution:

(a) The given program is rewritten as follows:

```
p(X,((a(X) :- Pa),(b(X) :- Pb))) :- a(X,Pa),b(X,Pb).
a(X,((c(X) :- Pc),(d(X) :- Pd))) :- c(X,Pc),d(X,Pd).
b(X,(e(X) :- Pe)) :- e(X,Pe).
c(1,true).
c(2,true).
d(X,true).
e(1,true).
```

When the goal $p(X, Proof)$ is evaluated, *Proof* unifies with $(a(X) :\text{-} Pa), (b(X) :\text{-} Pb)$. Then the goal $a(X, Pa)$ is executed, causing Pa to unify with $(c(X) :\text{-} Pc), (d(X) :\text{-} Pd)$. Then the goal $c(X,Pc)$ is executed and is unified with $c(1, true)$. Next, the goal $d(1, Pd)$ unifies with $d(X, true)$, after which $b(1, Pb)$ is executed, causing Pb to unify with $(e(1) :\text{-} Pe)$. Finally, $e(1, Pe)$ unifies with $e(1, true)$. Therefore, the goal $p(X, Proof)$ succeeds, and we have:

```
?- p(X,Proof).
X = 1
Proof = (a(1) :- (c(1) :- true),(d(1) :- true)),
        (b(1) :- (e(1) :- true)) ->
```

(b) We distinguish two cases:

1. If the clause is a unit clause, then we simply add an extra argument *true* to the formula.

2. If the clause is nonunit and has the form $A :\text{-} B$, then we first transform the body $B = (p(X), \ldots, q(Y))$ into two parts:

$$PA = (p(X) :\text{-} P, \ldots, q(Y) :\text{-} Q)$$
$$B1 = (p(X, P), \ldots, q(Y, Q)).$$

Then we add *PA* as an extra argument to the head *A* to obtain the new head *A1*. The transformed clause is thus *A1 :- B1*. The program is given below:

```
transform((A :- B),(A1 :- B1)) :- !,
    trans_body(B,PA,B1),
    add_argument(A,PA,A1).
transform(A,A1) :-
    add_argument(A,true,A1).

trans_body((B,Bs),((B :- PB),PBs),(B1,B1s)) :- !,
    add_argument(B,PB,B1),
    trans_body(Bs,PBs,B1s).
trans_body(B,(B :- PB),B1) :-
    add_argument(B,PB,B1).
```

```
add_argument(A,X,A1) :-
    A =.. [P|Xs], append(Xs,[X],Ys),
    A1 =.. [P|Ys].

append([],L,L).
append([H|T],L,[H|R]) :- append(T,L,R).
```

(c) An obvious advantage of the suggested method is its high efficiency due to the direct use of Prolog execution. This is also a weakness, because direct use of Prolog execution means that information is lost when failure occurs. Thus, the suggested technique does not provide failure proofs.

Supplementary problems

8.6   Some Prolog systems (e.g., MU-Prolog) avoid the problem of non-ground negated goals (see Section 8.3) by applying the following selection rule in goal evaluation. Given a goal of the form $A_1, A_2, \ldots, A_n$, if A_1 is a positive goal or a ground negative goal, then the system evaluates the goal in the same way as standard Prolog. If A_1 is a nonground negated goal (of the form $not(A)$), then the system delays its execution by swapping it with the next goal A_2 before trying to evaluate the goal again.

(a) Write a meta-procedure that performs the tasks of inspecting a goal and swapping its subgoals if necessary as described above.

(b) Comment on the advantages and disadvantages of this technique.

8.7   Some Prolog systems (such as Prolog by Gallaire and Lasserre (1982)) provide the built-in predicates that allow the user to specify the way of selecting clauses to be resolved with a goal.

(a) Write a meta-procedure that tests if a given simple goal is of a specific type, and if it is, selects the clauses that can resolve with the goal in ascending order of their length (i.e., number of subgoals in the clause).

(b) Comment on the advantages and disadvantages of using the facilities described above.

8.8   Write a Prolog program that receives an arithmetic equation and performs the following tasks:

- Count the number of unknowns (which are represented by non-numeric constant symbols) in the equation. (Hint: follow the procedure *extract_symbols* of Figure 8.4.)

- If the equation has no unknowns, then evaluate both sides and return "yes" if the equation holds, otherwise return "no".

- If the equation has only one unknown, then solve the equation and return the solution. For example, for the equation $1 + 2 * x = 3$, the returned solution is $x = 1$.

- If the equation has more than one unknown, solve one unknown in terms of the others. For example, for the equation $1 + 2 * x = 3 * y$, the returned solution should be $x = (3 * y - 1)/2$.

8.9 Write a meta-program that simulates a simple editor. Use a two-dimensional array to represent the rows and columns. The editor should be able to perform the following tasks:

- Move back and forth within the current line (row), and move to the previous line or the next line if they exist.

- Add a blank line after the current line.

- Add or insert a character at the current position.

- Delete the character at the current position or the character to its left (i.e., the effect of backspace).

- Delete the whole current line and move the cursor to the left end position.

8.10 Many sensory and diagnosis expert systems apply the forward-chaining reasoning technique, which works as follows. Given a set of rules and a list of symptoms that are represented as facts, the system uses the facts to establish the conditions of the rules. If a rule has one condition (i.e., a subgoal) satisfied, that condition is eliminated from the rule to give a new rule (the old rule is discarded if it is no longer useful). If a rule becomes a fact, then it is added to the list of facts to be used like other facts. When all facts have been used, the final list of facts is reported as the possible conclusions of the symptoms.

Write a meta-program that performs the forward-chaining reasoning process as described above.

Chapter 9

Building expert systems in Prolog

9.1 What is an expert system?

An expert system is a computer system that is capable of solving problems in some specific domain with the skill of human experts.

Basically, an expert system is a computer program. However, expert systems differ from ordinary computer programs in many aspects. First, expert systems deal with problems that are incomplete and unapparent. Hence, unlike conventional computer systems that employ well-defined algorithms to solve problems, expert systems apply logical deduction and heuristic search

397

to find answers. Second, like human experts, an expert system must be able to explain to the user how it arrived at a conclusion. Third, an expert system must be able to check and update its knowledge by learning either from human experts or simply from ordinary users.

The well-known expert systems in use are in the fields of medical diagnosis (MYCIN, CASNET, and CADUCEUS), molecular-structure analysis (DENDRAL), symbolic differentiation and integration (MACSYMA, SAINT, and MATHLAB), and speech understanding (HEARSAY I and II). Numerous other expert systems with very specialised domains are also being used in industry and laboratories.

9.2   Components of an expert system

The fundamental architecture of an expert system is depicted in Figure 9.1. From the inside out, an expert system consists of the following components:

- A *knowledge-base* that contains expert knowledge in some specific domain.

- An *inference engine* that manipulates the knowledge-base to find answers for given problems.

- An *explanation generator* that provides explanations to the user about how the system arrives at a conclusion.

- A *user-interface* that helps the system to communicate with the user. User's queries are converted into internal form to be processed by the system; conversely, the system's answers and explanations are translated into a language the user can understand.

In the expert systems written in Prolog, the inference engine, the explanation generator, and the user interface are meta-programs that form the control-knowledge of the system, which we shall study in the subsequent sections. The system's knowledge-base contains facts and rules that represent the system's knowledge in a particular field. This knowledge-base normally consists of two parts. The main part represents the expert knowledge in the system's specialised domain. For example:

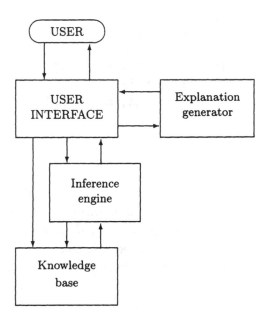

FIGURE 9.1 Architecture of an expert system.

A patient has symptoms of being infected by EB-virus if
    the patient has high temperature, and
    the patient has sore throat, and
    the patient's heterophil-agglutination test is positive.

EB-virus is classified as herpesvirus-4.
Herpesvirus-4 is transmitted by saliva.

The above expert knowledge is represented in the knowledge-base by the following facts and rules.

```
viral_infection(Patient,'EB-virus') :-
    temperature(Patient,high),
    symptoms(Patient,sore_throat),
    test(Patient,heteroagglu,positive).

classify('EB-virus',herpesvirus_4).
transmission(herpesvirus_4,saliva).
```

The second part of the knowledge-base represents specific-case information, which is usually organised into frames. For example:

```
patient_details([name: N, age: A, occupation: O]).
test_results([blood: B, munofluorescence: MF,
              heteroagglu: HA, microagglu: MA]).
```

The slots in the above frames are to be filled when the relevant information is supplied by the user.

Basically, the system works as follows. To answer a user's query, the system converts it into a Prolog query. The inference engine (which is a meta-interpreter) is then called to search the knowledge-base to find an answer for the query. During this searching process, if an unfilled frame is found, then the user is asked to supply required information. When an answer is found, it is translated into the user language and is presented to the user. If the user requests an explanation, then the explanation generator is called to form the explanation, which is also given to the user in the user language.

9.3   Building an expert system

The methods of building expert systems are so diverse that it requires a whole book to explore all aspects of the art (see, for example, Hayes-Roth, Waterman, and Lenat (1983)). In this section and the subsequent ones, we only present the techniques of building expert systems in Prolog. In particular, we show the development of ESSLN, a simple but powerful expert system shell that supports quantified queries, subtypes, and various user languages.

We begin with a general plan for building an expert system using Prolog. To develop an expert system, the following steps are to be followed:

1. Define the scope of the system. It is advisable that the narrower the scope is the more hopeful it will result in an effective and efficient system. After all, the word "expert" means something very specialised.

2. Collect expert knowledge by consulting human experts in the relevant field or by perusing the books in libraries.

3. Organise the collected expert knowledge into a Prolog knowledge-base by using the following hierarchical approach. First, we classify the potential problems into different classes. For each class of problems,

we list all the possible queries we can think of. Then, for each query we list the information required to answer the query. This is represented in the knowledge-base by a Prolog rule where the subgoals are to be considered as queries at the next level. The process is continued until all subgoals are either facts that can be obtained from the collected expert knowledge, or specific-case information, which is to be supplied by the user. Each piece of specific-case information is represented by a to-be-filled fact or frame in the knowledge-base.

4. Finally, we test the knowledge-base by putting queries to the system and verifying the answers.

Figure 9.2 shows the hierarchical structure of an expert system's knowledge-base.

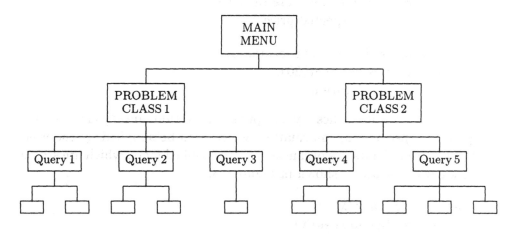

FIGURE 9.2 The hierarchical structure of an expert knowledge-base.

Following is a simple example that demonstrates the construction of an expert system's knowledge-base.

EXAMPLE 9.1   Let us develop the knowledge-base for an expert system that advises diners about the restaurants in town which suit them best.

First of all, we collect the names of the good restaurants in town with relevant details such as their specialties, price, and location, and whether or not they use MSG, chilli, or other special spices in their food. We then list the possible queries, which are not many in this case, as the scope of the system has been narrowed considerably. A possible query is the following:

Which restaurant suits me best ?

To answer the above query, the following rules are formed:

A restaurant suits you best *if*
    its specialties include your favourites, and
    its price is within your expectation, and
    its location is close to your location.

A restaurant's specialties include your favourites *if*
    your favourite dishes are among
    the ones in the restaurant's list of specialties.

A restaurant's price is within your expectation *if*
    its average price is not more than $ 5
        above your expected price.

A restaurant is close to your location *if*
    its location is less than 20 km
        from your location.

Here, "your" favourite dishes, "your" price expectation, and "your" location compose the specific-case information, which is to be supplied by the user. So, these expected data are organised into to-be-filled facts, which are stored in the knowledge-base as shown in Figure 9.3.

```
best_restaurant(X) :-
    serve_favourites(X),
    good_price(X),
    close_location(X).

serve_favourites(X) :-
    your_favourites(Y),
    specialties(X,Z),
    included(Y,Z).

good_price(X) :-
    your_price(Y),
    average_price(X,Z),
    Z =< Y + 5.
```

```prolog
close_location(X) :-
    your_location(Y),
    restaurant_location(X,Z),
    distance(Y,Z,D),
    D =< 20.

included([],_) :- !.
included([X|T],L) :- member(X,L),included(T,L).

specialties('Le Marecage',[chicken,duck,eel,frog]).
specialties('Le Tour d''Ivoire',[duck,pigeon,quail]).
specialties('Le Grand Couteau',[duck,frog,snake,snail]).

average_price('Le Marecage',25).
average_price('Le Tour d''Ivoire',40).
average_price('Le Grand Couteau',34).

restaurant_location('Le Marecage','Clamart').
restaurant_location('Le Tour d''Ivoire','Paris-15').
restaurant_location('Le Grand Couteau','Paris-17').

distance('Paris-15','Paris-18',15).
distance('Paris-18','Paris-17',8).
distance('Paris-18','Clamart',35).

tobe_filled(your_favourites(X)).
tobe_filled(your_price(X)).
tobe_filled(your_location(X)).
```

FIGURE 9.3 An expert knowledge-base for diners.

Note that the last three facts of the knowledge-base shown in Figure 9.3 can be combined into a single frame (see Subsection 6.3.2 of Chapter 6). We leave them separate for the convenience of producing explanations, which we shall explain in Section 9.5. An advantage of representing specific-case information separately is that they can be easily changed or deleted. A full diner expert system that makes use of the knowledge-base of Figure 9.3 is presented in Section 9.5.

9.4   Representation of uncertainty

In real life, there are many things even the experts are not completely sure if they are true or false. For example, if a patient has a high temperature, sore throat, and positive heterophil-agglutination test, then any experienced physician would believe with some 90% certainty that the patient has contracted some form of herpesvirus. There is still, however, a 10% possibility that the above common diagnosis is wrong.

Therefore, in some expert systems, it is necessary to express a degree of certainty of the rules and facts of the system's knowledge-base. A simple way of doing this is to declare a symbol "#", say, as an infix operator (by using the command :- $op(500, xfx, \#)$), and to present each clause of the knowledge-base in the following form:

```
A # C :- B1,...,Bn.
```

Where C is a real number between 0 and 1 that represents the degree of certainty of the rule, the above rule means that if $B_1, \ldots, B_n$ are all true, then we are $100C\%$ certain that A is true.

Following is an example of an expert system's knowledge that includes certainty assessment.

EXAMPLE 9.2   The following are some rules of a detective expert system's knowledge-base.

```
murder(X,Victim) # 0.9 :-
    motive_to_kill(X,Motive),
    appear_near(X,Victim),
    gave_false_alibi(X,Alibi).

motive_to_kill(suzie,insurance_beneficiary) # 1.
appear_near(suzie,'J.R.') # 0.8.
gave_false_alibi(suzie,grandma) # 0.9.
```

The first rule establishes that it is 90% certain that X murdered the victim if X had a motive to kill, X appeared to be near the victim at the time the murder occurred, and X gave a false alibi. The last three facts represent specific-case information with their associated degrees of certainty. The information includes: Suzie had a motive to kill, as she is the victim's life-insurance beneficiary, Suzie appeared to be near J.R. at the time J.R.

was murdered, and Suzie gave as her alibi her grandma who is blind, can't speak, and has a hearing problem as well.

If an expert system's knowledge-base contains certainty assessment, then the system's answer to every query is associated with a degree of certainty. For example, if we ask: "Who murdered J.R. ?", then the system's answer may be in the form: "I am 65% positive that Suzie murdered J.R.".

The degree of certainty associated with an answer is calculated as follows. Consider a goal A and a clause $A1 \# C$:- B, where A unifies with $A1$. Then, by the probability theory, we have:

$$P(A) = P(A/B) * P(B). \qquad (9.1)$$

Here, $P(A/B)$ is the probability of having A when B already happened. In this case, $P(A/B)$ has the value C given in the clause.

On the other hand, let $B = B_1, \ldots, B_n$ and assume that the events $B_1, \ldots, B_n$ are independent, we have:

$$P(B) = P(B_1) * \cdots * P(B_n). \qquad (9.2)$$

The formulas (9.1) and (9.2) are used to calculate the degree of certainty of goals in most cases.

EXAMPLE 9.3   Let us consider again the rules and facts shown in Example 9.2. The probability of the hypothesis that "Suzie murdered J.R." is calculated as follows:

$$
\begin{aligned}
P(\text{murder}&(\text{suzie},\text{'J.R.'})) \\
&= 0.9 * P(\text{motive\_to\_kill}(\text{suzie}, \text{insurance\_beneficiary})) \\
&\quad * P(\text{appear\_near}(\text{suzie}, \text{'J.R.'})) \\
&\quad * P(\text{gave\_false\_alibi}(\text{suzie}, \text{grandma})) \\
\\
&= 0.9 * 1 * 0.8 * 0.9 \\
&= 0.648.
\end{aligned}
$$

The probability formula (9.2) is applied only when the events $B_1, \ldots, B_n$ are independent (that is, the occurrence of one event does not affect the occurrence of the others). If the events $B_1, \ldots, B_n$ are not independent, then there are two different methods to estimate the degree of certainty of the combined event.

The first method is called the *liberal approach* because it is very generous in estimating the degree of certainty of $B = B_1, \ldots, B_n$. In fact, by the liberal method, we have:

$$P(B) = min(P(B_1), \ldots, P(B_n)). \qquad (9.3)$$

For example, with the murder case of Example 9.3, the liberal method gives:

$$\begin{aligned} P(\text{murder}(\text{suzie},'\text{J.R.}')) &= 0.9 * min(1, 0.8, 0.9) \\ &= 0.72. \end{aligned}$$

The second method is called the *conservative approach* because it minimises the degree of certainty of the combined event $B = B_1, \ldots, B_n$. By the conservative method, we have:

$$P(B) = max(0, P(B_1) + P(B_2, \ldots, B_n) - 1). \qquad (9.4)$$

For example, with the murder case of Example 9.3, the conservative method gives:

$$\begin{aligned} P(\text{murder}(\text{suzie},'\text{J.R}')) & \\ &= 0.9 * max(0, 1 + max(0, 0.8 + 0.9 - 1) - 1) \\ &= 0.9 * 0.7 \\ &= 0.63. \end{aligned}$$

Generally, in the case where the events are not independent, if they have a strong positive correlation, we use the liberal method, otherwise, we use the conservative method.

Let us now consider how to calculate the degree of certainty of a negated goal. Recall that in Prolog, the goal $not(A)$ succeeding means A is false for all values of the variables in A.

To calculate the probability $P(not(A))$, we find the set of all answers to the goal A with their associated degrees of certainty. Suppose that this set is:

$$L = [(A_1, C_1), \ldots, (A_n, C_n)].$$

Then we have

$$\begin{aligned} P(not(A)) &= (1 - P(A_1)) * \cdots * (1 - P(A_n)) \\ &= (1 - C_1) * \cdots * (1 - C_n). \end{aligned}$$

On the other hand, note that if the system allows the use of the predicate *non* introduced in Chapter 8, Section 8.4, then the probability of a goal $non(A)$ is calculated in the same way as for any positive goal. Finally, note that every system goal (with built-in predicate) is given a degree of certainty of 1 if it succeeds, and 0 if it fails.

9.5 Generation of explanations

There are two occasions when explanations may be requested by the user. The first occasion is when the user is asked to supply some specific information. The user may not see the relevance of the requested information, and so demands an explanation of the need to give that information. This case is studied through Example 9.4 below. The second kind of explanation the user may demand from the system is how the system arrived at a conclusion. This kind of explanation will be discussed through Example 9.5.

EXAMPLE 9.4   Suppose that you are using the diner expert system that is partly described in Example 9.1 to find a restaurant in Paris that suits you best. Following is a sample conversation between the system and the user. The user's entry is shown in italic.

> Q:> *Which restaurant suits me best ?*
>   > What are your favourites ? (List your favourite dishes
>   in the form [lobster, fish, clam, etc.]) : [*duck, frog*].
>   > What price per head are you willing to pay ? : *30.*
>   > Where do you live ? : *why.*
>   > Because
>   IF
>   your location is A,
>   the location of restaurant Le Marecage is B,
>   the distance from A to B is C,
>   C ≤ 20
>   THEN
>   restaurant Le Marecage is conveniently close to you
>   > Where do you live ? : *'Paris-18'.*
>
> A:> restaurant Le Grand Couteau suits you best.

Observe that the system abandoned the restaurant Le Marecage because it realised that it is possibly too far from your place. Instead, it finds a closer restaurant, Le Grand Couteau, which is also famous for duck soup and frog legs, and has prices you can afford.

To be able to produce the explanations as shown in Example 9.4, the system must maintain a list containing the rules used in the process of evaluating a goal. For example, when the system evaluates the goal *close_location('Le Marecage')*, it saves the clause:

```
close_location('Le Marecage') :-
    your_location(X),
    restaurant_location('Le Marecage',Y),
    distance(X,Y,D),
    D =< 20.
```

Then the system asks the user to fill in the goal *your_location*(*X*). If the user asks "why", then the system retrieves the above clause to produce an explanation of its request. The program that performs this task is shown in Figure 9.4.

```
ask_user(Goal,Rules) :-
    display_question(Goal),
    read(Answer),
    process_answer(Answer,Goal,Rules).

process_answer(why,Goal,[Rule|Rules]) :- !,
    display_rule(Rule),nl,
    ask_user(Goal,Rules).
process_answer(why,Goal,[]) :- !,
    nl,write('  > No more explanations!'),nl,
    ask_user(Goal,[]).
process_answer(X,Goal,_) :-
    var_list(Goal,[V]), V = X,
    assert(already_asked(Goal)).

display_question :- % see Figure 9.7
display_rule :-     % see Figure 9.5
var_list :-         % see Figure 8.2
```

FIGURE 9.4 Querying the user and generating explanations.

There are a few things in the program of Figure 9.4 that should be explained. First of all, the procedures *display_question* and *display_rule* display the questions and explanations in an English-like language. This can be done in two ways.

A straightforward (but tedious) way is to associate with each goal that is to be asked or explained an English sentence expressing the goal. When a goal needs to be displayed, its English expression is retrieved and displayed instead. The procedure *display_rule* is shown in Figure 9.5, and examples of *display_goal* and *display_question* are given in Figures 9.6 and 9.7, respectively.

A more sophisticated technique to display the questions and explanations in a language the user can understand is to associate with each predicate symbol in the system's knowledge-base a sentence in the user-language expressing that predicate. This technique is used in our ESSLN expert system shell and is discussed in detail in Section 9.10.

```
display_rule((A :- B)) :-
    member(B,[true,usergiven,nofact,system:R]),!,
    nl,write(' > Because'),
    nl,tab(8),display_goal(A),
    nl,write('    is '),write(B).
display_rule((A :- B)) :-
    copy((A,B),(A1,B1)),
    var_list((A1,B1),VL),bind_vars(VL,65),
    nl,write(' > Because'),
    nl,write('    IF'),  display_body(B1),
    nl,write('    THEN'),display_body(A1).

display_body((A,B)) :- !,
    nl,tab(8),display_goal(A),write(','),
    display_body(B).
display_body(A) :-
    nl,tab(8),display_goal(A).

bind_vars([],_) :- !.
bind_vars([X|VL],C) :-
    name(X,[C]),C1 is C+1,bind_vars(VL,C1).

display_goal :- % see Figure 9.6
member :-       % see Figure 2.13
copy :-         % see Figure 8.2
var_list :-     % see Figure 8.2
```

FIGURE 9.5 Displaying a rule.

```
display_goal(best_restaurant(X)) :- !,
    write_list(['restaurant ',X,' suits you best.']).
display_goal(serve_favourites(X)) :- !,
    write_list(['restaurant ',X]),
    write_list([' is famous for your favourite dishes']).
display_goal(good_price(X)) :- !,
    write_list(['restaurant ',X]),
    write_list([' charges reasonable prices']).
display_goal(close_location(X)) :- !,
    write_list(['restaurant ',X]),
    write_list([' is conveniently close to you']).
display_goal(your_favourites(X)) :- !,
    write_list(['your favourite dishes are ',X]).
display_goal(specialties(X,Y)) :- !,
    write_list(['restaurant ',X,' is famous for ',Y]).
display_goal(included(X,Y)) :- !,
    write_list(['dishes ',X,' are included in ',Y]).
display_goal(your_price(X)) :- !,
    write_list(['your price limit is ',X]).
display_goal(average_price(X,Y)) :- !,
    write_list(['average price at restaurant ',X]),
    write_list([' is ',Y]).
display_goal(your_location(X)) :- !,
    write_list(['your location is ',X]).
display_goal(restaurant_location(X,Y)) :- !,
    write_list(['the location of restaurant ',X]),
    write_list([' is ',Y]).
display_goal(distance(X,Y,D)) :- !,
    write_list(['the distance from ',X,' to ',Y]),
    write_list([' is ',D]).

display_goal(A) :- syst(A),write(A).

write_list([]) :- !.
write_list([X|T]) :- write(X),write_list(T).
syst :- % see Figure 9.13
```

FIGURE 9.6 Displaying of goals.

```
display_question(your_favourites(X)) :- nl,
    write(' > What are your favourites ?'),
    write(' (List your favourite dishes'), nl,
    write('   in the form [lobster,fish,clam,etc]): ').
display_question(your_price(X)) :- nl,
    write(' > What price per head are you willing'),
    write(' to pay ? : ').
display_question(your_location(X)) :- nl,
    write(' > Where do you live ? : ').
```

FIGURE 9.7 Displaying of questions.

Another thing which should be noted from the program of Figure 9.4 is that it assumes that the system's knowledge does not contain certainty assessment. If certainties are involved, then for every specific information supplied by the user, the user is asked to estimate the degree of certainty associated with the information. This can be realised by including an extra argument C representing the information's degree of certainty as shown in Figure 9.8.

```
ask_user(Goal,C,Rules) :-
    display_question(Goal),
    read(Answer),
    process_answer(Answer,Goal,C,Rules).

process_answer(why,Goal,_,Rules) :-
    % the same as in Figure 9.4.
process_answer(X,Goal,C,_) :-
    var_list(Goal,[V]), V = X,
    nl,write(' > Give a percentage on your certainty : '),
    read(C1), C is C1/100,
    assert(already_asked(Goal,C)).
```

FIGURE 9.8 Querying the user for specific information and certainty.

We now study the second kind of explanation the user may demand from the system. Consider the following example.

EXAMPLE 9.5   Let us continue Example 9.4 and assume that after the system recommends to you that the restaurant Le Grand Couteau suits you best, you want to know on what basis the system has drawn that advice. The conversation can continue as follows:

A : > restaurant Le Grand Couteau suits you best
  > *how.*
  > Because
    IF
        restaurant Le Grand Couteau is famous for your favourite dishes,
        restaurant Le Grand Couteau charges reasonable prices,
        restaurant Le Grand Couteau is conveniently close to you
    THEN
        restaurant Le Grand Couteau suits you best
  > *ok.*

The explanations given in Example 9.5 are extracted from the proof of the goal *best_restaurant*(X), which is shown below.

```
best_restaurant('Le Grand Couteau') :-
    (serve_favourites('Le Grand Couteau') :-
        (your_favourites([duck,frog]) :- usergiven),
        (specialties('Le Grand Couteau',
                    [duck,frog,snake,snail]) :- fact),
        (included([duck,frog],[duck,frog,snake,snail])
                    :- system:yes)),
    (good_price('Le Grand Couteau') :-
        (your_price(30) :- usergiven),
        (average_price('Le Grand Couteau',34) :- fact),
        (34 =< 30 + 5 :- system:yes)),
    (close_location('Le Grand Couteau') :-
        (your_location('Paris-18') :- usergiven),
        (restaurant_location('Le Grand Couteau','Paris-17')
                    :- fact),
        (distance('Paris-18','Paris-17',8) :- fact),
        (8 =< 20 :- system:yes)).
```

The program that extracts explanations from a goal's proof and displays them to the user is shown in Figure 9.9.

From this program, we see that if the user asks "*how*" the system arrives at a conclusion, then the system uses the proof of the related goal to generate the explanation. If the proof is a conjunction of proofs, then the system explains each of them, one after another. If the proof is a single proof of the form A :- *Proof*, then the system reconstructs a clause of the form A :- $B_1, \ldots, B_n$ by recollecting the body $(B_1, \ldots, B_n)$ from *Proof*, which may have the form $(B_1$:- $C_1), \ldots, (B_n$:- $C_n)$ or may be just a proof termination such as *fact*, *system:yes*, *usergiven*, or *noclause*. After the clause has been constructed, the procedure *display_rule* (Figure 9.5) is called to display it.

```
process_response(ok,_) :- !.
process_response(how,(ProofA,ProofB)) :- !,
    process_response(how,ProofA),
    read_response(Response),
    process_response(Response,ProofB).
process_response(how,(A :- Proof)) :- !,
    recollect_body(Proof,Body),
    display_rule((A :- Body)),
    read_response(Response),
    process_response(Response,Proof).
process_response(how,_) :-
    nl,write('   No more explanations for this goal.').

recollect_body(fact,true) :- !.
recollect_body(system:R,system:R) :- !.
recollect_body(usergiven,usergiven) :- !.
recollect_body(toofar,nonterminate) :- !.
recollect_body(noclause,nofact) :- !.
recollect_body((B : nottried),B) :- !.
recollect_body((B :- C),B) :- !.
recollect_body(((B :- C),Rest),(B,Bs)) :- !,
    recollect_body(Rest,Bs).
recollect_body(B,B).

read_response(R) :- nl,write('  > '),
    read(S),(member(S,[ok,how,more]),!,R = S;
    write('   Type ok., how. or more.'),
    read_response(R)).
```

FIGURE 9.9 Producing explanation for an answer.

We can now construct a full diner expert system using the programs shown
in Figures 9.3 to 9.9. The system's top-level control is shown in Figure 9.10.

```
diner_expert :-
    introduction,
    repeat,
        receive_query(Query),
        convert_query(Query,Goal),
        evaluate(Goal),
    terminate(Goal).

introduction :- cls,
  nl,write('HELLO ! I AM THE DINER EXPERT IN PARIS'),
  nl,write('YOU MAY ASK ME ABOUT PARIS RESTAURANTS'),
  nl,write('FOR EXAMPLE, YOU MAY ASK QUESTIONS LIKE'),
  nl,write('   Which restaurant suits me best?'),
  nl,write('   Which restaurant serves my favourite dishes?'),
  nl,write('   Which restaurant charges reasonable prices?'),
  nl,write('   Which restaurant is conveniently close to me?'),
  nl,write('etc.'),nl.

receive_query(Query) :- nl,write('Q:> '),
    read_string(100,S),list_text(T,S),scan_text(T,Query).

scan_text([],[]) :- !.
scan_text(T,[W|Ws]) :- append(L,[C|T1],T),
    member(C,[32,46,63]),!,name(W,L),scan_text(T1,Ws).

convert_query(['Which',restaurant,suits,me,best],
    best_restaurant(X)).
convert_query(['Which',restaurant,serves,my,favourite,
    dishes],serve_favourites(X)).
convert_query(['Which',restaurant,charges,reasonable,
    prices],good_price(X)).
convert_query(['Which',restaurant,is,conveniently,close,
    to,me],close_location(X)).
convert_query([bye],bye).
```

FIGURE 9.10 Top-level control of the diner expert system.

The system's operation is typical. After receiving a query in the form of a text string, the system scans the string to produce a list of words, which is then converted into a Prolog goal. The evaluation of a goal is performed by the procedure *evaluate* that uses a meta-interpreter similar to the one developed in Chapter 8, Section 8.7 (see Figures 8.15 and 8.16). The procedure *evaluate* is shown in Figure 9.11 below.

```
evaluate(Goal) :-
    prove(Goal,20,Result,Proof,[]),
    process_result(Goal,Result,Proof),!.
evaluate(_).

process_result(bye,_,_) :- !.
process_result(Goal,Result,Proof) :-
    nl,write('A:> '),
    (Result = no,write('No');
     Result = yes, display_goal(Goal)),
    read_response(Response),
    process_response(Response,Proof).

bye.
terminate(bye) :-
    retract(already_asked(X)),fail; true.

display_goal :-      % see Figure 9.6
read_response :-     % see Figure 9.9
process_response :- % see Figure 9.9
prove :-             % see Figure 9.12
```

FIGURE 9.11 Goal evaluation in the diner expert system.

The meta-interpreter used in this expert system has two extra features. First, there is a fifth argument *Rules*, which is used to store the rules employed in the evaluating process for the purpose of producing explanations (see Example 9.5). Second, if a goal does not unify with any clause in the knowledge-base, then it is possibly a specific-case information to be supplied by the user. The system checks this fact by calling the procedure *find_out* to test if the goal needs to be filled. If so, the system calls the procedure *ask_user* (Figure 9.4) to put the goal to the user, if it is not already asked. The modified meta-interpreter is shown in Figures 9.12 and 9.13.

```
prove(Goal,Depth,Result,Proof,Rules) :-
    prove_branch(Goal,Depth,Result,Proof,Rules),
    check_result(Goal,Depth,Result,Proof).
prove(Goal,Depth,no,FailProof,Rules) :-
    collect_failbranches(Goal,FailProof).

prove_branch(true,D,yes,fact,Rules) :- !.
prove_branch(A,0,lost,toofar,Rules) :- !.
prove_branch(not(A),D,NegResult,NegProof,Rules) :-
    prove(A,D,Result,Proof,Rules),!,
    invert(A,Result,NegResult,Proof,NegProof).
prove_branch((A;B),D,Result,Proof,Rules) :- !,
    (prove_branch(A,D,Result,Proof,Rules);
     prove_branch(B,D,Result,Proof,Rules)).
prove_branch((A,B),D,Result,(ProofA,ProofB),Rules) :- !,
    prove_branch(A,D,ResultA,ProofA,Rules),
    prove_conj(ResultA,B,D,Result,ProofB,Rules).
prove_branch(A,D,Result,(A :- system:Result),Rules) :-
    syst(A),!,
    (A,!,Result = yes; Result = no).
prove_branch(A,D,Result,(A :- Proof),Rules) :-
    not(clause(A,B)),!,
    find_out(A,Result,Proof,Rules).
prove_branch(A,D,Result,(A :- Proof),Rules) :-
    clause(A,B),D1 is D-1,
    prove_branch(B,D1,Result,Proof,[(A :- B)|Rules]).

find_out(A,yes,usergiven,Rules) :-
    tobe_filled(A),!,
    (already_asked(A),!; ask_user(A,Rules)).
find_out(A,no,noclause,_).

ask_user :- % see Figure 9.4
```

FIGURE 9.12 The meta-interpreter of the diner expert system.

```
invert(A,yes,no,SuccProof,(not(A) :- fails(SuccProof))).
invert(A,no,yes,FailProof,(not(A) :- succeeds(FailProof))).

prove_conj(yes,B,D,Result,Proof,Rules) :- !,
    prove_branch(B,D,Result,Proof,Rules).
prove_conj(RA, B,D,RA,B:nottried,Rules).

check_result(G,D,yes,_) :- !,
    (maxdepth(D),!; collect_failbranches(G,_)).
check_result(G,_,_,Proof) :-
    assert(failproof(G:Proof)),!,fail.

collect_failbranches(G,[FailBranch|Rest]) :-
    copy(G,G1),retract(failproof(G1:FailBranch)),!,
    collect_failbranches(G,Rest).
collect_failbranches(_,[]).

syst(A) :- functor(A,F,N),
        (system(F/N); member(F,[member,included])).

copy(A,B) :- assert(zzzz(A)),retract(zzzz(B)).
member(X,[X|_]) :- !.
member(X,[_|T]) :- member(X,T).
maxdepth(20).
```

FIGURE 9.13 The meta-interpreter of the diner expert system (continued).

9.6   A meta-interpreter for expert systems

In the preceding section, we have presented a simple meta-interpreter for expert systems that contain no certainty assessment. We now develop a more general meta-interpreter for expert systems using the same structure with the following changes.

1. In expert systems that contain certainties, the result of a goal's evaluation is not definitely "yes" or "no", but it is represented by a degree of certainty C. If $C = 1$, then the goal is considered to be definitely

true. If C is less than some predetermined threshold (0.20, say), then the goal is regarded as *false*.

2. The proof of a negated goal $not(A)$ is obtained in the following way. First, we find the successive answers of A that have proofs $P_1, \ldots, P_n$ with their associated degrees of certainty $C_1, \ldots, C_n$. Then, the proof of $not(A)$ takes the form

$$not(A) \ \# \ C \ :- \ (P_1, \ldots, P_n)$$

where $C = (1 - C_1) * \cdots * (1 - C_n)$. For efficiency, however, we cease to collect the proofs of A as soon as the product $(1 - C_1) * \cdots * (1 - C_i)$ becomes less than the predetermined threshold.

3. For any system goal A, its degree of certainty has value 1 if it succeeds, and 0 otherwise.

4. For any nonsystem goal A, if there is no clause in the knowledge-base that can be resolved with A, then the system checks if A represents a specific-case information to be supplied by the user. If so, the system asks the user for the required information together with its certainty estimation.

5. To be able to explain to the user the necessity of a specific information, the system maintains a list of rules that were used in the process of goal evaluation.

6. Finally, for efficiency, only nonduplicated answers and branch failure proofs are maintained.

The meta-interpreter with the above-described new features is shown in Figures 9.14 to 9.16.

```
prove(Goal,Depth,Certainty,Proof,Rules) :-
    prove_branch(Goal,Depth,Certainty,Proof,Rules),
    check_result(Goal,Depth,Certainty,Proof).
prove(Goal,Depth,0,FailProof,Rules) :-
    collect_failproof(Goal,Depth,FailProof).
```

```
prove_branch(true,D,1,fact,Rules) :- !.
prove_branch(A,0,0,nonterminate,Rules) :- !.
prove_branch(not(A),D,C,(not(A) # C :- Proof),Rules) :- !,
    copy(A,A1),collect_proof(A1,D,Rules,C,List),!,
    convert(List,Proof).
prove_branch((A,B),D,C,(ProofA,ProofB),Rules) :- !,
    prove_branch(A,D,CA,ProofA,Rules),
    prove_conj(CA,B,D,C,ProofB,Rules).
prove_branch(A,D,C,(A # C :- system:R),Rules) :-
    syst(A),!,(A, C = 1, R = true; not(A), C = 0, R = false).
prove_branch(A,D,C,(A # C :- Proof),Rules) :-
    not(find_clause((A # C),B)),!,
    find_out(A,C,Proof,Rules).
prove_branch(A,D,C,(A # C :- Proof),Rules) :-
    threshold(C0),
    find_clause((A # RC),B),D1 is D-1,
    detect_cut(B,B1,B2,Cut),
    (Cut = yes,
      prove_branch(B1,D1,C1,Proof1,[(A # RC :- B)|Rules]),
      (C1 < C0, C is RC*C1,return_proof(Proof1,B2,Proof);
       C1 >= C0,!,
       prove_branch(B2,D1,C2,Proof2,[(A # RC :- B)|Rules]),
       C is RC*C1*C2,conjunct(Proof1,Proof2,Proof));
     Cut = no,
       prove_branch(B,D1,CB,Proof,[(A # RC :- B)|Rules]),
       C is RC*CB).

detect_cut(B,B1,B2,yes) :- cutin(B,B1,B2),!.
detect_cut(_,_,_,no).

cutin(!,!,true) :- !.
cutin((!,B),!,B) :- !.
cutin((A,!),(A,!),true) :- !.
cutin((A,B),(A,As),Bs) :- cutin(B,As,Bs).
```

FIGURE 9.14 A meta-interpreter for expert systems (top level).

```
return_proof(Proof1,B,Proof) :-
    B = true,!, Proof1 = Proof;
    conjunct(Proof1,(B : nottried),Proof).

conjunct(A,fact,A) :- !.
conjunct((A,As),L,(A,Bs)) :- !,conjunct(As,L,Bs).
conjunct((A),L,(A,L)).

collect_proof(A,D,Rules,0,List) :-
    threshold(T),asserta(bag(1,[],D)),
    prove(A,D,C,P,Rules),
      once(retract(bag(C0,L,D))),
      C1 is C0* (1-C),asserta(bag(C1,[P|L],D)),
      C1 < 1-T, retract(bag(_,List,D)),remove(answer(A,D)),!.
collect_proof(A,D,_,C,List) :-
    retract(bag(C,List,D)),remove(answer(A,D)).

convert([P],P) :- !.
convert([P|L],(P,NP)) :- convert(L,NP).

prove_conj(C,B,D,0,(B : nottried),Rules) :-
    threshold(T), C < T,!.
prove_conj(CA,B,D,C,ProofB,Rules) :-
    prove_branch(B,D,CB,ProofB,Rules),
    C is CA*CB.

check_result(G,D,C,Proof) :-
    threshold(C0), C < C0,!,
    not((failproof((G1,D):_),instance(G,G1))),
    assert(failproof((G,D):Proof)),fail.
check_result(G,D,C,Proof) :-
    collect_failbranches(G,D,_),
    (answer(G1,D1),D1 < D,retract(answer(G1,D1)),fail;
    not((answer(G1,D),instance(G,G1))),save_answer(G,D)).
```

FIGURE 9.15 A meta-interpreter for expert systems (lower level).

```
collect_failproof(G,D,FailProof) :-
    collect_failbranches(G,D,FailList),
    not(answer(G,D)),convert(FailList,FailProof).

collect_failbranches(G,D,[FailBranch|Rest]) :-
    copy(G,G1),retract(failproof((G1,D):FailBranch)),!,
    collect_failbranches(G,D,Rest).
collect_failbranches(_,_,[]).

find_out(A,C,usergiven,Rules) :-
    tobe_filled(A) # 1,!,
    (already_asked(A,C),!; ask_user(A,C,Rules)).
find_out(A,0,nofact,_).

find_clause((A # RC),B) :- clause((A # RC),B).
find_clause((A # RC),B) :-
    code_world(X,api),
    clause((A # RC),B),
    code_world(_,X).

save_answer(Goal,Depth) :-
    assert(answer(Goal,Depth)).

syst(A) :- functor(A,F,N),
           (system(F/N),!;
            member(F,[member,append,var_list,tvar_list,
                      uninstantiated,instantiate])).

remove(A) :- retract(A),fail; true.

copy(A,B) :- assert(zzzz(A)),retract(zzzz(B)).
maxdepth(20).
threshold(0.2).

instance  :- % see Figure 8.3
ask_user   :- % see Figures 9.4 and 9.8
```

FIGURE 9.16 A meta-interpreter for expert systems (continued).

9.7 Expert system shells

Many expert systems differ from one another only in their knowledge-bases, while their other components are functionally similar. Therefore, one can build a system consisting of the three main components of most expert systems: the user interface, the inference engine, and the explanation generator, so that when an expert knowledge is added, the system can perform as an expert system. Such a system is called an *expert system shell*.

Expert system shells are designed to help nonprogrammers build their expert systems. An expert system shell normally takes care of the following tasks:

- Translate the expert knowledge expressed in some form of natural language into a form of internal representation to be stored in the system's knowledge-base. In the case of Prolog, the internal representation is in the form of Prolog rules and facts.

- Perform reasoning and searching to find answers for the user's queries. This is the function of the inference engine, which decides on the techniques and the strategies of searching. For example, some expert system shells allow the user to choose between forward and backward chaining strategies.

- Calculate the degree of certainty of goals during and at the end of each goal evaluating process. Again, some expert system shells allow the user to select the formula (of probability, liberal, or conservative approach) to be used in the calculation.

- Display the questions, answers, and explanations to the user in the language adopted between the system and the user.

Thus, by using an expert system shell, the builder of an expert system is freed of most technical problems and is allowed to concentrate on the matter of gathering knowledge and expressing it in the language accepted by the system.

In the remaining sections of this chapter, we present the construction of ESSLN, a multilingual expert system shell that supports quantified queries and subtypes. (For the theoretical basis of ESSLN, see Le (1989) and Le (1990).)

9.8   ESSLN: An expert system shell with logical negation

As we have mentioned in the preceding section, expert system shells are purposely designed to assist nonprogrammers building knowledge systems in the domains of their expertise. A large majority of the currently available expert system shells provide this assistance in the form of questioning the user to collect information, using a particular language, usually English, as a communicating language. This method certainly makes the user feel passive and lacking of freedom. Also, for most systems, the user is not allowed to ask negative or quantified questions.

ESSLN is a Prolog-based expert system shell designed to provide the user with much more freedom and power, including the ability to work in a language of his or her choice. In fact, besides the standard functions of an expert system shell, ESSLN has the following three special features:

- ESSLN allows knowledge and queries to be entered in any Latin-based language with little restriction.

- ESSLN supports negative and quantified queries in the forms similar to the following examples:

    Which suspect had *not* a motive to kill victim J.R.?
    Which suspect had a motive to kill *all* victims?
    Which suspect has *no* alibi?

- ESSLN allows entities' types to be partially ordered, that is, some types can be declared to be subtypes of other types. Thus, for a query such as "Which person had some contact with victim J.R.?" we may have the answer "All suspects had some contact with victim J.R.", where *suspect* is a subtype of the type *person* that includes victims, witnesses, and lawyers.

ESSLN's user interface is presented in Section 9.10, and the system's handling of subtypes is discussed in Section 9.11. In this section and the next one, we describe how the system handles negative and quantified queries. For convenience, we assume English is the user's language of choice.

ESSLN's inference engine operates within the framework of multitype logic (also called many-sorted logic, see, e.g., Enderton (1972)) in which every term has a *type* and every predicate is associated with a *domain*. Thus, in ESSLN, constant symbols and predicates' domains are stored as shown in the following examples:

```
constsymbol(suspect:'Alan Smith').
constsymbol(victim:'J.R.').
   .
   .
   .
domain(p2(S:X,T:Y)) :- type(S,suspect),type(T,victim).
domain(p8(S:X,T:Y)) :- type(S,suspect),type(T,alibi).
   .
   .
   .
type(T,T).
type(S,T) :- subtype(S,T).
```

The negation of a formula $p(S{:}X,\ T{:}Y)$ is represented in ESSLN by the goal $non(p(S{:}X,\ T{:}Y))$. The evaluation of this negated goal produces a proof for the formula $\exists_S X\ \exists_T Y \sim p(X,Y)$, where $\exists_S$ and $\exists_T$ are the existential quantifiers associated with the types S and T, respectively. Thus, in ESSLN positive and negative goals are evaluated in the same fashion. That is, in evaluating a positive goal A, the system finds a maximally general substitution for the variables of A such that A succeeds. Similarly, to evaluate a negative goal $non(A)$, the system searches for a maximally general substitution for the variables of A such that A fails. The procedure that performs negative goal evaluation is given in Figure 9.17, where the numbers of the form $\#C$ represent the rules' degree of certainty. The rules that have no associated certainty have their head predicates declared to be system predicates, and thus automatically have certainty degree of 1.

```
non(A) # 1 :- tvar_list(A,L),eval_non(A,L).

eval_non(A,L) # 1 :- not(A),!.
eval_non(A,L) # 1 :- eval(A),uninstantiated(L),!,fail.
eval_non(A,L) # 1 :- instantiate(A,L,VL),eval_non(A,VL).

eval(A) # 1 :- A,!.
uninstantiated(L) :- tvar_pure(L),unrestricted(L,0).
```

```
tvar_pure([]) :- !.
tvar_pure([T:V|TVs]) :- var(V),tvar_pure(TVs).

unrestricted([],_) :- !.
unrestricted([T:N|TVs],N) :-
    N1 is N+1,unrestricted(TVs,N1).

instantiate(A,L,VL) :- domain(A),instant(L,VL).

instant([X|Xs],Xs) :- get_term(X,Xs).
instant([X|Xs],[X|VL]) :- instant(Xs,VL).

get_term(T:V,TVs) :- constsymbol(T:V).
get_term(X,Xs) :- get_var(X,Xs).

get_var(T:V,[T:V|TVs]).
get_var(X,[Y|Xs]) :- get_var(X,Xs).

tvar_list(A,[]) :- ground(A),!.
tvar_list(A,L) :-  A =.. [P|Args],
    setof(T:X,(member(T:X,Args),var(X)),L).

ground(A) :- copy(A,B), A == B.
copy(A,B) :- assert(zzzz(A)),retract(zzzz(B)).

member(X,[X|_]).
member(X,[_|T]) :- member(X,T).
```

FIGURE 9.17 ESSLN's negation evaluator.

9.9   Quantified goals in ESSLN

Like LnProlog (see Section 8.6 of Chapter 8), ESSLN combines the two built-in predicates *not* and *non* to represent quantified goals. Following is a list of typical quantified goals and their representation in ESSLN. (Here, the symbols $\forall_T$ and $\exists_T$ are the universal and existential quantifiers associated with a given type T.)

Quantified goal	Representation in ESSLN
$\forall_S X \; p(X)$	`not(non(p(S:X)))`
$\forall_S X \sim p(X)$	`not(p(S:X))`
$\exists_S X \; \forall_T Y \; p(X,Y)$	`p(S:X,T:_),not(non(p(S:X,T:Y)))`
$\exists_S X \; \forall_T Y \sim p(X,Y)$	`non(p(S:X,T:_)),not(p(S:X,T:Y))`

The operational meanings of the above-listed goals are elucidated below.

1. The goal $not(non(p(S{:}X)))$ succeeds if and only if $non(p(S{:}X))$ fails. That is, there are no values for X of type S such that $p(S{:}X)$ is false. Equivalently, $p(S{:}X)$ is true for every value of X of type S.

2. The goal $not(p(S{:}X))$ succeeds if and only if $p(S{:}X)$ fails. That is, there are no values for X of type S such that $p(S{:}X)$ is true. Equivalently, $p(S{:}X)$ is false for every value of X of type S.

3. The goal $p(S{:}X, T{:}\_),not(non(p(S{:}X, T{:}Y)))$ succeeds with an answer $(X = X0)$ if and only if $p(S{:}X, T{:}Z)$ succeeds with an answer $(X = X0, Z = Z0)$ and $not(non(p(S{:}X0, T{:}Y)))$ succeeds. This means that $p(S{:}X0, T{:}Y)$ is true for every value of Y of type T.

4. The goal $non(p(S{:}X, T{:}\_)),not(p(S{:}X, T{:}Y))$ succeeds if and only if $non(p(S{:}X, T{:}Z))$ succeeds with an answer $(X = X0, Z = Z0)$ and $not(p(S{:}X0, T{:}Y))$ succeeds. This means $p(S{:}X0, T{:}Y)$ is false for every value of Y of type T.

Thus, in ESSLN, quantified goals can be interpreted like any ordinary goals. However, to facilitate the task of explaining quantified queries' answers, we place the goals of the forms $(A,not(non(A1)))$ and $(non(A),not(A1))$ under the common form $all(A, B)$ and interpret them as follows:

To prove a goal $all(A, B)$ do
    prove A first;
    if A fails (i.e., having certainty 0),
        then $all(A, B)$ fails and its failure proof is that of A;
    if A succeeds,
        but its joined goal B had been obtained before, then ignore it;
        otherwise, prove B and return its proof and degree of certainty
            as those of $all(A, B)$.

The above interpreting algorithm is expressed by the clauses shown in Figure 9.18, which are added to the meta-interpreter of Figure 9.14.

```
prove_branch(all(A,B),D,C,(all(A,B) # C :- Proof),Rules) :-
    !,prove_all(A,B,D,C,Proof,Rules).

prove_all(A,B,D,C,Proof,Rules) :-
    prove(A,D,CA,ProofA,Rules),
    check_all(CA,ProofA,B,D,C,Proof,Rules).
prove_all(A,B,D,_,_,_) :-
    remove(answer(A,D)),remove(save_all(B,D)),fail.

check_all(0,ProofA,B,D,0,ProofA,Rules) :- !.
check_all(_,_,B,D,C,ProofB,Rules) :-
    not((save_all(B1,D),instance(B,B1))),
    asserta(save_all(B,D)),
    prove_branch(B,D,C,(B # C :- ProofB),Rules).
```

FIGURE 9.18 ESSLN's interpretation of conjunctive quantified goals.

Also, to enable the detection and suppression of duplicated answers to quantified queries, these answers must be trimmed before being saved. So, the procedure *save_answer* of Figure 9.16 is modified as follows:

```
save_answer(Goal,Depth) :-
    trim_answer(Goal,Goal1),assert(answer(Goal1,Depth)).

trim_answer(all(A,B),all(_,B)) :- !.
trim_answer((A,B),(A1,B1)) :- !,
    trim_answer(A,A1), trim_answer(B,B1).
trim_answer(A,A).
```

9.10   ESSLN's user interface

In this section, we explain how ESSLN accepts knowledge and queries in various user languages and converts them into Prolog and vice versa.

At the start, after displaying its banner, ESSLN asks the user to choose a language to be used in the conversation between the system and the user. If the chosen language is known to the system, then it switches itself to that language. Otherwise, the system "learns" the new language by asking the user to translate a number of sentences from a language known to both the system and the user to the new language; these sentences will be used to produce advice and explanations to the user. Through this translation, the system learns the keywords of the new language that are equivalent to "all", "every", "not", "no", "some", and "which" in English, and their locations in a full sentence. (The implementation of this feature is straightforward but rather tedious and is not included in this book.)

Then, the system instructs the user about how to structure the sentences in entering information and queries. These structural rules are very simple and are given below:

- Each sentence contains a unit of information in which the objects and their types are indicated by words beginning with an underscore. Such a word must precede a variable (starting with a capital letter) or a constant (starting with a small letter or being enclosed between single quotation marks) or a standard expression (i.e., a number, a numeric expression such as $(X + 1)$, or a list expression such as $[X \mid Y]$). In particular, standard expressions are allowed not to be preceded by a type-word (because their types are obvious).

- Each sentence is terminated by one of the following delimiters:

    : is read "if" (or its equivalent in other languages)
    , is read "and" (or its equivalent in other languages)
    . terminates a piece of information (i.e., a rule or a fact)
    ? terminates a query.

- The keyword *not* (or its equivalent in other languages) appearing in a sentence will make that sentence to be translated into a negated goal.

- Any of the quantifying adjectives *all, every, some*, and *no* (or their equivalents in other languages) preceding a type-word is associated with that word. In queries, the keyword *which* plays a similar role.

- If a piece of information (i.e., a rule or a fact) is associated with a degree of certainty C, then the sentence must begin with the word $\% D$, where $D = 100C$. Any rule or fact with no specified certainty is assumed to have 100% of certainty.

EXAMPLE 9.6   Let us first consider a knowledge-base with no certainty assessment. This knowledge-base contains information on supplier-part relations, and is written in English.

```
_agent X is a fractional supplier :
    _agent X not supply some _item.
_agent 'Adams & Sons' supply _item b1.
_agent 'Adams & Sons' supply _item b2.
_agent 'Adams & Sons' supply _item b3.
_agent 'Johnny Ltd' supply _item b1.
_agent 'Johnny Ltd' supply _item b2.
_agent 'Mitre 10' supply _item b1.
```

The above information can be either entered directly, line by line, from the terminal, or loaded into ESSLN's database from a file. (The *load* command and other special queries are discussed at the end of this section.) This information is converted by ESSLN into the following Prolog knowledge-base.

```
p1(A:B) # 1 :- non(p2(A:B,C:D)).

p2(agent:'Adams & Sons',item:b1) # 1.
p2(agent:'Adams & Sons',item:b2) # 1.
p2(agent:'Adams & Sons',item:b3) # 1.
p2(agent:'Johnny Ltd',item:b1) # 1.
p2(agent:'Johnny Ltd',item:b2) # 1.
p2(agent:'Mitre 10',item:b1) # 1.

predicate([(agent,A:B),is,a,fractional,supplier],p1(A:B)).
predicate([(agent,A:B),supply,(item,C:D)],p2(A:B,C:D)).
predicate([(agent,A:B),not,supply,(item, C:D)],
          non(p2(A:B,C:D))).

domain(p1(A:B)) :- type(A,agent).
domain(p2(A:B,C:D)) :- type(A,agent),type(C,item).

constsymbol(agent:'Adams & Sons').
constsymbol(agent:'Johnny Ltd').
constsymbol(agent:'Mitre 10').
constsymbol(item:b1).
constsymbol(item:b2).
constsymbol(item:b3).
```

Observe that ESSLN detects the keyword *not* in the first sentence and learnt where it should be placed in this sentence. This knowledge is saved in the third predicate definition. It is usually difficult to know where to add the keyword *not* (or its equivalents in other languages) to a sentence to negate the sentence. ESSLN learns this from the information supplied by the user, including the negative queries. Note also that in the definition of each predicate, the type-variable A in a pair such as ($agent,A{:}B$) is designed to handle subtypes effectively and efficiently, as we shall see in Section 9.11.

Now with the above given knowledge-base, we can enter various queries and obtain the system's responses and explanations as shown below:

```
Q:> which _agent is a fractional supplier?
A:> agent Johnny Ltd is a fractional supplier
 -> how.
  > Because
    IF
      agent Johnny Ltd not supply item b3
    THEN
      agent Johnny Ltd is a fractional supplier
 -> more.
A:> agent Mitre 10 is a fractional supplier
 -> how.
  > Because
    IF
      agent Mitre 10 not supply item b2
    THEN
      agent Mitre 10 is a fractional supplier
 -> ok.
```

Here, the arrow-prompt indicates that the system is waiting for the user to accept the result (by entering "ok.") or to request an explanation (by entering "how."). Following are the system's responses to quantified queries.

```
Q:> which _agent supply all _item?
A:> agent Adams & Sons supply all item
 -> how.
```

```
    > Because
      IF
        agent Adams & Sons not supply some item is false
      THEN
        agent Adams & Sons supply all item
   -> ok.
Q:> which _agent supply no _item?
A:> no agent supply no item
   -> ok.
```

The explanation to the first quantified query above shows that because the goal $non(p2(agent: 'Adams \& Sons', item: Y))$ fails (that is, having certainty 0), the goal $not(non(p2(agent: 'Adams \& Sons', item: Y)))$ succeeds, and hence, the goal $all(p2(S:X, T:\_), not(non(p2(S:X, T:Y))))$ succeeds with the answer $(S:X = agent: 'Adams \& Sons')$.

Since ESSLN accepts quantified information, we may enter the following knowledge:

```
Q:> _agent 'Rossianno Co' supply no _item.
Q:> _agent 'Yoshima Kuru' supply all _item.
```

The result is the addition of the following facts:

```
non(p2(agent:'Rossianno Co',item:A)) # 1.
p2(agent:'Yoshima Kuru',item:A) # 1.
```

Of course, before entering the above sentences (or any other information), one must check the knowledge-base to avoid storing conflicting information. The answers to the previous quantified queries are now as follows:

```
Q:> which _agent supply no _item?
A:> agent Rossianno Co supply no item
  -> how.
    > Because
      IF
        agent Rossianno Co supply some item is false
      THEN
        agent Rossianno Co supply no item
```

```
 -> how.
  > Because
      agent Rossianno Co supply some item
    is nofact
 -> ok.
Q:> which _agent supply all _item?
A:> agent Adams & Sons supply all item
 -> more.
A:> agent Yoshima Kuru supply all item
 -> ok.
```

This time the explanations show that because the goal $p2(agent:'Rossianno\ Co',item:Y)$ fails, the goal $not(p2(agent:'Rossianno\ Co',item:Y))$ succeeds, hence the goal $all(non(p2(S:X,T:\_)),not(p2(S:X,T:Y)))$ succeeds with an answer $(S:X = agent:'Rossianno\ Co')$.

EXAMPLE 9.7 Let us now consider a knowledge-base that contains certainty assessment. Following is a portion of a detective expert system knowledge-base:

```
%90 _suspect X murdered _victim Y :
    _suspect X had a motive to kill _victim Y,
    _suspect X had the potential to kill _victim Y.

%80 _suspect X had a motive to kill _victim Y :
    _suspect X had a serious conflict with _victim Y.

%95 _suspect X had a motive to kill _victim Y :
    _suspect X is the life-insurance beneficiary of _victim Y.

%60 _suspect X had a motive to kill _victim Y :
    _suspect X had a secret known to _victim Y.

%90 _suspect X had the potential to kill _victim Y :
    _suspect X might appear near _victim Y,
    _suspect X has no _alibi.

_suspect 'Alan Smith' had a serious conflict with
    _victim 'J.R.'.
```

```
_suspect 'Sue R.' is the life-insurance beneficiary of
    _victim 'J.R.'.
_suspect 'Sue.R.' had a secret known to _victim 'W.K.'.

%90 _suspect 'Sue R.' might appear near _victim 'J.R.'.
%70 _suspect 'Alan Smith' might appear near _victim 'J.R.'.

_suspect 'Alan Smith' has _alibi 'John Cooper'.
_suspect 'Alan Smith' has _alibi 'Peter Falk'.
```

The above knowledge is converted into the following Prolog rules and facts:

```
p1(A:B,C:D) # 0.9 :- p2(A:B,C:D), p3(A:B,C:D).

p2(A:B,C:D) # 0.8 :- p4(A:B,C:D).
p2(A:B,C:D) # 0.95 :- p5(A:B,C:D).
p2(A:B,C:D) # 0.6 :- p6(A:B,C:D).
p3(A:B,C:D) # 0.9 :- p7(A:B,C:D),
    all(non(p8(A:B,E:F)),not(p8(A:B,E:G))).

p4(suspect:'Alan Smith',victim:'J.R.') # 1.
p5(suspect:'Sue R.',victim:'J.R.') # 1.
p6(suspect:'Sue R.',victim:'W.K.') # 1.
p7(suspect:'Sue R.',victim:'J.R.') # 0.9.
p7(suspect:'Alan Smith',victim:'J.R.') # 0.7.
p8(suspect:'Alan Smith',alibi:'John Cooper') # 1.
p8(suspect:'Alan Smith',alibi:'Peter Falk') # 1.

predicate([(suspect,A:B),murdered,(victim,C:D)],p1(A:B,C:D)).
predicate([(suspect,A:B),had,a,motive,to,kill,(victim,C:D)],
    p2(A:B,C:D)).
predicate([(suspect,A:B),had,the,potential,to,kill,
    (victim,C:D)],p3(A:B,C:D)).
predicate([(suspect,A:B),had,a,serious,conflict,with,
    (victim,C:D)],p4(A:B,C:D)).
predicate([(suspect,A:B),is,the,'life-insurance',beneficiary,
    of,(victim,C:D)],p5(A:B,C:D)).
predicate([(suspect,A:B),had,a,secret,known,to,(victim,C:D)],
    p6(A:B,C:D)).
```

```
predicate([(suspect,A:B),might,appear,near,(victim,C:D)],
    p7(A:B,C:D)).
predicate([(suspect,A:B),has,(alibi,C:D)],p8(A:B,C:D)).

domain(p1(A:B,C:D)) :- type(A,suspect),type(C,victim).
domain(p2(A:B,C:D)) :- type(A,suspect),type(C,victim).
domain(p3(A:B,C:D)) :- type(A,suspect),type(C,victim).
domain(p4(A:B,C:D)) :- type(A,suspect),type(C,victim).
domain(p5(A:B,C:D)) :- type(A,suspect),type(C,victim).
domain(p6(A:B,C:D)) :- type(A,suspect),type(C,victim).
domain(p7(A:B,C:D)) :- type(A,suspect),type(C,victim).
domain(p8(A:B,C:D)) :- type(A,suspect),type(C,alibi).

constsymbol(suspect:'Alan Smith').
constsymbol(victim:'J.R.').
constsymbol(suspect:'Sue R.').
constsymbol(victim:'W.K.').
constsymbol(alibi:'John Cooper').
constsymbol(alibi:'Peter Falk').
```

Observe again that in the definition of each predicate, the type-variable in a pair such as (*suspect*, *A*:*B*) is designed to handle subtypes.

Having built the above knowledge-base, we can now find out who murdered 'J.R.' by entering the following query, to which ESSLN's answers and explanations are shown below.

```
Q:> which _suspect murdered _victim 'J.R.'?
A:> I am 69% positive that
    suspect Sue R. murdered victim J.R.
 -> how.
  > Because
    IF
      suspect Sue R. had a motive to kill victim J.R.
         with 95% certainty
      suspect Sue R. had the potential to kill victim J.R.
         with 81% certainty
    THEN
      suspect Sue R. murdered victim J.R. with 69% certainty
 ->
```

Here, the conclusion's certainty is obtained by the probability calculation $(0.9 * 0.95 * 0.81) * 100 = 69.2$ (truncated). If we continue to query the system, we will have the following display, where the explanation of the negatively quantified goal "Sue R. has no alibi" is worth noting:

```
-> how.
 > Because
   IF
     suspect Sue R. is the life-insurance beneficiary of
        victim J.R.
   THEN
     suspect Sue R. had a motive to kill victim J.R.
        with 95% certainty
-> how.
 > Because
     suspect Sue R. is the life-insurance beneficiary of
        victim J.R.
   is fact
-> ok.
-> how.
 > Because
   IF
     suspect Sue R. might appear near victim J.R.
        with 90% certainty
     suspect Sue R. has no alibi
   THEN
     suspect Sue R. had the potential to kill victim J.R.
        with 81% certainty
-> how.
 > Because
     suspect Sue R. might appear near victim J.R.
   is fact with 90% certainty
-> ok.
-> how.
   Because
   IF
     suspect Sue R. has some alibi is false
   THEN
     suspect Sue R. has no alibi
```

```
-> how.
  Because
    suspect Sue R. has some alibi
  is nofact


-> ok.
```

The following queries show the system's behaviour in processing negative and quantified goals.

```
Q:> which _suspect had not a motive to kill _victim 'J.R.'?
A:> all suspect had a motive to kill victim J.R.
 -> ok.
Q:> which _suspect had a motive to kill all _victim?
A:> suspect Sue R. had a motive to kill all victim
 -> how.
  > Because
    IF
      suspect Sue R. had not a motive to kill some victim
        is false
    THEN
      suspect Sue R. had a motive to kill all victim
 -> how.
  > Because
    IF
      using the substitution [victim : _9455]
      evaluating negation shows suspect Sue R. had not a
        motive to kill some victim is false
    THEN
      suspect Sue R. had not a motive to kill some victim
        is false
 ->
```

If we continue to ask for more explanations, the system will get very deep into its knowledge-base to provide the facts that Sue R. is the life-insurance beneficiary of J.R. on the one hand, and she also had a secret known to the victim W.K., on the other hand.

Let us now have an insight into ESSLN's user interface. The system's top-level control is quite typical and is shown below.

```
essln :- initialise,
         repeat,
             receive_query(Q,C),
             process_query(Q,C),
         terminate(Q).
```

During the initialising phase, the system performs the following routine tasks:

- Displaying the system's banner and menus;

- Creating a workspace for the user and bringing in pre-prepared tools;

- Learning a new language from the user if required;

- Switching itself to the user's language of choice.

Figures 9.19 and 9.20 show ESSLN's first two screens.

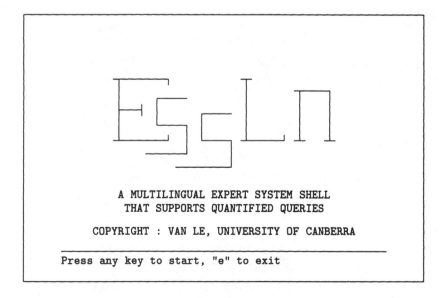

FIGURE 9.19 ESSLN's front banner.

```
PLEASE CHOOSE A LANGUAGE FOR OUR CONVERSATION

1. Algerian          9. Pilipino
2. Dutch            10. Portuguese
3. English          11. Romanian
4. French           12. Senegalese
5. Indonesian       13. Spanish
6. Italian          14. Swedish
7. Moroccan         15. Vietnamese
8. Norwegian        16. Other


Your language of choice:
```

FIGURE 9.20 ESSLN's language list.

In the rest of a working session, the system repeatedly receives inputs from the user and processes the requests. If the input is a unit of knowledge, then it is stored in the system's knowledge-base; if it is a query, then the system evaluates the query and provides answers to the user.

To receive knowledge or a query from the user, the system reads the input sentence into a string S, then converts it into a list Q of tokens, each of which contains the ASCII codes of the characters of a word. The procedure *receive_query* is shown in Figures 9.21 and 9.22.

```
receive_query(Q,C) :-
    nl, write('Q:> '),readstring($ $,S,C),
    list_text(T,S),scan_text(T,Q),!.
receive_query(_,_) :- error_query,fail.

readstring(R,S,C) :-
    read_string(100,R1),concat(R,R1,S1),
    (endstring(R1,C1),!, S = S1, C = C1;
     nl,tab(8),readstring(S1,S,C)).
```

FIGURE 9.21 ESSLN's *receive_query* procedure.

```
endstring(S,C) :- string_length(S,N),
    M is N-1, nth_char(M,S,C), end_char(C).
end_char(C) :- C = 46; C = 63.  % period or ?

scan_text([],[]) :- !.
scan_text(T,[W|L]) :-
    append(_,[C|T1],T), C \= 32,!,  % skip spaces
    get_word([C|T1],W,T2), scan_text(T2,L).

get_word([C|T],C,T) :- member(C,[58,44,46,63]),!.
get_word([C|T],[C],T) :- C = 61,!. % (=)
get_word([C|T],[C|W],T2) :-
    bracket(C,C1),!,get_chars(0,C1,T,W,T2).
get_word([C|T],[C|W],T2) :-
    valid_start(C),!,get_chars(1,32,T,W,T2).

get_chars(K,C1,[C|T],[C|W],T2) :-
    valid_char(K,C,C1),!,get_chars(K,C1,T,W,T2).
get_chars(0,39,[39|T],[],T) :- !.
get_chars(0,C,[C|T],[C],T) :- (C = 41; C = 93),!. % ) or ]
get_chars(1,C1,[C|T],[],[C|T]) :-
    member(C,[32,61,58,44,46,63]). % (space = : , . ?)

valid_start(C) :- valid(C); C = 37.  % (%)
valid_char(K,C,C1) :- K = 0,!, C \= C1; K = 1, valid(C).

bracket(39,39).   bracket(40,41).   bracket(91,93).
```

FIGURE 9.22 ESSLN's *receive_query* procedure (continued).

The list Q of tokens returned by the procedure *receive_query* represents a query of one of the following categories:

- Special queries that can be processed immediately;

- Supplied information that must be converted into Prolog clauses before being stored in the system's knowledge-base;

- General queries that must be converted into Prolog queries to be passed to the system's meta-interpreter for evaluation.

The procedure that handles special queries is quite straightforward and will be discussed later (Figure 9.28). Besides the above-mentioned special queries, if the list Q is terminated with a period (ASCII code 46), then it is converted into a Prolog clause to be stored in the knowledge-base. The procedure *convert_clause* (Figures 9.23 and 9.24) uses *append* to extract from the list Q a unit of information P, which is terminated by either a colon (ASCII code 58) or a comma (44) or a period (46), and *converts* it into a Prolog formula A. The variables in A are compared with those previously found in VS so that variables representing the same symbol are unified; any new variables are added to VS to make the new list $VS1$.

The procedure *convert* processes the first unit of information differently from the rest of the input list, because the clause's head contains a certainty assessment in the form $\# \, C$, and its variables are always assumed to be universally quantified. Thus, if P is the first unit of information, then the procedure *convert_atom* returns three major lists: $P1$ is a list of words translated from P that expresses a relation to be represented by some formula $A1$; the list NP is the same as $P1$ except that all arguments are replaced with distinct variables, and the keyword *not*, if it exists, is left where it is so that NP will be used to express the negated sentence; finally, the list $[E,Nt,No,All]$ contains quantification indicators, each of which is set to 1 if the associated quantification is found. The formula $A1$ can be returned by the goal $predicate(P1, A1)$, if the system already knows the sentence; otherwise, the system learns the new sentence and generates a new predicate to construct the formula $A1$ (see procedure *construct* in Figure 9.24). Now if one of the indicators No or Not is set, then the returned formula A is $non(A1)$ (that has universally quantified variables in the case of No, and is ground in the case of Not); otherwise, the formula A is plainly $A1$. The list of arguments AL, which is also returned by the procedure *convert_atom*, is used to store the constant symbols.

Note that ESSLN does not allow a single unit of input to contain more than one of the keywords *not, no*, and *all* (or their equivalents in other languages; see procedures *quantify* and *bad_atom* in Figure 9.24), because any such sentence can always be restructured to comply with the rule. (We shall see later, however, that answers to user's queries may contain various combinations of *not, no*, and *all*.)

```
process_query(Q,46) :- !,
    convert_clause(c,[],Q,E),
    store_clause(E).

convert_clause(S,VS,Q,E) :-
    append(P,[C|Rest],Q),member(C,[58,44,46]),!,P \= [],
    convert(S,P,VS,VS1,A),        % [ :  ,  .]
    (C = 58,!, E = (A :- B), convert_clause(t,VS1,Rest,B);
     C = 44,!, E = (A,B), convert_clause(t,VS1,Rest,B);
     C = 46,!, E = A).

convert(c,[[37|N]|P],VS,VS1,(A # C)) :- !,
    list_text(N,T),int_text(I,T),C is I/100,
    convert(h,P,VS,VS1,A).
convert(c,P,VS,VS1,(A # 1)) :- !,
    convert(h,P,VS,VS1,A).

convert(h,P,VS,VS1,A) :- !,
    convert_atom(P,VS,VS1,NP,P1,AL,_,[0,0,0,0],[_,Nt,No,All]),
    (bad_atom(Nt,No,All),!,fail;
    (predicate(P1,A1),!; construct(P1,A1)),
    (No = 1,!,A = non(A1); quantify([_,Nt,0,0],NP,_,A1,A)),
    store_constants(AL)).

convert(t,P,VS,VS1,A) :-
    convert_atom(P,VS,VS1,NP,P1,AL,P2,[0,0,0,0],QL),
    (predicate(P1,A1),!; construct(P1,A1)),
    quantify(QL,NP,P2,A1,A),
    store_constants(AL).

store_constants([]) :- !.
store_constants([T:A|AL]) :-
    (atom(A),not(constsymbol(T:A)),!,
        assert(constsymbol(T:A)); true),
    store_constants(AL).
```

FIGURE 9.23 Processing a clause.

```
quantify([_,0,0,0],_,_,A,A) :- !.
quantify([0,0,1,0],_,_,A,not(A)) :- !.
quantify([0,0,0,1],_,_,A,not(non(A))) :- !.
quantify([1,0,0,1],_,P,A,all(A,not(non(B)))) :- !,
    predicate(P,B).
quantify([1,0,1,0],_,P,A,all(non(A),not(B))) :- !,
    predicate(P,B).
quantify([_,1,0,0],NP,_,A,non(A)) :- !,
    (predicate(NP,_),!;
     functor(A,F,N),copy_clause(_,NP,VL,_),
     A1 =.. [F|VL],assert(predicate(NP,non(A1)))).
quantify([_,Nt,No,All],_,_,_,_) :-
    (bad_atom(Nt,No,All); unknown_concept),!,fail.

construct([Find|P1],tobe_filled(A)) :-
    trans_word(find,Find),!,construct(P1,A).
construct(P1,A) :- copy_clause(P1,P2,VL,TL),
    generate_symbol(P), E =.. [P|VL],
    assert(predicate(P2,E)),convert(TL,Types),
    assert((domain(E) :- Types)),predicate(P1,A).

copy_clause([],[],[],[]) :- !.
copy_clause([(T,S:A)|P1],[(T,R:V)|P2],[R:V|VL],
    [type(R,T)|TL]) :- !,copy_clause(P1,P2,VL,TL).
copy_clause([W|P1],[W|P2],VL,TL) :-
    copy_clause(P1,P2,VL,TL).

bad_atom(Nt,No,All) :-
    Nt+No+All > 1,
    nl,write('A:> '),write_word('Bad clause!'),nl,tab(4),
    write_word('Use no more than one of "not","no","all".').

store_clause((A # C :- B)) :- !,assert((A # C :- B)).
store_clause((non(A) # C)) :- !,domain(A),assert((non(A) # C)).
store_clause((A # C)) :- domain(A),assert((A # C)).
generate_symbol :- % see Figure 8.6
```

FIGURE 9.24 Processing a clause (continued).

```
convert_atom([Q,[95|W]|Rest],VS,VS1,[(T,S:V)|NP],
   [(T,S1:V1)|P1],[T:V1|AL],[(T,S1:V2)|P2],[E,Nt,No,All],QL) :-
   universal(Q),!,name(T,W),
   convert_atom(Rest,VS,VS1,NP,P1,AL,P2,[E,Nt,No,1],QL).
convert_atom([Q,[95|W]|Rest],VS,VS1,[(T,S:V)|NP],
   [(T,S1:V1)|P1],[T:V1|AL],[(T,S1:V2)|P2],[E,Nt,No,All],QL) :-
   neguniversal(Q),!,name(T,W),
   convert_atom(Rest,VS,VS1,NP,P1,AL,P2,[E,Nt,1,All],QL).
convert_atom([Q,[95|W]|Rest],VS,VS1,[(T,S:V)|NP],
   [(T,S1:V1)|P1],[T:V1|AL],[(T,S1:V1)|P2],[E,Nt,No,All],QL) :-
   existential(Q),!,name(T,W),
   convert_atom(Rest,VS,VS1,NP,P1,AL,P2,[1,Nt,No,All],QL).
convert_atom([Q|Rest],VS,VS1,[Q1|NP],P1,AL,P2,
   [E,Nt,No,All],QL) :-
   negation(Q,Q1),!,
   convert_atom(Rest,VS,VS1,NP,P1,AL,P2,[E,1,No,All],QL).
convert_atom([[95|W],[C|L]|Rest],VS,VS1,[(T,S:V)|NP],
   [(T,S1:V1)|P1],[T:V1|AL],[(T,S1:V1)|P2],[E,Nt,No,All],QL) :-
   capital(C),!,name(X,[C|L]),name(T,W),
   (member((X,T,S1:V1),VS),!,VS2 = VS; VS2 = [(X,T,S1:V1)|VS]),
   convert_atom(Rest,VS2,VS1,NP,P1,AL,P2,[1,Nt,No,All],QL).
convert_atom([[95|W],A|Rest],VS,VS1,[(T,S:V)|NP],
   [(T,S1:A1)|P1],[T:A1|AL],[(T,S1:A1)|P2],[E,Nt,No,All],QL) :-
   !, aterm(A,VS,E,A1,VS2,E1),name(T,W),
   convert_atom(Rest,VS2,VS1,NP,P1,AL,P2,[E1,Nt,No,All],QL).
convert_atom([W|Rest],VS,VS1,[(T,S:V)|NP],
   [(T,S1:W1)|P1],[T:W1|AL],[(T,S1:W1)|P2],[E,Nt,No,All],QL) :-
   special_term(W,VS,E,T,W1,VS2,E1),
   convert_atom(Rest,VS2,VS1,NP,P1,AL,P2,[E1,Nt,No,All],QL).
convert_atom([W|Rest],VS,VS1,[W1|NP],[W1|P1],AL,[W1|P2],
   QL0,QL) :-
   !,name(W1,W),
   convert_atom(Rest,VS,VS1,NP,P1,AL,P2,QL0,QL).
convert_atom([],VS,VS,[],[],[],[],QL,QL).
```

FIGURE 9.25 Conversion of a unit of information.

```
universal(Q) :- name(Q1,Q),
    (trans_word(all,Q1);trans_word(every,Q1)),!.
existential(Q) :- name(Q1,Q),
    (trans_word(some,Q1);trans_word(which,Q1)),!.
negation(Q,Q1) :- name(Q1,Q),trans_word(not,Q1),!.
neguniversal(Q) :- name(Q1,Q),trans_word(no,Q1),!.


capital(C) :- 65 =< C, C =< 90.


aterm(W,VS,E,W1,VS,E) :- atomname(W,W1),!.
aterm(W,VS,E,W1,VS2,E1) :- special_term(W,VS,E,_,W1,VS2,E1).


atomname([39|W],W1) :- name(W1,W).
atomname([C|W],W1) :- 96 < C, C < 123,name(W1,[C|W]).


special_term(W,VS,E,T,W1,VS,E) :-    % integer number
    list_text(W,S),int_text(W1,S),!,trans_word(number,T).
special_term([C|W],VS,E,T,W1,VS2,E1) :-
    (C = 40,!,trans_word(number,T); % ( for numeric expression
     C = 91,  trans_word(list,T)),  % [ for list
    list_text([C|W],S),string_term(S,W1),
    list_var_symbols([C|W],0,[],WVS),
    (WVS = [],!, VS = VS2, E = E1;
     var_list(W1,WVL), match_vars(WVS,WVL,VS,VS2), E1 = 1).


match_vars([],[],VS,VS) :- !.
match_vars([X|XL],[V|VL],VS,VS2) :-
    (member((X,T,S:V),VS),!,match_vars(XL,VL,VS,VS2);
     match_vars(XL,VL,[(X,T,S:V)|VS],VS2)).


unknown_concept :- nl,write('A:> '),
    write_word('I dont know this concept. Check your typing'),
    nl,tab(4),write_word('If new concept, please teach me').

var_list :-          % see Figure 8.2
list_var_symbols :- % see Figure 8.13
```

FIGURE 9.26 Recognition of quantification and terms.

Unlike the first unit of information of an input list, any subsequent unit of information may contain existentially or universally (positively or negatively) quantified variables. To handle this, the procedure *convert_atom* returns an extra list *P2*, which is a copy of *P1* except that those variables that are universally quantified (positively or negatively) are different. The returned formula *A* is then constructed by combining the formulas representing *P1* and *P2* in accordance with the quantification indicators *E, Nt, No,* and *All*. This is shown in Figure 9.24. Details of the procedure *convert_atom* are shown in Figures 9.25 and 9.26.

On the other hand, if the input list *Q* is terminated with a question mark (ASCII code 63), then it is converted into a Prolog query to be passed to the system's meta-interpreter (see Figures 9.14 to 9.16) for evaluation. The conversion of a query is similar to that of a clause's subgoals, except that no predicate symbols or constant symbols need to be stored. The procedure *convert_query* is shown in Figure 9.27.

```
process_query(Q,63) :-
    convert_query([],Q,G),
    evaluate(G).

convert_query(VS,Q,G) :-
    append(P,[C|Rest],Q),member(C,[44,63]),!,P \= [],
    convert(g,P,VS,VS1,A),       % [ , ?]
    (C = 44,!, G = (A,B), convert_query(VS1,Rest,B);
     C = 63,!, G = A).

convert(g,P,VS,VS1,A) :-
    convert_atom(P,VS,VS1,NP,P1,_,P2,[0,0,0,0],QL),
    (predicate(P1,A1),!, quantify(QL,NP,P2,A1,A);
     error_query,!,fail).

error_query :-
    nl,write('A:> '),write_word('Illegal query !').

convert_atom :- % see Figure 9.25
quantify :-     % see Figure 9.24
evaluate :-     % see Figure 9.29
```

FIGURE 9.27 Processing a user query.

We now return to the system's process of special queries. For convenience, the system allows the following special forms of commands to be processed directly:

- Declaration of individual constant symbols, besides those extracted from the input clauses (e.g., _agent 'Rossianno Co'.);

- Declaration of subtypes (e.g., _contractor is _agent.);

- Request for displaying of constants of a specified type (e.g., _agent?);

- Request for listing of part or the whole of the knowledge-base (e.g., list predicate., list base.);

- Request for loading an existing file that contains knowledge in some user-language into the knowledge-base (e.g., load 'c:supplier.dat'.);

- Request for saving the current knowledge-base in some specified file (e.g., save 'c:supplier.ari'.);

- Request for loading an existing file that contains knowledge in Prolog language, which might be previously saved by ESSLN, into the knowledge-base (e.g., reload 'c:supplier.ari'.).

The system's handling of subtypes will be discussed in the next section. Other special commands listed above are processed in a simple way, and the procedure that performs these tasks is given in Figure 9.28. Note that when loading an existing file written in some user-language, the system expects the file to be terminated by the keyword "*bye*" (or its equivalent in other languages), as if it is entered directly from the keyboard. Note also that the first clause in Figure 9.28 must be the first clause of the procedure *process_query* (see Figures 9.23 and 9.27) so that special queries are processed immediately. (For the definition of *atomname* see Figure 9.26.) Following are some examples of special queries:

```
Q:> _agent 'Rossianno Co'.
Q:> _agent ?
agent Adams & Sons ->
agent Johnny Ltd ->
agent Mitre 10 ->
agent Rossianno Co ->
```

```
process_query(Q,_) :- special_query(Q),!.

special_query([[95|W],A,46]) :- !,
    atomname(A,A1),
    name(T,W),assert(constsymbol(T:A1)).
special_query([[95|W],63]) :- !,
    name(T,W),constsymbol(T:X),
    nl,write_list([T,' ',X,' ->']),get0(13).
special_query([[95|W],X,[95|W1],46]) :-
    name(Is,X),trans_word(is,Is),!,
    name(T,W),name(T1,W1),process_subtype(T,T1).
special_query([Q|R]) :-
    name(Q1,Q),trans_word(W,Q1),
    member(W,[bye,list,load,save,reload]),!,
    process_special_query(W,R).

process_special_query(bye,_) :- !.
process_special_query(list,R) :- !,
    (R = [46],!,nl,listing;
     R = [P,46],name(N,P),
     nl,(trans_word(base,N),listing('#'),!; listing(N))).
process_special_query(load,[[39|N],46]) :- !,
    name(Filename,N),
    see(Filename),
    repeat,
        receive_query(Q,C),
        process_query(Q,C),
    end(Q),seen.
process_special_query(save,[[39|N],46]) :- !,
    name(Filename,N),
    tell(Filename),listing,told.
process_special_query(reload,[[39|N],46]) :- !,
    (retract(symbol_index(_)),!; true),
    name(Filename,N),reconsult(Filename).

end([Q,46]) :- name(Q1,Q),trans_word(bye,Q1).
```

FIGURE 9.28 Processing special queries.

Let us now study the last phase of a goal's evaluation in ESSLN. The meta-interpreter for expert systems shown in Figures 9.14 to 9.18 is the core of ESSLN's inference engine. The goal evaluating process is shown in Figures 9.29 and 9.30.

```
evaluate(Goal) :-
    prove(Goal,20,Certainty,Proof,[]),
    process_result(Goal,Certainty,Proof),!,
    clear_workspace.
evaluate(_) :-
    terminate_message,
    clear_workspace.

process_result(Goal,Certainty,Proof) :-
    print_answer(Goal,Certainty),
    read_response(Response),
    process_response(Response,Proof).

print_answer(Goal,0) :- !,
    nl,write('A:> '),
    copy(Goal,Goal1),display_goal(Goal1,no).
print_answer(Goal,Certainty) :-
    nl,write('A:> '),
    write_goal_certainty(Certainty),
    copy(Goal,Goal1),display_goal(Goal1,yes).

terminate_message :-
    nl,tab(4),write_word('No (more) answers !').
clear_workspace :-
    abolish(answer/2),
    abolish(save_all/2),
    abolish(failproof/1).

prove :-          % see Figure 9.14
display_goal :-   % see Figure 9.31
process_response :- % see Figure 9.34
```

FIGURE 9.29 ESSLN's evaluation of goals.

```
write_goal_certainty(C) :-
    C =:= 1,!;
    C1 is C*100,float_text(C1,T,fixed(0)),int_text(C2,T),
    write_word('I am'),
    write_list([' ',C2,'% ']),write_word('positive that'),
    nl,tab(4).

write_rule_certainty(C) :-
    (var(C); C =:= 1),!;
    C =:= 0,!,write_word('is false');
    C1 is C*100,float_text(C1,T,fixed(0)),int_text(C2,T),
    write_word(with),
    write_list([' ',C2,'% ']),write_word(certainty).

read_response(R) :-
    nl,write(' -> '), read(S),
    (trans_word(T,S),
    member(T,[ok,how,more]),!,R = T;
    write_word('   Type ok., how. or more.'),
    read_response(R)).

write_word(W) :- trans_word(W,W1),write(W1).
write_list([]) :- !.
write_list([X|T]) :- write(X),write_list(T).
```

FIGURE 9.30 ESSLN's evaluation of goals (continued).

ESSLN's procedure *display_goal* (which is shown in Figures 9.31 and 9.32) is much more sophisticated than the one given in Figure 9.6. In fact, here we have various types of goals, including the ones representing quantified goals, to be converted back to sentences in the user language. For example, consider a goal of the form $all(A, not(non(B)))$, where A and B have the form $p(S{:}X, T{:}Y)$ and $p(S{:}X, T{:}Z)$, respectively. This goal represents the formula $\exists_S X \, \forall_T Y \, p(X, Y)$. If the existentially quantified variable X is uninstantiated, then it should be read "all" (or its equivalent in other languages) when the answer $R = yes$, and "no" when $R = no$, whereas the universally quantified variable Z is always read "all". So, we indicate this to the procedure *print_goal* (see Figure 9.32) by binding all variables of A with an appropriate quantifier Q before sending the goal B to *print_goal*.

```
display_goal(all(A,not(non(B))),R) :- !,
    univ_quantify(R,Q),univ_quantify(yes,Q1),
    tvar_list(A,VL),bind_vars(VL,Q),
    print_goal(B,Q1).
display_goal(all(non(A),not(B)),R) :- !,
    univ_quantify(R,Q),univ_quantify(no,Q1),
    tvar_list(A,VL),bind_vars(VL,Q),
    print_goal(B,Q1).
display_goal(not(non(A)),R) :- !,
    (R = no,!,univ_quantify(some,Q),print_goal(non(A),Q);
     univ_quantify(yes,Q), print_goal(A,Q)).
display_goal(not(A),R) :- !,
    (R = no,!,univ_quantify(some,Q),print_goal(A,Q);
     ground(A),!,print_goal(non(A),_);
     univ_quantify(no,Q), print_goal(A,Q)).
display_goal(non(A),R) :- !,
    (R = no,!,univ_quantify(yes,Q),print_goal(A,Q);
     univ_quantify(R,Q), print_goal(non(A),Q)).
display_goal((A,B),no) :- !,
    (ground((A,B)),!,write_word(no); write_word(none)).
display_goal((A,B),yes) :- !,
    display_goal(A,yes),
    nl,tab(4),display_goal(B,yes).
display_goal(A,R) :-
    (R = no,ground(A),!,print_goal(non(A),_);
     univ_quantify(R,Q),print_goal(A,Q)).

univ_quantify(yes,Q) :- trans_word(all,Q).
univ_quantify(no,Q) :- trans_word(no,Q).
univ_quantify(some,Q) :- trans_word(some,Q).

bind_vars([],_) :- !.
bind_vars([T:Q|Xs],Q) :- bind_vars(Xs,Q).

tvar_list :-  % see Figure 9.17
```

FIGURE 9.31 ESSLN's displaying of goals.

```
print_goal(non(A),Q) :- !,domain(A),
    (predicate(PNA,non(A)),!,print_phrase(PNA,Q);
     predicate(PA,A),negate_quantify(Q,Q1,W),
     print_phrase([W|PA],Q1)).
print_goal(A,Q) :- domain(A),
    predicate(Phrase,A),
    print_phrase(Phrase,Q).

print_phrase([],_) :- !.
print_phrase([(T,S:X)|Rest],Q) :- !,
    (var(X),!,write_list([Q,' ',S,' ']);
     quantifier(X),!,write_list([X,' ',S,' ']);
     write_list([T,' ',X,' '])),
    print_phrase(Rest,Q).
print_phrase([W|Rest],Q) :-
    write_list([W,' ']),
    print_phrase(Rest,Q).

negate_quantify(Q,Q1,W) :-
    trans_word(deny,W),
    (trans_word(some,Q),trans_word(all,Q1);
     trans_word(all,Q),trans_word(some,Q1)).

quantifier(X) :- trans_word(W,X),member(W,[all,no,some]).
```

FIGURE 9.32 ESSLN's displaying of goals (continued).

For example, consider the query

```
which _agent supply all _item ?
```

which is translated into the goal

```
all(p2(S:X,T:Y),not(non(p2(S:X,T:Z))))
```

where the predicate *p2* is defined by

```
predicate([(agent,A:B),supply,(item,C:D)],p2(A:B,C:D)).
```

Note first that in the above predicate definition, the definite types *agent* and *item* are used to recognise the input query, while the variable types A and C are used to construct the output sentence. Here, we have four cases as shown below:

1. The goal fails (that is, having certainty 0) and $S{:}X$ is uninstantiated. In this case, the appropriate quantifier for X is *no*. So, after binding the variable X with the value "no", we pass the pair $(p2(S{:}no, T{:}Z), all)$ to the procedure *print_goal*. This procedure checks the domain of $p2$ to bind the type S to *agent* and T to *item*, and consults the predicate definition to obtain the phrase

   ```
   [(agent,agent:no),supply,(item,item:Z)]
   ```

   This phrase and the quantifier $Q = all$ are passed to the procedure *print_phrase*. As a result, the following sentence is displayed:

   ```
   no agent supply all item.
   ```

2. The goal succeeds with $S{:}X$ uninstantiated. Then, the appropriate quantifier for X is *all* (while the quantifier for Z is still *all*). So, the same process as in case 1 will produce the phrase:

   ```
   [(agent,agent:all),supply,(item,item:Z)]
   ```

   which is displayed as:

   ```
   all agent supply all item.
   ```

3. The goal succeeds with $S{:}X$ instantiated to *contractor:X*, say, where *contractor* has been declared to be a subtype of *agent*. Then, the procedure *domain* only checks the subtype, and the same process would produce the phrase:

   ```
   [(agent,contractor:all),supply,(item,item:Z)]
   ```

   which is then displayed as:

   ```
   all contractor supply all item.
   ```

4. The goal succeeds and $S{:}X$ is instantiated to some constant, *agent:'Adams & Sons'*, say, then the constructed phrase would be:

```
[(agent,agent:'Adams & Sons'),supply,(item,item:Z)]
```

which is displayed as:

```
agent Adams & Sons supply all item.
```

Let us now consider another typical quantified query:

```
_agent 'Johnny Ltd' supply all _item ?
```

This query is translated into the following goal:

```
not(non(p2(S:'Johnny Ltd',T:X)))
```

where the predicate symbol *p2* has been defined before. For this query, there are only two possible answers. If the answer is $R = no$ (i.e., certainty $C = 0$), then we use the quantifier $Q = some$ (or its equivalent in other languages) and the pair $(non(p2(S:'Johnny\ Ltd', T:X)), some)$ is passed to the procedure *print_goal*. This procedure then calls *domain* to bind S to *agent* and T to *item*, and consults the predicate definitions to obtain the phrase for the negated goal:

```
[(agent,agent:'Johnny Ltd'),not,supply,(item,item:X)]
```

This phrase is passed to procedure *print_phrase* together with the quantifier $Q = some$. As a result, the following sentence is displayed:

```
agent Johnny Ltd not supply some item.
```

In case the procedure *print_goal* fails to find an appropriate sentence for the negated goal $non(p2(agent:'Johnny\ Ltd', item:X))$, it would call the procedure *negate_quantify* to obtain the alternative quantifiers $Q1 = all$ and $W = deny$. Consequently, the output sentence would be:

```
deny agent Johnny Ltd supply all item.
```

If the answer to the given goal is $R = yes$ (i.e., its certainty is greater than the predetermined threshold), then the pair $(p2(S:'Johnny\ Ltd', T:X), all)$ is passed to the procedure *print_goal* instead, and the following sentence will be displayed:

```
agent Johnny Ltd supply all item.
```

Note that the only circumstance under which we may have a ground goal of the form *not*(*A*) is when it appears within a proof of *non*(*A*). ESSLN's handling of other types of goals is similar to the process described above.

Let us now go back to the meta-interpreter of Figures 9.14 to 9.16, where the procedure *ask_user* (Figure 9.8) is called to put a request to the user for needed information. This request is displayed by the following procedure:

```
display_question(Goal) :-
    trans_word(which,Q),
    nl,print_goal(Goal,Q),
    write('? ').
```

If the user demands an explanation for the need of the requested information, then the system must display the rule containing the required information. The procedure *display_rule* of ESSLN is slightly different from the one given in Figure 9.5, and is shown in Figure 9.33. Like procedure *display_goal*, the procedure *display_rule* must handle quantified goals specifically.

Finally, the procedure *process_response* is similar to the one given in Figure 9.9, except that here we have to collect the degree of certainty associated with each goal in the proof for displaying. The procedure *process_response* is shown in Figures 9.34 and 9.35. Here, the procedures *read_response*, *write_rule_certainty* (Figure 9.30), and *display_goal* (Figure 9.31) have been defined previously.

Note that the words that are actually displayed are translated from English into the user's language by the procedure *trans_word*. For example, if the language used is French, then we have:

```
trans_word('Because','Parce que').
trans_word('IF','SI').
trans_word('THEN','ALORS').
trans_word('No more explanations for this',
           'Pas davantage d''explications pour ceci').
```

```prolog
display_rule((A # C :- true)) :- !,
    copy(A,A1),
    nl,write(' > '),write_word('Because'),
    nl,tab(6),display_rule_body(A1,65,_),
    nl,tab(4),write_word('is true'),
    write_rule_certainty(C).
display_rule((A # C :- B)) :-
    copy((A,B),(A1,B1)),
    nl,write(' > '),write_word('Because'),
    nl,tab(4),write_word('IF'),
    nl,tab(6),display_rule_body(B1,65,NextChar),
    nl,tab(4),write_word('THEN'),
    nl,tab(6),display_rule_body(A1,NextChar,_),
    write_rule_certainty(C).

display_rule_body(all(A,not(non(B))),Char,NextChar) :- !,
    tvar_list(A,VL),bind_var_char(VL,Char,NextChar),
    univ_quantify(yes,Q),print_goal(B,Q).
display_rule_body(all(non(A),not(B)),Char,NextChar) :- !,
    tvar_list(A,VL),bind_var_char(VL,Char,NextChar),
    univ_quantify(no,Q),print_goal(B,Q).
display_rule_body(not(non(A)),Char,Char) :- !,
    univ_quantify(yes,Q),print_goal(A,Q).
display_rule_body(not(A),Char,Char) :- !,
    univ_quantify(no,Q),print_goal(A,Q).
display_rule_body((A,B),Char,NextChar) :- !,
    display_rule_body(A,Char,Char1),
    nl,tab(6),display_rule_body(B,Char1,NextChar).
display_rule_body(A,Char,NextChar) :-
    tvar_list(A,VL),bind_var_char(VL,Char,NextChar),
    print_goal(A,_).

bind_var_char([],Char,Char) :- !.
bind_var_char([T:X|Xs],Char,NextChar) :-
    name(X,[Char]),Char1 is Char + 1,
    bind_var_char(Xs,Char1,NextChar).
```

FIGURE 9.33 ESSLN's displaying of rules.

```
process_response(ok,_) :- !.
process_response(more,_) :- !,fail.
process_response(how,(Proof1,Proof2)) :- !,
    process_response(how,Proof1),
    read_response(Response),
    process_response(Response,Proof2).
process_response(how,(A # C :- Proof)) :- !,
    recollect_body(Proof,Body),
    display_proof((A # C :- Body)),
    read_response(Response),
    process_response(Response,Proof).
process_response(how,End) :-
    nl,tab(4),write_word('No more explanations for this'),
    read_response(Response),
    process_response(Response,End).

recollect_body(B,(B,1)) :-
    member(B,[fact,system:true,usergiven]),!.
recollect_body(B,(B,0)) :-
    member(B,[nofact,system:false,nonterminate]),!.
recollect_body((B:nottried),(B:nottried,0)) :- !.
recollect_body((B # C :- D),(B,C)) :- !.
recollect_body(((B # C :- D),Rest),((B,Bs),(C,Cs))) :-
    recollect_body(Rest,(Bs,Cs)).

display_proof((A # C :- (B,1))) :-
    member(B,[fact,system:true,usergiven]),!,
    nl,write(' > '),write_word('Because'),
    nl,tab(6),copy(A,A1),display_goal(A1,yes),
    nl,tab(4),write_word(is),write(' '),write_word(B),
    write(' '),write_rule_certainty(C).
display_proof((A # 0 :- (B,0))) :-
    member(B,[nofact,system:false,nonterminate]),!,
    nl,write(' > '),write_word('Because'),
    nl,tab(6),copy(A,A1),display_goal(A1,some),
    nl,tab(4),write_word(is),write(' '),write_word(B).
```

FIGURE 9.34 ESSLN's explanation generator.

```
display_proof((A # C :- Body)) :-
    nl,write(' > '),write_word('Because'),
    nl,tab(4),write_word('IF'),
    nl,tab(6),display_proof_body(Body),
    nl,tab(4),write_word('THEN'),
    nl,tab(6),display_proof_body((A,C)).

display_proof_body(((B,Bs),(C,Cs))) :- !,
    display_proof_body((B,C)),
    nl,tab(6),display_proof_body((Bs,Cs)).
display_proof_body((B:nottried,C)) :- !,
    write('...').
display_proof_body((B,C)) :-
    (C = 0,!,Q = some; Q = yes),
    copy(B,B1),display_goal(B1,Q),
    write_rule_certainty(C).

write_rule_certainty :- % see Figure 9.30
display_goal :-         % see Figure 9.31
```

FIGURE 9.35   ESSLN's displaying of explanations.

9.11   Subtypes in ESSLN

As in classic many-sorted logic, relations in ESSLN that have different domains are represented by different predicate symbols, even in the case where one domain is contained in another. So, when a type S is declared to be a subtype of another type T, each relation having a component defined on T generates a restricted relation having the corresponding component defined on S. For example, consider the following information entered by the user:

```
Q:> _person 'John Cooper' had some contact with
        _person 'Peter Falk'.
Q:> _suspect 'Alan Smith' had some contact with
        _victim 'J.R.'.
```

Although the above two sentences describe the same relationship, they involve different domains, which are unrelated at this stage. So, this information is stored in the following facts.

```
p9(person:'John Cooper',person:'Peter Falk') # 1.
p10(suspect:'Alan Smith',victim:'J.R.') # 1.

predicate([(person,A:B),had,some,contact,with,(person,C:D)],
    p9(A:B,C:D)).
predicate([(suspect,A:B),had,some,contact,with,(victim,C:D)],
    p10(A:B,C:D)).

domain(p9(A:B,C:D)) :- type(A,person),type(C,person).
domain(p10(A:B,C:D)) :- type(A,suspect),type(C,victim).
```

Then, we have the following query and answer:

```
Q:> which _person had some contact with _person 'J.R.'?
A:> no person had some contact with person J.R.
 -> how.
  > Because
       some person had some contact with person J.R.
    is nofact
 -> ok.
```

Now, if we declare *suspect* and *victim* to be subtypes of *person*, by entering the following information:

```
Q:> _suspect is _person.
Q:> _victim is _person.
```

then ESSLN establishes a number of new relations that are restrictions of relation *p9* to the subdomains, and we have the following new information stored in the knowledge-base.

```
subtype(suspect,person).
subtype(victim,person).

predicate([(suspect,A:B),had,some,contact,with,(person,C:D)],
    p11(A:B,C:D)).
predicate([(person,A:B),had,some,contact,with,(suspect,C:D)],
    p12(A:B,C:D)).
predicate([(suspect,A:B),had,some,contact,with,(suspect,C:D)],
    p13(A:B,C:D)).
```

```
predicate([(victim,A:B),had,some,contact,with,(person,C:D)],
    p14(A:B,C:D)).
predicate([(person,A:B),had,some,contact,with,(victim,C:D)],
    p15(A:B,C:D)).
predicate([(victim,A:B),had,some,contact,with,(suspect,C:D)],
    p16(A:B,C:D)).
predicate([(victim,A:B),had,some,contact,with,(victim,C:D)],
    p17(A:B,C:D)).

domain(p11(A:B,C:D)) :- type(A,suspect),type(C,person).
    .
    .
    .
domain(p17(A:B,C:D)) :- type(A,victim),type(C,victim).

p9(A:B,C:D) # 1 :- p11(A:B,C:D).
    .
    .
    .
p15(A:B,C:D) # 1 :- p10(A:B,C:D).
```

Having been taught the above subtype relations, the system is now able to recognise *suspects* and *victims* as *persons*, as shown in the following answers:

```
Q:> which _person had some contact with some _person?
A:> person John Cooper had some contact with person
        Peter Falk
 -> more.
A:> person Alan Smith had some contact with person J.R.
 -> how.
   > Because
     IF
       suspect Alan Smith had some contact with person J.R.
     THEN
       person Alan Smith had some contact with person J.R.
 -> how.
     Because
     IF
       suspect Alan Smith had some contact with victim J.R.
     THEN
       suspect Alan Smith had some contact with person J.R.
```

```
-> how.
  Because
    suspect Alan Smith had some contact with victim J.R.
  is fact
->
```

The system's handling of subtypes becomes more significant when it provides a subtype as an answer to a query, as shown in the following example.

```
Q:> all _suspect had some contact with _victim 'W.K.'.
Q:> which _person had some contact with some _victim?
A:> person Alan Smith had some contact with victim J.R.
 -> more.
A:> all suspect had some contact with victim W.K.
 ->
```

The system's ability to recognise that not all persons had some contact with victim W.K., but only the subset of suspects that has *all* members having had some contact with victim W.K., is due to the reservation of the type variables in the predicates representation as shown below.

```
predicate([(person,A:B),had,some,contact,with,(victim,C:D)],
    p15(A:B,C:D)).

domain(p15(A:B,C:D)) :- type(A,person),type(C,victim).

type(T,T).
type(S,T) :- subtype(S,T).

subtype(suspect,person).
```

So, when the answer *p15(suspect:X,victim:'W.K.')* is translated back to the user language, the system is able to produce the sentence "all suspect had some contact with victim W.K.".

The procedure *process_subtype*, which is called by procedure *special_query* to establish the restricted relations *p11* to *p17* as shown above, is given in Figure 9.36. Observe that the restriction of a relation to some subdomain may happen to be the restriction of another relation to the same subdomain. Therefore, each time a type is declared to be a subtype of another type, all

```
process_subtype(T1,T2) :-
    not(subtype(T1,T2)),
    asserta(subtype(T1,T2)),
    subtype(S,T),
      clause(predicate(Phrase,A),true),
        append(W,[(T,R:X)|Rest],Phrase),
        append(W,[(S,R:X)|Rest],Phrase1),
        process_subphrase(Phrase1,R,S,T,A),
    fail.
process_subtype(_,_).

process_subphrase(Phrase,R,S,T,A) :-
    clause(predicate(Phrase,A1),true),!,
      not(clause((A # 1),A1)),
      assert((A # 1 :- A1));
    generate_symbol(P1),
    A =.. [P|L1], A1 =..[P1|L1],
    assert(predicate(Phrase,A1)),
    assert((A # 1 :- A1)),
    clause(domain(A),Types),conv(TL,Types),
    append(W,[type(R1,T)|Rest],TL), R == R1,!,
    append(W,[type(R1,S)|Rest],TL1),conv(TL1,Types1),
    assert((domain(A1) :- Types1)).

conv([X|T],(X,R)) :- T \== [],!,conv(T,R).
conv([X],(X)).
```

FIGURE 9.36 ESSLN's processing of subtypes.

types that are ordered by the subtype relation must be reconsidered. In the procedure of Figure 9.36, we do this by using *asserta* to store the new subtype fact on top of the others, then scan all subtype facts by using a fail-controlled loop. For each pair (S, T) where S is a subtype of T, and each predicate that has an argument defined on T, we replace T by S (using *append*) to obtain a new relation expressing phrase, then call *process_subphrase* to generate a new predicate, if it does not already exist, and to establish its relation with the original predicate, again if this does not exist.

Solved problems

9.1 Use the tools supplied in Section 9.5 of this chapter to develop an expert system that performs the task of a course advisor for students of some computer science course at your university. The system should be able to advise students on academic matters such as what units to take in the next semester, what prerequisites a specific unit requires, and what books to buy. The system would be more effective if it takes into account the user's personal abilities and habits. For simplicity, however, we assume the system is designed to assist ordinary students on common matters.

Solution:

This system can be developed along the lines of the diner expert system that was presented in Section 9.5. We reuse almost all components of the diner expert system and only add an expert knowledge-base on courses and related matters. In the following, we show only part of this knowledge-base. To answer a query such as "Which units should I enrol next semester?", the following rules are formed.

> You should enrol in unit X *if*
> unit X is part of your course,
> you have not done unit X,
> you meet the prerequisites of unit X,
> and unit X is available next semester.

> Unit X is part of your course *if*
> you are doing the course C, and
> *either* unit X is one of the core units
> of the course C.
> *or*   unit X is an elective unit of the course
> and you are interested in doing it.

> You have done the unit X *if*
> your completed units are L,
> which include the unit X.

> You meet the prerequisites of unit X *if*
> *either* the prerequisite units for X are L,
> your completed units are $L1$, and
> L is included in $L1$
> *or*   unit X requires no prerequisites at all.

The above rules are represented in Prolog as follows.

```
enrol_unit(X) :-
    program_unit(X),
    not(complete(X)),
    meet_prerequisite(X),
    available(X).

program_unit(X) :-
    your_course(C),
    core_units(C,L),
    member(X,L).
program_unit(X) :-
    your_course(C),
    elective_units(C,L),
    your_interest(X,L).

complete(X) :-
    your_complete_units(L),
    member(X,L).

meet_prerequisite(X) :-
    prerequisite_units(X,L),
    your_complete_units(L1),
    included(L,L1).
meet_prerequisite(X) :-
    not(prerequisite_units(X,_)).
```

Other information on the computer science course, including the course's compulsory and elective units, prerequisites of the units, and the list of units available next semester, are given below. Here, "your course", "your interest", and "your completed units" are user-supplied information and are represented by to-be-filled facts.

```
core_units('Computer-Science',
    [ics,dma,dsa,is1,is2,is3,ps2,se1,os,pm,
    co1,co2,cp,es]).

elective_units('Computer-Science',
    [car,cau,cme,cc,idb,dbs,dc,dcn,es,gst,
    icg,lbs,lc,ai,rtca,st,se2,tc,vlsi]).
elective_units('Mathematics',
    [ma1,ma2,ma3,lp,or,mm,as,hm,la,fp]).
```

```
prerequisite_units(se1,[dsa,is1]).
prerequisite_units(dsa,[ics,dma]).
      .
      .
      .
prerequisite_units(cp,[is3,os,pm]).

available(se1).
      .
      .
available(cp).

included([],_).
included([X|T],L) :- member(X,L),included(T,L).

tobe_filled(your_course(X)).
tobe_filled(your_interest(X,L)).
tobe_filled(your_complete_units(L)).
```

Finally, queries and answers are handled by the following processes.

```
% USER QUERIES
convert_query(['Which',units,should,'I',enrol,next,semester],
    enrol_unit(X)).
convert_query(['Is',unit,X,available,next,semester],
    available(X)).
convert_query(['What',are,the,prerequisites,for,unit,X],
    prerequisite_units(X,L)).
convert_query(['What',are,the,core,units,for,X],
    core_units(X,L)).
convert_query(['What',are,the,elective,units,for,X],
    elective_units(X,L)).
convert_query([bye],bye).

% SYSTEM QUERIES
display_question(your_course(X)) :- nl,
    write('  > What course are you doing? ').
display_question(your_interest(X,L)) :- nl,
    write('  > What unit of the following that you are'),
    write(' interested in?'),
    nl,write('  '),write(L),nl,write('  ').
display_question(your_complete_units(L)) :- nl,
    write('  > What units have you completed? '),
    nl,write('    List the units in this form'),
    write(' [ics,dma,...]'),nl,write('    ').
```

```
% SYSTEM EXPLANATIONS
display_goal(enrol_unit(X)) :- !,
    write_list(['You should enrol in unit ',X]).
display_goal(program_unit(X)) :- !,
    write_list(['The unit ',X,' is a unit in your course']).
display_goal(not(complete(X))) :- !,
    write_list(['You have not done the unit ',X]).
display_goal(complete(X)) :- !,
    write_list(['You did the unit ',X]).
display_goal(meet_prerequisite(X)) :- !,
    write_list(['You did the prerequisite for the unit ',X]).
display_goal(available(X)) :- !,
    write_list(['Unit ',X,' is available next semester']).
display_goal(your_course(X)) :- !,
    write_list(['You are doing the course ',X]).
display_goal(core_units(C,L)) :- !,
    write_list(['The core units of the course ',C,' are ']),
    (length(L,N),N > 7,!,nl,tab(8); true), write(L).
display_goal(elective_units(C,L)) :- !,
    write_list(['The elective units of the course ',C,' are ']),
    (length(L,N),N > 7,!,nl,tab(8); true), write(L).
display_goal(your_interest(X,L)) :- !,
    write_list(['You chose ',X,' among the units ']),
    (length(L,N),N > 7,!,nl,tab(8); true), write(L).
display_goal(your_complete_units(L)) :- !,
    write_list(['You have completed the units ']),
    (length(L,N),N > 7,!,nl,tab(8); true), write(L).
display_goal(prerequisite_units(X,L)) :- !,
    write_list(['The prerequisites for ',X,' are ',L]).
display_goal(not(prerequisite_units(X,L))) :- !,
    write_list(['Unit ',X,' requires no prerequisites']).
display_goal(included(X,L)) :- !,
    write_list(['The units ',X,' are among ']),
    (length(L,N),N > 7,!,nl,tab(8); true), write(L).
display_goal(member(X,L)) :- !,
    write_list(['Unit ',X,' is among the units ']),
    (length(L,N),N > 7,!,nl,tab(8); true), write(L).
display_goal(succeeds([(complete(X) :- B)|_])) :-
    write_list(['Unit ',X,' is not among your completed units']).
display_goal(succeeds([(prerequisite_units(X,_) :- B)|_])) :-
    write_list(['Unit ',X,' has no prerequisites']).
```

Following is part of a typical conversation conducted by the system.

```
Q:> Which units should I enrol next semester?

  > What course are you doing? 'Computer-Science'.

  > What units have you completed?
    List the units in this form [ics,dma,...].
    [ics,dma,is1,co1,co2].

A:> You should enrol in unit dsa
  > more.

A:> You should enrol in unit is2
  > how.
  > Because
    IF
        The unit is2 is a unit in your course
        You have not done the unit is2,
        You did the prerequisites for the unit is2
        Unit is2 is available next semester
    THEN
        You should enrol in unit is2
  > ok.
```

9.2 Earthquake prediction is a very difficult task. Much of the research in this field is done in the United States, Japan, and China. The Japanese, in particular, have more than two hundred years of experience in earthquake analysis, and they have published a huge number of reports on the symptoms of earthquake. These reports include both scientific analyses and legends such as unusual behaviour of animals, appearance of fish that are not usually seen in the area, disappearance of rats in the region, and coming out of snakes, centipedes and worms in large number.

Design a knowledge-base containing a number of symptoms of earthquake in a form that can be used by ESSLN (Section 9.8) to predict if there will be an earthquake in some particular region. (Consult the book "Earthquake prediction" by Tsuneji Rikitake (1976).)

Solution:

This is a major project that requires much more space than this part can provide. In the following, we give a small part of the knowledge-base in order to show its form. The reader is warned that for a PC system, it is likely that this knowledge-base will cause stack-overflow.

%60 there will be an earthquake in the _region X:
    there are reported unusual behaviour of animals
        within and around the _region X,
    there are noticed unusual changes in land and
        weather in _region X,
    there are reported changes in seismic wave
        velocities in _region X,
    there are reported unusual geomagnetic and
        geoelectric effects in _region X.

there are reported unusual behaviour of animals
    within and around the _region X:
    there are reports on animal unrest in _region Y,
    _region Y is close to _region X.

there are noticed unusual changes in land and
    weather in _region X:
    there are reports on land deformation in _region X.
there are noticed unusual changes in land and
    weather in _region X:
    there are reports on unusual changes in gravity
    in _region X.

there are reported changes in seismic wave
    velocities in _region X:
    there are significant changes of Vp/Vs ratio in _region X.

there are reported changes in seismic wave
    velocities in _region X:
    there are significant changes in Vs
    anisotropy in _region X.

there are reported unusual geomagnetic and
    geoelectric effects in _region X:
    there are reports on significant changes in
    geomagnetic field in _region X.
there are reported unusual geomagnetic and
    geoelectric effects in _region X:
    there are reports on significant changes in
    seismomagnetic effect in _region X.
there are reported unusual geomagnetic and
    geoelectric effects in _region X:
    there are reports on anomalous changes in
    earth current in _region X.

```
there are reports on animal unrest in _region X:
    there are reports on appearance of fish normally
    unseen in _region X.
there are reports on animal unrest in _region X:
    there are reports on disappearance of rats
    in _region X.
there are reports on animal unrest in _region X:
    there are reports that frogs snakes centipedes
    and worms coming out in large number in _region X.
```

9.3 *Forward chaining.* In all expert systems presented in this chapter, in order to find information, the system starts with a goal, and traces backward to find out if the goal is deducible from any facts. This inference method is called *backward chaining*. Backward chaining inference is most effective when the user already has some form of information and only asks the system either to confirm it or to fill it with details. In many application systems such as medical diagnosis and image recognising systems, the user only has some facts and wants to know what can be deduced from these facts. In this case, the system must start with the facts and use the rules in its knowledge-base to arrive at some conclusions. This method is called *forward chaining*. Prolog is most suitable for implementing backward-chaining systems, thanks to its resolution mechanism. It is not difficult, however, to implement forward-chaining systems in Prolog.

Given a knowledge-base in the form of a Prolog program, you are asked to write a Prolog program that receives a list of facts and returns a second list of facts that are deduced from the given facts by using the rules in the knowledge-base. Test your program on the following knowledge-base and the given facts [e,f].

```
a :- b.        % 1
a :- c.        % 2
b :- e,f.      % 3
c :- e,g.      % 4
p(1) :- b.     % 5
q(X) :- p(X).  % 6
r :- a,s.      % 7
```

Solution:

Basically, the forward-chaining method works as follows. Given a fact F and a rule A :- $B_1, \ldots, B_n$, if F unifies with a subgoal B_i (for convenience, let us assume $i = 1$) by the unifier θ, then we have two cases:

(i) If $n = 1$, then we obtain a new fact $A\theta$. In this case, for any rule A' :- B' in the knowledge-base, if its head A' is an instance of $A\theta$, then the rule is redundant and so removed from the knowledge-base.

(ii) If $n > 1$, then we obtain a new rule $(A$:- $B_2, \ldots, B_n)\theta$.

In either case, if A is an instance of $A\theta$ (i.e., the unifier has no effect on A), then we remove the rule A :- $B_1, \ldots, B_n$. Otherwise, we replace it with the restricted rule A :- $non(F\theta), B_1, \ldots, B_n$.

Applying the above inference rule to the given knowledge-base and the fact $[e, f]$, we have the following step-by-step process.

1. Take fact e from the given facts. Apply fact e to rules 3 and 4 to obtain new rules b :- f and c :- g; the old rules are discarded. Fact e becomes a used fact and the knowledge-base becomes:

```
c :- g.        % 1    Unused facts: [f]
b :- f.        % 2
a :- b.        % 3    Used facts:   [e]
a :- c.        % 4
p(1) :- b.     % 5
q(X) :- p(X).  % 6
r :- a,s.      % 7
```

2. Take fact f from the unused facts and apply it to rule 2. We have a new fact b. Fact f becomes a used fact and the knowledge-base becomes:

```
c :- g.        % 1    Unused facts: [b]
a :- b.        % 2
a :- c.        % 3    Used facts:   [f,e]
p(1) :- b.     % 4
q(X) :- p(X).  % 5
r :- a,s.      % 6
```

3. Take fact b from the unused facts and apply it to rules 2 and 4 to obtain the new facts a and $p(1)$. The old rules are removed, and so is rule 3. Thus the knowledge-base becomes:

```
c :- g.        % 1    Unused facts: [p(1),a]
q(X) :- p(X).  % 2
r :- a,s.      % 3    Used facts:   [b,f,e]
```

4. Take fact $p(1)$ from the unused facts and apply it to rule 2 to obtain a new fact $q(1)$. The old rule is replaced with $q(X) :\!\!- non(p(1)), p(X)$. Thus the knowledge-base now becomes:

```
c :- g.                    % 1  Unused facts: [q(1),a]
r :- a,s.                  % 2
q(X) :- non(p(1)),p(X).    % 3  Used facts: [p(1),b,f,e]
```

5. Take fact $q(1)$ from the unused facts. This fact does not match with any rule, so it is simply added to the set of used facts. We now have:

```
c :- g.                    % 1
r :- a,s.                  % 2
q(X) :- non(p(1)),p(X).    % 3

% Unused facts: [a]
% Used facts:   [q(1),p(1),b,f,e]
```

6. Take fact a from the unused facts and apply it to rule 2. We obtain a new rule $r :\!\!- s$, and the knowledge-base becomes:

```
r :- s.                    % 1
c :- g.                    % 2
q(X) :- non(p(1)),p(X).    % 3

% Unused facts: []
% Used facts:   [a,q(1),p(1),b,f,e]
```

As there are no more unused facts, the process terminates with success and the obtained facts are $a, q(1), p(1), b, f, e$.

The process presented above is now expressed in the following general algorithm.

To find *NewFacts* from *GivenFacts* using forward chaining do
    collect other facts in the knowledge-base and
    store them together with the given facts, then
    apply forward-chaining procedure to obtain *NewFacts*.

In applying forward chaining to obtain *NewFacts* do
    take an unused fact F, and match F with the rules
    in the knowledge-base to obtain new facts or new rules,
    move fact F to the set of used facts, and
    continue until no more unused facts;
    finally, collect the used facts and return them as *NewFacts*.

To match a fact F with the rules in the knowledge-base do
take a rule $A :\text{-} B_1, \ldots, B_n$ from the knowledge-base
and apply the inference rule stated at the beginning of
this solution.

To facilitate the matching process, we represent each rule of a knowledge-base
in the form $rule((A :\text{-} [B_1, \ldots, B_n]))$. For example, the given knowledge-base
is stored as shown below.

```
rule((a :- [b])).
rule((a :- [c])).
rule((b :- [e,f])).
rule((c :- [e,g])).
rule((p(1) :- [b])).
rule((q(X) :- [p(X)])).
rule((r :- [a,s])).
```

The Prolog program of the above algorithm is shown below.

```
forward_chain(GFacts,FFacts) :-
    collect_facts(GFacts,IFacts),
    forward(IFacts,[],FFacts),!.

forward([F|Fs],UFs,Facts) :-
    match_rules(F,Fs,UFs,NFs),
    forward(NFs,[F|UFs],Facts).
forward([],Facts,Facts).

match_rules(F,Fs,UFs,NFs) :-
    rule(Rule),
    match_rule(F,Rule,Fs,UFs,IFs),
    match_rules(F,IFs,UFs,NFs).
match_rules(F,NFs,UFs,NFs).

match_rule(F,(A :- B),Fs,UFs,IFs) :-
    copy((A,B),(A1,B1)),
    select(F,B1,B2),not(member(non(F),B2)),
    new_rule(F,(A,B),(A1,B2),Fs,UFs,IFs).

new_rule(F,(A,B),(A1,[]),Fs,UFs,IFs) :- !,
    new_fact(A1,Fs,UFs,IFs),
    replace_rule(F,(A,B),A1),
    remove_rules(A1).
```

```
new_rule(F,(A,B),(A1,B1),Fs,_,Fs) :-
    replace_rule(F,(A,B),A1),
    asserta(rule((A1 :- B1))).

new_fact(A,Fs,UFs,[A|Fs]) :-
    not(member(A,Fs)),not(member(A,UFs)),!.
new_fact(_,Fs,_,Fs).

replace_rule(F,(A,B),A1) :-
    retract(rule((A :- B))),
    (instance_of(A,A1),!;
     assert(rule((A :- ([non(F)|B]))))).

remove_rules(A1) :-
    rule((A :- B)),instance_of(A,A1),
    retract(rule((A :- B))),
    fail; true.

collect_facts(Fs,IFs) :-
    setof(F,fact(F),L),!,
    append(Fs,L,IFs).
collect_facts(Fs,Fs).

select :-      % see Figure 2.16
append :-      % see Figure 2.21
instance_of :- % see page 348
```

9.4 In Problem 9.3, we have studied the implementation of forward chaining in Prolog. A combination of forward and backward chaining can be realised in the following way. First, a fact is used to match with a subgoal of some rule in the forward-chaining pattern; then backward inference is used to establish the goal in the head of this rule. If the goal succeeds, then it is saved as a new fact (if it does not already exist). This process is repeated until there are no more unused facts.

Write a Prolog program to perform the above-described *two-way* inference procedure.

Solution:

It is interesting to note that the *two-way inference procedure* is much easier to implement in Prolog than the forward-chaining procedure. The two-way inference algorithm is as follows.

To find *NewFacts* from *GivenFacts* using two-way chaining do
    store the given facts together with any other facts
    in the knowledge-base, then
    apply two-way chaining to obtain *NewFacts*.

In applying two-way chaining to obtain *NewFacts* do
    take an unused fact from the store,
    use this fact to match the rules in order to generate new facts,
    then continue until no more unused facts;
    finally, collect the stored facts to return as *Newfacts*.

To use a fact *F* in generating new facts do
    for each rule in the knowledge-base
    if *F* matches a subgoal of the rule then
      prove the goal in the head of the rule;
      if the goal succeeds then store it as a new fact
        (if it does not already exist).

The program is shown below. With the knowledge-base and the initial facts given in Problem 9.3, this program produces the same answer.

```
twoway_chain(GFacts,FFacts) :-
    store_facts(GFacts),
    twoway(FFacts),!.

twoway(Facts) :-
    fact(F),
    match_rules(F),
    twoway(Facts).
twoway(Facts) :-
    fact(_),twoway(Facts);
    setof(F,saved_fact(F),Facts).

match_rules(F) :-
    rule(Rule),
    match_rule(F,Rule),
    fail.
match_rules(F) :-
    retract(fact(F)),
    assert(saved_fact(F)).
```

```
match_rule(F,(A :- B)) :-
    member(F,B),prove(A),
    (not(fact(A)),not(saved_fact(A)),!,
     asserta(fact(A));true).

prove(A) :- fact(A); saved_fact(A).
prove(A) :- rule((A :- B)),prove(B).
prove([A|B]) :- prove(A),prove(B).
prove([]).

store_facts([F|Fs]) :-
    asserta(fact(F)),store_facts(Fs).
store_facts([]) :-
    abolish(saved_fact/1).

member :- % see Figure 2.13
select :- % see Figure 2.16
append :- % see Figure 2.21
```

Supplementary problems

9.5 Develop a diner expert system that can advise the user on all matters about the restaurants in your city. (Hint: follow the lines of Example 9.1.) Explain how this system can be developed using ESSLN.

9.6 Continue Example 9.7 and develop a detective expert system that can solve various murder cases. Consult Agatha Christie's books for sample cases.

9.7 Develop an expert system that provides diagnoses on fish diseases. Following is a sample rule. If a salmon shows the following symptoms:

- Red necrotic lesions of the abdominal musculature and exophthalmos;

- Erythema at the bases of the fins and around the vent;

- Hemorrhaging along the length of the intestinal tract;

then the diagnosis is "vibriosis of salmon" (synonym: salt-water furunculosis) (Sindermann, (1977)).

9.8 Develop an expert system that provides diagnosis on bacterial infections of the human skin, and advice on treatment. The following is an example. If the following symptoms exist:

- Itching and burning in hairy areas;
- Pustules in the hair follicles;
- Inflammation of surrounding skin area;

then the diagnosis is *folliculitis*. Folliculitis is caused by staphylococcal infection of hair follicles. There are three forms of folliculitis. Sycosis is usually propagated by the autoinoculation and trauma of shaving. Gram-negative folliculitis usually develops from antibiotic-treated acne. Pseudo-folliculitis is caused by ingrowing hairs in the beard area and on the nap.

Treatment:

- Topical 2% mupirocin;
- Polymyxin B in combination with bacitracin or oxytetracycline.

Application:

- Cleanse the area gently with chlorhexidine;
- Apply saline or aluminum subacetate soaks or compresses to the involved area for 15 minutes twice daily.

(Consult the book "Current Medical Diagnosis & Treatment", by Shroeder et al. (1989).)

Chapter 10

Natural language processing in Prolog

10.1 Natural language processing

The term *natural language* is commonly used to refer to some restricted form of a human language. Natural languages are designed to enable ordinary users to communicate with computer systems.

Certainly, it would be ideal if a full human language could be used in user-machine conversation. But this is too difficult, due to the complexity and ambiguity of most human languages. Generally, in any human language, the structure of sentences is highly intricate, and each sentence (or even each word) may have several different meanings. Very often, the context of a sentence extends beyond the sentence. Humans do not find these problems serious, because they have acquired an enormous knowledge of the language and its usage, through many years of practice. No contemporary computers have attained the capacity and the speed to store and to scan such immense knowledge.

Therefore, to be able to build computer systems that can understand some form of human language, we must restrict the language to some processable structures, and limit its interpretation to a manageable range of options.

In modern linguistics, logic has been used to formalise human languages. As Prolog originates in logic, it is the most suitable programming language for natural language processing. In fact, Prolog was primarily designed, by Colmerauer, for natural language translation.

Basically, the task of processing a natural language consists of the following phases.

- *Lexical analysis*: the input sentence is read into a list of tokens, each of which represents an atomic entity of the language.

- *Syntactic analysis*: the list of tokens is parsed for recognition of the sentence's grammatical structure.

- *Semantic analysis*: the sentence is converted into a form of internal representation, and the system's interpreter is called upon to interpret the sentence, and to respond to it if so required.

In Chapter 4 (Figure 4.9), we have given the procedure *read_sentence* that reads an input sentence into a list of words. In this chapter, we shall describe the task of parsing a sentence according to some given grammar, and the process of interpreting and responding to the query expressed by the sentence. We shall also provide (in Section 10.6) a simple but powerful database query-answering system that is able to recognise and answer queries such as the following:

> Which agents supply all items?
> Which agents supply most items?
> Few agents supply most items?

10.2 Context-free grammars

A grammar is a set of rules that define the legal structures in a language. A grammar is said to be *context-free* if its constituents are mutually structurally independent, that is, the structure of one part has no influence on that of any other part.

A context-free grammar can be described hierarchically in the same way as a Prolog description of a world. Following is a sample description of a context-free grammar in a notation called *definite clause grammar* (DCG) notation.

EXAMPLE 10.1   To recognise a sentence such as "the president has a cat", we define a context-free grammar as follows.

```
sentence --> noun_phrase, verb_phrase.
noun_phrase --> determiner, noun.
verb_phrase --> verb, noun_phrase.

determiner --> [the].
determiner --> [a].

noun --> [president].
noun --> [cat].

verb --> [has].
```

FIGURE 10.1 A context-free grammar.

In this grammar, the rules state that a *sentence* is composed of a *noun-phrase*, followed by a *verb-phrase*. A noun-phrase is composed of a *determiner*, followed by a *noun*, and a verb-phrase has a *verb*, followed by a noun-phrase. The last five rules list the atomic entities of the language.

The syntax of the symbols used in the above grammar is similar to that of predicate symbols in Prolog. Generally, the left-hand side of the symbol "-->" (which is read "is composed of") represents a grammatical constituent of the language and the right-hand side gives its definition. The terminal entities are to be enclosed between square brackets.

Most Prolog systems accept the above-given grammar (via *consult* or *reconsult*) and convert it into a Prolog procedure called *a context-free grammar parser*, which is shown on the next page. This conversion is quite straightforward: two arguments are added to each nonterminal so that in each clause, the pairs of arguments propagate from the head predicate to the last subgoal of the clause, and the symbol "-->" is replaced with the neck symbol ":-" (a procedure that performs this conversion is given in Problem 10.2).

```
sentence(S,R) :-
    noun_phrase(S,T), verb_phrase(T,R).
noun_phrase(S,T) :-
    determiner(S,N), noun(N,T).
verb_phrase(T,R) :-
    verb(T,N),noun_phrase(N,R).

determiner([the|R],R).
determiner([a|R],R).

noun([president|R],R).
noun([cat|R],R).

verb([has|R],R).
```

In each atomic formula of the above procedure, the first argument represents the input list of tokens, and the second argument contains the tokens left over after a specified grammatical element has been extracted. For example, the first rule is read:

> The list S contains a sentence with leftover R *if*
> > S contains a noun-phrase with leftover T, and
> > T contains a verb-phrase with leftover R.

The syntax of definite clause grammar also allows the inclusion of non-converted subgoals by enclosing them with curly brackets. That is, any subgoals that are enclosed between curly brackets are unchanged after the rules are converted into Prolog clauses.

Having obtained the above context-free grammar parser, we can now parse some sentences by entering the following queries:

```
?- sentence([the,president,has,a,cat],[]).
yes

?- sentence([the,president,has,a,cat,suit],R).
R = [suit] ->
yes
```

```
?- sentence([the,president,has,a,wild,cat],R).
no

?- noun([wild,cat],R).
no
```

The last two queries show that the sentence "the president has a wild cat" is not recognised in the described grammar, because "wild" is not a legal noun.

We can also use the above parser to generate all legal sentences in the given grammar. There are sixteen sentences, many of which do not really make sense, including the sentence "the cat has a president". This is done by entering the following query:

```
?- sentence(S,[]).
S = [the,president,has,the,president] ->;
    .
    .
    .
S = [a,cat,has,a,cat] ->;
no
```

Context-free grammars are easy to define, but they lack some essential potency. First, context-free grammars ignore any structural interdependence of the constituents of a sentence. Thus, with a context-free grammar, one cannot describe the influence of a subject-noun on a verb form or that of a determiner on a noun's plurality (many Latin-based languages such as Indonesian, Malaysian, and Vietnamese do not have this problem). Second, parsing a sentence using a context-free grammar parser does not explicitly show the structure of the sentence.

To overcome these weaknesses, context-free grammar is extended (by Colmerauer (1978)) into a more general form called *definite clause grammar*, which is studied in the next section.

10.3   Definite clause grammars

Definite clause grammar is an extension of context-free grammar in which nonterminals are allowed to contain arguments that represent the interinfluence of components of a sentence.

Following is an example of a definite clause grammar.

EXAMPLE 10.2   To recognise the following sentences:

"the president has a cat".
"many cats have a president".

we extend the grammar given in Figure 10.1 into a definite clause grammar as shown in Figure 10.2. Here, each nonterminal has an argument representing the plurality of the component it defines. In any rule, if two nonterminals share the same variable in their arguments, then the defined components must have the same plurality. For example, "the president" and "has" are singular, whereas "many" and "cats" are plural.

```
sentence --> noun_phrase(P),verb_phrase(P).
noun_phrase(P) --> determiner(P),noun(P).
verb_phrase(P) --> verb(P),noun_phrase(_).

determiner(_) --> [the].
determiner(sgular) --> [a].
determiner(plural) --> [many].

noun(sgular) --> [president].
noun(sgular) --> [cat].
noun(plural) --> [cats].

verb(sgular) --> [has].
verb(plural) --> [have].
```

FIGURE 10.2 A definite clause grammar.

Again, most Prolog systems accept the above definite clause grammar and convert it into a Prolog procedure as shown on the next page. Then, we can parse the given sentences by entering the following queries:

```
?- sentence([the,president,has,a,cat],[]).
yes

?- sentence([many,cats,have,a,president],[]).
yes
```

```
sentence(S,R) :-
    noun_phrase(P,S,T),verb_phrase(P,T,R).
noun_phrase(P,S,T) :-
    determiner(P,S,N),noun(P,N,T).
verb_phrase(P,T,R) :-
    verb(P,T,N),noun_phrase(Q,N,R).

determiner(P,[the|R],R).
determiner(sgular,[a|R],R).
determiner(plural,[many|R],R).

noun(sgular,[president|R],R).
noun(sgular,[cat|R],R).
noun(plural,[cats|R],R).

verb(sgular,[has|R],R).
verb(plural,[have|R],R).
```

Also, as before we can use the parser to generate all legal sentences in the grammar, and this time there are 36 sentences altogether.

We now turn to the question of constructing a parse tree for a given sentence. This is done by adding to each nonterminal of the grammar an extra argument that represents the tree structure of the specified constituent of the grammar. Thus, the grammar given in Figure 10.2 is modified again to include parse trees as shown in Figure 10.4. Here, the first rule states that the parse tree of a sentence has the form s(*NP*, *VP*), where *NP* and *VP* are parse trees of the constituent noun-phrase and verb-phrase, respectively. The parse trees of lower-level components are defined in the same way.

Now parsing a sentence returns a parse tree if the sentence's structure is recognised in the given grammar. For example:

```
?- sentence(S,[the,president,has,a,cat],[]).
S = s(np(dt(the),n(president)),vp(v(has),np(dt(a),n(cat)))) ->
yes

?- sentence(S,[many,cats,have,a,president],[]).
S = s(np(dt(many),n(cats)),vp(v(have),np(dt(a),n(president))))
->
yes
```

The above parse trees are shown in Figure 10.3. Observe that although the given grammar defines only one sentence structure, we have a large number of combinations with a small vocabulary.

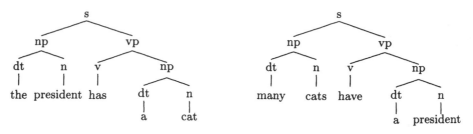

FIGURE 10.3 Parse trees of sentences.

```
sentence(s(NP,VP)) -->
    noun_phrase(P,NP),verb_phrase(P,VP).
noun_phrase(P,np(D,N)) -->
    determiner(P,D),noun(P,N).
verb_phrase(P,vp(V,NP)) -->
    verb(P,V),noun_phrase(_,NP).

determiner(_,dt(the)) --> [the].
determiner(sgular,dt(a)) --> [a].
determiner(plural,dt(many)) --> [many].

noun(sgular,n(president)) --> [president].
noun(sgular,n(cat)) --> [cat].
noun(plural,n(cats)) --> [cats].

verb(sgular,v(has)) --> [has].
verb(plural,v(have)) --> [have].
```

FIGURE 10.4 A definite clause grammar that generates parse trees.

The parse tree of a sentence can be used to identify components of the sentence. For example, given the grammar described in Figure 10.4, and that we wish to construct a sentence in which the subject is specific but the object is not, and the subject and object are not the same, we can define such a restricted form of sentence as follows.

```
restricted_sentence(S) :-
  sentence(s(np(dt(the),n(N1)),vp(_,np(dt(D),n(N2)))),S,[]),
  D \= the, N1 \= N2.
```

Then, the following query returns only a few sentences.

```
?- restricted_sentence(S).
S = [the,president,has,a,cat] ->;
S = [the,president,has,many,cats] ->;
S = [the,cat,has,a,president] ->;
S = [the,cat,has,many,cats] ->;
S = [the,cats,have,a,president] ->;
S = [the,cats,have,a,cat] ->;
no
```

Parse trees are very useful in database query languages where a tree structure can be used to identify specific components such as "airline number", "departure", and "destination". However, the information that can be extracted from a parse tree is limited to structural aspects. In the next section, we study another form of internal representation that facilitates the interpretation of the input sentence.

10.4   Logical representation of sentences

Logic has been used as a formalised form of languages in Mathematics and Philosophy. In this section, we present logical form as a first-stage representation of natural language sentences for the purpose of interpreting them.

Consider the following English sentences:

Every man loves a woman.
Some men love all women.
Some men love no women.

In typed logic (also called many-sorted logic), the above sentences are formulated into the following logical formulas, where the symbols $\forall_m$ and $\exists_w$ are the universal and existential quantifiers associated with the types *man* and *woman*, respectively, and the symbol "$\sim$" represents logical negation.

$$\forall_m X \; \exists_w Y \; love(X,Y)$$
$$\exists_m X \; \forall_w Y \; love(X,Y)$$
$$\exists_m X \; \forall_w Y \; \sim love(X,Y)$$

In our Prolog representation, the above formulas are written as follows:

```
all(man:X,exist(woman:Y,love(man:X,woman:Y))).
exist(man:X,all(woman:Y,love(man:X,woman:Y))).
exist(man:X, no(woman:Y,love(man:X,woman:Y))).
```

We shall see in the next sections that the inclusion of types in the above formulas facilitates the task of interpreting them as well as the translation of answers back to the user language. Following are some more typical sentences that can be used in database query languages.

Which agents supply most items?
Few agents supply all items?
Most agents supply few items?

These sentences are represented by the following formulas.

```
exist(agent:X,most(item:Y,supply(agent:X,item:Y))).
few(agent:X,all(item:Y,supply(agent:X,item:Y))).
most(agent:X,few(item:Y,supply(agent:X,item:Y))).
```

Thus, in our representation, the logical form of a sentence is either an atomic formula or a logical formula of the form $quant(E,F)$, where $quant$ is one of the quantifiers *all, exist, no, most*, and *few*; E is a term of the form *Type : X*; and F is a logical formula.

Note

In English, the article "the" is often used as a special quantifier that expresses a *unique existence*. In most French textbooks of modern mathematics, the symbol used to denote *unique existence* is $\exists!$ from which the Prolog's cut symbol probably originates.

A definite clause grammar that is designed to parse the sentences of the above-described form and to produce their logical representation is given in Figure 10.5. In this grammar, besides the argument P that represents the plurality of grammatical constituents of a sentence, other arguments represent the logical components that compose the sentence's logical form. The first few rules are read as follows.

The logical form S of a sentence is
> a logical formula that relates an entity E to a formula VP, where
> the relation and the entity E are determined by a noun-phrase,
> and the formula VP is established by a verb-phrase.

The logical formula NP that relates an entity E to a formula F,
in a way determined by a noun-phrase
either has the form $quant(E,F)$, where $quant$ is a quantifier that
> represents a determiner, and E is a term representing a noun;

or is F itself, if there is no determiner, and the term E
> represents a noun that is specified by a proper-noun.

The logical formula VP established by a verb-phrase
that is imputed to an entity X is
> a formula that relates an entity Y to a formula F, where
> the formula F is formed by a verb and the entities X, Y, and
> the relation between Y and F is determined by a noun-phrase.

The remaining rules are straightforward. Perhaps there is one more thing that should be noted, that is, a negative verb-phrase beginning with "does not" or "do not" is represented by a formula of the form $non(F)$, where F is the logical form of its positive part.

```
sentence(S) -->
    noun_phrase(P,S,E,VP),verb_phrase(P,E,VP).

noun_phrase(P,NP,E,F) -->
    determiner(P,NP,E,F),noun(P,E).
noun_phrase(P,F,E,F) -->
    noun(P,E),proper_noun(P,E).

verb_phrase(P,X,VP) -->
    verb(P,F,X,Y),noun_phrase(_,VP,Y,F).
verb_phrase(P,X,VP) -->
    neg_verb(P,F,X,Y),noun_phrase(_,VP,Y,F).

determiner(P,all(E,F),E,F) -->
    [W],{once(member(W:P,
    [all:plural,every:sgular,each:sgular]))}.
```

```
determiner(P,exist(E,F),E,F) -->
    [W],{member(W,[some,which])}.
determiner(P,no(E,F),E,F) --> [no].
determiner(plural,A,E,F) -->
    [W],{member(W,[most,few]), A =.. [W,E,F]}.

noun(sgular,T:X) -->
    [T],{member(T,[agent,item])}.
noun(plural,agent:X) --> [agents].
noun(plural,item:X) -->  [items].

proper_noun(sgular,T:X) -->
    [X],{proper_name(T:X)}.

verb(sgular,supply(X,Y),X,Y) --> [supplies].
verb(plural,supply(X,Y),X,Y) --> [supply].
neg_verb(P,non(F),X,Y) -->
    negation(P),verb(plural,F,X,Y).

negation(sgular) --> [does,not].
negation(plural) --> [do,not].

proper_name(N) :- constsymbol(N).
member(X,[X|_]).
member(X,[_|T]) :- member(X,T).
```

FIGURE 10.5 A definite clause grammar that generates logical forms.

Observe from the procedure of Figure 10.5 that in the rules that define determiners, the goal `member(W:P,[all:plural,every:sgular,each:sgular])` is enclosed within the goal *once* (see Figure 10.12 for the definition of *once*), so that only one term will be chosen during the course of translating a goal back to the user language. Following are some examples of parsing using the grammar given in Figure 10.5.

```
?- sentence(S,[which,agents,supply,most,items],[]).
S = exist(agent:_0154,most(item:_0260,
    supply(agent:_0154,item:_0260))) ->
yes
```

```
?- sentence(S,[few,agents,supply,all,items],[]).
S = few(agent:_018C,all(item:_0230,
    supply(agent:_018C,item:_0230))) ->
yes


?- sentence(S,[most,agents,supply,few,items],[]).
S = most(agent:_0180,few(item:_0284,
    supply(agent:_0180,item:_0284))) ->
yes
```

The first sentence given above represents a query to which a possible answer is the following:

```
most(item:_0A62,supply(agent:'Adams & Sons',item:_0A62)).
```

where the constant symbol 'Adams & Sons' is defined by:

```
constsymbol(agent:'Adams & Sons').
```

Then, the parser of Figure 10.5 can be used to translate the answer back to the user language as follows:

```
?- sentence(most(item:Y,
    supply(agent:'Adams & Sons',item:Y)),Ans,[]).
Y = _0038
Ans = [agent,'Adams & Sons',supplies,most,items] ->
```

Observe that the plurality compatibility defined in the grammar has enabled the return of the right word "supplies", instead of "supply".

10.5   Interpretation of logical formulas

We now consider how to interpret the logical formulas established in the preceding section. This task consists of translating the formulas into Prolog goals and defining rules to evaluate these goals.

In Chapter 9, we have discussed the interpretation of some of the logical formulas mentioned above in the environment of a multilingual expert system shell, where a parser is not useful, as the grammar of the language in use is assumed to be unknown. For easy reference, we give a summary of Prolog representation of those formulas already studied. In the table below, A and $A1$ are identical formulas except for some variable names; for example, $A = p(X, Y)$ and $A1 = p(X, Y1)$. In general, X, Y, $Y1$ ... stand for collections of typed variables. Also, the predicate *non* represents the logical negation defined in Chapter 9 (Section 9.8).

Logical formula	Prolog representation
`exist(X,A)`	`A`
`exist(X,all(Y,A))`	`(A,not(non(A1)))`
`exist(X,no(Y,A))`	`(non(A),not(A1))`
`all(X,A)`	`not(non(A))`
`all(X,exist(Y,A))`	`not((non(A),not(A1)))`
`all(X,no(Y,A))`	`not(A)`
`no(X,all(Y,A))`	`not((A,not(non(A1))))`
`no(X,no(Y,A))`	`not((non(A),not(A1)))`

The operational meanings of the first four formulas listed above have been given in Chapter 9, Section 9.9. The remaining formulas are the negated form of the above ones. Note that the above representation contains no explicit reference to type predicates. Thus, it can be used as a general scheme of representing quantified queries for databases.

We now consider Prolog representation of the logical formulas that contain the relative quantifiers *most* and *few*. We begin with the predicates *most* and *few* that are expressed as follows.

$most(X, Y, A)$: For most X, A is true for some Y.
$few(X, Y, A)$: For few X, A is true for some Y.

We shall explain shortly how, for programming convenience, the Prolog term $most(X, Y, A)$ can be used to represent both the general formula $most(X, exist(Y, A))$ and the special one $most(X, A)$, where A contains no variables other than X. The definitions of *most* and *few* are given below.

$most(X, Y, A)$ is true *if*
> the set of X such that A is true for some Y
> is large compared with its complementary set.

$few(X, Y, A)$ is true *if*
> the set of X such that A is true for some Y
> is small compared with its complementary set.

Here, the concept of being "large" or "small" is conventional. For the database that we use for experiments in the next section, we assume "most" means 84% (an arbitrary choice) or more, and "few" means 16% or less. Prolog definitions of the predicates *most* and *few* are given in Figure 10.6.

```
most(X,Y,A) :-
    complement(X,Y,A,L1,L2),
    large(L1,L2).

few(X,Y,A) :-
    complement(X,Y,A,L1,L2),
    large(L2,L1).

complement(X,Y,A,L1,L2) :-
    (setof(X,Y^A,L1),!; L1 = []),
    (setof(X,(constsymbol(X),
     not(member(X,L1))),L2),!; L2 = []).

large(L1,L2) :-
    length(L1,N1),length(L2,N2),
    N1 >= 5*N2.
```

FIGURE 10.6 Definition of predicates *most* and *few*.

Note that in the formulas $most(X, Y, A)$ and $few(X, Y, A)$, we can let $Y = 0$ to indicate that A contains no variables other than X. In this case, the goal $setof(X, Y\char`\^A, L)$ has the same effect as $setof(X, A, L)$. Thus, the formula $most(X, 0, A)$ merely means that "A is true for most X". Similarly, the formula $few(X, 0, A)$ means "A is true for few X".

Following are typical formulas that contain the quantifiers *most* and *few*.

Logical formula	Prolog representation
exist(X,most(Y,A))	(A,most(Y1,0,A1))
exist(X,few(Y,A))	(non(A),few(Y1,0,A1))
all(X,most(Y,A))	not((non(A),not(most(Y1,0,A1))))
all(X,few(Y,A))	not((A,not(few(Y1,0,A1))))
no(X,most(Y,A))	not((A,most(Y1,0,A1)))
no(X,few(Y,A))	not((non(A),few(Y1,0,A1)))
most(X,most(Y,A))	most(X,Y,(A,most(Y1,0,A1)))
most(X,few(Y,A))	most(X,Y,(non(A),few(Y1,0,A1)))

Here, as in the previous list, A and $A1$ are atomic formulas of the form $A = p(X,Y)$ and $A1 = p(X,Y1)$, where X, Y, and $Y1$ are typed variables. We note again that the listed representation contains no explicit reference to type predicates, and so, it can be used as a general scheme of representing quantified queries for databases. The operational meanings of the first three formulas in the list are given below.

- The goal $p(S{:}X, T{:}_-), most(T{:}Z, 0, p(S{:}X, T{:}Z))$ succeeds with an answer $X = X0$ if and only if $p(S{:}X, T{:}Y)$ succeeds with an answer $X = X0$, $Y = Y0$ and $most(T{:}Z, 0, p(S{:}X0, T{:}Z))$ succeeds. That is, $p(S{:}X0, T{:}Z)$ is true for most values of Z of type T.

- The goal $non(p(S{:}X, T{:}_-)), few(T{:}Z, 0, p(S{:}X, T{:}Z))$ succeeds with an answer $X = X0$ if and only if $non(p(S{:}X, T{:}Y))$ succeeds with an answer $X = X0$, $Y = Y0$ and $few(T{:}Z, 0, p(S{:}X0, T{:}Z))$ succeeds. That is, $p(S{:}X0, T{:}Z)$ is true for only few values of Z of type T.

- The goal $not((non(p(S{:}X, T{:}_-)), not(most(T{:}Z, 0, p(S{:}X, T{:}Z)))))$ succeeds if and only if $(non(p(S{:}X, T{:}_-)), not(most(T{:}Z, 0, p(S{:}X, T{:}Z))))$ fails. That is, for every value of X of type S, either $non(p(S{:}X, T{:}Y))$ fails, which means $p(S{:}X, T{:}Y)$ is true for all values of Y of type T, or $most(T{:}Z, 0, p(S{:}X, T{:}Z))$ succeeds, which means $p(S{:}X, T{:}Z)$ is true for most values of Z of type T.

The remaining goals in the list are interpreted in the same way as described above.

In summary, we have the following general scheme of representing quantified formulas in Prolog, which is presented in Figures 10.7 and 10.8.

```
translate(exist(X,exist(Y,A)),A,(X,Y,A)) :- !.
translate(exist(X,all(Y,A)),(A,not(non(A1))),
    (X,all(Y1,A1))) :- !, copy((X,Y,A),(X1,Y1,A1)),X = X1.
translate(exist(X,no(Y,A)),(non(A),not(A1)),
    (X,no(Y1,A1))) :- !, copy((X,Y,A),(X1,Y1,A1)),X = X1.
translate(exist(X,most(Y,A)),(A,most(Y1,0,A1)),
    (X,most(Y1,A1))) :- !, copy((X,Y,A),(X1,Y1,A1)),X = X1.
translate(exist(X,few(Y,A)),(non(A),few(Y1,0,A1)),
    (X,few(Y1,A1))) :- !, copy((X,Y,A),(X1,Y1,A1)), X = X1.
translate(exist(X,A),A,(X,A)) :- !.
```

FIGURE 10.7 Prolog representation of logical formulas.

```
translate(all(X,exist(Y,A)),not((non(A),not(A1))),_) :- !,
   copy((X,A),(X1,A1)), X = X1.
translate(all(X,all(Y,A)),not(non(A)),_) :- !.
translate(all(X,no(Y,A)),not(A),_) :- !.
translate(all(X,most(Y,A)),not((non(A),not(most(Y1,0,A1)))),_)
   :- !, copy((X,Y,A),(X1,Y1,A1)), X = X1.
translate(all(X,few(Y,A)),not((A,not(few(Y1,0,A1)))),_) :- !,
   copy((X,Y,A),(X1,Y1,A1)), X = X1.
translate(all(X,A),not(non(A)),_) :- !.
translate(no(X,exist(Y,A)),not(A),_) :- !.
translate(no(X,all(Y,A)),not((A,not(non(A1)))),_) :- !,
   copy((X,A),(X1,A1)), X = X1.
translate(no(X,no(Y,A)),not((non(A),not(A1))),_) :- !,
   copy((X,A),(X1,A1)), X = X1.
translate(no(X,most(Y,A)),not((A,most(Y1,0,A1))),_) :- !,
   copy((X,Y,A),(X1,Y1,A1)), X = X1.
translate(no(X,few(Y,A)),not((non(A),few(Y1,0,A1))),_) :- !,
   copy((X,Y,A),(X1,Y1,A1)), X = X1.
translate(no(X,A),not(A),_) :- !.

translate(most(X,exist(Y,A)),most(X,Y,A),_) :- !.
translate(most(X,all(Y,A)),few(X,Y,non(A)),_) :- !.
translate(most(X,no(Y,A)),few(X,Y,A),_) :- !.
translate(most(X,most(Y,A)),most(X,Y,(A,most(Y1,0,A1))),_)
   :- !, copy((X,Y,A),(X1,Y1,A1)), X = X1.
translate(most(X,few(Y,A)),most(X,Y,(non(A),few(Y1,0,A1))),_)
   :- !, copy((X,Y,A),(X1,Y1,A1)), X = X1.
translate(most(X,A),most(X,0,A),_) :- !.
translate(few(X,exist(Y,A)),few(X,Y,A),_) :- !.
translate(few(X,all(Y,A)),most(X,Y,non(A)),_) :- !.
translate(few(X,no(Y,A)),most(X,Y,A),_) :- !.
translate(few(X,most(Y,A)),few(X,Y,(A,most(Y1,0,A1))),_)
   :- !, copy((X,Y,A),(X1,Y1,A1)), X = X1.
translate(few(X,few(Y,A)),few(X,Y,(non(A),few(Y1,0,A1))),_)
   :- !, copy((X,Y,A),(X1,Y1,A1)), X = X1.
translate(few(X,A),few(X,0,A),_) :- !.
translate(A,A,_).
```

FIGURE 10.8 Prolog representation of logical formulas (continued).

10.6   A database query-answering system

We now have enough materials to form a simple but powerful query-answering system that can accept and answer rather sophisticated queries.

By putting together the language parser of Figure 10.5, the logical formula translator of Figures 10.6 to 10.8, and the logical negation evaluator given in Figure 9.17, which is again shown below (in Figures 10.9 and 10.10), we obtain a complete query-answering system that handles all the queries described in the preceding section.

```
non(non(A)) :- !,A.
non(A) :- tvar_list(A,L),eval_non(A,L).

eval_non(A,L) :- not(A),!.
eval_non(A,L) :- eval(A),uninstantiated(L),!,fail.
eval_non(A,L) :- instantiate(A,L,VL),eval_non(A,VL).

eval(A) :- A,!.
uninstantiated(L) :- tvar_pure(L),unrestricted(L,0).

tvar_pure([]) :- !.
tvar_pure([T:V|TVs]) :- var(V),tvar_pure(TVs).

unrestricted([],_) :- !.
unrestricted([T:N|TVs],N) :-
    N1 is N+1,unrestricted(TVs,N1).

instantiate(A,L,VL) :- domain(A),instant(L,VL).

instant([X|Xs],Xs) :- get_term(X,Xs).
instant([X|Xs],[X|VL]) :- instant(Xs,VL).

get_term(T:V,TVs) :- constsymbol(T:V).
get_term(X,Xs) :- get_var(X,Xs).

get_var(T:V,[T:V|TVs]).
get_var(X,[Y|Xs]) :- get_var(X,Xs).
```

FIGURE 10.9 A logical negation evaluator.

```
tvar_list(A,[]) :- ground(A),!.
tvar_list(A,L) :-  A =.. [P|Args],
    setof(T:X,(member(T:X,Args),var(X)),L).

ground(A) :- copy(A,B), A == B.
copy(A,B) :- assert(zzzz(A)),retract(zzzz(B)).
```

FIGURE 10.10 A logical negation evaluator (continued).

Note that in the procedure of Figure 10.9, the first clause is logically un-necessary, but it is added to improve the efficiency of evaluation. Also, the predicate *domain* is to be defined in the application database and the predicate *member* has been defined in Figure 2.13.

Following is the top-level control of our query-answering system.

```
dbqas :-
    repeat,
        receive_query(Q),
        process_query(Q,R),
        print_answer(R),
    terminate(Q).

process_query(Q,R) :-
    once(sentence(S,Q,[])),
    translate(S,T,A),
    call(T),response(A,R).
process_query([e],[e]) :- !.
process_query(_,[no]) :-
    not(answer([yes])).
process_query(_,_) :-
    abolish(answer/1),fail.

response(confirm,[yes]) :- !,
    assert(answer([yes])).
response(A,R) :-
    transback(A,B),
    once(sentence(B,R,[])),
    not(answer(R)),assert(answer(R)).
```

FIGURE 10.11 Top-level control of a query-answering system.

```
transback((T:X,A),all(T:X,B)) :-
    var(X),!,transback(A,B).
transback((_,A),B) :- !,transback(A,B).
transback(A,A).

terminate(Q) :- Q = [e]; (get0('e),nl,dbqas).
once(P) :- P,!.
```

FIGURE 10.12 Control of a query-answering system (continued).

Here, the procedure *receive_query* reads a query in some natural language
and stores the words in a list Q (the definitions of procedures *receive_query*
and *print_answer* have been given in Problem 5.3 of Chapter 5). The query
Q is first parsed for grammatical structure, by the procedure *sentence*. The
result is a logical formula S which is translated into a Prolog goal T and
an answer form A (which may be a single variable if Q is a confirming
query). If the evaluation of T succeeds (causing the instantiation of A),
then the answer A is converted back into a response sentence R (by the
same procedure *sentence*). Note from Figure 10.12 that if the variable X
in an answer A is uninstantiated, then the answer is made into the form
all(T:X,B). To avoid producing duplicate answers, we save the responses in
the form *answer(R)* and check every obtained response before returning it.

Also, in order to handle the database-management queries, such as the
deletion of existing facts and the addition of new facts, we add the following
clauses to the parser and the translator as shown in Figures 10.13 and 10.14.

```
sentence(S) -->
    command(S,F),fact(F).

command(add(S),S) --> [add].
command(append(S),S) --> [append].
command(delete(S),S) --> [delete].

fact(constsymbol(T:X)) --> noun(_,T:X),[X].
fact(F) --> sentence(F).
```

FIGURE 10.13 Part of a grammar to handle database-management queries.

```
translate(add(A),asserta(B),_)    :- !,trans(A,B).
translate(append(A),assertz(B),_) :- !,trans(A,B).
translate(delete(A),retract(B),_) :- !,trans(A,B).

trans(all(X,A),B) :- !,trans(A,B).
trans(no(X,A),non(B)) :- !,trans(A,B).
trans(A,A).
```

FIGURE 10.14 Translation of database-management queries.

We now present some tests on the above-established query-answering system. We take a sample database on suppliers and parts as shown below.

```
supply(agent:'Adams & Sons',item:b1).
supply(agent:'Adams & Sons',item:b2).
supply(agent:'Adams & Sons',item:b3).
supply(agent:'Adams & Sons',item:b4).
supply(agent:'Adams & Sons',item:b5).
supply(agent:'Adams & Sons',item:b6).
supply(agent:'Johnny Ltd',item:b1).
supply(agent:'Johnny Ltd',item:b2).
supply(agent:'Johnny Ltd',item:b3).
supply(agent:'Johnny Ltd',item:b4).
supply(agent:'Johnny Ltd',item:b5).
supply(agent:'Mitre 10',item:b1).
supply(agent:'Yoshima Kuru',item:X).
non(supply(agent:'Rossianno Co',item:X)).

constsymbol(agent:'Adams & Sons').
constsymbol(agent:'Johnny Ltd').
constsymbol(agent:'Mitre 10').
constsymbol(agent:'Rossianno Co').
constsymbol(agent:'Yoshima Kuru').

constsymbol(item:b1).    constsymbol(item:b2).
constsymbol(item:b3).    constsymbol(item:b4).
constsymbol(item:b5).    constsymbol(item:b6).
```

FIGURE 10.15 Portion of a supplier-part database.

Observe that the database of Figure 10.15 contains two special clauses that express the facts that agent Yoshima Kuru supplies all items and agent Rossianno Co supplies no items. It is important to note that any negative fact, such as the one given in the above supplier-part database, should be placed in front of the logical negation evaluator of Figures 10.9 and 10.10 (which is normally hidden in another data world) to improve the efficiency of evaluation. Also the negative facts must be brought into memory by the use of *consult*, instead of *reconsult*, because a *reconsult* command will substitute them for the definition of *non* in the logical negation evaluator.

   We now list some interesting query answers of the system.

```
?- dbqas.

Q:> which agents supply item b1?
A:> agent Adams & Sons supplies item b1
A:> agent Johnny Ltd supplies item b1
A:> agent Mitre 10 supplies item b1
A:> agent Yoshima Kuru supplies item b1
A:> no

Q:> which agents do not supply item b2?
A:> agent Rossianno Co does not supply item b2
A:> agent Mitre 10 does not supply item b2
A:> no

Q:> which agents supply all items?
A:> agent Adams & Sons supplies all items
A:> agent Yoshima Kuru supplies all items
A:> no

Q:> which agents supply most items?
A:> agent Adams & Sons supplies most items
A:> agent Johnny Ltd supplies most items
A:> agent Yoshima Kuru supplies most items
A:> no

Q:> which agents supply few items?
A:> agent Rossianno Co supplies few items
A:> agent Mitre 10 supplies few items
A:> no
```

```
Q:> which agents do not supply most items?
A:> agent Rossianno Co does not supply most items
A:> agent Mitre 10 does not supply most items
A:> no

Q:> most agents supply most items?
A:> no

Q:> few agents supply few items?
A:> no
```

Now we make some changes to the database by using the following queries:

```
Q:> delete agent 'Rossianno Co' supplies no items.
A:> yes

Q:> add agent 'Rossianno Co' supplies all items.
A:> yes

Q:> add agent 'Extra Co'.
A:> yes

Q:> add agent 'Extra Co' supplies all items.
A:> yes
```

The effect of the above database-management queries is the removal of the fact non(supply(agent:'Rossianno Co',item:X)) and the addition of the following facts to the database:

```
supply(agent:'Rossianno Co',item:X).
constsymbol(agent:'Extra Co').
supply(agent:'Extra Co',item:Y).
```

Then we have the following answers:

```
Q:> most agents supply most items?
A:> yes

Q:> few agents supply few items?
A:> yes
```

The following command adds the fact `supply(agent:X,item:b1)` to the database, thus changing the answer to a previous query as shown below:

```
Q:> add all agents supply item b1.
A:> yes

Q:> which agents supply item b1?
A:> all agents supply item b1
```

Finally, the addition of the fact `supply(agent:X,item:Y)` to the database produces the following interesting answer:

```
Q:> add all agents supply all items.
A:> yes

Q:> which agents supply all items?
A:> all agents supply all items
```

We shall study other forms of queries that begin with *what, where*, etc., in Problem 10.4.

Solved problems

10.1 Consider the following French verse (by Henri de Regnier):

> le trottoir de la rue est sonore a mon pas,
> les jardins etroits sont fleuris de lilas.

Write a definite clause grammar to parse the above sentences. Ensure that the grammar can be used to recognise the following variant sentences:

> la rue etroite est fleurie comme un jardin,
> mon pas est sonore sur le trottoir de lilas.

Solution:

We first observe that in French nouns have gender, that is, every noun is either masculine or feminine. For example, the garden (le jardin) is male, while the road (la rue) is female. Gender and plurality of a noun are carried to any adjectives that define the noun. Also, an adjective may be placed before or after the noun it defines, but the adjectives in the given sentences are normally placed after the nouns they define.

The structure of the given sentences is quite standard, namely, a sentence is composed of a noun-phrase followed by a verb-phrase. A noun-phrase is composed of a noun part which may be followed by a qualification part. A noun part begins with a determiner which is followed by a noun and possibly an adjective. A qualification part begins with one of the qualifiers *à, de, dans, comme, sur,* etc., which is followed by a noun or a noun-phrase. A verb-phrase in the given sentences begins with the verb *être* (to be) which is followed by an adverb-phrase. An adverb-phrase is composed of an adjective followed by a qualification part.

The definition of a grammar for the given sentences is given below, where each nonterminal has two arguments: P represents plurality, and G represents gender of a component of the sentence.

```
sentence --> noun_phrase(P,G),verb_phrase(P,G).

noun_phrase(P,G) --> noun_part(P,G).
noun_phrase(P,G) --> noun_part(P,G),qualify_part.

noun_part(P,G) --> determiner(P,G),noun_form(P,G).
noun_form(P,G) --> noun(P,G).
noun_form(P,G) --> noun(P,G),adjective(P,G).

qualify_part --> qualifier,noun(_,_).
qualify_part --> qualifier,noun_phrase(_,_).

verb_phrase(P,G) --> verb(P,G),adv_phrase(P,G).
adv_phrase(P,G) --> adjective(P,G),qualify_part.

determiner(s,m) --> [W],{member(W,[le,mon,un])}.
determiner(s,f) --> [W],{member(W,[la,ma,une])}.
determiner(p,m) --> [W],{member(W,[les,mes])}.

noun(s,m) --> [W],{member(W,[trottoir,jardin,pas,lilas])}.
noun(s,f) --> [rue].
noun(p,m) --> [jardins].

adjective(s,m) --> [W],{member(W,[etroit,fleuri])}.
adjective(s,f) --> [W],{member(W,[etroite,fleurie])}.
adjective(s,_) --> [sonore].
adjective(p,m) --> [W],{member(W,[etroits,fleuris])}.

qualifier --> [W],{member(W,[de,dans,a,comme,sur])}.
verb(s,_) --> [est].    verb(p,_) --> [sont].
```

After loading the above-defined grammar, we can parse the given sentences by entering the following queries.

```
?- sentence([le,trottoir,de,la,rue,est,sonore,a,mon,pas],[]).
yes

?- sentence([les,jardins,etroits,sont,fleuris,de,lilas],[]).
yes

?- sentence([la,rue,etroite,est,fleurie,comme,un,jardin],[]).
yes

?- sentence([mon,pas,est,sonore,sur,le,trottoir,de,lilas],[]).
yes
```

10.2 Write a Prolog program to convert a definite clause grammar into a Prolog procedure that can be used as a parser. Ensure that any subgoals enclosed between curly brackets are unchanged after the rules are converted into Prolog clauses.

Solution:

Assume that the given grammar is stored in a file *Filename*, and we wish to convert it into a Prolog procedure to be stored in Prolog's database. We do this by reading and converting one rule at a time. Thus, the top-level control of the converting procedure is quite standard as shown below.

```
consult_parser(Filename) :-
    see(Filename),read_rules,seen.

read_rules :-
    read(Rule),
    convert_rule(Rule,Clause),
    assert(Clause),
    read_rules.
read_rules.
```

To convert a rule $(P \dashrightarrow Q)$ into a Prolog clause $P1 :- Q1$, we first add two variables X, Y to the arguments of P to obtain $P1$, then we use the variables X, Y to convert the body Q into $Q1$. In converting a component A of Q into a subgoal of $Q1$ using the variables X, Y, we consider the following cases.

If A is an ordinary component that is followed by other components As, then we add two variables X, Z to the arguments of A, and use Z, Y to convert As. If A is the last component of the rule, then we add the variables

X, Y to its arguments.

If A is a list of terminals such as $[a, b, c]$ which is followed by other components As, then we let $X = [a, b, c | Z]$, and we use Z, Y to convert As. If a list $[a, b, c]$ is the last component of the rule, then we simply let $X = [a, b, c | Y]$.

For any component of the form $\{A\}$, we simply remove the brackets and let $X = Y$. The procedure *convert_rule* is given below.

```
convert_rule((A --> B),(A1 :- B1)) :-
    add_arguments(A,[X,Y],A1),
    convert_goals(B,[X,Y],B1).

convert_goals((A,As),[X,Y],Bs) :-
    append(A,Z,X),!,
    convert_goals(As,[Z,Y],Bs).
convert_goals((A,As),[X,Y],(B,Bs)) :- !,
    add_arguments(A,[X,Z],B),
    convert_goals(As,[Z,Y],Bs).
convert_goals(A,[X,Y],true) :-
    append(A,Y,X),!.
convert_goals(A,[X,Y],B) :-
    add_arguments(A,[X,Y],B).

add_arguments({A},[X,X],A) :- !.
add_arguments(A,[X,Y],B) :-
    A =.. [P|Xs], append(Xs,[X,Y],Ys),
    B =.. [P|Ys].
```

The predicate *append* has been defined in Figure 2.21. Observe from the above program that the goal *append(A,Z,X)* is used to test if A is a list, and if $A = [a, b, c]$, say, then the result of this goal is $X = [a, b, c | Z]$. Note also that any rule containing a list of terminals as its last component is converted into a Prolog clause with a *true* last subgoal. This is logically indifferent. But if we want to exclude these *true* subgoals, then we can remove the third clause of procedure *convert_goals* and add the following clauses at the top of the corresponding procedures.

```
convert_rule((A --> B),(A1)) :-
    append(B,Y,X),!,
    add_arguments(A,[X,Y],A1).

convert_goals((A,As),[X,Y],B) :-
    append(As,Y,Z),!,
    add_arguments(A,[X,Z],B).
```

10.3 Consider the procedure *complement* of Figure 10.6. This procedure receives three terms X, Y, A and returns two lists: the list $L1$ contains all terms X such that A is true for some Y, and the list $L2$ is the complement of $L1$. Run the procedure on the supplier-part database given in Figure 10.15 to find the following sets.

(a) The set of items supplied by agent 'Johnny Ltd', and its complement. The set of items supplied by agent 'Mitre 10', and its complement. The set of items supplied by agent 'Yoshima Kuru', and its complement.

(b) The set of items not supplied by agent 'Adams & Sons', and its complement. The set of items not supplied by agent 'Mitre 10', and its complement. The set of items not supplied by agent 'Rossianno Co', and its complement.

(c) The set of agents that supply most items, and its complement. The set of agents that supply few items, and its complement.

(d) The set of agents that do not supply some item, and its complement. The set of agents that do not supply most items, and its complement. The set of agents that do not supply few items, and its complement.

Solution:

We note first that in all answers to the queries presented in this solution, for neatness, the variables' internal forms, such as X = _0038, are not shown.

(a) The expression "agent X supplies item Y" is represented by the formula *supply(agent:X, item:Y)*. So, the queries for part (a) are as follows.

```
?- complement(item:Y,0,
     supply(agent:'Johnny Ltd',item:Y),L1,L2).
L1 = [item:b1,item:b2,item:b3,item:b4,item:b5]
L2 = [item:b6] ->

?- complement(item:Y,0,
     supply(agent:'Mitre 10',item:Y),L1,L2).
L1 = [item:b1]
L2 = [item:b2,item:b3,item:b4,item:b5,item:b6] ->

?- complement(item:Y,0,
     supply(agent:'Yoshima Kuru',item:Y),L1,L2).
L1 = [item:_01EC]
L2 = [] ->
```

The answer to the last query shows agent 'Yoshima Kuru' supplies all items, as every term of the form `item:X` is a member of the list *L1*.

(b) The expression "agent X does not supply item Y" is represented by the formula *non(supply(agent:X, item:Y))*. So, the queries for part (b) are expressed as follows.

```
?- complement(item:Y,0,
   non(supply(agent:'Adams & Sons',item:Y)),L1,L2).
L1 = []
L2 = [item:b1,item:b2,item:b3,item:b4,item:b5,item:b6] ->

?- complement(item:Y,0,
   non(supply(agent:'Mitre 10',item:Y)),L1,L2).
L1 = [item:b2,item:b3,item:b4,item:b5,item:b6]
L2 = [item:b1] ->

?- complement(item:Y,0,
   non(supply(agent:'Rossianno Co',item:Y)),L1,L2).
L1 = [item:_01FC,item:_0218]
L2 = [] ->
```

We observe that in the answer to the last query of part (b), *L1* contains two elements, one is returned by the negative fact in the database, and the other is produced by the logical negator. This is logically acceptable, as the two answers represent the same thing. But if we want to eliminate the duplication, we need only add a cut to the right-hand side of the negative fact.

(c) The expression "agent X supplies most items" is represented by the formula *most(item:Z,0, supply(agent:X, item:Z))*. The expression "agent X supplies few items" has a similar representation. So, the queries for part (c) are as follows.

```
?- complement(agent:X,item:Y,(supply(agent:X,item:Y),
   most(item:Z,0,supply(agent:X,item:Z))),L1,L2).
L1 = [agent:'Adams & Sons',agent:'Johnny Ltd',
      agent:'Yoshima Kuru']
L2 = [agent:'Mitre 10',agent:'Rossianno Co'] ->

?- complement(agent:X,item:Y,(non(supply(agent:X,item:Y)),
   few(item:Z,0,supply(agent:X,item:Z))),L1,L2).
L1 = [agent:'Mitre 10',agent:'Rossianno Co']
L2 = [agent:'Adams & Sons',agent:'Johnny Ltd',
      agent:'Yoshima Kuru'] ->
```

(d) The first query for part (d) is similar to those in part (b).

```
?- complement(agent:X,item:Y,
   non(supply(agent:X,item:Y)),L1,L2).
L1 = [agent:'Johnny Ltd',agent:'Mitre 10',
   agent:'Rossianno Co']
L2 = [agent:'Adams & Sons',agent:'Yoshima Kuru'] ->
```

To find the remaining sets required in part (d), we note first that the expressions "agent X does not supply most items" and "agent X does not supply few items" are represented, respectively, by the following formulas (compare with part (c)):

$$not(most(item:Z,0, supply(agent:X, item:Z))),$$
$$not(few(item:Z,0, supply(agent:X, item:Z))).$$

So the remaining sets required in part (d) are obtained by using the following queries.

```
?- complement(agent:X,item:Y,(non(supply(agent:X,item:Y)),
   not(most(item:Z,0,supply(agent:X,item:Z)))),L1,L2).
L1 = [agent:'Mitre 10',agent:'Rossianno Co']
L2 = [agent:'Adams & Sons',agent:'Johnny Ltd',
   agent:'Yoshima Kuru'] ->
```

```
?- complement(agent:X,item:Y,(supply(agent:X,item:Y),
   not(few(item:Z,0,supply(agent:X,item:Z)))),L1,L2).
L1 = [agent:'Adams & Sons',agent:'Johnny Ltd',
   agent:'Yoshima Kuru']
L2 = [agent:'Mitre 10',agent:'Rossianno Co'] ->
```

10.4 Assume that the supplier-part database given in Figure 10.15 contains information on the agents' bases of the following form:

```
base(agent:AgentName,city:CityName).
```

Extend the definite clause grammar given in Figure 10.5 so that the query-answering system described in Section 10.6 can recognise and answer the following forms of queries on the supplier-part database.

where is agent 'Adams & Sons' based ?
what does agent 'Johnny Ltd' supply ?

Solution:

The following rules are added to the grammar to define the structure of the new query sentences.

```
sentence(S) -->
    query_part(M,S,E,F),proposition(M,E,F).

query_part(M,exist(E,F),E,F) -->
    query_term,aux_verb(M).

proposition(M,E,F) -->
    noun_phrase(_,_,N,_),verb(M,F,N,E).

query_term --> [W],{member(W,[where,what])}.

aux_verb(passive) --> [is].
aux_verb(active) --> [does].

verb(passive,base(X,Y),X,Y) --> [based].
verb(active,supply(X,Y),X,Y) --> [supply].
verb(sgular,base(X,Y),X,Y) --> [is,based,in].

noun(sgular,city:X) --> [city].
```

Now assume the database contains the following additional facts:

```
base(agent:'Adams & Sons',city:'London').
base(agent:'Johnny Ltd',city:'New York').
base(agent:'Mitre 10',city:'Sydney').
base(agent:'Rossianno Co',city:'Milan').
base(agent:'Yoshima Kuru',city:'Tokyo').

constsymbol(city:'London').
constsymbol(city:'New York').
constsymbol(city:'Sydney').
constsymbol(city:'Milan').
constsymbol(city:'Tokyo').
```

We can enter the following queries to test the modified grammar.

```
Q:> where is agent 'Adams & Sons' based?
A:> agent Adams & Sons is based in city London

Q:> what does agent 'Adams & Sons' supply?
A:> agent Adams & Sons supplies item b1
A:> agent Adams & Sons supplies item b2
A:> agent Adams & Sons supplies item b3
A:> agent Adams & Sons supplies item b4
```

```
A:> agent Adams & Sons supplies item b5
A:> agent Adams & Sons supplies item b6
A:> no

Q:> where is agent 'Mitre 10' based?
A:> agent Mitre 10 is based in city Sydney

Q:> what does agent 'Mitre 10' supply?
A:> agent Mitre 10 supplies item b1
A:> no

Q:> where is agent 'Yoshima Kuru' based?
A:> agent Yoshima Kuru is based in city Tokyo

Q:> what does agent 'Yoshima Kuru' supply?
A:> agent Yoshima Kuru supplies all items
A:> no

Q:> where is agent 'Rossianno Co' based?
A:> agent Rossianno Co is based in city Milan

Q:> what does agent 'Rossianno Co' supply?
A:> no
```

10.5 In Chapter 4, we have developed the procedure *readline* that reads a line of text into a list of characters (see Figure 4.8), and the procedure *tokenize* that extracts the tokens from a list of characters (see Problem 4.8). Let us now write a definite clause grammar to describe the terms and rules in Prolog. This grammar together with the procedures *readline* and *tokenize* mentioned above can be used in place of the built-in predicates *read_string* and *string_term* of Arity-Prolog, if they are not available in other systems.

Solution:

Recall that a Prolog term is either a variable, a constant, a list, or a compound term. Formally, compound terms are represented in prefix form, but Prolog also allows infix form terms. We also note that, in order to convert a list of tokens into a Prolog term, we must maintain a list of variable names so that any occurrences of the same variable name will be converted into the same (internal) variable. Thus, the definition of a Prolog term is as follows:

```
term(T,VL,VL1) --> formal_term(T,VL,VL1).
term(T,VL,VL1) --> infix_term(T,VL,VL1).
```

```
formal_term(T,VL,VL1) --> variable(T,VL,VL1).
formal_term(T,VL,VL1) --> constant(T,VL,VL1).
formal_term(T,VL,VL1) --> list(T,VL,VL1).
formal_term(T,VL,VL1) --> prefix_term(T,VL,VL1).

variable(V,VL,VL1) -->
    [X],{variable_name(X,V,VL,VL1)}.
constant(T,VL,VL) -->
    [X],{(constsymbol(X,T);number(X,T))}.

list([],VL,VL) --> ['[',']'].
list([T|L],VL,VL1) --> ['[',
    term(T,VL,VL2),tail(L,VL2,VL1).

tail([],VL,VL) --> [']'].
tail([T|L],VL,VL1) -->
    [','],term(T,VL,VL2),tail(L,VL2,VL1).
tail(L,VL,VL1) -->
    ['|'],variable(L,VL,VL1),[']'].
tail(L,VL,VL1) -->
    ['|'],list(L,VL,VL1),[']'].

prefix_term(T,VL,VL1) -->
    functer(F),['('],
    arguments(Args,VL,VL1),[')'],
    {T =.. [F|Args]}.

functer(X) -->  [X],{functsymbol(X)}.

arguments([Arg],VL,VL1) -->
    term(Arg,VL,VL1).
arguments([A|Args],VL,VL1) -->
    term(A,VL,VL2),[','],
    arguments(Args,VL2,VL1).

infix_term(T,VL,VL1) --> rightas_term(T,VL,VL1).
infix_term(T,VL,VL1) --> bracket_term(T,VL,VL1).

rightas_term(T,VL,VL1) -->
    formal_term(T,VL,VL1).
rightas_term(T,VL,VL1) -->
    formal_term(A,VL,VL2),[F],{operator(F)},
    rightas_term(B,VL2,VL1),
    {T =.. [F,A,B]}.
```

```
bracket_term(T,VL,VL1) -->
    ['('],rightas_term(T,VL,VL1),[')'].
bracket_term(T,VL,VL1) -->
    ['('],rightas_term(A,VL,VL2),[')',F],{operator(F)},
    rightas_term(B,VL2,VL1),
    {T =.. [F,A,B]}.
bracket_term(T,VL,VL1) -->
    ['('],rightas_term(A,VL,VL2),[')',F],{operator(F)},
    bracket_term(B,VL2,VL1),
    {T =.. [F,A,B]}.

variable_name(X,V,VL,VL1) :-
    name(X,[C|L]),
    ((capital(C); C = 95, L \= []),
        (member((X,V),VL),!,VL1 = VL;
                        VL1 = [(X,V)|VL]);
        C = 95,L = [],VL1 = [(X,V)|VL]).

constsymbol(X,X) :- atom_name(X).
constsymbol(X,T) :- char_string(X,T).

functsymbol(X) :- atom_name(X); system(X/N);
    member(X,[abs,exp,ln,log,sqrt,acos,asin,
            atan,cos,sin,tan]).

atom_name(X) :- name(X,[C|L]),'a =< C, C =< 'z.
char_string(X,T) :- name(X,[C|L]),
    C = '', string(L,R), name(T,R).
capital(C) :- 'A =< C, C =< 'Z.

string([''],[]).
string([H|T],[H|R]) :- string(T,R).

number(X,T) :- name(X,[C|L]),
    ('0 =< C, C =< '9),chars_int([C|L],0,T).

chars_int([],N,N).
chars_int([C|L],M,N) :-
    M1 is 10*M + C - '0,chars_int(L,M1,N).

operator(F) :-
member(F,[is,':','+','-','*','/','=','<','>','^',mod]);
member(F,['->','\=','==','@<','@>','=<','>=','//']);
member(F,['=:=','=\=','\==','@=<','@>=','=..','-->']).
```

Here, as usual, the procedure *member* is defined in Figure 2.13. Now recall that a Prolog rule is composed of a head that is an atomic formula (the structure of which is the same as that of a prefix-term or a constant symbol), followed by the neck symbol ':-' and terminated with a body which is a conjunction of atomic formulas. Thus, the definition of a Prolog rule is as follows:

```
rule((A :- B),VL,VL1) -->
    head_term(A,VL,VL2),[(':-')],
    conj_term(B,VL2,VL1).

head_term(T,VL,VL1) --> constant(T,VL,VL1).
head_term(T,VL,VL1) --> prefix_term(T,VL,VL1).

conj_term(T,VL,VL1) --> term(T,VL,VL1).
conj_term((A,B),VL,VL1) --> term(A,VL,VL2),[','],
    conj_term(B,VL2,VL1).
```

For example, by taking the following sample list of tokens, we have the parsing result that follows (where the display of L is not shown).

```
sample(1,[length,'(','[','H','|','T',']',',',',','N',')',(':-'),
    length,'(','T',',',',','M',')',',',',','N',is,'M','+','1']).

?- sample(1,L),rule(R,[],V,L,[]).
R = length([_0420|_0424],_0824) :- length(_0424,_0E98),
_0824 is _0E98 + 1
V = [('M',_0E98),('N',_0824),('T',_0424),('H',_0420)] ->
```

Supplementary problems

10.6 Provide additional rules to the grammar of Figure 10.5 so that the extended grammar can be used to parse the following queries.

> what items are supplied by agent 'Adams & Sons'?
> what items are supplied by most agents?
> which agents are based in city 'London'?

Write the logical formulas of the above sentences that will be produced by the extended parser. Execute the parser to confirm your answers, then run the database query-answering system of Figure 10.11, on the supplier-part database given in Figure 10.15 and Problem 10.4, to obtain the responses to the given queries.

10.7 Consider lists of tokens representing products of polynomials of the form `['(',P,')',*,'(',Q,')']`, where P and Q consist of polynomial symbols such as the following:

$$6,*,x,\char`\^,3,+,24,*,x,\char`\^,2,+,x,+,15$$

(a) Write a definite clause grammar to parse the above-described products of polynomials. The parser should return an expression of the form `(P)*(Q)`, where P and Q are polynomial expressions.

(b) Write a supporting procedure that receives the polynomials P and Q, performs the multiplication of P and Q, and returns the product polynomial in simplified form.

10.8 Write a Prolog program to translate simple French sentences of the form given in Problem 10.1 into English. Use the following vocabulary:

le trottoir	: the sidewalk,	la rue	: the road,
mon pas	: my step,	le jardin	: the garden,
lilas	: lilac,	sonore	: sounding,
etroit	: narrow,	fleuri	: in bloom.

(Hint: develop two parsers similar to the one given in Problem 10.1, so that each parser returns a parse tree for the input sentence, and write a procedure to convert between parse trees.)

10.9 Design a database to store information on concerts that are to be staged in your city. Develop a simple database query-answering system to answer queries on the location, time, performers, and price of the concerts.

10.10 Design a database to store students' records of a particular course in your university. Develop a database query-answering system that is capable of handling simple queries on students' information, such as: current programme, passed units, course completion, and number of students in a particular unit. (Hint: follow the development of the system described in Section 10.6.)

Chapter 11

System simulation
in Prolog

11.1   What is simulation?

Simulation is the process of imitating the operation of a system for the purpose of studying certain aspects of the system.

Simulation has been widely used in many fields of research and has been shown to be an effective method of problem-solving and decision making. This method is particularly useful when the system under study is not yet built or actual experiments are prohibitively costly.

To facilitate the task of simulation, several computer-aided simulation systems have been built to provide the special environment and programming languages needed in simulation. For discrete-event simulation, the well-known systems include GASP, GPSS, SIMULA, SIMSCRIPT, and ECSL.

These systems provide excellent means for simulation programming, but they require expertise in their languages, which is not easy to attain. More recently available simulation systems such as TIM (using Smalltalk) and SIM2 (Pascal) are based on a new trend of programming, namely the *object-oriented programming* approach.

In this chapter, we present the technique of simulation programming in Prolog, using the object-oriented modelling approach. We shall also discuss the construction of POSS (Prolog-based Object-oriented Simulation System), a simple but powerful simulation system that combines the object-oriented modelling concept with the powerful nondeterministic unification mechanism of Prolog. It turns out that several typical simulation problems, which normally result in very complex programs in the above-mentioned traditional simulation languages, can be programmed quite straightforwardly in POSS.

11.2   Object-oriented simulation models

In object-oriented simulation modelling, an operational system is considered to be a collection of objects that interact by sending messages to each other. Each object in the system has its own patterns of reaction to specific types of messages. When an object receives a message, it may perform some domestic work before responding to the message. Thus, in general, an object-oriented simulation model consists of a number of object descriptions of the following form:

> Object : Object-name
>> Message type 1 :   Domestic work
>> Responses;
>>
>> $\vdots$
>>
>> Message type n :   Domestic work
>> Responses;

In some systems, there may be messages that do not require responses. For example, joining a queue changes only the queue's contents, and freeing an object only makes the object available again; these messages require no responses from the objects. In particular, *queues* are classified as *passive objects*, as they never send any messages to other objects. Passive objects with routine domestic work (such as queues) need not have explicit object descriptions, as their domestic work can be handled by the underlying simulation system.

EXAMPLE 11.1   Consider the simulation of a single-runway airport, which is to be built in a newly established town. Aircraft requesting permission to land or take off are placed in queues. When the runway is clear, the first aircraft waiting to land is allowed to proceed. Only when there are no aircraft waiting in the air for landing, is the first aircraft waiting to take off allowed to enter the runway.

Suppose the aircraft's interarrival times have a negative exponential distribution with a mean of 10 minutes. Fifty percent of the aircraft request landing and 50% need to take off. Landing times have a normal distribution with a mean of 20 minutes and a standard deviation of 4 minutes. Take-off times also have a normal distribution with a mean of 15 minutes and a standard deviation of 3 minutes.

The system model is shown below. Here, for simplicity, we first use a single queue for both landing and taking-off aircraft, with aircraft waiting for landing having higher priority. In the next section, we shall compare this model with its modified version where waiting aircraft are placed in two separate queues.

Object : Aircraft

  Arrive :
    Request: 50% landing (higher priority), 50% takeoff;
    Next arrival: negative exponential distribution of mean 10.

    Aircraft joins queue in order of arrival time and priority.
    Aircraft waits to take the runway for required service.
    Next aircraft arrives.

Object : Runway

  Provide service :
    Landing time: normal distribution with $\mu = 20$, $\sigma = 4$;
    Take-off time: normal distribution with $\mu = 15$, $\sigma = 3$.

    After service is completed, the runway becomes available.

Simulation time: 8 hours (480 minutes).

Initial state: runway is free and no aircraft are waiting.

Start message: the first aircraft arrives.

Histogram form: waiting times for runway, classified into 7 classes
of width 10, starting from 0.

11.3   Prolog simulation models

Once an object-oriented model for a given system has been built, it can be
directly translated into a Prolog program in which each object description
is expressed by a unit clause of the form:

```
object(Time,Object,Methods)
```

where **Methods** is a list of message-response patterns. Here, we represent
each response to a message in the form of a quadruple:

```
(Time,Priority,Object,Message)
```

where the arguments represent, respectively, the *time* the message is to be
sent, its *priority* among messages that are available for sending at the current time, the *object* that will receive the message, and details of the *message*.

Thus, a Prolog simulation model consists of a number of object-description
clauses of the following general form:

```
object(Time,object_name,
  [(message_type1 :-
      do(domestic_work1),
      respond([(response11),...,(response1p)])),
      .
      .
      .
    (message_typen :-
      do(domestic_workn),
      respond([(responsen1),...,(responsenq)]))]).
```

To complete the model, we need only add the procedures that define the
domestic work, the *simulation time*, the *initial state*, the *start message*, and
any *statistic specifications*.

EXAMPLE 11.2   The single-runway airport model given in Example 11.1 is
translated into the following Prolog program.

```prolog
% SIMULATION MODEL OF A SINGLE-RUNWAY AIRPORT
% Time unit = 1 minute

object(Time,aircraft,
  [(arrive(I) :-
     do((request(Service,Priority),
        next_arrival(Time,I,NTime,NI))),
     respond([(Time,Priority,runway,queue(aircraft(I))),
        (Time,Priority,runway,seize(aircraft(I):Service)),
        (NTime,np,aircraft,arrive(NI))]))]).

object(Time,runway,
  [(seize(Aircraft:Service) :-
     do((serve_time(Service,ST),NTime is Time + ST)),
     respond([(NTime,np,runway,release(Aircraft))]))]).

request(Service,Priority) :- P is random,
    (P < 0.5, Service = takeoff, Priority = 1,!;
              Service = landing, Priority = 0).

next_arrival(CurTime,I,NextTime,NI) :-
    expon(10,AT), NextTime is CurTime + AT,
    NI is I + 1.

serve_time(takeoff,Time) :- normal(15,3,Time).
serve_time(landing,Time) :- normal(20,4,Time).

simulation_time(0,480).
initial_state([free(aircraft),free(runway)]).
start_message([(Time,np,aircraft,arrive(I))]) :-
    next_arrival(0,0,Time,I).
histogram_form((wait-time,runway,(7,0,10))).
```

FIGURE 11.1 Simulation model of a single-runway airport.

Note from the program of Figure 11.1 that the message *queue(aircraft(I))* is to be sent to the (implicit) queue *runway* (which is created internally when a *queue* message is sent to it for the first time), whereas the message *seize(aircraft(I):Service)* will be sent to both the object *runway* and the queue *runway*. Thus, the message *seize* will have two effects: occupying the object *runway* and changing the queue *runway* (recording waiting time and queue length statistics). A full study of the system's internal operation will be presented in Section 11.7 and details of the effect of *queue* and *seize* messages will be given in Section 11.8.

We can now run the Prolog model of Figure 11.1 by entering the following query to POSS, where the indicator *nosnap* indicates that no snapshots are required. The simulation results are shown in Figure 11.2.

```
?- simulate(nosnap).

            . . .
            . . .
    . . .   . . .           . . .
    . . .   . . .   . . .   . . .
    . . .   . . .   . . .   . . .
    . . .   . . .   . . .   . . .           . . .
    . . .   . . .   . . .   . . .   . . .   . . .
 . . . . . . . . . . . . . . . . . . . . . . . . . . . . . . .
    0    10   20   30   40   50   60

Frequency of wait - time for runway

Utilization of runway is 96%
Average use - time of runway is 19
Average wait - time for runway is 23
Average queue length of runway is 6
```

FIGURE 11.2 Result of a simulation run on the model of Figure 11.1.

It should be pointed out that simulation runs normally require a great deal of memory. If the user's Prolog system does not provide enough memory, then the simulation run can be broken down to several successive runs with shorter intervals. To do this, we simply change the simulation time to simulation_time(0,200), say, and execute a series of commands of the following form:

```
?- simulate(nosnap).
         .
         .
         .
?- sim_cont(400).
         .
         .
         .
?- sim_cont(480).
```

The final result would be the same as that produced by a single run as shown in Figure 11.2. This result shows on average an aircraft has to wait for 23 minutes before being allowed to use the runway for landing or takeoff. As mentioned before, we first used a single queue for both landing and taking-off aircraft to explain the point that the same message can be sent simultaneously to an object and its associated queue.

Obviously, it is more useful to know the waiting time for landing and takeoff separately. To achieve this we simply replace the queueing response in the program of Figure 11.1 by the following:

```
(Time,Priority,queue(Service),queue(aircraft(I)))
```

Thus, aircraft requesting the runway service for landing or takeoff are placed in separate queues. This, however, causes the problem that the message *seize(aircraft(I):Service)* cannot reach the queues. So, we must insert the following response:

```
(Time,0,queue(Service),leaveq(Aircraft))
```

as an additional response to the message *seize(Aircraft:Service)* for the *runway*. This response is to be sent to the relevant queue to change its contents and to record appropriate statistics.

With the above-described changes to the Prolog program of Figure 11.1, we now make another run on the (modified) model, and the result is shown in Figure 11.3. These results show that the take-off queue is much longer than the landing one, and waiting time in the take-off queue is almost seven times that in the landing queue.

```
?- simulate(nosnap).
        ...
        ...  ...
        ...  ...
        ...  ...  ...
        ...  ...  ...  ...
        ...  ...  ...  ...             ...
        ...  ...  ...  ...        ...  ...
.........................................................
        0    10   20   30   40   50   60
```

Frequency of wait - time for runway

Utilization of runway is 97%
Average use - time of runway is 20
Average wait - time for queue(landing) is 5
Average wait - time for queue(takeoff) is 34
Average queue length of queue(landing) is 1
Average queue length of queue(takeoff) is 8

FIGURE 11.3 Simulation result of a single-runway airport with two queues.

11.4   Realisation of nondeterminism

Nondeterminism is an important aspect of simulation. Typically, a system may have several objects of the same type, of which more than one could be available at a certain time. So, when a message is sent to these available objects, one of them is chosen (nondeterministically) to receive the message.

The Prolog language, with its unification and backtracking mechanisms, allows nondeterminism to be realised with ease. In fact, in a Prolog simulation program, a class of objects of the same type can be represented by a common term *ObjectName(N)*, where N runs over the indices of objects in the class. Then one can refer to an arbitrary object of the class by using the term *ObjectName(_)*.

EXAMPLE 11.3   Suppose that the future airport described in Example 11.1 will have two runways. Now, aircraft requesting permission to land or take off are placed in separate queues with the landing queue having higher priority than the take-off queue. The first aircraft in the queues will be allowed to take whichever runway is available at the time.

The Prolog program for this simulation problem is the same as the one given in Example 11.2 (the two-queue version) except that *runway* is replaced with *runway(N)* and the initial state and statistic specifications are changed accordingly. For completion, we list the full program in Figure 11.4.

```
object(Time,aircraft,
  [(arrive(I) :-
    do((request(Service,Priority),
        next_arrival(Time,I,NTime,NI))),
    respond([(Time,Priority,queue(Service),queue(aircraft(I))),
        (Time,Priority,runway(_),seize(aircraft(I):Service)),
        (NTime,np,aircraft,arrive(NI))]))]).

object(Time,runway(N),
  [(seize(Aircraft:Service) :-
    do((serve_time(Service,ST),NTime is Time + ST)),
    respond([(Time,0,queue(Service),leaveq(Aircraft)),
        (NTime,np,runway(N),release(Aircraft))]))]).

request(Service,Priority) :- P is random,
    (P < 0.5, Service = takeoff, Priority = 1,!;
            Service = landing, Priority = 0).
next_arrival(CurTime,I,NextTime,NI) :- expon(10,AT),
    NextTime is CurTime + AT, NI is I + 1.

serve_time(takeoff,Time) :- normal(15,3,Time).
serve_time(landing,Time) :- normal(20,4,Time).

simulation_time(0,480).
initial_state([free(aircraft),free(runway(1)),free(runway(2))]).
start_message([(Time,np,aircraft,arrive(I))]) :-
    next_arrival(0,0,Time,I).
histogram_form((wait-time,runway(_),(7,0,5))).
statistic_focus(wait-time,runway(_)).
statistic(wait-time,runway(_),nil).
```

FIGURE 11.4 Simulation of a two-runway airport with two queues.

The statistic specifications given in the program of Figure 11.4 indicate that the histogram is used to tally waiting times for both runways, but their average will not be calculated.

A simulation run of the model given in Figure 11.4 produces the result shown in Figure 11.5.

```
?- simulate(nosnap).


        ...
        ...
        ...  ...
        ...  ...
        ...  ...
        ...  ...
        ...  ...  ...
        ...  ...  ...      ...        ...
        ...  ...  ...      ...        ...
        ...  ...  ...      ...        ...
        ...  ...  ...  ...  ...  ...  ...
        ...  ...  ...  ...  ...  ...  ...
    ...........................................
        0    5   10   15   20   25   30

Frequency of wait - time for runway(_)

Utilization of runway(1) is 81%
Average use - time of runway(1) is 18
Utilization of runway(2) is 76%
Average use - time of runway(2) is 16
Average wait - time for queue(landing) is 3
Average wait - time for queue(takeoff) is 20
Average queue length of queue(landing) is 0
Average queue length of queue(takeoff) is 1
```

FIGURE 11.5 Result of a simulation run on the model of Figure 11.4.

The following example demonstrates that nondeterministic selection of objects can be easily nested.

EXAMPLE 11.4   At the next World Expo, one of the American attractions will be a simulated trip on Mars. There will be two vehicles to take the passengers around: a boat that can accommodate three people and a jeep that can take four passengers. Each passenger buys one or two tickets and joins a single queue to enter whichever vehicle that has a vacant place. The time a passenger spends in the boat is between 15 and 25 minutes, and in the jeep is between 10 and 20 minutes. After leaving a vehicle, if the passenger still has a ticket, then he or she will rejoin the queue to enter the other vehicle; otherwise, the passenger just leaves. Visitors are expected to arrive in a uniform pattern between 0 and 3 minutes. The purpose of simulation is to estimate the average queue length, average waiting time in queue, and the utilisation of the vehicles. The model is given below.

Object : Passenger

Arrive :

Passenger buys 1 or 2 tickets.

Next arrival: uniform distribution 0-3 minutes.

Passenger joins a single queue with no priority.

Passenger waits to enter one of the two vehicles.

Next passenger arrives.

Object : Vehicle (boat 1-3, jeep 1-4)

Take passenger with 2 tickets :

Time spent: in boat 15-25 minutes; jeep 10-20 minutes.

Next vehicle: boat $\rightarrow$ jeep; jeep $\rightarrow$ boat.

After spending time in the vehicle, passenger leaves it;

rejoins the queue; and

waits to enter the next vehicle.

Take passenger with 1 ticket :

Time spent in vehicle is as above.

After spending time in vehicle, passenger leaves system.

Simulation time : 2 hours (120 minutes).

Initial state : both vehicles are free and no passengers waiting.

Start message : first passenger arrives.

Histogram form : waiting times in 7 classes of width 10, from 0.

The above model is translated into the program of Figures 11.6 and 11.7.

```
% SIMULATION MODEL OF A SIMULATED JOURNEY ON MARS

object(Time,passenger,
  [(arrive(I) :-
    do((buy(Tickets),next_arrival(Time,I,NTime,NI))),
    respond([(Time,np,vehicle(_),queue(pass(I))),
      (Time,np,vehicle(_),seize(pass(I):Tickets)),
      (NTime,np,passenger,arrive(NI))]))]).

object(Time,vehicle(V:N),
  [(seize(Pass:2) :-
    do((spend_time(V,ST),LTime is Time + ST,
      next_vehicle(V,NV))),
    respond([(LTime,np,vehicle(V:N),release(Pass)),
      (LTime,np,vehicle(_),queue(Pass)),
      (LTime,np,vehicle(NV:_),seize(Pass:1))])),
  (seize(Pass:1) :-
    do((spend_time(V,ST),LTime is Time + ST)),
    respond([(LTime,np,vehicle(V:N),release(Pass))]))]).

buy(Tickets) :- uniform(1,2,Tickets).
next_arrival(CurTime,I,NextTime,NI) :-
    uniform(0,3,AT), NextTime is CurTime + AT,
    NI is I + 1.
next_vehicle(boat,jeep).
next_vehicle(jeep,boat).
spend_time(boat,Time) :- uniform(15,25,Time).
spend_time(jeep,Time) :- uniform(10,20,Time).

simulation_time(0,120).
initial_state(States) :-
    setup(3,boat,[free(passenger)],BStates),
    setup(4,jeep,BStates,States).
start_message([(Time,np,passenger,arrive(I))]) :-
    next_arrival(0,0,Time,I).
```

FIGURE 11.6 Simulation model of a simulated journey on Mars.

```
histogram_form((wait-time,vehicle(_),(7,0,10))).
statistic_focus(wait-time,vehicle(_)).
statistic_focus(use-time,vehicle(boat:_)).
statistic_focus(use-time,vehicle(jeep:_)).
statistic_focus(queue,vehicle(_)).
capacity(vehicle(boat:_),3).
capacity(vehicle(jeep:_),4).

setup(0,_,States,States) :- !.
setup(N,V,States,FStates) :- N1 is N - 1,
    setup(N1,V,[free(vehicle(V:N))|States],FStates).
```

FIGURE 11.7 Simulation model of a simulated journey on Mars (continued).

Observe from the model of Figure 11.6 that a seat in any vehicle is represented by the common term *vehicle(V:N)*, where *V* can be *boat* or *jeep* and *N* is the seat number in the vehicle. At first a passenger refers to an arbitrary vehicle as *vehicle(_)*. Then, when the vehicle *V* is known, an arbitrary place in the vehicle is referred to as *vehicle(V:_)*. A simulation run of the above model is shown below and in Figure 11.8.

```
?- simulate(nosnap).
                            . . .
                            . . .
           . . .            . . .
           . . .            . . .
           . . .            . . .
           . . .     . . .  . . .  . . .
           . . .  . . .  . . .  . . .  . . .
           . . .  . . .  . . .  . . .  . . .  . . .
           . . .  . . .  . . .  . . .  . . .  . . .
           . . .  . . .  . . .  . . .  . . .  . . .
           . . .  . . .  . . .  . . .  . . .  . . .
           . . .  . . .  . . .  . . .  . . .  . . .
           . . .  . . .  . . .  . . .  . . .  . . .
           . . .  . . .  . . .  . . .  . . .  . . .
........................................................
        0    10   20   30   40   50   60

Frequency of wait - time for vehicle(_)
```

```
Average wait - time for vehicle(_) is 27
Average queue length of vehicle(_) is 21
Utilization of vehicle(jeep:_) is 94%
Average use - time of vehicle(jeep:_) is 15
Utilization of vehicle(boat:_) is 87%
Average use - time of vehicle(boat:_) is 19
```

FIGURE 11.8 Result of a simulation run on the model of Figures 11.6 and 11.7.

11.5   Multiobject requirement

Another typical situation in simulation is when a message requires the availability of several objects before being sent to all of them simultaneously. In conventional simulation languages such as GPSS and SIMULA, this type of problem requires quite complex arrangements involving testing of the objects' availability, followed by seizing the objects and preventing the interference of other messages.

In POSS, we simply refer to the relevant objects as a group of objects by using the following general form of response:

```
(Time,Priority,(Object1,...,Objectm),Message).
```

Again, each object of the group can be (arbitrarily) chosen from a number of objects of the same type that happen to be available at the time. The following example demonstrates an application of this technique.

EXAMPLE 11.5   A harbour has several berths and tugs to help ships dock for loading and unloading their cargos. There are two large berths for big ships, and three small berths for small ships. Also there are three tugs of the same kind. Big ships require a large berth and two tugs to dock, while small ships must dock at small berths using only one tug.

Ships arrive almost regularly at intervals between 10 and 30 minutes. About 40% of the ships are large ones. A large ship uses two tugs, takes between 20 and 30 minutes to dock, and takes between one and two hours to load or unload cargo. A small ship uses one tug, takes between 15 and 20 minutes to dock, and spends between 40 and 90 minutes at a small berth.

The purpose of simulation is to estimate the average waiting times of large and small ships, and using time of the two kinds of berth. The model is shown below.

Object : Ship

Arrive:

Ship type: 40% large, require 1 large berth and 2 tugs;
            60% small, require 1 small berth and 1 tug.
Next arrival: uniform distribution 10-30 minutes.

Ship waits to use appropriate berth and tugs.
Next ship arrives.

Object : Berth (large: 1-2; small: 1-3)

Dock ship:
Time required: large 60-120 minutes; small 40-90 minutes.

After being used, berth becomes available.

Object : Tug

Pull ship:
Time required: large 20-30 minutes; small 15-20 minutes.

After being used, tug becomes available.

Simulation time: 8 hours (480 minutes).
Initial state: all berths and tugs are available, no ships waiting.
Start message: first ship arrives.
Histogram form: wait times for large berth (and 2 tugs), classified
        into 7 classes of width 5, starting from 0.
Histogram form: wait times for small berth (and 1 tug), classified
        into 7 classes of width 5, starting from 0.
Statistics: use time of large and small berths.
            no use time for tugs.

The above model is translated into the Prolog program shown in Figures 11.9 and 11.10. Observe from this program that `BerthTugs` is an arbitrary group of either `(berth(large:_),tug(_),tug(_))` or `(berth(small:_),tug(_))`, depending on whether the ship is large or small.

```
% SIMULATION MODEL OF A SHIP-DOCK SYSTEM
% Time unit = 1 minute

object(Time,ship,
  [(arrive(I) :-
     do((ship_type(Type,BerthTugs),
         next_arrival(Time,I,NTime,NI))),
     respond([(Time,np,BerthTugs,seize(ship(I):Type)),
       (NTime,np,ship,arrive(NI))]))]).

object(Time,berth(Type:N),
  [(seize(Ship:Type) :-
     do((berth_time(Type,BT),LTime is Time + BT)),
     respond([(LTime,np,berth(Type:N),release(Ship))]))]).

object(Time,tug(N),
  [(seize(Ship:Type) :-
     do((tug_time(Type,TT),FTime is Time + TT)),
     respond([(FTime,np,tug(N),release(Ship))]))]).

ship_type(Type,BerthTugs) :-
    P is random,
    (P < 0.4,!, Type = large,
     BerthTugs = (berth(large:_),tug(_),tug(_));
     Type = small, BerthTugs = (berth(small:_),tug(_))).

next_arrival(CurTime,I,NextTime,NI) :-
    uniform(10,30,AT), NextTime is CurTime + AT,
    NI is I + 1.

berth_time(large,Time) :- uniform(60,120,Time).
berth_time(small,Time) :- uniform(40,90,Time).

tug_time(large,Time) :- uniform(20,30,Time).
tug_time(small,Time) :- uniform(15,20,Time).
```

FIGURE 11.9 Simulation model of a ship-dock system.

```
simulation_time(0,480).
initial_state(States) :-
    setup_berths(2,large,[free(ship)],AStates),
    setup_berths(3,small,AStates,BStates),
    setup_tugs(3,BStates,States).
start_message([(Time,np,ship,arrive(I))]) :-
    next_arrival(0,0,Time,I).

histogram_form((wait-time,
    (berth(large:_),tug(_),tug(_)),(7,0,5))).
histogram_form((wait-time,
    (berth(small:_),tug(_)),(7,0,5))).

statistic_focus(wait-time,(berth(large:_),tug(_),tug(_))).
statistic_focus(wait-time,(berth(small:_),tug(_))).
statistic_focus(use-time,berth(large:_)).
statistic_focus(use-time,berth(small:_)).
statistic(use-time,tug(_),nil).
capacity(berth(large:_),2).
capacity(berth(small:_),3).

setup_berths(0,_,States,States) :- !.
setup_berths(N,Type,States,NStates) :-
    N1 is N - 1,
    setup_berths(N1,Type,
        [free(berth(Type:N))|States],NStates).

setup_tugs(0,States,States) :- !.
setup_tugs(N,States,NStates) :-
    N1 is N - 1,
    setup_tugs(N1,[free(tug(N))|States],NStates).
```

FIGURE 11.10 Simulation model of a ship-dock system (continued).

The result of a simulation run on the model of Figures 11.9 and 11.10 is
shown in Figure 11.11. Here, the statistic specifications indicate that wait
times for large berth (with two tugs) and small berth (with one tug) are
collected. Also, use times of large and small berths are recorded separately,
but use times of tugs are not collected.

```
?- simulate(nosnap).

        ...
        ...
        ...
        ...
        ...
        ...         ...                   ...
.....................................................
        0    5   10   15   20   25   30
```

Frequency of wait - time for berth(large:_),tug(_),tug(_)

```
        ...
        ...
        ...
        ...
        ...
        ...
        ...
        ...
        ...   ...
        ...   ...
        ...   ...              ...
.....................................................
        0    5   10   15   20   25   30
```

Frequency of wait - time for berth(small:_),tug(_)

Utilization of berth(small:_) is 64%
Average use - time of berth(small:_) is 67
Utilization of berth(large:_) is 45%
Average use - time of berth(large:_) is 74
Average wait - time for berth(large:_),tug(_),tug(_) is 7
Average wait - time for berth(small:_),tug(_) is 2

FIGURE 11.11 Result of a simulation run on the model of Figures 11.9 and 11.10.

11.6   Implementation of rendez-vous

In an object-oriented simulation model, *rendez-vous* between two objects is realised by arranging for each object to send a message in the form:

```
(Time,Priority,Object1,waitfor(Object2,Message)).
```

The first message is kept in the system states until the second matching message arrives. Then the two messages are sent (simultaneously) to the related objects.

EXAMPLE 11.6   A motor repair shop employs two mechanics to carry out repair work. The first mechanic receives a motor, removes its casing, and passes the casing to the second mechanic for cleaning, while he inspects and repairs the motor. When the first mechanic completes repairing and the second one finishes cleaning the casing (if one finishes first, then he must wait for the other), they exchange the parts so that the first mechanic will dry paint the casing while the second one cleans the engine. After finishing dry painting, the first mechanic will take the next motor and repeat the process, unless the second mechanic has already finished cleaning the engine, in which case the first mechanic will take the cleaned engine and replace the casing to it, before turning his attention to the next motor.

Motors are brought in at intervals of between 30 and 45 minutes. About 30% of the motors require minor repairs, 50% major repairs, and the rest only need adjustment. Service times are uniformly distributed in the following patterns. Removing casing: 5-10 min; minor repair: 15-30 min; major repair: 30-60 min; adjustment: 10-20 min; dry painting casing: 10-20 min; cleaning casing: 10-30 min; cleaning engine: 20-30 min; and assembling: 10-20 min. The purpose of simulation is to estimate the time a motor must wait before being serviced by each mechanic and the average use time of each mechanic. The model is given below, in which queue statistics are not collected.

Object : Motor

Arrive :

Service: 30% minor repair, 50% major repair, 20% adjustment.
Next arrival: uniform distribution 30-45 minutes.

Motor waits for mechanic 1 to start service.
Next motor arrives.

Object : Mechanic 1

Provide service:

Removing casing needs 5-10 min; minor-repair: 15-30 min; major-repair: 30-60 min; adjustment: 10-20 min.

After removing the casing, passes it to mechanic 2 for cleaning. After repairing motor, mechanic 1 waits for mechanic 2.

Wait for mechanic 2:

Dry-painting needs 10-20 min.

After finishing painting, mechanic 1 is available.

Perform assembly:

Assembling needs 10-20 min.

After assembling motor, mechanic 1 is available.

Object : Mechanic 2

Clean casing:

Cleaning casing needs 10-30 min.

After cleaning casing, mechanic 2 waits for mechanic 1.

Wait for mechanic 1:

Cleaning engine needs 20-30 min.

After cleaning engine, passes it to mechanic 1 for assembling; Mechanic 2 becomes available.

Simulation time: 8 hours (480 minutes).
Initial state: both mechanics are free, no motors are waiting.
Start message: first motor arrives.
Histogram form: waiting times for mechanic 1 classified into 6 classes of width 20, starting from 20.

The above model is translated into the Prolog program shown in Figures 11.12 and 11.13. Observe from this program that both the casing and the engine of a motor are represented by the same term *c(Motor)*, which in general simply means a copy of (the message representing) the motor.

```
% SIMULATION MODEL OF A MOTOR REPAIR SHOP

object(Time,motor,
  [(arrive(I) :-
     do((need(Service),next_arrival(Time,I,NTime,NI))),
     respond([(Time,1,mechanic(1),seize(motor(I):Service)),
       (NTime,np,motor,arrive(NI))]))]).
object(Time,mechanic(1),
  [(seize(Motor:Service) :-
     do((repair(Service),
        serve_time(remove-casing,RT),CTime is Time + RT,
        serve_time(Service,ST),WTime is CTime + ST)),
     respond([(CTime,1,mechanic(2),seize(c(Motor):clean-casing)),
       (WTime,1,mechanic(1),waitfor(mechanic(2):c(Motor)))])),
   (waitfor(mechanic(2):c(Motor)) :-
     do((serve_time(paint-casing,PT),FTime is Time + PT)),
     respond([(FTime,np,mechanic(1),release(Motor))])),
   (seize(Engine:assemble) :-
     do((serve_time(assemble,AT),ATime is Time + AT)),
     respond([(ATime,np,mechanic(1),release(Engine))]))]).

object(Time,mechanic(2),
  [(seize(c(Motor):clean-casing) :-
     do((serve_time(clean-casing,CT),WTime is Time + CT)),
     respond([(WTime,1,mechanic(2),waitfor(mechanic(1):Motor))])),
   (waitfor(mechanic(1):Motor) :-
     do((serve_time(clean-engine,ET),ATime is Time + ET)),
     respond([(ATime,np,mechanic(2),release(c(Motor))),
       (ATime,0,mechanic(1),seize(c(Motor):assemble))]))]).

need(Service) :- P is random,
    (P < 0.3, Service = minor-repair,!;
     P < 0.8, Service = major-repair,!;
             Service = adjustment).
next_arrival(CurTime,I,NextTime,NI) :-
    uniform(30,45,AT), NextTime is CurTime + AT,
    NI is I + 1.
```

FIGURE 11.12 Simulation model of a motor repair shop.

```
repair(Service) :-
    member(Service,[minor-repair,major-repair,adjustment]).
serve_time(remove-casing,Time) :- uniform(5,10,Time).
serve_time(minor-repair,Time) :- uniform(15,30,Time).
serve_time(major-repair,Time) :- uniform(30,60,Time).
serve_time(adjustment,Time) :- uniform(10,20,Time).
serve_time(paint-casing,Time) :- uniform(10,20,Time).
serve_time(clean-casing,Time) :- uniform(10,30,Time).
serve_time(clean-engine,Time) :- uniform(20,30,Time).
serve_time(assemble,Time) :- uniform(10,20,Time).

simulation_time(0,240).
initial_state([free(motor),
    free(mechanic(1)),free(mechanic(2))]).
start_message([(Time,np,motor,arrive(I))]) :-
    next_arrival(0,0,Time,I).
histogram_form((wait-time,mechanic(1),(6,20,20))).
```

FIGURE 11.13 Simulation model of a motor repair shop (continued).

The result of a simulation run on the above model is shown below.

```
?- simulate(nosnap).
        . . .
        . . .
        . . .   . . .
        . . .   . . .                   . . .
        . . .   . . .           . . . . . .   . . .
  ....................................................
        20   40   60   80   100  120

Frequency of wait - time for mechanic(1)

Average wait - time for mechanic(1) is 67
Average wait - time for mechanic(2) is 2
Utilization of mechanic(1) is 89%
Average use - time of mechanic(1) is 42
Utilization of mechanic(2) is 79%
Average use - time of mechanic(2) is 63
```

11.7   POSS: A Prolog-based object-oriented simulation system

In the preceding sections, we have described a simple technique of developing Prolog simulation programs. Let us now explain how those developed simulation models are executed by the simulation system POSS.

POSS is a Prolog-based object-oriented simulation system which was developed at the University of Canberra, for the purpose of research and teaching in simulation and VLSI design.

POSS executes an object-oriented simulation model (as described in Section 11.3) by performing the following cycle:

Repeat
Select the next message to be sent to an available object or
group of objects;
Send the message and obtain responses from the object(s);
Insert the responses into the list of scheduled messages;
Until time is up.

In order to perform the above execution cycle and to collect statistical data in a simulation run, POSS maintains the following facilities:

- A clock that shows the current time;

- A list of scheduled messages in ascending order of time and priority (top-priority messages are given priority 0);

- A list of states of the objects in the system;

- A list of histograms as required;

- A statistic board that stores statistical information on the objects.

At the beginning, POSS obtains the initial information such as start and stop times, the initial state, the start message, and other specifications on histograms and statistics, from the user-supplied Prolog model. Then, the system executes the above-given cycle, updating the clock accordingly, until the clock shows time is up. At the start of each cycle, if the snap-indicator is set, then POSS displays a snapshot of the system's current state (a sample display is shown in Figure 11.19 of Section 11.8). At the end, besides producing a last snapshot and a final report on the simulation run, POSS also saves the system's last state to be used in any continued simulation runs. The top-level control of POSS is shown in Figure 11.14.

```
simulate(Snap) :-
    simulation_time(Start,Stop),initial_state(States),
    start_message(Messs),histogram_specification(Hist),
    simul_run((Start,Stop,Messs,States,Hist,[],Snap)).

simul_run((CT,ST,Messs,States,Hist,Statistics,Snap)) :-
    CT >= ST,!,
    store((CT,ST,Messs,States,Hist,Statistics,Snap)),
    snap_shot(Snap,CT,Messs,States,Hist,Statistics),
    report(CT,Hist,Statistics).
simul_run((CT,ST,Messs,States,Hist,Statistics,Snap)) :-
    snap_shot(Snap,CT,Messs,States,Hist,Statistics),
    select_message(CT,Mess,Messs,RMesss,States),!,
    send_message(CT,Mess,RMesss,States,Hist,Statistics,
        NxT,NMesss,NStates,NHist,NStatistics),
    simul_run((NxT,ST,NMesss,NStates,NHist,
        NStatistics,Snap)).

histogram_specification(HistList) :-
    findall(Hist,histogram_form(Hist),HistList).
```

FIGURE 11.14 POSS's top-level control.

POSS's procedure of selecting the next message for sending is simple, yet powerful. The system begins by finding the first message that can be sent to an available object or group of objects. If this message is on schedule or is a future message (that is, its scheduled time is greater than or equal to the current time, which assures it has highest priority among all messages that can be sent at the same time) or if priority is not involved, then the message is selected. Otherwise, the system inspects all messages that compete for one or more of the objects available to the first message found above, and selects the one with highest priority. During this course of selection, Prolog's unification and backtracking mechanisms are used to determine the appropriate available objects.

The procedure *select_message* is shown in Figure 11.15. In this procedure, *general_message(M)* refers to the messages such as *queue(_)*, *leaveq(_)*, *release(_)*, and *waitfor(_)*, which are always sent to the specified objects, irrespective of their current states.

```
select_message(CT,Mess,Messs,RMesss,States) :-
    member((T,P,O,M),Messs),
    (available(O,O1,States); general_message(M)),!,
    select_mess(CT,(T,P,O,M),O1,Mess,Messs,RMesss).

available((O,Os),(O1,Os1),States) :- !,
    select(free(O1),States,NStates),not(not(O = O1)),!,
    available(Os,Os1,NStates).
available(O,O1,States) :-
    member(free(O1),States),not(not(O = O1)).

select_mess(CT,(T,P,O,M),O,(T,P,O,M),Messs,RMesss) :-
    (CT =< T; P = np),!,
    select((T,P,O,M),Messs,RMesss).
select_mess(CT,_,O,(T1,P1,O1,M1),Messs,RMesss) :-
    findall((P,T,Ob,M),(among(Ob,O),member((T,P,Ob,M),Messs),
        T =< CT),List), sort(List,[(P1,T1,O1,M1)|_]),
    select((T1,P1,O1,M1),Messs,RMesss).
```

FIGURE 11.15 POSS's selection of next message.

Also in the procedure of Figure 11.15, *among(Ob, O)* means *Ob* is one or more objects of the object(s) *O*. In fact, we have:

```
among(A,(A,As)).
among(X,(A,As)) :- among(X,As).
among((A,B),(A,As)) :- among(B,As).
among(A,(A)) :- A \= (B,C).
```

We next consider how POSS sends a message to an object or a group of objects and obtains their responses. This is a key event in a simulation run, as it causes four important effects: updating of the clock time, changing the simulated system's state, adding new messages to the list of scheduled messages, and updating the system's collection of statistics.

The procedure *send_message* is shown in Figure 11.16. Note that the messages *queue(_)* and *leaveq(_)* do not change the system's state and generate no responses. This is shown in the first two clauses of the procedure *update_states*. The remaining clauses define the effect of *seize(_)*, *release(_)*, *waitfor(_)*, and other user-defined messages.

```prolog
send_message(CT,(ET,POM),Messs,States,Hist,Statistics,
    NT,NMesss,NStates,NHist,NStatistics) :-
    max(CT,ET,NT),
    update_states(NT,PT,(ET,POM),Messs,States,NMesss,NStates),
    update_statis(NT,PT,POM,Hist,Statistics,NHist,NStatistics).

update_states(CT,ET,(ET,_,_,queue(_)),Messs,States,
    Messs,States) :- !.
update_states(CT,WT,(_,_,_,leaveq(_)),Messs,States,
    Messs,States) :- !.
update_states(CT,ET,(ET,_,(O,Os),seize(M:W)),Messs,States,
    NMesss,NStates) :- !,
    update_states(CT,ET,(ET,_,O,seize(M:W)),Messs,States,
    MMesss,MStates),update_states(CT,ET,(ET,_,Os,seize(M:W)),
    MMesss,MStates,NMesss,NStates).
update_states(CT,ET,(ET,_,O,seize(M:W)),Messs,States,
    NMesss,[busy(O,M,CT)|NStates]) :- !,
    send(CT,O,seize(M:W),Responses),
    insert_list(Responses,Messs,NMesss),
    select(free(O),States,NStates).
update_states(CT,BT,(_,_,O,release(M)),Messs,States,
    Messs,[free(O)|NStates]) :- !,
    select(busy(O,M,BT),States,NStates).
update_states(CT,ET,(ET,_,O,waitfor(O1:M)),Messs,States,
    NMesss,NStates) :-
    select(wait(O1,O,M1),States,NStates),!,
    send(CT,O,waitfor(O1:M),Resp),
    insert_list(Resp,Messs,MMesss),
    send(CT,O1,waitfor(O:M1),Resp1),
    insert_list(Resp1,MMesss,NMesss).
update_states(CT,ET,(ET,_,O,waitfor(O1:M)),Messs,States,
    Messs,[wait(O,O1,M)|States]) :- !.
update_states(CT,ET,(ET,_,O,M),Messs,States,NMesss,States) :-
    send(CT,O,M,Responses),
    insert_list(Responses,Messs,NMesss).
```

FIGURE 11.16 POSS's procedure of sending messages.

Here, the procedure *send* gets responses from a single object by obtaining its *methods* (which is a list of message-response pairs), and applying the message to the methods to retrieve the responses. The system then executes the required domestic work to complete the responses, before returning them. Observe that an object may inherit the methods of its ancestors (or super-objects). The procedure is presented in Figure 11.17.

```
:- op(500,xfx,isa).

send(Time,Object,Message,Responses) :-
    obtain(Time,Object,Methods),
    apply(Message,Methods,Responses).

obtain(Time,Object,Methods) :-
    inherit(Object,AncObj),
    object(Time,AncObj,Methods).

apply(A,Methods,Responses) :-
    member((A :- do(B),respond(Responses)),Methods),
    call(B).

inherit(Object,Object).
inherit(Object,AncObj) :-
    Object isa SupObj,
    inherit(SupObj,AncObj).
```

FIGURE 11.17 POSS's procedure of sending messages (continued).

Finally, the task of collecting statistics is straightforward but rather tedious. The message *queue(M)* adds member *M* to a queue, whereas the message *leaveq(M)* removes the member *M* from a queue and records waiting time in the histograms as well as in the statistics board. The message *release(M)* only updates using time of an object. These tasks are shown in Figure 11.18, where the subprocedures *update_queue*, *update_histogram*, and *update_time* are quite ordinary, and the purpose of the goal *statistic_focus(queue,O1)* is to generalise the reference to queue, if so indicated.

```
update_statis(CT,ET,(P,O,queue(M)),Hist,Statistics,
   Hist,Statistics) :- !,
   (queue(_,O,_,_,_),!;
   (statistic_focus(queue,O1), not(not(O = O1)),!; O = O1),
     assert(queue(O,O1,O,O,[]))),
   update_queue(CT,ET,O,(P,ET,M),1).
update_statis(CT,WT,(_,O,M),Hist,Statistics,NHist,NStatistics):-
   (M = leaveq(A); M = seize(A:W)),!,
   update_queue(CT,WT,O,(_,WT,A),-1),
   update_histogram(CT,WT,(wait-time,O),Hist,NHist),
   update_time(wait-time,CT,WT,O,Statistics,NStatistics).
update_statis(CT,BT,(_,O,release(_)),Hist,Statistics,
   NHist,NStatistics) :- !,
   update_histogram(CT,BT,(use-time,O),Hist,NHist),
   update_time(use-time,CT,BT,O,Statistics,NStatistics).
update_statis(_,_,_,Hist,Statistics,
   Hist,Statistics) :- !.
```

FIGURE 11.18 POSS's statistics collection.

The remaining procedures of POSS contain merely routine tasks (including statistical calculation and report printing) and can be inspected from the system supplied with this book.

11.8 Simulation programming with POSS

POSS is designed to support object-oriented simulation programming in Prolog. Simulation using POSS has the following advantages.

- The simulation program has declarative style and contains no explicit controls;

- The program style is uniform and is very close to the form of a system model;

- Nondeterministic choice, multiobject accession, and rendez-vous are standard;

- The small number of built-in messages makes it easy to learn.

In fact, simulation programming in POSS is almost reduced to system modelling. The small number of built-in messages is provided merely for the purpose of statistics collection. We now give a summary of the built-in messages in POSS and their statistical effects. The following messages are assumed to be sent to a specified object (or a group of objects or a queue).

queue(M) : message M joins the specified queue.
> Internally, the message is added to the specified queue and queue length is incremented. Also the duration of the previous queue length is recorded to be used in the final calculation of average queue length. If the queue does not exist, then it is created to contain the message M.

leaveq(M) : message M leaves the specified queue.
> Internally, the message is removed from the specified queue and queue length is decremented. Also the duration of the previous queue length is recorded. Waiting time in the queue is collected to be used in updating wait-time histograms and statistics.

seize(M:W) : message M waits to be sent to the specified object or group of objects when they become available. When the objects receive this message, they become *busy*. If the object has an associated queue (bearing the same name), then the effect of *seize(_)* on the queue is the same as *leaveq(_)*.

release(M) : message M releases the specified object.
> This object becomes *free*, and the duration of the message's occupation is collected to be used in updating use-time histograms and statistics.

waitfor(O1:M) : the specified object O waits for object $O1$ to pass the message M. This message is kept until a matching message *waitfor(O:M1)* arrives, then both messages are sent to the appropriate objects.

seton(M) : message M sets the specified object free, irrespective of its current state.

setoff(M) : message M sets the specified object off, irrespective of its current state.

dropout(M) : message M drops out of the specified queue.
> The waiting message that matches M is removed from the list of scheduled messages as well as from the specified queue, and queue length is decremented.

Besides the above-listed built-in messages, the user can also refer to a queue's length or the shortest queue in the system by using the following goals:

queue_length(QName,N) : length of *QName* is N.
shortest_queue(QList,QName,N) : the shortest queue in *QList* is *QName* that has length N.

We shall explain the application of the above extra features of POSS in Problems 11.2 and 11.3. POSS also provides three statistical functions that are frequently used in simulation. In the following goals, the returned value X is an integer obtained from the specified distribution.

uniform(A,B,X) : uniform distribution in the range $A - B$.
expon(M,X)   : negative exponential distribution of mean M.
normal(M,S,X) : normal distribution of mean M and standard deviation S.

In conclusion, we summarise the basic technique of developing a simulation program using POSS.

In order to develop a Prolog simulation program to be run by POSS, the following steps should be followed.

1. Identify the relevant objects in the simulated system and their patterns of interaction.

2. Develop a system model reflecting the patterns of object interaction in the style described in Section 11.2.

3. Translate the model of step 2 into a Prolog program using the form set out in Section 11.3.

4. Run the simulation program by entering the following query to POSS:

    ?- simulate(snap).

5. Inspect the snapshots displayed by POSS to check the program's correctness. (The snapshot running can be continued by pressing any key, and stopped by using <Ctrl-Break>.) Correct the program and the model if necessary.

6. When the snapshots show the model evolves in an expected manner, perform a full simulation run by entering the query:

    ?- simulate(nosnap).

7. If the simulation run is aborted due to lack of memory, then reduce the stop time in the program and rerun the program with a series of continued commands:

```
?- simulate(nosnap).
        .
        .
        .
?- sim_cont(400).
        .
        .
?- sim_cont(480).
```

Note that we can request snapshot displays during continued simulation runs by using the command *sim_cont(400,snap)*. An example of snapshot display of the two-runway airport program (Figure 11.4) is shown in Figure 11.19.

```
?- sim_cont(400,snap).

Time       : 328
Messages   : 320,1,runway(_A448),seize(aircraft(31):takeoff)
             328,0,runway(_C354),seize(aircraft(32):landing)
             332,np,runway(1),release(aircraft(30))
             334,np,runway(2),release(aircraft(29))
             336,np,aircraft,arrive(33)
States     : busy(runway(1),aircraft(30),315)
             busy(runway(2),aircraft(29),312)
             free(aircraft)
Histograms: wait-time,runway(_88E8),[16,4,3,0,1,1,5],0,5
Statistics: wait-time,queue(takeoff),413,14
             use-time,runway(1),246,14
             wait-time,queue(landing),70,16
             use-time,runway(2),244,14
Queues     : q(320,queue(takeoff),413,1,[(1,320,aircraft(31))])
             q(328,queue(landing),70,1,[(0,328,aircraft(32))])
Counters   :
```

FIGURE 11.19 A snapshot display of POSS.

The snapshot displayed in Figure 11.19 shows that the aircraft 31 and 32 are waiting to take off and to land, respectively, while the runways are being used by aircraft 29 and 30. Runway 1 will be cleared first, by aircraft 30, and is expected to be used by aircraft 32, which has higher priority than aircraft 31. The display also shows the current states of the queues, histograms, and statistics collections.

A final note on using POSS is that we must remove any queues and system states saved from previous runs before making a new simulation run. This can be done by using the system goals *abolish(queue/5)* and *abolish(state/1)* or their equivalents in the Prolog system being used.

Solved problems

11.1 Consider a computer system that has a multiplexor linking its central processing unit (CPU) with four stations, one at a time. Each station is connected to a terminal. Messages from a terminal must wait at the connected station to be transmitted to the CPU. When the station is polled by the multiplexor, only the first waiting message is transmitted, and when response is complete, the station is closed and the multiplexor polls the next station. If no messages are waiting at the polled station, the multiplexor closes the station immediately and polls the next station. The polling pattern is 1-2-4-3-4-2-4-1-3-4-2-4-3-4.

Messages arriving from the terminals have interarrival times distributed exponentially with mean 3 seconds. About 14.3% of messages are from terminal 1, 31.4% from terminal 2, 21.3% from terminal 3, and the rest from terminal 4. Also 20% of messages are enquiries with a fixed length of 50 characters; the rest are data with 10% having 30 characters, 70% having 50 characters, and the rest having 80 characters. Responses to enquiry and data messages have lengths of 50 and 20 characters, respectively. CPU processing time of enquiries is between 0.5 and 1 second, and of data is 0.001 second per character, while transmission rate is 20 characters per second. The multiplexor takes 0.5 second to poll a station and 0.001 second to realise that no messages are waiting at a station.

Write a simulation program in POSS to simulate the above-described computer system, using only the built-in messages *queue(_)*, *leaveq(_)*, *seize(_)*, and *release(_)*. The purpose of simulation is to estimate the time a message must wait at a station before being processed and the average queue length at each station.

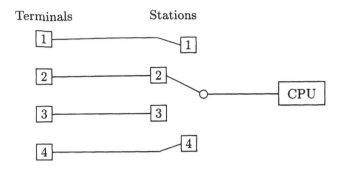

Solution:

In this given system, the relevant objects are the messages, the stations, and the multiplexor (called the poller). The terminals only serve as the source of the messages and the CPU is identified with the multiplexor. The system model is simple and is given below.

Object : Message

    Arrive:

        From terminal: 14.3% from terminal 1; 31.4% from terminal 2;
            21.3% from terminal 3; and 33% from terminal 4.
        Message type: 20% enquiries of length 50; 80% data, of which
            10% have length 30; 70% length 50; 20% length 80.
        Next arrival: negative exponential of mean 3 seconds.

        Message joins station's queue.
        Message waits to enter the station.
        Next message arrives.

Object : Poller

    Poll station:

        Station to poll: 1-2-4-3-4-2-4-1-3-4-2-4-3-4.
        Polling time: 0.5 second; inspecting time: 0.001 second.

        Poller polls station.
        After inspecting station, poller waits (with high authority)
            to close the station.

Object : Station (1-4)

    Transmit message:

Transmit time: 0.05 second per character.
Processing time: uniform distribution 0.5-1 second for enquiries;
    0.01 second per character for data.

Message leaves station queue.
After transmission is complete, station is available.

Closed by poller:
    Next round of polling: as above.

Poller starts to poll next station.

Simulation time: 3 minutes.
Initial state: all stations are closed, no messages are waiting.
Start messages: poller polls first station, first message arrives.
Histogram form: waiting times in queue 4, classified into 7
    classes of width 1 second, starting from 0.
Statistics: wait-time in each queue;
    wait-time and use-time of stations are not collected.

The above model is translated into the following program.

```
% SIMULATION OF A COMPUTER MULTIPLEXOR
% Time unit = 100th of second

object(Time,message,
  [(arrive(I) :-
      do((terminal(N),message_type(Type),
          next_arrival(Time,I,NTime,NI))),
      respond([(Time,1,queue(N),queue(message(I))),
          (Time,1,station(N),seize(message(I):Type)),
          (NTime,1,message,arrive(NI))]))]).

object(Time,poller,
  [(poll(I) :-
      do((poll_station(I,N),poll_time(Time,PTime,CTime))),
      respond([(PTime,1,station(N),release(poller)),
          (CTime,0,station(N),seize(poller:I))]))]).

object(Time,station(N),
  [(seize(message(I):Type) :-
      do(transmit_time(Type,Time,FTime)),
      respond([(Time,1,queue(N),leaveq(message(I))),
          (FTime,1,station(N),release(message(I)))])),
```

```
    (seize(poller:I) :-
        do(I1 is (I mod 14) + 1),
        respond([(Time,1,poller,poll(I1))])])]).

next_arrival(Time,I,NTime,NI) :-
    expon(300,AT), NTime is Time + AT,
    NI is I + 1.

terminal(N) :- P is random,
    (P < 0.143,!, N is 1; P < 0.457,!, N is 2;
     P < 0.670,!, N is 3; N is 4).

message_type((Type,Length)) :- P is random,
    (P < 0.2,!, Type = enquiry, Length = 50;
     Type = data, Q is random,
     (Q < 0.1,!, Length = 30;
      Q < 0.8,!, Length = 50; Length = 80)).

transmit_time((enquiry,Length),Time,FTime) :-
    uniform(50,100,PT),
    FTime is Time + 5*(Length + 50) + PT.
transmit_time((data,Length),Time,FTime) :-
    FTime is Time + 5*(Length + 20) + Length.

poll_station(I,N) :-
    member((I:N),
    [1:1,2:2,3:4,4:3,5:4,6:2,7:4,8:1,9:3,
    10:4,11:2,12:4,13:3,14:4]).

poll_time(Time,ETime,CTime) :-
    ETime is Time + 50,
    CTime is ETime + 1.

simulation_time(0,18000).
initial_state([free(poller),free(message),
    busy(station(1),poller,0),busy(station(2),poller,0),
    busy(station(3),poller,0),busy(station(4),poller,0)]).
start_message([(0,1,poller,poll(1)),
    (Time,1,message,arrive(I))]) :-
    next_arrival(0,0,Time,I).
histogram_form((wait-time,queue(4),(7,0,100))).
statistic(wait-time,station(_),nil).
statistic(use-time,station(_),nil).
```

A simulation run of the above model produces the following results (if the model is run with a PC-Prolog system, it will be necessary to make several continued simulation runs as suggested in the last section of this chapter):

```
?- simulate(nosnap).
```

```
                                          . . .
                                          . . .
                                          . . .
                                          . . .
                                          . . .
                         . . .            . . .
       . . .  . . .  . . .  . . .      . . .  . . .
...........................................................
       0    100  200  300  400  500  600
```

Frequency of wait - time for queue(4)

```
Average wait - time for queue(1) is 2571
Average wait - time for queue(2) is 3619
Average wait - time for queue(3) is 1713
Average wait - time for queue(4) is 1398
Average queue length of queue(1) is 1
Average queue length of queue(2) is 4
Average queue length of queue(3) is 0
Average queue length of queue(4) is 1
```

11.2 Consider again the computer system described in Problem 11.1. This time write a simulation program in POSS to estimate the utilisation of the stations in transmitting and responding to messages from the terminals. (Hint: use the built-in messages *seton(_)* and *setoff(_)* of POSS, as described in Section 11.8.)

Solution:

We note first that the model developed in Problem 11.1 cannot be used to estimate the utilisation of the stations, as a large proportion of the stations' busy-time is due to the poller's occupation.

In order to study the use of the stations in processing the messages from the terminals, we use four station gates to simulate polling operation of the multiplexor. The system model is modified as follows.

Object : Message

Arrive:

Terminal, message type and next arrival are as in Problem 11.1.

Message joins station's queue.
Message waits to get through the station gate.
Next message arrives.

Object : Poller

Poll station:

Station to be polled and polling time are as in Problem 11.1.

Poller opens station gate.
After inspecting station, poller waits (with high authority)
    to close the gate.

Object : Station gate (1-4)

Receive message:

Message leaves the queue.
Message closes the gate behind it.
Message enters station to be transmitted.

Receive poller:

Next round of polling: as in Problem 11.1.

Poller closes the station gate.
Poller starts polling next station.

Object : Station (1-4)

Transmit message:

Transmit time and process time are as in Problem 11.1.

After transmission is complete, station is available.
Message opens the station gate.

Simulation time: 3 minutes.
Initial state: all stations are free but their gates are not open;
        no messages are waiting.
Start messages: poller polls first station, first message arrives.
Histogram form: waiting times in queue 4, classified into 7
        classes of width 1 second, starting from 0.
Statistics: wait-time in each queue and utilisation of each station;
        wait-times for stations are not collected;
        no statistics for station gates.

The simulation program is shown below, where the procedures *terminal*, *message_type*, *next_arrival*, *transmit_time*, *poll_station*, and *poll_time* are the same as in the program of Problem 11.1.

```
% SIMULATION OF A COMPUTER MULTIPLEXOR USING GATES
% Time unit = 100th of second

object(Time,message,
   [(arrive(I) :-
       do((terminal(N),message_type(Type),
           next_arrival(Time,I,NTime,NI))),
       respond([(Time,1,queue(N),queue(message(I))),
               (Time,1,stngate(N),wait(message(I):Type)),
               (NTime,1,message,arrive(NI))]))]).

object(Time,poller,
   [(poll(I) :-
       do((poll_station(I,N),poll_time(Time,PTime,CTime))),
       respond([(PTime,1,stngate(N),seton(poller(I))),
               (CTime,0,stngate(N),wait(poller(I):_))]))]).

object(Time,stngate(N),
   [(wait(message(I):Type) :-
       do(true),
       respond([(Time,1,queue(N),leaveq(message(I))),
               (Time,0,stngate(N),setoff(message(I))),
               (Time,1,station(N),seize(message(I):Type))])),
    (wait(poller(I):_) :-
       do(I1 is (I mod 14) + 1),
       respond([(Time,0,stngate(N),setoff(poller(I))),
               (Time,1,poller,poll(I1))]))]).

object(Time,station(N),
   [(seize(message(I):Type) :-
       do(transmit_time(Type,Time,FTime)),
       respond([(FTime,1,station(N),release(message(I))),
               (FTime,1,stngate(N),seton(message(I)))]))]).

simulation_time(0,18000).
initial_state([free(poller),free(message),free(station(1)),
    free(station(2)),free(station(3)),free(station(4))]).
start_message([(0,1,poller,poll(1)),
    (Time,1,message,arrive(I))]) :-
    next_arrival(0,0,Time,I).
```

```
histogram_form((wait-time,queue(4),(7,0,100))).
statistic(_,stngate(_),nil).
statistic(wait-time,station(_),nil).
```

A simulation run of the above modified model gives the following results:

```
?- simulate(nosnap).
```

```
                                                    . . .
                                                    . . .
                                                    . . .
                                                    . . .
                                                    . . .
                              . . .                 . . .
        . . .         . . .           . . .         . . .
. . . . . . . . . . . . . . . . . . . . . . . . . . . . . . . . . . . . . . . .
         0     100   200   300   400   500   600
```

```
Frequency of wait - time for queue(4)
```

```
Utilization of station(1) is 16%
Average use - time of station(1) is 500
Utilization of station(2) is 23%
Average use - time of station(2) is 467
Utilization of station(3) is 17%
Average use - time of station(3) is 454
Utilization of station(4) is 26%
Average use - time of station(4) is 434
Average wait - time for queue(1) is 2863
Average wait - time for queue(2) is 3787
Average wait - time for queue(3) is 2719
Average wait - time for queue(4) is 1223
Average queue length of queue(1) is 1
Average queue length of queue(2) is 4
Average queue length of queue(3) is 1
Average queue length of queue(4) is 0
```

11.3 The Healthy Fast-Food Bar has been at Pialligo for many years to serve the staff and workers of the nearby factories during lunch time. It has recently received many complaints about the delay in waiting to buy lunch at the bar, particularly since lunch break has been cut down to a mere one hour.

In order to improve the service, it is necessary to study the present system to see how long customers have to spend in the bar to obtain lunch and how many customers are turned away due to its crowdedness.

At present the bar has four servers and two cash registers; two servers share a cash register and are not allowed to use the other one.

When customers arrive, they enter the waiting area if it is not already full. They choose the foods and required quantities from a list of hot foods and then join the shortest of the four queues. (Of course, if they choose nothing, they will leave the bar immediately.) After taking an order, the server goes to the food buffer to begin filling the order. If the buffer does not have enough food for the current order, the server will press a button to signal the kitchen to supply more, and ask the customer to wait and turn to serve the next customer. But when the buffer is replenished, the server will serve those customers waiting for her as soon as she finishes serving her current customer.

After filling an order, the server waits for her cash register to be available, then uses it for payment. Customers leave the queue and the bar only after having paid for their takeaway food.

The bar's waiting area can have at most 16 people. Customers are expected to arrive at intervals of between 0 and 2 minutes. They choose from 0 to 5 hamburgers, 0 to 6 chicken pieces, and 0 to 3 packs of chips, in a uniform pattern. A server takes from 3 to 6 minutes to fill an order, but needs only one minute to realise that the food buffer has insufficient food; also she needs 2 minutes to process a customer's payment. The kitchen requires from 5 to 10 minutes to prepare the foods, but they always prepare in advance so that the foods can be supplied as soon as possible when requested. The buffer's replenished levels are 20 hamburgers, 20 chicken sticks, and 30 packs of chips.

Solution:

In this system, besides the objects shown in the given picture, we also have a kitchen signal which is used to indicate to the cook that the food buffer needs replenishment. There are two things that make this system differ slightly from the ones we have studied so far. First, a customer does not leave the queue until his required service is complete. Second, when a customer leaves the bar, not only the queue length is decremented, but the total number of people in the bar is also reduced. Thus, a customer has some extra domestic work to perform before leaving the bar. The system model is shown below.

KITCHEN

FOOD BUFFER

A	B	C

SERVERS

①   ②   ③   ④

IN   OUT

Object : Customer

Arrive:

Foods required: 0-5 hamburgers, 0-6 chickens, 0-3 chips.

Queue to join: the shortest queue.

Next arrival: uniform distribution 0-2 minutes.

Customer joins the chosen queue.

Customer waits for server to be served.

Next customer arrives.

Arrive:

Restaurant is full or no foods required.

Next customer arrives.

Leave:

Total number of people in the bar is decremented.

Customer leaves the queue.

Object : Server (1-4)

Serve customer:

Order filling needs 3-6 minutes.

Register used: 1 for servers 1-2; 2 for servers 3-4.

After filling order, server waits to use the register.

Serve customer:
>Buffer does not have enough foods; time required is 1 min.
>
>Server sets buffer off for self-reminding.
>Server sets kitchen signal on.
>After telling the customer to wait, server is available.
>Server and customer wait for buffer to be refilled.

Object : Register (1-2)

Payment:
>Paying time is 2 minutes;
>
>After payment is complete, register is available;
>Server becomes available; and
>Customer leaves the bar.

Object : Cook

Supply:
>Food preparation time is between 5 and 10 minutes.
>
>After preparing foods, the cook waits for kitchen signal.

Object : Kitchen signal

Get the cook:
>Replenish levels: 20 hamburgers, 20 chickens, and 30 chips.
>
>The cook sets kitchen signal off.
>The cook sets buffer on.
>The cook starts preparing new supply.

Object : Buffer

Get waiting server and customer:
>Customer is served again by the server.

Simulation time: 1 hour (60 minutes).
Initial state: all servers and registers are free;
>the buffer is full and the cook is available.

Start messages: the cook starts supply and first customer arrives.
Histogram form: waiting times in any queue, classified into 7
>classes of width 3 minutes, starting from 6.

Statistics: wait-time in any queue and for any register;
>wait-times for servers are not collected;
>use-times of registers are not collected.

The program is given below.

```
% SIMULATION OF A FAST-FOOD BAR
% Time unit = 1 minute

object(Time,customer,
  [(arrive(I) :-
      do((determine(Queue,Foods),
          next_arrival(Time,I,NTime,NI))),
      respond([(Time,1,serveq(Queue),queue(customer(I))),
          (Time,1,server(Queue),seize(customer(I):Foods)),
          (NTime,np,customer,arrive(NI))])),
    (arrive(I) :-
      do((restaurant_full,next_arrival(Time,I,NTime,NI))),
      respond([(NTime,np,customer,arrive(NI))])),
    (leave(Cust:N) :-
      do(leave_restaurant),
      respond([(Time,np,serveq(N),leaveq(Cust))]))]).

object(Time,server(N),
  [(seize(Cust:Foods) :-
      do((buffer_plenty(Foods,Time,FTime),register(N,R))),
      respond([(FTime,1,register(R),seize(server(N):Cust))])),
    (seize(Cust:Foods) :-
      do(buffer_low(Foods,Time,WTime)),
      respond([(Time,0,buffer,setoff(server(N))),
          (Time,0,kitchen_signal,seton(server(N))),
          (WTime,0,server(N),release(Cust)),
          (WTime,0,buffer,wait(server(N):(Cust:Foods)))]))]).

object(Time,register(R),
  [(seize(server(N):Cust) :-
      do(pay_bill(Time,FTime)),
      respond([(FTime,np,register(R),release(server(N))),
          (FTime,np,server(N),release(Cust)),
          (FTime,np,customer,leave(Cust:N))]))]).

object(Time,cook,
  [(supply :-
      do(prepare_time(Time,FTime)),
      respond([(FTime,0,kitchen_signal,wait(cook))]))]).
```

```
object(Time,kitchen_signal,
  [(wait(cook) :-
      do(replenish_buffer),
      respond([(Time,0,kitchen_signal,setoff(cook)),
               (Time,0,buffer,seton(cook)),
               (Time,0,cook,supply)]))]).

object(Time,buffer,
  [(wait(Server:Cust) :-
      do(true),
      respond([(Time,0,Server,seize(Cust))]))]).

determine(Queue,(Hamb,Chick,Chips)) :-
    counter(custin_room,N), N < 16,
    choose_foods((Hamb,Chick,Chips)),
    Hamb + Chick + Chips > 0,
    change_counter(custin_room,1),
    choose_queue(Queue).

choose_foods((Hamb,Chick,Chips)) :-
    uniform(0,5,Hamb),
    uniform(0,6,Chick),
    uniform(0,3,Chips).

choose_queue(N) :-
    shortest_queue([serveq(1),serveq(2),
    serveq(3),serveq(4)],serveq(N),_).

restaurant_full :-
    counter(custin_room,N), N >= 16,!,
    change_counter(lost_customers,1).
restaurant_full.

leave_restaurant :-
    change_counter(custin_room,-1).

next_arrival(Time,I,NTime,NI) :-
    uniform(0,2,AT), NTime is Time + AT,
    NI is I + 1.

counter(custin_room,0).
counter(lost_customers,0).
buffer(20,20,30).
```

```
buffer_plenty((Hamb,Chick,Chips),Time,FTime) :-
    buffer(Bham,Bchk,Bchp),
    NBham is Bham - Hamb,  NBham >= 0,
    NBchk is Bchk - Chick, NBchk >= 0,
    NBchp is Bchp - Chips, NBchp >= 0,!,
    retract(buffer(Bham,Bchk,Bchp)),
    assert(buffer(NBham,NBchk,NBchp)),
    uniform(3,6,ST), FTime is Time + ST.

buffer_low((Hamb,Chick,Chips),Time,FTime) :-
    buffer(Bham,Bchk,Bchp),
    (Bham < Hamb; Bchk < Chick; Bchp < Chips),!,
    FTime is Time + 1.

register(N,R) :- R is (N//3) + 1.

pay_bill(Time,PTime) :- PTime is Time + 2.

prepare_time(Time,FTime) :-
    uniform(5,10,PT), FTime is Time + PT.

replenish_buffer :-
    retract(buffer(_,_,_)), assert(buffer(20,20,30)).

change_counter(Name,I) :-
    retract(counter(Name,N)), N1 is N + I,
    assert(counter(Name,N1)).

simulation_time(0,60).
initial_state([free(customer),free(cook),
    free(register(1)),free(register(2)),
    free(server(1)),free(server(2)),
    free(server(3)),free(server(4)),
    free(buffer)]).
start_message([(0,1,cook,supply),
    (Time,1,customer,arrive(I))]) :-
    next_arrival(0,0,Time,I).
histogram_form((wait-time,serveq(_),(7,6,3))).
statistic_focus(wait-time,serveq(_)).
statistic_focus(wait-time,register(_)).
statistic_focus(use-time,server(_)).
statistic(wait-time,server(_),nil).
statistic(use-time,register(_),nil).
capacity(server(_),4).
```

A simulation run of the above program produces the following result that shows the number of lost customers should be a serious concern to the restaurant's owner.

```
?- simulate(nosnap).
```

```
                                 ...
                       ...       ...
                       ...       ...
                       ...       ...
                       ...  ...  ...
                       ...  ...  ...
          ...  ...  ...  ...  ...  ...
          ...  ...  ...  ...  ...  ...  ...
          ...  ...  ...  ...  ...  ...  ...
     ..........................................
          6    9   12   15   18   21   24
```

Frequency of wait - time for serveq(_)

Average wait - time for serveq(_) is 16
Utilization of server(_) is 88%
Average use - time of server(_) is 5
Average wait - time for register(_) is 0
Average queue length of serveq(1) is 3
Average queue length of serveq(2) is 3
Average queue length of serveq(3) is 2
Average queue length of serveq(4) is 2
Total number of lost_customers is 9
Total number of custin_room is 16

Supplementary problems

11.4 A local branch of the New-Bank has three tellers and two general staff. During peak hours, customers arrive with interarrival times uniformly distributed between 0 and 5 minutes. Customers join a single queue and wait for service. About 80% of customers only need normal transactions that can be done at a teller and take from 2 to 4 minutes. The rest of the customers require special service of the general staff that takes from 5 to 15 minutes.

Write a simulation program in POSS to estimate the time customers have to wait in the queue, the average queue length, and the utilisation of the staff at the tellers and the enquiry counter.

11.5 A flying school uses computers with large screens and sound effects to provide simulated flying lessons. There are four machines simulating small aircraft and two machines for large aircraft. Two instructors are available to help the students. Students arrive, from another class, with interarrival times exponentially distributed with the mean equal to 2 minutes. They join a single queue and wait for a required machine and an instructor to be available. A student only needs the instructor at the beginning for basic operational procedures; after that the student can follow the system's instructions, and the instructor may help other students. About 30% of students come to learn to fly large commercial aircraft, and the rest want to learn to fly light planes. Training on a large machine takes from 20 to 30 minutes, and on a small machine from 10 to 20 minutes. An instructor takes about 5 minutes to explain basic procedures to any student.

Write a simulation program in POSS to study the operation of the above-described system.

11.6 A manufacturing assembly line has two groups of workers. Jobs arrive almost regularly every 2 to 3 hours. Each job is divided into two parts to be done by the two worker-groups, and they are done in two stages. Group 1 takes from 1 to 1.5 hours to work on part 1 during stage 1, and group 2 takes from 45 minutes to 2 hours to work on part 2 in stage 1. At the end of stage 1, the two parts must be compared and matched before the workers start doing stage 2. Group 1 takes from 40 minutes to 1 hour to complete stage 2 of part 1, and group 2 needs exactly 1 hour to finish stage 2 of part 2. At the end, the two parts are combined and group 1 needs about 15 minutes to finalise the job.

Write a simulation program in POSS to estimate the delay time of jobs' start and the utilisation of each group of workers.

11.7 The manager of a rock band is planning a concert in Canberra. He has identified the following activities in his preparation.

ACTIVITY	TIME (weeks)
1. Select a site	2 - 4
2. Hire engineers	1 - 3
3. Hire supporting acts	3 - 8
4. Organise program	1 - 2
5. Organise transportation	1 - 3
6. Prepare sound system	2 - 3
7. Hire ticket agents	1 - 2
8. Advertise and sell tickets	7 - 8
9. Rehearsal	2 - 4

The sequence of the above activities is shown in the following graph. Write a simulation program in POSS to estimate the total time required to complete the concert's preparation. (Hint: treat the concepts of planning and testing as objects; arrange a number of test messages to be sent through the planning network and for each test, record the total preparation time; calculate the average preparation time at the end. No built-in messages are needed in this problem.)

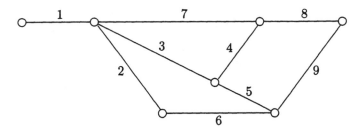

11.8 A downtown car park is to be built and is planned to have four gates: gate 1 will be attended by an assistant whose duty is to punch bulk tickets of regular customers and to show them the nearest place they can park their cars; all other gates are automatic.

Customers arriving at the car park will choose the gates to enter in the following pattern:

(a) Regular customers who hold bulk tickets usually enter gate 1, unless its queue currently contains more than three cars. In that case the customer might look around to see if there is any free automatic gate. If he finds a free automatic gate, he may prefer to enter that gate and be willing to pay cash. (If there is no free gate at that time or the customer does not have ready cash, then he would still choose gate 1.)

(b) Nonregular customers can only enter the automatic gates, but if all queues contain more than three cars, then they would drive on to the next nearby car park. Otherwise, they would choose to enter the free gate if there is any; if not, they would join the shortest queue.

It is expected that customers' interarrival times are exponentially distributed with a mean of 30 seconds. About 25% of the total of potential customers will be issued with bulk tickets. The probability that a regular customer may choose to enter a free automatic gate when the assistant-attended gate queue has more than three cars is 0.2. The time required to get through a gate is from 60 to 90 seconds for gate 1, and from 50 to 90 seconds for other gates.

Write a simulation program in POSS to estimate the time customers have to wait at the gates and the average queue lengths during a half an hour of peak time. (Hint: this problem sounds complex but its solution is very simple.)

Appendix A

Theory of unification and resolution

A.1 Unification

Unification is the process of making two terms or two atomic formulas identical. Syntactically, terms and atomic formulas have the same form, so, for convenience, they are commonly called *simple expressions.*

In order to make two simple expressions identical, one replaces their variables with appropriate terms. For example, consider the following two simple expressions:

$$likes(X, husband(Y)), \qquad likes(mother(Z), Z)$$

where X, Y, Z are variables. If we let

$$X = mother(husband(Y))$$
$$Z = husband(Y)$$

then both expressions become

$$likes(mother(husband(Y)), husband(Y))$$

which is called a *common instance* of the two given expressions. The set of equations of replacement is called a *substitution.*

In general, a *substitution* is a finite (possibly empty) set of equations of the form

$$\theta = \{X_1 = T_1, \dots, X_k = T_k\}$$

where $X_1, \dots, X_k$ are distinct variables and $T_1, \dots, T_k$ are terms whose variables do not include any of the $X_1, \dots, X_k$. If E is a simple expression and θ is the above-given substitution, then $E\theta$ denotes the simple expression obtained from E by replacing all occurrences in E of each variable X_i with T_i. $E\theta$ is called an *instance* of E. Now, given a second substitution

$$\rho = \{Y_1 = S_1, \dots, Y_h = S_h\}$$

such that no variable X_i of θ appears in ρ (on any side of the equations).

Then $\theta\rho$ denotes the substitution obtained from θ by replacing all occurrences in $T_1,\ldots,T_k$ of each variable Y_j with S_j, and then adding ρ to it. That is,

$$\theta\rho = \{X_1 = T_1\rho,\ldots,X_k = T_k\rho,\ Y_1 = S_1,\ldots,Y_h = S_h\}.$$

Observe that the substitution $\theta\rho$ imposes more severe constraint on the variables than θ. Hence, we say that the substitution θ is *more general* than the substitution $\theta\rho$, and that $\theta\rho$ is an *instance* of θ.

We can now give the formal definition of unification.

Definition 1

(a) A *unifier* of two simple expressions E, F is a substitution θ such that $E\theta = F\theta$. If two simple expressions have a unifier, they are said to be *unifiable*; we also say that E *is unified with* F by the unifier θ.

(b) A *most general unifier*, abbreviated as *mgu*, of two simple expressions E, F is a unifier θ that is more general than any unifier of E, F.

For example, let E and F be the two simple expressions given above, where the substitution

$$\theta = \{X = mother(husband(Y)),\quad Z = husband(Y)\}$$

has been shown to be a unifier of E, F. It can be verified that the substitution

$$\sigma = \{X = mother(husband(ann)),\quad Z = husband(ann),\quad Y = ann\}$$

is another unifier of E, F, and that, by letting $\rho = \{Y = ann\}$, we have $\sigma = \theta\rho$. Thus, the unifier θ is more general than σ. In fact, θ is the *mgu* of E, F as a result of the unification algorithm shown below.

Robinson (1965) proved that: *If two simple expressions are unifiable, then they have an mgu which is unique up to variable renaming and which can be computed by a unification algorithm.*

Given two simple expressions, and since the variables in one expression are initially unrelated to those in the other expression, we can always assume that the variables of one expression are renamed so that the two expressions contain disjoint sets of variables. The unification algorithm is given below.

Set two pointers pointing at the beginning of two expressions.
Set $\theta = \{\}$.
Repeat
    Move pointers in parallel to the right until
    either a mismatch is found or both expressions exhausted.
    If a mismatch occurs **then**
        If one pointer points at a variable X and the other
           at a term T that contains no occurrence of X
           then set $\theta = \theta\{X = T\}$ and replace all occurrences
              of X in the expressions with T
        else set $\theta = nil$ (indicating failure).
until $\theta = nil$ or both expressions are exhausted.
Return θ.

Note that the unification algorithm of Robinson assumes that all functions are one-to-one. That is, if $f(X) = f(Y)$ then $X = Y$. So, the programmer must ensure that all functions defined in his or her program are one-to-one. For example, if the program contains a function *mother*, then it is assumed that everyone in the world described by the program is the single child of his or her mother. In fact, when it comes to unifying *mother*(*ann*) and *mother*(*sue*), say, Prolog will fail, since it ignores the possibility that these terms represent the same person. Likewise, for a query such as $?1 + 2 = 2 + 1$, Prolog's answer will be "no". Thus, functions in logic programming are used for construction of data structures, rather than for computation. As for computation, Prolog provides the side-effect predicates "*is*" and "=:=" for this purpose.

A.2 SLD-resolution

SLD-resolution stands for Selected Linear resolution for Definite clauses. In the environment of a given logic program, SLD-resolution is used as a goal-reduction procedure which, for a given goal G, generates a goal G' such that, under some constraint of variables, G is true if G' is true. Thus, evaluating G is reduced to evaluating G'. In particular, if $G' = \Box$, the empty goal, then G is a true fact.

SLD-resolution consists of

- A selection rule that selects a subgoal from a given goal;

- An inference rule based on clause resolution.

The procedure works as follows.

Definition 2 Let S be a selection rule. Given a goal $G = A_1, \ldots, A_n$ and a clause $C = (A :\text{-} B_1, \ldots, B_m)$, if a subgoal A_i is selected from the goal G, by use of the selection rule S, and A_i is unified with A by the mgu θ, then we obtain a new goal

$$G' = (A_1, \ldots, A_{i-1}, B_1, \ldots, B_m, A_{i+1}, \ldots, A_n)\theta$$

which is called a *derived goal* (or a *resolvent*) of G and C via θ, and by use of S.

For example, suppose that we want to answer the query "Is there any woman who likes someone's husband?" by way of evaluating the following goal

$$woman(X), likes(X, husband(Y)).$$

To do this, we search the available logic program for related information, and assume that we find the following clause

$$likes(mother(Z), Z) :- good(Z).$$

Now the subgoal $likes(X, husband(Y))$ of the given goal is selected and is unified with the head of the above clause by the mgu

$$\theta = \{X = mother(husband(Y)), \quad Z = husband(Y)\}$$

Then we obtain the following derived goal

$$(woman(X), good(Z))\theta$$

which is (after variable substitution)

$$woman(mother(husband(Y))), good(husband(Y)).$$

Thus, the initial goal has been reduced to the above goal, which can be read as "Find someone whose mother-in-law is a woman and whose husband is good".

If this process is continued, assuming that the logic program contains the following facts:

$woman(mother(V))$.	% Every mother is a woman
$good(husband(ann))$.	% Ann's husband is good

then we obtain the following subsequently derived goals with the corresponding mgus shown in the right column.

$good(husband(Y))$	$\theta_1 = \{V = husband(Y)\}$
$\square$	$\theta_2 = \{Y = ann\}$

The empty goal's occurrence indicates that the goal evaluating process has succeeded, and an answer to the query is obtained by restricting the substitution $\theta\theta_1\theta_2$ to the variables of the initial goal. That is

$$X = mother(husband(ann))$$
$$Y = ann$$

Therefore, the answer to the initial query is "Yes! Ann's mother-in-law likes Ann's husband".

The process presented in the above example is now formally described in the following definition.

Definition 3 Let S be a selection rule, P a logic program, and G a goal.

(a) A *derivation* of G in (P, S) is a (finite or infinite) sequence of triples (G_i, C_i, θ_i), where $G_0 = G$ and for each $i = 0, 1, 2, \ldots$ C_i is a copy of a clause in P with all variables renamed by names not occurring before, and G_{i+1} is a derived goal of G_i and C_i via θ_i, and by use of S.

(b) A *refutation* of G in (P, S) is a finite derivation (G_i, C_i, θ_i) of G in (P, S) that ends with an empty goal. In this case, the restriction θ of $\theta_0 \ldots \theta_k$ to the variables of G is called an *answer* to the query $?G$. (If $\theta = \{\}$, then the answer is simply "true".)

(c) We say that G *succeeds* in (P, S) if it has a refutation in (P, S), and that G *fails* otherwise.

When S is the only selection rule involved, we simply write P in place of (P, S).

Note that the above-described process of evaluating a goal is purely syntactical. That is, symbols are manipulated by an algorithm with no concern about what they mean. This task can therefore be carried out by a machine.

However, two questions arise naturally:

- Is the found answer correct?

- Is there any answer that is missed out by the procedure?

The first question is about the *soundness* (that is, *correctness*) of the goal evaluating procedure in use, and the second concerns its *completeness*. It turns out that the answers to the above questions are "yes" and "no", respectively. In fact, Clark (1979) proved that:

The SLD-resolution procedure is both sound and complete. That is, given a selection rule S, a logic program P, and a goal G,

(a) If G succeeds in (P, S) with an answer θ, then $G\theta$ is true in P.

(b) If there exists a substitution σ such that $G\sigma$ is true in P, then G succeeds in (P, S) with an answer θ which is more general than σ (i.e., σ is an instance of θ).

The above proposition assures us that the choice of the selection rule does not affect the existence of an answer to a given query. It is the method of searching for a refutation that has a crucial effect on the finding of an answer. This searching task is very complex and is still a big problem for logic programming researchers. Prolog, for the sake of efficiency, adopts a straightforward strategy that facilitates its implementation, but loses the completeness. This incompleteness of Prolog is discussed in Appendix B.

Appendix B

Pure-Prolog interpreter

Prolog's goal evaluation procedure is an adaptation of SLD-resolution with a very simple selection rule and a trivial search strategy. In Prolog:

- The selection rule is to select the leftmost subgoal in the goal;
- The search rule is to choose the next clause in the program in the appearing order of clauses.

The figure on the next page shows a flowchart of pure-Prolog's evaluation procedure (which is adapted from Colmerauer's *Prolog in 10 Figures*, Association for Computing Machinery Inc., 1985). There are three loops in the chart: the outer loop represents *derivation* of goals, the inner one represents *backtracking* when a success or a failure occurs, and the lower loop represents *searching* clauses for unification. Two functions are called: function *copy* makes a copy of a clause in the program with variables renamed by names not occurring before, and function *unify* returns the mgu of two simple expressions if they are unifiable; otherwise it returns *nil* (which should be distinguished from {}) to indicate that a unifier was not found. The variable k_i represents a clause index. Note also that $h(C)$ denotes the head of C, $b(C)$: body of C, $h(G_i)$: head of G_i, and $t(G_i)$: tail of G_i.

Thus in Prolog the order of the clauses in a program is crucial. This falls short of what is intended for a logic programming system, that is, to allow the clauses to be arranged in any order. However, the simplicity of the selection and search rules makes Prolog's execution very efficient and easy to be traced for debugging and for providing explanations in expert systems.

Lloyd (1984) showed that: *the pure-Prolog goal evaluation procedure is sound but incomplete.*

In fact, the following example shows that no matter how the program's clauses are arranged, Prolog is unable to find an answer, which does exist. The program defines paths between places in a garden:

$p(a, b).$	% There is a path from a to b
$p(c, b).$	% There is a path from c to b
$p(x, y) :- p(y, x).$	% Paths are two-way
$p(x, z) :- p(x, y), p(y, z).$	% Paths are connectable

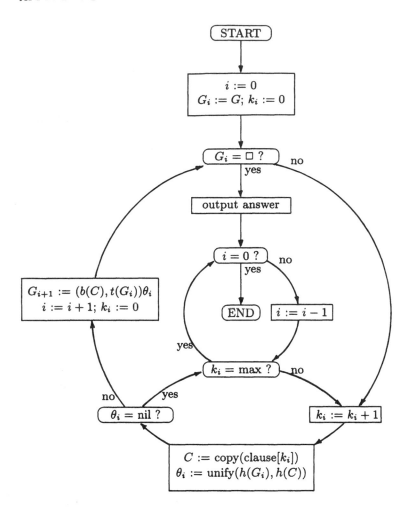

For the query ?- $p(a, c)$, SLD-resolution would find a refutation that confirms the given goal, which means "There is a path from a to c". However, Prolog is unable to find any answer (and it is stuck in an infinite loop), because it uses only one of the last two clauses (whichever precedes) in its derivation process, irrespective of the clauses's ordering.

In conclusion, pure-Prolog is an efficiency-oriented logic programming system based on SLD-resolution. Its trade-in for execution efficiency is completeness. This is not a serious problem, however, provided that the programmer is fully aware of it and takes caution in the ordering of clauses and of subgoals in each clause of his or her program.

Appendix C

Prolog predefined functions and predicates

;	Disjunction of goals.
!	The cut goal: cut all alternative search paths.
X == Y	Test if two terms X and Y are identical.
X \== Y	Test if two terms X and Y are not identical.
X = Y	Attempt to unify term X with term Y.
X \= Y	Test if two terms X and Y are nonunifiable.
X =:= Y	Test if the values of two terms X and Y are equal.
X =\= Y	Test if the values of two terms X and Y are not equal.
X < Y	Test if the value of term X is less than that of term Y.
X > Y	Test if the value of term X is greater than that of term Y.
X =< Y	Test if the value of term X is less than or equal to that of term Y.
X >= Y	Test if the value of term X is greater than or equal to that of term Y.
X @< Y	Test if term X is alphabetically before term Y.
X @> Y	Test if term X is alphabetically after term Y.
X @=< Y	Test if term X is alphabetically before or the same as term Y.

X @>= Y	Test if term X is alphabetically after or the same as term Y.
X + Y	Addition.
X − Y	Subtraction.
X * Y	Multiplication.
X / Y	Division, the result is a floating-point number.
X // Y	Integer division, the result is an integer.
X mod Y	Remainder of integer division.
X ^ Y	X to the power Y.
X =.. L	Convert term X to list L or vice versa.
[Filename]	Read clauses from Filename into the database as with the *consult* predicate. −Filename uses the *reconsult* predicate.
abolish(Name/Arity)	Remove from the database all clauses with the specified Name and Arity.
abort	Abort the current process and return to the interpreter.
abs(X)	Absolute value of X.
acos(X)	Arc cosine of X.
arg(N, Term, X)	Unify X with the Nth-argument of Term (arguments are numbered from 1 upward).
arg0(N, Term, X)	Unify X with the Nth-argument of Term (arguments are numbered from 0 upward).
argrep(Term, N, Arg, Newterm)	Replace the Nth-argument of Term with Arg to give Newterm.

asin(X)	Arc sine of X.
assert(Clause)	Add Clause at the end of an appropriate procedure.
asserta(Clause)	Add Clause at the beginning of an appropriate procedure.
assertz(Clause)	The same as assert.
atan(X)	Arc tangent of X.
atom(X)	Test if X is an atom (i.e., a mnemonic symbol).
atomic(X)	Test if X is an atomic data type (i.e., a constant symbol).
bagof(X, G, L)	Collect all instances of X for which the goal G succeeds and return them in an unordered list L.
call(G)	Execute the goal G.
clause(Head, Body)	Unify Head and Body with the head and body of a clause. Head must be instantiated.
cls	Clear the screen and move the cursor to the upper left corner.
code_world(Old, New)	Arity/Prolog: unify Old with the name of current code world, then change the code world to New.
concat(String1, String2, Result)	Arity/Prolog: concatenate two strings and return the new string in Result.
consult(Filename)	Read clauses from Filename into the database.
cos(X)	Cosine of X.
create_world(Worldname)	Arity/Prolog: create a new world named Worldname.
delete_world(Worldname)	Arity/Prolog: Delete the world named Worldname.

display(Term)	Write Term in prefix Polish form to the standard output device.
end_of_file	Represents the end-of-file marker.
exp(X)	e to the power X.
fail	This goal always fails.
findall(X, G, L)	As bagof(X, G, L), but all free variables are assumed to be existentially quantified.
float(X)	Test if X is a floating-point number.
float_text(Float, Text, Format)	Arity/Prolog: convert a floating-point number to a string according to Format or vice versa.
functor(Term, Func, Arity)	Return Term's functor and arity; or construct Term with given functor and arity.
get(Char)	Read the next character from the standard input device, skipping nonprinting characters (including space), and unify its ASCII code with Char.
get0(Char)	Read the next character from the standard input device and unify its ASCII code with Char. get0 does not skip nonprinting characters.
halt	Exit from the interpreter.
integer(X)	Test if X is an integer.
int_text(N, String)	Arity/Prolog: convert integer N to a string or vice versa.
X is E	Evaluate E and unify its value with X.
length(L, N)	Return the length N of a list L.
listing	Write to standard output all clauses in the current code world.

listing(Name)   Write to standard output all clauses in the
                        current code world with head predicate Name.

listing(Name/Arity)   Write to standard output all clauses in the
                        current code world with head predicate Name and
                        arity equals Arity.

listing([Name/Arity,...])   Write to standard output all clauses in the
                        current code world with head predicate Name and
                        arity given in the list.

list_text(List, String) Arity/Prolog: convert List of characters to an atom
                        or to a String, or vice versa.

ln(X)   Natural logarithm of X.

log(X)   Decimal logarithm of X.

name(Atom, List)   Convert List of character codes to Atom or vice
                        versa.

nl   Write a new line to the standard output device.

nonvar(X)   Test if X is not an uninstantiated variable.

nospy(Name/Arity)   Remove a spy point from the specified predicate.

not(P)   Succeeds if P fails; fails if P succeeds.

notrace   Turn the debugger off.

nth_char(N, String, Char) Arity/Prolog: return the ASCII code of the
                        (N+1)-th character of the string.

number(X)   Test if X is either an integer or a floating-point
                        number.

op(Prec, Assoc, Op)   Define operator Op to have precedence Prec, and
                        associativity Assoc.

put(C)   Write the character of ASCII code C to standard
                                ouput.

read(Term)   Read a term from standard input.

read_string(MaxLength, String) Arity/Prolog: read a string of specified
                                maximum length from standard input.

reconsult(Filename)   Read clauses from Filename into the database,
                                replacing any predicates that are already present
                                in the database with those clauses that also occur
                                in the file.

repeat   Always succeeds, and when encountered during
                                backtracking, always succeeds again.

retract(Clause)   Remove Clause from the database.

see(Filename)   Open Filename for reading and make it the current
                                input stream.

seeing(X)   Return in X the name of the file that was opened
                                for reading by *see*.

seen   End input from the current open file and close the
                                file; return to the default input stream.

setof(X, G, L)   Collect all instances of X for which the goal G
                                succeeds into an ordered list with no duplication.

shell   Enter the DOS environment while maintaining the
                                current program state. To return to Prolog environ-
                                ment, type "exit".

shell(DOS command)   Enter DOS and execute the DOS command, then
                                return to Prolog environment immediately.

sin(X)   Sine of X.

sort(L,L1)   Sort list L and eliminate any duplication to produce
                                list L1

spy(Name/Arity)   Specify a predicate as a spy point for debugging.

sqrt(X)   Square root of X.

string(X)   Arity/Prolog: test if X is a string.

string_length(String, Length)   Arity/Prolog: return the length of String.

string_term(String, Term)   Arity/Prolog: convert String into a term.

system(P)   Test if P is a system predicate.

tab(N)   Write N spaces to standard output.

tan(X)   Tangent of X.

tell(Filename)   Open Filename for writing and make it the current
                         output stream.

telling(X)   Return in X the name of the file that was opened
                         for writing by *tell*.

told   Close the file that is currently open for writing;
                         return to the default output stream.

trace   Turn the debugger on.

true   This goal always succeeds.

var(X)   Test if X is an uninstantiated variable.

write(Term)   Write Term to standard output.

The ASCII character set

0		32		64	@	96	`	128	Ç	160	á	192	└	224	α
1	☺	33	!	65	A	97	a	129	ü	161	í	193	⊥	225	β
2	☻	34	"	66	B	98	b	130	é	162	ó	194	┬	226	Γ
3	♥	35	#	67	C	99	c	131	â	163	ú	195	├	227	π
4	♦	36	$	68	D	100	d	132	ä	164	ñ	196	─	228	Σ
5	♣	37	%	69	E	101	e	133	à	165	Ñ	197	┼	229	σ
6	♠	38	&	70	F	102	f	134	å	166	ª	198	╞	230	μ
7	•	39	'	71	G	103	g	135	ç	167	º	199	╟	231	τ
8	◘	40	(	72	H	104	h	136	ê	168	¿	200	╚	232	Φ
9	○	41	)	73	I	105	i	137	ë	169	⌐	201	╔	233	θ
10	◙	42	*	74	J	106	j	138	è	170	¬	202	╩	234	Ω
11	♂	43	+	75	K	107	k	139	ï	171	½	203	╦	235	δ
12	♀	44	,	76	L	108	l	140	î	172	¼	204	╠	236	∞
13	♪	45	−	77	M	109	m	141	ì	173	¡	205	=	237	φ
14	♫	46	.	78	N	110	n	142	Ä	174	«	206	╬	238	∈
15	☼	47	/	79	O	111	o	143	Å	175	»	207	╧	239	∩
16	►	48	0	80	P	112	p	144	É	176	▒	208	╨	240	≡
17	◄	49	1	81	Q	113	q	145	æ	177	▓	209	╤	241	±
18	↕	50	2	82	R	114	r	146	Æ	178	█	210	╥	242	≥
19	‼	51	3	83	S	115	s	147	ô	179	│	211	╙	243	≤
20	¶	52	4	84	T	116	t	148	ö	180	┤	212	╘	244	⌠
21	§	53	5	85	U	117	u	149	ò	181	╡	213	╒	245	⌡
22	▬	54	6	86	V	118	v	150	û	182	╢	214	╓	246	÷
23	↨	55	7	87	W	119	w	151	ù	183	╖	215	╫	247	≈
24	↑	56	8	88	X	120	x	152	Ÿ	184	╕	216	╪	248	°
25	↓	57	9	89	Y	121	y	153	Ö	185	╣	217	┘	249	•
26	→	58	:	90	Z	122	z	154	Ü	186	║	218	┌	250	•
27	←	59	;	91	[	123	{	155	¢	187	╗	219	█	251	√
28	∟	60	<	92	\	124			156	£	188	╝	220	▄	252	ⁿ
29	↔	61	=	93	]	125	}	157	¥	189	╜	221	▌	253	²
30	▲	62	>	94	^	126	~	158	₨	190	╛	222	▐	254	∎
31	▼	63	?	95	_	127	△	159	ƒ	191	┐	223	▀	255	

Appendix E

Prolog operators precedence

Operator	Type	Precedence
:-	$xfx,\ fx$	1200
?-	fx	1200
;	xfy	1100
,	xfy	1000
not	fy	900
is, =.. and all comparing predicates	xfx	700
+ −	$yfx,\ fx$	500
:	xfy	500
* /	yfx	400
mod	xfx	300
∧	xfy	200

Type notation	Meaning
xfx	Infix nonassociative
xfy	Infix right-associative
yfx	Infix left-associative
fx	Prefix nonassociative
fy	Prefix right-associative
xf	Postfix nonassociative
yf	Postfix left-associative

Appendix F

List of defined procedures

Appendix G

The diskettes

G.1 Contents of the diskettes

The two diskettes accompanying this book contain all the programs presented in the book. For easy search, each program is stored in a file named after the chapter and the figure or the problem in which the program occurs. For example, the file `\chap4\figure9.pro` contains the program given in Figure 4.9 of Chapter 4, and the file `\chap6\problm5.pro` has the program presented in Problem 6.5 of Chapter 6. For programs that spread over several figures, we store the whole program in the file named after the first figure in which the program occurs.

Each file in the diskettes also contains the instructions on how to run the program and to perform experiments with the program. Sample test data are also included in the files to facilitate the experiments. Thus, the diskettes are ready for use in the practical sessions.

The diskettes also contain the three complete systems described in the text, namely LnProlog, ESSLN, and POSS. LnProlog and ESSLN were originally written in Arity-Prolog, taking advantage of the built-in predicates provided for database partition and string handling. But we have added other versions of LnProlog and ESSLN that are written in standard Prolog (expectably, these versions run slightly slower than the original ones). Thus the diskettes contain the following versions of LnProlog, ESSLN, and POSS.

- `\chap8\lnprolog.ari` contains the original version of LnProlog that employs the six special built-in predicates of Arity-Prolog listed on page 365 of Chapter 8, Section 8.5.

- `\chap8\lnprolg2.ari` contains the original version of LnProlog with its own debugger and tracer as described in Section 8.8 and Problem 8.2, respectively.

- `\chap8\lnprolog.std` contains Version A of LnProlog, which is written in standard Prolog and which can be run on most Prolog systems.

- `\chap8\lnprolg2.std` contains Version A2 of LnProlog, which is written in standard Prolog and has its own debugger and tracer, as `lnprolg2.ari`.

- \chap9\essln0.ari contains the original version of ESSLN, which is written in Arity-Prolog 4.0 (that has some features unavailable in the later versions).

- \chap9\essln.ari contains ESSLN's Version 1, which is also written in Arity-Prolog, but it can be run with the later versions of Arity-Prolog.

- \chap9\essln.std contains ESSLN's Version 2, which is written in standard Prolog, and can be run with most Prolog systems.

- \chap11\poss.pro contains the simulation system POSS, which is (originally) written in standard Prolog.

G.2 How to use the diskettes

The following instructions apply to Prolog systems under MS-DOS (for other operating systems, use the equivalent commands). To use the diskettes, follow the following steps:

1. If your directory does not have the file **mcopy.exe**, then generate this file by using the command:

   ```
   copy /b c:\dos\xcopy.exe mcopy.exe
   ```

2. Make a new directory in your hard disk and copy all files and subdirectories of the diskettes into that directory. For example, make a directory called **c:\v1prolog**, then place the first diskette in drive A and enter the following command:

   ```
   mcopy a: c:\v1prolog\ /s /e
   ```

   Then repeat the command with the second diskette.

3. For each file, read and follow the instructions at the beginning of the file to run the program in the file and to perform experiments with the program. For most programs, the instructions are straightforward. For a small number of programs that require screen handling, system testing, and random-number generating (such as LnProlog, ESSLN, and POSS), the instructions include essential commands to make the

programs work in your Prolog system. So, for those programs, it is recommended that the reader study the instructions thoroughly and take any required actions before running the programs.

Bibliography

Aho, A., and Corasick, M. (1975). Efficient string matching: an aid to bibliographic search. *Communications of the ACM*, Vol. 18, No. 6, 333-340.

Ait-Kaci, H., and Nasr, R. (1986). LOGIN: a logic programming language with built-in inheritance. *Journal of Logic Programming*, Vol. 3, No. 3, 185-215.

Amble, T. (1987). *Logic Programming and Knowledge Engineering*. Addison-Wesley, Reading, Massachusetts.

Arity Corporation (1986). *The Arity/Prolog Programming Language*. Arity Corporation, Concord, Massachusetts.

Backus, J. (1978). Can programming be liberated from the von Neumann style? A functional style and its algebra of programs. *Communications of the ACM*, Vol. 21, No. 8, 613-641.

Ballard, D. H., and Brown, C. M. (1982). *Computer Vision*. Prentice-Hall, Englewood Cliffs, New Jersey.

Barklund, J. (1988). What is a meta-variable in Prolog? *Proceedings of the Workshop on Meta-Programming in Logic Programming*. University of Bristol, Bristol, England, June, 281-292.

Birtwistle, G. M., Dahl, O.-J., Myhrhaug, B., and Nygaard, K. (1973). *SIMULA begin*. Petrocelli-Charter, Philadelphia.

Borland International (1986). *Turbo-Prolog: The Natural Language of AI*. Borland, Scotts Valley, California.

Brachman, R. J., and Schmolze, J. G. (1985). An overview of the KL-ONE Knowledge Representation System. *Cognitive Science*, Vol. 9, No. 2, 171-216.

Bratko, I. (1990). *Prolog Programming for Artificial Intelligence*. Addison-Wesley, Reading, Massachusetts.

Broda, K., and Gregory, S. (1984). PARLOG for discrete-event simulation. *Proceedings of the Second International Logic Programming Conference.* Uppsala University Press, Sweden.

Bruffaerts, A., and Henin, E. (1988). Proof trees for negation-as-failure: yet another Prolog meta-interpreter. *Proceedings of the Workshop on Meta-Programming in Logic Programming.* University of Bristol, Bristol, England, June, 133-146.

Buchanan, B. G., and Shortliffe, E. H. (1984). *Rule-based Expert Systems: The MYCIN Experiments of the Stanford Heuristic Programming Project.* Addison-Wesley, Reading, Massachusetts.

Burkholder, L. (1987). PROLOG for the people. *AI Expert*, Vol. 2, 63-84.

Byrd, L. (1980). Understanding the control flow of Prolog programs. *Proceedings of the Logic Programming Workshop*, Debrecen, Hungary, July, 127-138.

Chan, D. (1988). Constructive negation based on the completed database. *Proceedings of the Fifth International Symposium on Logic Programming.* IEEE, Seattle, Washington, August.

Chan, D., and Wallace, M. (1988). A treatment of negation during partial evaluation. *Proceedings of the Workshop on Meta-Programming in Logic Programming.* University of Bristol, Bristol, England, June.

Charniak, E., and McDermott, D. (1985). *Introduction to Artificial Intelligence.* Addison-Wesley, Reading, Massachusetts.

Clancey, W., and Bock, C. (1982). MRS/NEOMYCIN: representing meta-control in predicate calculus. *Stanford Heuristic Programming Project.* Report No. HPP-82-31.

Clark, K. L. (1978). Negation as failure. In *Logic and Databases*, H. Gallaire and J. Minker, eds. Plenum Press, New York, 293-322.

Clark, K. L. (1979). *Predicate Logic as a Computational Formalism.* Research Report 79/59, Department of Computing, Imperial College, London, England.

Clark, K. L., and McCabe, F. G. (1979). The control facilities of IC-Prolog. In *Expert Systems in the Micro Electronic Age*, D. Michie, ed. Edinburgh University Press, Edinburgh, Scotland.

Clark, K. L., and McCabe, F. G. (1982). Prolog: a language for implementing expert systems. *Machine Intelligence*, Vol. 10, 455-470.

Clark, K. L., and Tarnlund, S. A., eds. (1982). *Logic Programming*. Academic Press, New York.

Clocksin, W. F., and Mellish, C. S. (1981). *Programming in Prolog*. Springer-Verlag, New York/Berlin.

Cohn, A. G. (1983). Improving the expressiveness of many-sorted logic. *Proceedings of AAAI-83*, Washington D. C., 84-87.

Colmerauer, A. (1978). Metamorphosis grammars. In *Natural Language Communication with Computers*, Lecture Notes in Computer Science, L. Bole ed. Springer-Verlag, New York/Berlin, 133-189.

Colmerauer, A. (1982). Infinite trees and inequalities in Prolog. In *Logic Programming*, K. L. Clark and S. A. Tarnlund, eds. Academic Press, New York.

Colmerauer, A. (1985). Prolog in ten figures. *Communications of the ACM*, Vol. 28, No. 12, 1296-1310.

Date, C. J. (1986). *An Introduction to Database Systems*, 4th ed. Addison-Wesley, Reading, Massachusetts.

Davis, R. (1980). Meta-rules: reasoning about control. *Artificial Intelligence Journal*, Vol. 15, 179-222.

Enderton, H. B. (1972). *A Mathematical Introduction to Logic*. Academic Press, New York.

Evans, T. G. (1968). A heuristic program to solve geometric analogy problems. In *Semantic Information Processing*, M. Minsky, ed. MIT Press, Cambridge, Massachusetts.

Fikes, R. E., and Kehler, T. P. (1985). The role of frame-based representation in reasoning. *Communications of the ACM*, Vol. 28, No. 9, 904-920.

Frisch, A. M. (1985). An investigation into inference with restricted quantification and a taxonomic representation. *SIGART Newsletter*, Vol. 91, 28-31.

Futo, I., and Szeredi, J. (1982). A discrete simulation system based on artificial intelligence methods. In *Discrete Simulation and Related Fields*,
A. Javor, ed. North-Holland, Amsterdam.

Gabbay, D. M., and Sergot, M. J. (1986). Negation as inconsistency. *Journal
of Logic Programming*, Vol. 3, No. 1, 1-36.

Gallaire, H., Minker, J., and Nicolas, J. M. (1978). An overview and introduction to logic and data bases. In *Logic and Data Bases*, H. Gallaire
and J. Minker, eds. Plenum Press, New York, 3-32.

Gallaire, H., and Lasserre, C. (1982). Meta-level control for logic programs.
In *Logic Programming*, K. L. Clark and S. A. Tarnlund, eds. Academic
Press, New York, 173-188.

Giannesini, F., Kanoui, H., Pasero, R., and van Caneghem, M. (1986).
Prolog. Addison-Wesley, Reading, Massachusetts.

Goldberg, A., and Robson, D. (1983). *Smalltalk-80: The Language and Its
Implementation*. Addison-Wesley, Reading, Massachusetts.

Gomory, R. E. (1966). The travelling salesman problem. *Proceedings of
the IBM Scientific Computing Symposium on Combinatorial Problems*.
IBM Data Processing Division, New York, 93-121.

Gordon, G. (1978). *System Simulation*. Prentice-Hall, Englewood Cliffs,
New Jersey.

Gries, D. (1981). *The Science of Programming*. Springer-Verlag, New York/
Berlin.

Harmon, P., and King, D. (1985). *Expert Systems*. Wiley, New York.

Hayes, P. J. (1979). The logic of frames. In *Frame Conceptions and Text
Understanding*, D. Metzing, ed. Gruyter, New York/Berlin, 46-60.

Hayes-Roth, F., Waterman, D. A., and Lenat, D. B. (1983). *Building Expert
Systems*. Addison-Wesley, Reading, Massachusetts.

Huber, M., and Varsek I. (1987). Extended Prolog for order-sorted resolution. *Proceedings of Symposium on Logic Programming*. IEEE, San
Francisco, Sept.

Irani, K. B., and Shin, D. G. (1985). A many-sorted resolution based on an extension of a first-order language. *Proceedings of IJCAI.* W. Kaufmann, Karlsruhe, Germany.

Kowalski, R. A. (1974). Predicate logic as a programming language. *Proceedings of IFIP* 74. North-Holland, Amsterdam.

Kowalski, R. A. (1979). *Logic for Problem Solving.* North-Holland, Amsterdam.

Kreutzer, W., and McKenzie, B. (1989). *Programming for Artificial Intelligence, Methods, Tools and Applications.* Addison-Wesley, Reading, Massachusetts.

Lassez, J-L., and Marriott, K. (1986). *Explicit Representation of Terms Defined by Counter Examples.* Research Report, RC 11915 (No. 53222). IBM, Thomas J. Watson Research Center, Yorktown Heights, New York, May.

Le, T. V. (1989). ESSLN: an expert system shell with logical negation. *Proceedings of AJAIC*, Melbourne, Nov., 163-172.

Le, T. V. (1990). A logical negation evaluator for standard Prolog. *Proceedings of ACSC-13*, Melbourne, Feb., 186-195.

Le, T. V. (1991). MLESS: A multilingual expert system shell that supports negative and quantified queries. *Proceedings of the First World Congress on Expert Systems*, Orlando, Florida, Dec., 1659-1671.

Le, T. V. (1991). *User Guide to POSS: A Prolog-based Object-oriented Simulation System.* Technical Report, University of Canberra, Canberra, Australia.

Le, T. V. (1992). Discrete-event simulation with POSS. *Proceedings of the Third International Conference on AI, Simulation and Planning in High Autonomy Systems*, Perth, Australia, July, 94-101.

Le, T. V. (1992). A general scheme of representing negative and quantified queries for deductive databases. *Proceedings of the First International Conference on Information and Knowledge Management*, Baltimore, Maryland, Nov.

Lloyd, J. W. (1984). *Foundations of Logic Programming*. Springer-Verlag, New York/Berlin.

Lloyd, J. W., and Hill, P. M. (1988). Analysis of meta-programs. *Proceedings of the Workshop on Meta-Programming in Logic Programming*. University of Bristol, Bristol, England, June, 27-41.

Logic Programming Associates (1989). *Prolog++: An Object-Oriented Extension to Prolog*. Logic Programming Associates Ltd., London.

Maier, D., and Warren, D. S. (1988). *Computing with Logic: Logic Programming with Prolog*. Benjamin-Cummings, Menlo Park, California.

Malpas, J. (1987). *Prolog: A Relational Language and Its Applications*. Prentice-Hall, Englewood Cliffs, New Jersey.

Marcus, C. (1986). *Prolog Programming*. Addison-Wesley, Reading, Massachusetts.

Martelli, A., and Montanari, U. (1982). An efficient unification algorithm. *ACM Transactions on Programming Languages and Systems*, Vol. 4, 258-282.

McVitie, D. G., and Wilson, L. B. (1969). Three procedures for the stable marriage problem. Algorithm 411, *Collected Algorithms*. Association for Computing Machinery, New York.

McVitie, D. G., and Wilson, L. B. (1971). The stable marriage problem. *Communications of the ACM*, Vol. 14, No. 7, 486-492.

Mellish, C. S. (1982). An alternative to structure sharing in the implementation of a Prolog interpreter. In *Logic Programming*, K. L. Clark and S. A. Tarnlund, eds. Academic Press, New York.

Mishra, P. (1984). Towards a theory of types in PROLOG. *Proceedings of the International Symposium on Logic Programming*, Atlantic City, New Jersey, Feb.

Mycroft, A., and O'Keefe, R. (1984). A polymorphic type system for PROLOG. *Artificial Intelligence*, Vol. 23, 295-307.

Naish, L. (1985). All solutions predicates in Prolog. *Proceedings of the Symposium on Logic Programming*, Boston, Massachusets, July.

Naish, L. (1986). Negation and quantifiers in NU-Prolog. *Proceedings of the Third International Conference on Logic Programming*. Imperial College, London, July.

Nilsson, M. (1984). Prolog as a tool for optimising Prolog unification. *Proceedings of the Second International Logic Programming Conference*, Uppsala, Sweden.

Poole, D. L., and Goebel, R. (1986). Gracefully adding negation and disjunction to Prolog. *Proceedings of the Third International Conference on Logic Programming*. Imperial College, London, July.

Rikitake, T. (1976). *Earthquake Prediction*. Elsevier, Amsterdam/New York.

Robinson, J. A. (1965). A machine-oriented logic based on the resolution principle. *Journal of the ACM*, Vol. 12, 23-41.

Roussel, P. (1975). *PROLOG: Manuel de Reference et d'Utilisation*. University of Aix-Marseilles, Luminy, France.

Rowe, N. C. (1988). *Artificial Intelligence through Prolog*. Prentice-Hall, Englewood Cliffs, New Jersey.

Sakai, K., and Miyachi, T. (1985). *Incorporating Naive Negation Into Prolog*. ICOT Pre-Publication Report, Tokyo, Japan.

Sammut, C. A., and Sammut, R. A. (1983). The implementation of UNSW-Prolog. *Australian Computer Journal*, Vol. 15, 58-64.

Schmidt-Schauss, M. (1985). A many-sorted calculus with polymorphic functions based on resolution and paramodulation. *Proceedings of the 9th IJCAI*. W. Kaufmann, Karlsruhe.

Schnupp, P., and Bernhard, L. W. (1986). *Productive Prolog Programming*. Prentice-Hall, Englewood Cliffs, New Jersey.

Schroeder, S. A., Krupp, M. A., Tierney, L. M., Jr. and McPhee, S. (1989). *Current Medical Diagnosis and Treatment*. Appleton & Lange, San Matleo, California.

Sergot, M. (1982). Prospects for representing the law as logic programs. In *Logic Programming*, K. L. Clark, and S. A. Tarnlund, eds. Academic Press, London, 3-18.

Sergot, M., and Vasey, P. (1986). *Qualified Answers, Open Worlds and Negation*. Technical Report, Imperial College, London, March.

Shapiro, E. Y. (1983). *Algorithmic Program Debugging*. MIT Press, Cambridge, Massachusetts.

Shortliffe, E. H. (1976). *MYCIN: Computer-based Medical Consultation*. Elsevier, Amsterdam/New York.

Sindermann, C. J. (1977). *Disease Diagnosis and Control in North American Marine Aquaculture*. Elsevier, Amsterdam/New York.

Stabler, E. P. (1986). Object-oriented programming in Prolog. *AI Expert*, Oct.

Sterling, L., Bundy, A., Byrd, L., O'Keefe, R., and Silver, B. (1982). Solving symbolic equations with PRESS. In *Computer Algebra*, J. Calmet, ed. Lecture Notes in Computer Science No. 144. Springer-Verlag, New York/Berlin.

Sterling, L., and Shapiro, E. (1987). *The Art of Prolog*. MIT Press, Cambridge, Massachusetts.

Taha, H. A. (1982). *Operations Research*. Macmillan, New York.

van Emden, M. H., and Kowalski, R. A. (1976). The semantics of predicate logic as programming language. *Journal of the ACM*, Vol. 23, No.4, 733-742.

van Emden, M. H. (1984). An interpreting algorithm for Prolog programs. In *Implementations of Prolog*, J. A. Campbell, ed. Horwood, Chichester, 93-110.

van Harmelen, F. (1988). A classification of meta-level architectures. *Proceedings of the Workshop on Meta-Programming in Logic Programming*. University of Bristol, Bristol, England, June, 87-94.

Vasey, P. (1986). Qualified answers and their application to transformation. *Proceedings of the Third International Conference on Logic Programming*. Imperial College, London, July.

Walker, A. (1986). Syllog: an approach to Prolog for non-programmers. In *Logic Programming and Its Applications*, M. van Caneghem and D. H. D. Warren, eds. Ablex, Norwood, New Jersey, 32-49.

Walker, A., McCord, M., Sowa, J. F., and Wilson, W. G. (1987). *Knowledge Systems and Prolog*. Addison-Wesley, Reading, Massachusetts.

Wallace, M. (1987). Negation by constraints: a sound and efficient implementation of negation in deductive databases. *Proceedings of the Symposium on Logic Programming*. IEEE, San Francisco, Sept.

Walther, C. (1983). A many-sorted calculus based on resolution and paramodulation. *Proceedings of the 8th IJCAI*. W. Kaufmann, Karlsruhe.

Walther, C. (1987). Many-sorted calculus based on resolution and paramodulation. *Research Notes in AI*. Pitman, London.

Warren, D. H. D. (1977). *Implementing Prolog - Compiling Predicate Logic Programs*. D.A.I. Research Report 39. University of Edinburgh, Edinburgh, Scotland.

Warren, D. H. D., Pereira, L. M., and Pereira, F. C. N. (1977). *PROLOG - The Language and Its Implementation Compared with LISP*. SIGPLAN Notices, Vol. 12, No. 8.

Weizenbaum, J. (1966). ELIZA - a computer program for the study of natural language communication between men and machines. *Communications of the ACM*, Vol. 9, 36-45.

Winston, P. H. (1984). *Artificial Intelligence*, 2d ed. Addison-Wesley, Reading, Massachusetts.

Wirth, N. (1976). *Algorithms + Data Structures = Programs*. Prentice-Hall, Englewood Cliffs, New Jersey.

Yalcinalp, L. V., and Sterling, L. (1988). An integrated interpreter for explaining Prolog's successes and failures. *Proceedings of the Workshop on Meta-programming in Logic Programming*. University of Bristol, Bristol, England, June, 147-159.

Zaniolo, C. (1984). Object-oriented programming in Prolog. *Proceedings of the International Symposium on Logic Programming*. IEEE, Atlantic City, Feb.

Index